CHILD ABUSE and NEGLECT

CHILD ABUSE
and NEGLECT

Monica L. McCoy,
Converse College

Stefanie M. Keen,
University of South Carolina, Upstate

Psychology Press
Taylor & Francis Group

New York   Hove

Psychology Press
Taylor & Francis Group
270 Madison Avenue
New York, NY 10016

Psychology Press
Taylor & Francis Group
27 Church Road
Hove, East Sussex BN3 2FA

© 2009 by Taylor & Francis Group, LLC
Psychology Press is an imprint of Taylor & Francis Group, an Informa business

Printed in the United States of America on acid-free paper
10 9 8 7 6 5 4 3 2 1

International Standard Book Number-13: 978-0-8058-6244-7 (Hardcover)

Library of Congress Cataloging-in-Publication Data

McCoy, Monica L. (Monica Louise)
    Child abuse and neglect : a guide for mandated reporters / Monica L. McCoy, Stefanie M. Keen.
-- 1st ed.
        p. cm.
    ISBN 978-0-8058-6244-7 (hardback)
    1. Child abuse--United States. 2. Child abuse--Law and legislation--United States. I. Keen, Stefanie
M. II. Title.

HV6626.52.M336 2009
362.76--dc22   2008039011

Visit the Taylor & Francis Web site at
http://www.taylorandfrancis.com

and the Psychology Press Web site at
http://www.psypress.com

I dedicate this book to my mother, Julie McCoy, and to the memory of my father, Gary McCoy, who gave me the priceless gift of a happy childhood.

Monica L. McCoy

To Hannah and Leah, you are my sunshine.

Stefanie M. Keen

Contents

PART III LEGAL ISSUES

PART IV WHAT HAPPENS NEXT

Preface

Our purpose in writing this book was to create a textbook that was appropriate for an undergraduate course in child abuse and neglect. There is a demand for this type of information because students preparing to enter many disciplines (psychology, education, social work, premed) are aware that they will be mandated reporters for child maltreatment, while also realizing that they are not prepared to meet this obligation. In order to fulfill this role, students need education about what maltreatment entails, how to recognize and report it, and how the issue is handled by child protective services and the courts. The current research indicates that many professionals who are mandated reporters think that their training in this area has not been adequate. It is our hope that having a textbook grounded in research and the law will provide a more adequate preparation for those who are now, or will become, mandated reporters of child maltreatment.

The text is divided into four main sections. In Part I, we provide background information on the problem of child maltreatment. This includes a brief history of child maltreatment as well as an introduction to some of the research limitations in the field. The second chapter in Part I covers many of the possible risk factors for child maltreatment. It is difficult for some students to understand how a parent could harm his or her own child. It is our hope that by considering many of the factors a family may be dealing with, students will recognize how maltreatment can occur, even among families who love their children. The final chapter in Part I covers mandated reporting in-depth. It is good to fully understand the role of a mandated reporter before learning about the different forms of maltreatment covered in Part II of the text. Chapters 4 to 9 cover each type of maltreatment (physical abuse, neglect, psychological maltreatment, sexual abuse, fetal abuse, and Munchausen by proxy syndrome) in detail. For each form of maltreatment, we provide definitions, estimates of incidence, and possible consequences. As appropriate, we cover issues and controversies that are relevant to that form of maltreatment. Part III deals with legal issues related to child maltreatment. Chapter 10 focuses on forensic interviewing, and Chapter 11 covers the legal system as it pertains to child maltreatment. While mandated reporters have less to do with this part of the process, it is still valuable information for them to have. For instance, knowing how suggestible children are to certain forms of questioning should make mandated reporters realize that they should not attempt to interview children about allegations of maltreatment unless they have been trained to do so. Finally, Part IV examines what occurs after a report of child maltreatment is made and prevention efforts. Chapter 12 details what happens to a child after child protective services receives a report of maltreatment. Although mandated reporters are not involved in this process, it is natural to be concerned about what happens after a reporter sets the investigative process in motion. Finally, the last chapter addresses the more optimistic issue of the prevention of child maltreatment.

While mandated reporters are required to notice and report child maltreatment, it would be better for everyone if the problem could be prevented.

The book has several features that have been included to deepen understanding about child maltreatment. The first time an important term or unfamiliar word is used, it appears in boldface type, and it is defined at the end of the chapter. At the end of the book, you will find a glossary of all the terms defined throughout the book. Many chapters have "Focus on Research" boxes. This feature allowed us to go into depth about representative research studies and to explain research methodologies that may be unfamiliar to students. We have also used "Case Example" sections throughout the text, some fictional and some real. We added these for two reasons. First, students tend to find case studies interesting and easier to grasp than more theoretical material. Second, the cases provide them with a starting point to engage in discussion with their classmates about the many gray areas in this field. Finally, the "Legal Example" sections explain, in detail, legal cases and judicial rulings that have had a significant impact on how child maltreatment cases are handled by the courts. By studying these cases, we hope students gain a deeper appreciation for the legal complexities surrounding child maltreatment. At the end of each case example and at the end of every chapter, they will find discussion questions related to the material they have just read. Thinking about these questions, and discussing their answers with their peers, will help to test and expand their knowledge of the material.

We realize that no textbook can answer all of the questions students will ever have about child maltreatment. However, the goal of this book is to help future mandated reporters be better prepared to meet the challenges of fulfilling that role.

Acknowledgments

A large number of people helped to make this book possible. We would like to take this opportunity to acknowledge the professional and personal support that we received while working on this book.

Our Professional Colleagues and Institutions

    The Psychology Department at Converse College: Dr. William Baker, Dr. Rich Keen, and Dr. Jan LeFrancois. Many thanks for being supportive throughout this entire process.

    Converse College, for granting a sabbatical leave to get this project started.

    Dr. Narina Nunez, for her guidance on research about child maltreatment.

    Jennifer Gray, for enthusiastic support of early versions, and her willingness to try out new material in the classroom.

    Angela Robinson, investigative supervisor with the Spartanburg County Department of Social Services, for taking the time to talk with us about child protective services and for helping us to understand the child protective process.

    Shannon Wardlow, interlibrary loan officer extraordinaire, for her cheerful and professional assistance in locating sources. We could not have done this without her assistance.

    Bill Herrick, executive director of the Children's Advocacy Center of Spartanburg, for his encouragement and his assistance with photographs.

Our Families

    A special thanks to Julie McCoy for her tireless proofreading, and for her constant encouragement. Not only did she correct many errors, she kept me from giving up when the project seemed overwhelming.

    A special thanks also to Rich Keen. His patience and support during this project has been seemingly endless. Thank you for always being a stable presence and for taking up the slack when I was too immersed to know which end was up.

Our Reviewers

    Further thanks are directed toward the reviewers who made many helpful suggestions during the writing process. Special thanks to Alice Yick Flanagan of Capella University and Marietta A. Veeder of Utah State University for their thoughtful feedback on our final draft.

Our Publisher

Finally, we would like to thank the professionals at Taylor & Francis for their assistance with this project: Lori Handleman, Rebecca Larsen, Kurt Roediger, and most especially, Christopher Myron and Debra Riegert. Their patience and guidance have made this project possible.

About the Authors

Monica L. McCoy, Ph.D., is an associate professor of psychology at Converse College in Spartanburg, South Carolina. She earned her bachelor's degree in psychology from Grove City College and her master's degree in experimental psychology from Villanova University. She then obtained her Ph.D. in experimental/developmental psychology, with a minor in statistics, from the University of Wyoming. Dr. McCoy currently teaches a broad range of undergraduate courses, including child abuse and neglect, human growth and development, statistics, general psychology, and senior seminar. Dr. McCoy's research has focused on determining what factors impact juror decisions in cases of alleged child maltreatment. She is also interested in exploring what the general public knows about child abuse and neglect, and how mandated reporters become educated about maltreatment. In addition to her work at the college, Dr. McCoy has served as a guardian ad litem, and she has offered training for others who serve as court advocates for abused children and for volunteers at the local children's shelter.

Stefanie M. Keen, Ph.D. is an assistant professor of psychology at the University of South Carolina Upstate in Spartanburg, South Carolina. She earned her bachelor's degree in psychology from the State University of New York at Binghamton, and her Ph.D. in clinical psychology from Indiana University. Dr. Keen currently teaches a variety of undergraduate courses including child abuse and neglect, developmental psychology, abnormal psychology, and trauma: society and the individual. She is also engaged in an active research program related to the psychological effects of traumatic stress including child maltreatment, intimate partner violence, and military-related trauma. Dr. Keen previously worked at the National Center for Posttraumatic Stress Disorder within the VA Boston Healthcare System, where she was engaged in both clinical work and research with military veterans.

PART I

Introduction/Purpose

CHAPTER 1

Introduction

The purpose of this textbook is to provide you with an overview of **child maltreatment**. This umbrella term includes both the abuse and the neglect of children. **Child abuse** is the term used for acts of commission—things a parent or caretaker does to a child that are inappropriate. Child abuse can include such diverse acts as beating, sexually assaulting, or verbally abusing a child. In each case, the adult is doing something to the child that is defined as maltreatment. Conversely, **child neglect** is the term used for acts of omission—things a parent or caretaker fails to do for a child when appropriate care would require that such things be done. Child neglect can include failure to provide for a child's physical, emotional, medical, or educational needs. In cases of child neglect, the parent fails to provide for the child even the minimum necessary for adequate care. Together, child abuse and child neglect make up child maltreatment. While most researchers in the field would agree to this terminology, it is important for readers of this literature to note that child abuse is also sometimes used synonymously with child maltreatment. In other words, when some authors write of child abuse, they often mean both abuse and neglect. I will also follow this usage largely because abuse is often a less awkward term than maltreatment. On the other hand, child neglect is not used to include child abuse; so when you see that term, you can be fairly certain that the focus is on acts of omission. The problem of confusing terminology is something we will need to keep in mind as we explore the literature on child maltreatment. This particular field is plagued with definitional issues. For example, what one author means by "sexual abuse" may be quite different from what another means by the same term. To be as clear as possible, I will begin each chapter that focuses on a type of maltreatment by establishing a working definition for that form of maltreatment. When you read other authors' chapters, you must be attentive to the definitions they are working with.

Many students become frustrated by the lack of definitional consistency in the field of child maltreatment. Although it does not make the situation any easier to deal with, it is helpful to note that the field is a new one. Certainly, the mistreatment of children is not new; all of recorded history includes references to acts we would today define as maltreatment. However, the professional examination of child maltreatment has a fairly short history. Many date the beginning of the professional research in this field to the early 1960s.

A BRIEF HISTORY OF CHILD MALTREATMENT

Although we definitely hear more about child abuse today than we did in the past, this does not mean it is a new phenomenon. The psychohistorian Lloyd deMause edited *The History of Childhood* in 1974, which he began with the now familiar quotation:

> The history of childhood is a nightmare from which we have only recently begun to awake. The further back in history one goes, the lower the level of child care and the more likely children are to be killed, abandoned, beaten, terrorized and abused.

> **DeMause, 1974, p. 1**

Ancient History

Historical research seems to support this rather grim statement. A study of ancient history reveals that **infanticide** (the act of killing an infant) was practiced in many societies. While we still use this term today, there are two important differences to note between ancient and modern usage. First, modern developmental psychologists define "infancy" as the period covering only the first year or two of life. In ancient times, the term infancy covered a much longer range, being identified as the period between birth and seven years. Second, while infanticide is clearly illegal today, in ancient times it was often condoned by society. The historians TenBensel, Rheinberger, and Radbill (1997) noted that in ancient times children did not have the right to live until that right was bestowed upon them by their father. If the father withheld this right, then the infants were abandoned. In some cases, even fathers could not grant their child the right to live. For instance, the Roman Law of Twelve Tables actually required that any "dreadfully deformed" child be put to death, no matter what the parents' desires were for that child. Reasons for infanticide included population control, appeasement of god(s), limitation of family size, and a way for an unwed mother to deal with shame. Allowing the murder of infants for any of these reasons suggests that children did not have even the most basic right—the right to life. Children who were permitted to live were considered to be the property of their fathers. As such, the rule of the father over the child was nearly complete. There is ample evidence that it was even socially acceptable in certain circles in ancient Greece for fathers to allow other men to use their sons sexually (Kahr, 1991). The respected philosopher Aristotle wrote, "The justice of a master or a father is a different thing from that of a citizen, for a son or a slave is property and there can be no injustice to one's own property."

Middle Ages

During the Middle Ages, laws forbidding infanticide were passed. It is not clear whether the laws were carefully enforced, but the idea was taking hold that the child at least had the right to live. This does not mean that the Middle Ages was a glorious time for children. The widespread poverty of this time made children a liability. There are horrific stories of children who were severely mistreated by their parents in order to bring more money into their household. Some children were actually sold for profit by their own parents. Other children were mutilated so that they would be more effective beggars. While wealthy strangers may have turned their back on a healthy child who was begging in the streets, it was harder to ignore a child who was blind or missing a limb; therefore, a child who was injured or deformed was likely to have more success on the streets.

Reformation

A dramatic change in the view of children occurred as a result of the Reformation of the 16th century. This religious movement, marked by a rise in Protestantism, had a significant impact on how children were regarded. On a positive note, children were seen as fragile creatures of God who needed to be safeguarded. As persons created in God's image, they had a soul and the right to life. On the other hand, all humans were born marked with the stain of original sin. These beliefs led to a resurgence of interest in educating children in a way that would overcome the stain of original sin. Parents and teachers were urged to use strict discipline in the hopes of molding the children into moral human beings (Stone, 1977). John Robinson, a pastor of the Pilgrim Fathers in Holland, wrote, "Surely there is in all children a stubbornness, and stoutness of mind arising from natural pride, which must in the first place be broken and beaten down" (Stone, 1977, p. 116). The general acceptance of this approach was clear when the birch rod became a symbol of education. The normative view seemed to be an acceptance of the saying "Spare the rod and spoil the child." Flogging became the normal punishment for any academic lapse, and records of the beatings reveal that they were often quite harsh. Children were whipped, generally with a bundle of birches, on their bare buttocks until they bled. Other teachers used a ferula (a flat piece of wood that had a rounded end with a hole in the middle) to hit students on the hand or mouth which resulted in a painful blister (Stone, 1977). The beatings extended even into the college years. Students working toward their bachelor's degree in the early 1600s could be flogged, not only by the college head but also by their deans and even their tutors.

While this paints a very bleak picture of childhood during the Reformation, there is some good news being reported in recent scholarship. Moran and Vinovskis (1986) found that this harsh child-rearing strategy may have been true of the prevailing public opinion, but many parents were resistant to using harsh discipline and instead raised their children with love and affection. This is also an important reminder that at any point in time, there will be great diversity in how children are treated, no matter what the current prevailing public opinion is.

Enlightenment

It was not until the Enlightenment that things begin to improve for children in terms of the generally accepted views of child rearing. The next shift in how childhood was viewed has been largely attributed to the writings of John Locke and Jean-Jacques Rousseau. Locke saw children as **tabula rasa**, which means blank slate. Locke viewed children not as innately flawed, but simply as blank or neutral. If children are tabulae rasae, then parents and teachers need only to shape children, mold them into whatever is good; there is no need to eliminate innate badness. Certainly, this would suggest that a kinder, gentler parent and educator was required. Rousseau's philosophy went even further by saying that children were noble savages, neither evil nor blank, but endowed with an innate sense of right and wrong. Rousseau believed that a parent's training would only interfere with a child's innate, orderly, moral development. Instead of forcing or molding a child, an adult needs to be sensitive to a child's needs (Berk, 1997). Children should be permitted to grow with very little constraint by parents or teachers.

Industrial Revolution

This shift in the view of human nature, from evil to neutral to good, does not mean that children have been treated gently since the Enlightenment! In fact, some of the saddest stories about the mistreatment of children come from the 19th century and the Industrial Revolution. Although the Industrial Revolution brought relief from hard labor for many, it was merely a new age of abuse for poor children who were brought into the labor force. Even very young children were forced to work long hours in horrific conditions where they were exposed to occupational hazards.

Some of the most compelling child labor stories in the U.S. were about the "breaker boys," who worked in the anthracite coal industry. The job for these boys was to pick impurities, like slate, out of the coal before it was sold. In order to do this, the boys sat on benches that were suspended over the conveyor belts that carried the coal. They spent their days bent over, picking through the coal in order to remove any impurities. The air was thick with coal dust that settled in their lungs and led to harsh coughs. Their hands were covered with cuts and calluses from dealing with the rough and sharp material. The long days of their work were filled with noise and danger. Boys who fell from their suspended benches suffered burns, cuts, and occasionally death by suffocation. Some adults indicated that the work done by the breaker boys was even more dangerous than working in the mines (Hindman, 2002).

These abuses continued in the U.S. until child labor laws were passed and enforced. By the late 1800s, advocates for children began pushing for legislation that would protect children. By 1900, all industrialized states had some law that dealt with child labor, but the laws at this time varied substantially in terms of the rules they proposed and the seriousness of their enforcement. This discrepancy led advocates to fight for a federal law to protect children in the workforce. Initial attempts at passing and sustaining a federal child labor law were not successful for a variety of reasons, including charges that they were unconstitutional or that they gave the federal government too much power. The issue was not resolved until 1941, when the U.S. Supreme Court upheld the Fair Labor Standards Act, which limited child labor. In many ways, the passing of this federal law was anticlimatic, because most child labor in the U.S. had been eliminated by that time (Hindman, 2002). Children living in the U.S. today are well protected by the child labor laws. With only a few exceptions (acting, newspaper delivery, some types of family businesses), children under the age of 14 are not permitted to work. Between the ages of 14 and 15, work for pay is limited by law. When school is in session, young adolescents may work a maximum of 3 hours per day and no more than 18 hours per week. When school is not in session, they can work no more than 40 hours per week. Some dangerous jobs like coal-mining, roofing, and logging may only be done by adults. Although the enforcement of the child labor laws in the U.S. is not perfect, it is generally considered to be fairly good. While these laws were directed at eliminating child maltreatment at work, they were not relevant to what went on in the home.

Looking at maltreatment from a historical perspective can give us hope when we consider how far we have come in protecting children. Although children today still suffer from abuse and neglect, many would argue that the lot of children is far better now than it has ever been. The progress we have made is, to a large degree, the result of the work of child advocates. Although some may judge the response to child maltreatment as too slow and too little, there have always been people who were willing to fight for children, and progress has been made.

RESPONDING TO CHILDREN IN CRISIS

History is peppered with notes that in some cases children were protected or treated gently. Over 6,000 years ago in Mesopotamia, there was a patron goddess for orphans who was believed to protect any child who did not have parents (TenBensel et al., 1997). Continuing concern for orphans is seen in the presence of orphanages throughout recorded history. For example, both Athens and Rome had homes for orphans. In the 12th century, Pope Innocent III established some of the first foundling houses to care for children who had been left behind in the wake of the Crusades. A more personal illustration can be found in the writings of Sir Thomas Moore, who lived from 1478 to 1535 and who clearly did not reflect the punitive approach to child rearing that was prevalent during his lifetime. He wrote to his children:

> I never could endure to hear you cry. You know, for example, how often I kissed you, how seldom I whipped you. My whip was invariably a peacock's tail. Even this I

wielded hesitantly and gently, so that sorry welts might not disfigure your tender seats. Brutal and unworthy to be called father is he who does not himself weep at the tears of his child.

(Stone, 1977, pp. 119–120)

Colonial America

Despite these flashes of benevolence, the widespread recognition of and response to child abuse is a modern phenomenon. In colonial America, the father had nearly complete control over his wife and his children. Strict discipline was considered to be appropriate and was justified by looking to the harsh justice meted out in the Bible. It was also permissible to turn a child over to another household as an indentured servant or an apprentice (who would receive training). The earliest recorded cases of child abuse involved masters and their apprentices. In severe cases of abuse a child might be released from indentures, and in fatal cases a master could be punished. However, prosecutions for child abuse were rare and differed from modern cases in that they did not involve parents (Jones, 1978).

The first recorded cases of child abuse charges against parents occurred in the 1670s and involved removing children from unsuitable homes. Study of these cases reveals that the homes were labeled "unsuitable" because the parents were not instilling the proper values (religious training and a strong work ethic) in their children. It was not until the 1820s that child neglect cases appeared in court. These cases, like the early abuse cases, rarely involved parents. Instead, child neglect charges were generally related to children living in institutions such as alms houses. For the most part, parents were allowed to treat their own children as they saw fit (Jones, 1978).

The Case of Mary Ellen

Even though the earliest records of criminal cases of child abuse in the U.S. date back to the mid-1600s, the public recognition of child maltreatment in the U.S. is often tied to the case of Mary Ellen Wilson in the 1870s. The story of Mary Ellen's early life is a sad one. According to public records, Mary Ellen was the biological daughter of Francis "Fanny" Connor and Thomas Wilson. While Thomas may have known about the birth of his daughter, he never had the chance to meet her. Mr. Wilson, a soldier in the Civil War, was killed in May of 1864. As a young widow, Fanny Connor was not able to survive on the benefits she received from the government, so she went to work as a laundress and paid a woman named Mary Score to care for her daughter. After placing Mary Ellen with Ms. Score, Fanny would visit her daughter and act in a loving way toward her. However, after a short time, Fanny stopped showing up to visit her daughter, and she failed to send money for her care. After Mary Score had not received payment for three weeks, she left Mary Ellen at the Department of Charities and Corrections on July 7, 1865. This was the first time the young Mary Ellen turned out to be a survivor. Despite the 85% death rate for infants in orphanages in New York at that time, Mary Ellen survived.

In 1866, when Mary Ellen was approximately 18 months of age (her exact birth date was never known), she was indentured to Mary and Thomas McCormack. Although Mary McCormack had given birth to three children prior to this time, none of them had survived. At the alms house, Mr. Thomas McCormack alleged that Mary Ellen was his daughter and that her birth was the result of an affair he had with her mother. He was never asked to prove this claim, and the adoption was permitted without any proof of his paternity. Seven months after the adoption, Thomas McCormack died of cholera, and Mary McCormack subsequently married a man named Francis Connolly (Shelman & Lazoritz, 2005). Mary Ellen was living with Francis

Figure 1.1   Mary Ellen. Photo Credit: The George Sim Johnston Archives of the New York Society for the Prevention of Cruelty to Children.

and Mary Connolly in 1873 when her plight came to the attention of Etta Wheeler, a Methodist missionary who visited with the poor in New York. During Etta's visits with a dying woman, she heard about a young girl, Mary Ellen, who was beaten and whipped by her mother in the same tenement house. The dying woman told Ms. Wheeler about the small child, who was frequently heard crying and screaming amidst the sounds of beatings. The pitiful sounds moved the ill woman to beg Etta Wheeler to find help for the girl. Ms. Wheeler was moved by the plight of Mary Ellen and attempted to have her removed from this abusive home. She was not successful in obtaining assistance from the police or from any benevolent societies that existed at that time (TenBensel et al., 1997; Watkins, 1990).

It is at this point that the story gets a bit confused. What we do know is that Ms. Wheeler approached Henry Bergh, who was the president of the American Society for the Prevention of Cruelty to Animals (ASPCA). After hearing about the case, Mr. Bergh sent a man to investigate Ms. Wheeler's claims. While pretending to be a census taker, this gentleman gained access to every room in Mary Ellen's home and was able to see the child in person. His report corroborated the story told by Etta Wheeler. Based on this information, Mr. Bergh was able to use his influence to have the child removed from her home by police officers the next day. Mary Ellen's story has grown to include the myth that she was protected under the existing animal protection laws. It has been said that Bergh argued for Mary Ellen to be considered an animal and given the rights any other animal would have, because she could not get aid as a child. This makes a good story, and it points out the fact that the American Society for the Prevention of Cruelty to Animals predates the **Society for the Prevention of Cruelty to Children** (SPCC), but it is not exactly what happened. Instead, it seems that Mr. Bergh advocated for Mary Ellen as a prominent citizen, not as head of the American Society for the Prevention of Cruelty to Animals. Mr. Bergh also used his influence to get the case covered by *The New York Times* (Watkins, 1990).

When Mary Ellen was brought before Judge Lawrence, he listened to her story as well as testimony from Ms. Wheeler, neighbors, and the investigator for the New York Society for the Prevention of Cruelty to Animals. Judge Lawrence agreed that Mary Ellen needed to be rescued,

Figure 1.2 Etta Wheeler. Photo Credit: The George Sim Johnston Archives of the New York Society for the Prevention of Cruelty to Children.

and he appointed himself her temporary guardian. Not only did Judge Lawrence work to protect Mary Ellen, he punished Mrs. Connolly. After being found guilty of felonious assault, she was sentenced to one year of hard labor in the penitentiary (Watkins, 1990).

When no relatives could be found to take Mary Ellen, she was placed into a home for children until Ms. Wheeler again intervened and had Mary Ellen placed with Ms. Wheeler's mother. Because of the deprivation of her early life, there was much Mary Ellen had to learn. For example, Etta Wheeler's mother remarked that because the child had so rarely been outside, she did not know how to walk on uneven ground. She also had no experience with peers or appropriate discipline. However, Mary Ellen seemed to thrive in her new surroundings. Unfortunately, less than five months later, her new guardian died of tuberculosis. Mary Ellen was then taken in by Etta's sister and brother-in-law, Elizabeth and Darius Spencer. There are not many details available about Mary Ellen's subsequent life, but we do know that when she was 24 years, old she married a widower, Lewis Schutt, who had two sons, and Mary Ellen and Lewis subsequently had two daughters. We also know that Mary Ellen named her firstborn "Etta," in honor of the woman who had rescued her, and her second daughter was named Florence. Both of her daughters went to college and became teachers. When asked about their mother, Etta and Florence said that she did not talk much about her childhood, but that she still carried the physical scars from the years of abuse. They also added that she was never a very strict disciplinarian with them! Mary Ellen lived to be 92 years old, a success story for child protection (Shelman & Lazoritz, 2005).

Largely as a result of the attention garnered by the Mary Ellen case, the Society for the Prevention of Cruelty to Children was founded in New York. Very quickly, this type of society spread across the nation. By 1900 there were 161 societies that had as their primary mission the protection of children (National Association of Counsel for Children, n.d.).

Juvenile Court

Not long after the case of Mary Ellen, there was a major change in how children were treated by the legal system in the U.S. In 1899 the first juvenile court was founded in Illinois, and by 1920 all but three states had **juvenile court** systems. These court systems were established to deal with cases of juvenile delinquency as well as with children who were neglected or dependent on the state. With regard to delinquency, this court's goal was to rehabilitate youthful offenders by keeping them separate from adult criminals and by focusing more on treatment than on punishment. Even though these were humanitarian goals, things did not work as smoothly as hoped. Because the focus was to be on helping children, it was deemed unnecessary to grant the juveniles the protective rights that adult defendants have in criminal court. Unfortunately this resulted in children, who had neither lawyers nor other constitutional rights granted to adults, receiving harsher sentences than their adult counterparts in criminal court. Instead of treatment or guidance, delinquents were simply being locked away.

In re Gault. The practice of denying due process rights to juveniles was modified after the pivotal case *In re Gault* (1967). Gerald Francis Gault, a 15-year-old boy, was found guilty of making lewd remarks over the telephone. If an adult had been found guilty of such a crime, the maximum sentence would have been a fine of $50 or two months in jail. Gerald Gault was sentenced to five years in a state industrial school in Arizona. So the "gentler" system of the juvenile court was planning to incarcerate a child for years for making what amounted to a dirty phone call. Clearly, the court was not working as intended—a move that was supposed to help children was in fact hurting them. After this case, juveniles were granted due process rights such as the right to an attorney, the notice of charges, the right to cross-examine witnesses, and the right to remain silent (Sagatun & Edwards, 1995). Although the early cases heard in juvenile court dealt more with delinquency than dependency, the use of this court to protect children has grown steadily, and today most child maltreatment cases are heard in this court (see chapter 10).

Prince v. Massachusetts. Another major legal step for the protection of children was the 1944 Supreme Court ruling in *Prince v. Massachusetts*. This ruling confirmed that states do have the right to interfere in family relationships to protect children. The highest court in the land said that the government had the right to intervene in a family in order to protect the children, even when challenged with claims of religious freedom. The facts of this case revolved around Sarah Prince, a Jehovah's Witness, who was convicted for violating the child labor laws. Ms. Prince had custody of her nine-year-old niece, Betty M. Simmons, and she had the child distributing religious literature. She claimed that her rights to exercise her religious freedom as guaranteed by the Fourteenth Amendment were being violated by the child labor laws. In his majority opinion, Justice Rutledge wrote:

> And neither rights of religion nor rights of parenthood are beyond limitation. Acting to guard the general interest in youth's well being, the state as parens patriae may restrict the parent's control by requiring school attendance, regulating or prohibiting the child's labor, and in many other ways. Its authority is not nullified merely because the parent grounds his claim to control the child's course of conduct on religion or conscience. ...the state has a wide range of power for limiting parental freedom and authority in things affecting the child's welfare; and that this includes, to some extent, matters of conscience and religious conviction.

(p. 5)

One important term that may be unfamiliar is the Latin phrase, **parens patriae** (pa-renz pa-tree). The translation is "father of his country," and it asserts that the state is the ultimate guardian for children and the mentally incompetent. While the care of children is entrusted to their parents, the state is the final guardian. Whereas historically fathers had nearly total control of their children, the state was now clearly saying that it had the ultimate say in child rearing.

Professional Publications Related to Child Maltreatment

As the public and the legal system began to move forward in child protection, it also became an area of interest for professionals to study and write about. The article that truly seemed to spur the research in this field was "The Battered-Child Syndrome." This paper was written in 1962 by five medical doctors: Kempe, Silverman, Steele, Droegemueller, and Silver, and it was published in the very well respected *Journal of the American Medical Association*. In this paper, Kempe et al. defined battered-child syndrome and described its incidence, clinical manifestations, and psychiatric aspects. A good portion of the article was devoted to techniques used to evaluate children, and this section was focused on the use of radiologic examination. It was the invention and application of pediatric x-rays that most aided doctors in moving from having a hunch about physical abuse to having concrete proof of maltreatment. Kempe et al. concluded their report by stating, "Above all, the physician's duty and responsibility to the child requires a full evaluation of the problem and a guarantee that the expected reposition of trauma will not be permitted to occur" (p. 24). Many believe that this article created the study of child maltreatment as a distinct academic field. This statement is supported by an examination of the number of papers related to child maltreatment that were published in the years before and after Kempe et al.'s paper. In the decade prior to Kempe et al.'s article, only nine articles had been published that dealt primarily with child maltreatment. In contrast, in the decade following, 260 such articles were published (Dorne, 2002). This information explosion continues at an amazing rate. If you type the term "child maltreatment" into the **PsycINFO** search engine and limit it to 2007, you get 172 hits for just that one year. If you search the decade 1997–2007, you will get 1,618 entries! What professionals and students today need to do is to attempt to digest this information while keeping in mind that it is still a new field of study.

Kempe et al.'s article not only spurred a dramatic increase in research, it was also the reason that the **Children's Bureau** hosted a symposium focused on child abuse in 1962. It was at this conference that professionals began to set up the standards for the mandatory reporting of child abuse by professionals (see chapter 3).

Although most researchers agree that Kempe et al.'s article was a land-breaking publication, it was not the first professional publication on child abuse. A century before it appeared, a French physician by the name of Ambroise Tardieu wrote fairly extensively about child maltreatment. In the 1860s Tardieu described the negative effects of child labor, the severity of physical abuse committed by some parents, the problem of infanticide, and even the sexual abuse of both female and male children (Labbe, 2005). Clearly, Tardieu was a man ahead of his time. Many things that are believed to be true concerning child abuse today were noted in Tardieu's 37-page article. For instance, Tardieu noted that the victims who suffered the most serious injuries were the very young; that bruises on abused children's bodies varied in coloration, indicating that they occurred at different times; that many of the marks on the children were in the shape of fingers; that there were a "frightening multiplicity" of wounds; and that doctors should inform the police if they see such injuries (Knight, 1986).

Although Tardieu's paper was very thorough, it did not radically changed the way physicians interpreted suspicious injuries in children. In 1888, twenty-eight years after the publication of Tardieu's paper, Dr. Samuel West published an article in the *British Medical Journal* examining severe swelling in the membranes surrounding the bones of several infants in the same family. This article on differential diagnosis (selecting the correct diagnosis when several options are possible) considered scurvy, syphilis, and rickets as possible causal factors. That the injuries could be the result of trauma inflicted by parents was not even mentioned, despite the fact that none of the natural diseases discussed adequately explained the symptoms (Knight, 1986).

Considering that it took a hundred years for the explosion of professional writing on child maltreatment to begin after it was first addressed in the professional literature, it becomes clear that more than interest and attention must be present for a topic to become popular: society has to be ready to hear about the issue and act on it.

Federal Law in the United States

The Social Security Act of 1935 includes a section (521) on Child Welfare Services within the Title IV—Grants to States for Aid to Dependent Children. This section outlines the willingness of the federal government to help fund agencies "establishing, extending, and strengthening, especially in predominantly rural areas, public welfare services (hereinafter in this section referred to as child-welfare services) for the protection and care of homeless, dependent and neglected children and children in danger of becoming delinquents" (The Social Security Act, Part 3, Section 521, a). While this law marks the beginning of the practice of child protection being partially funded by the federal government, it is striking that there is no mention of physical abuse.

This also illustrates the fact that the federal government does not have direct control over how states respond to children in need. However, Congress does have the right to decide how money should be spent to further national welfare. Therefore, the federal government can influence policy and practice by insisting that the states follow certain rules if they wish to be eligible for funding (Myers, 2002).

It was not until 1974 that the first federal law on child abuse was passed in the U.S., the Child Abuse Prevention and Treatment Act (CAPTA). This legislation provided states with funding for the investigation and prevention of child abuse as long as the states had mandated reporting laws. The act also established the **National Clearinghouse on Child Abuse and Neglect** (NCCAN) to serve as a clearinghouse for information about child maltreatment. Since this time, the federal government has maintained an active role in the prevention and treatment of child abuse by funding states for complying with federal guidelines. Today, in order to receive federal funding, states must comply with the Keeping Children and Families Safe Act of 2003. The funding and regulations are constantly adjusted and updated, but it seems clear that the federal government will continue to play an active role in protecting children.

RESEARCH ON MALTREATMENT

This textbook is based on the existing research on child maltreatment. Great strides have been made in understanding abuse and its consequences, but there is still much to learn. Progress has been impeded by how difficult it is to conduct research in this area. There are several concerns about research methodology that must be kept in mind as you consider the information presented in this book.

Only Identified Children Are Studied

First, the research on maltreated children is conducted on *identified* children. If you read an article that is comparing neglected children to nonneglected children, you need to remember a few things about the children in the groups that are being compared. If we know children in the neglected group have been neglected, then someone has labeled them this way. So, research on neglected children does not include children who are being neglected but have not yet been identified as victims. It is certainly possible that children who are suffering undetected neglect may differ from those who have been identified. This may have led you to the next possible problem: are there unidentified neglected children in our nonneglected group? One or two such children in a large study should not cause any major problems, but researchers should not lose sight of the fact that these are difficult groups to clearly identify .

Because not all victims of maltreatment are known as children, some researchers have worked with a **retrospective design**. These studies collect data in the present that are based on recollections of the past. In these cases, adults are asked to recall their past and any maltreatment they suffered, and then answer questions about their present situations. The most obvious limitation of this research is that we all have faulty memories. The memory of our past is not like a video recording. Instead of being perfect records, our memories are biased by our life experiences, our current mood, and even the situation we are recalling. Furthermore, even if a person does accurately recall abuse, it is not a given that he or she will report the maltreatment. Just as children may be ashamed or unwilling to report abuse while it is happening, adults may also keep secrets for myriad reasons. Adults may deny being abused as children because they do not want to recall the painful events, because they are ashamed, or because they do not want to make their families look bad. On the other hand, and probably less common, it is also possible that a person would report a history of abuse when no maltreatment was actually suffered. For instance, a man who is currently charged with abusing his children may report that he too was a victim of abuse in an attempt to excuse or explain his current behavior. Finally, it is evident that there is not likely to be any corroborating evidence of abuse years after it allegedly occurred. For all of these reasons, one must be careful when interpreting data that has been collected retrospectively.

Problems with Separating Different Forms of Maltreatment

A further research concern arises when we want to compare the effects of different types of maltreatment. Take, for instance, a researcher who wants to study the impact of sexual abuse, physical abuse, emotional abuse, and neglect on attachment (the emotional bond between child and caregiver). This design assumes that we can identify children who suffer from just one type of maltreatment and compare them to others who suffer from one other type of abuse. If a parent is beating a child, can we truly say there is no emotional abuse involved? Unfortunately, as you will learn throughout this text, many children suffer simultaneously from multiple types of abuse. However, grouping maltreated children together also has its disadvantages, as a child who is raped is likely to be affected quite differently from a child who is not fed consistently.

Effects of Maltreatment May Not Be Immediately Obvious

Also, when determining the effects of abuse, one needs to consider timing. Imagine that a researcher is interested in aggressive behavior among preschool boys who were the victims of physical abuse. This researcher may measure aggression among boys who come to the attention of **child protective services** (CPS) when their abuse has been discovered. Imagine further that he finds no differences in aggressiveness between the physically abused boys and a comparison group of nonabused boys. Does this mean the boys have not learned aggressive behavior from their parents? Is it possible that children who are not initially aggressive as a result of abuse may become aggressive later in life when they are physically stronger? Could it be the case that boys only recently removed from abusive homes may be in shock and somewhat withdrawn at the time of the study and that this behavior will change later? Questions like these point to the importance of **longitudinal research**. This is research that follows participants for a long period of time: years, decades, a lifetime. Although this type of research provides excellent data, it takes years to complete, and it is costly. Of course, even with the necessary time and money, one would still need to find participants who are willing to be a part of a continuing study and who will stay with the project. Attrition among participants can be a major impediment to longitudinal research. It is not unusual for participants to drop out, move away, or even die.

Difficulty Separating the Effects of Poverty and Maltreatment

Yet another concern about the research on child maltreatment is the fact that abuse is very often confounded with poverty. This means that many children who are identified as victims of maltreatment are also living in poverty. Therefore, if researchers find that maltreated children exhibit language delays, we need to know if these delays are due to the maltreatment or to the poverty. Researchers work to control this problem by carefully selecting their control (nonabused) groups. If most of the children in the maltreated group live below the poverty line, then the same percentage of children in the control group should be from families with similarly low incomes.

Socioeconomic status (SES) is only one variable that researchers need to consider when they are selecting a comparison group. Other issues that should be considered include the make-up of the family, family dysfunction, age and sex of child, and environmental stresses. If we want to say that something about a group of children is the result of the maltreatment they suffered, then we must be confident that the groups we are comparing differ only in terms of maltreatment status. As you can imagine, this makes devising appropriate control groups an extremely challenging prospect.

Inability to Make Causal Statements

Another aspect of research on child maltreatment makes it difficult to make causal statements— to say this act *caused* this effect. We cannot make causal statements based on **correlational research**, and much of the research in this field is, of necessity, correlational. In a correlational research study, an experimenter measures two variables to determine if they are related. The researcher does not manipulate anything. I can ask, for example, if there is a relationship between the number of hours a child is left alone and vocabulary at age three. I may find that the two variables are related: as hours left alone increase, vocabulary decreases. This would be a negative correlation, which means as one variable goes up, the other goes down. Now, it may be tempting and even correct to say that being left alone for many hours *causes* a decrease in vocabulary, but we do not know this to be true from correlational work. Is it not possible that children with low vocabularies are left alone more often? That is, could it be that having a low vocabulary causes people to leave you alone more often? It could also be that some other, unexamined factor causes both of these things. Perhaps parents with low education are forced to work long hours to make ends meet. These parents may also have a lower vocabulary than more educated parents and feel that it is less important to speak to their children, so the children are alone more and speak less as a result of their parents' educational level. Children who are left alone for a large number of hours but have parents who make speaking to them while they are at home a priority may have perfectly adequate vocabularies.

It is only when we conduct an **experiment** that we can be confident about cause-and-effect relationships. In an experiment, participants are randomly assigned to groups, and the groups are treated identically except for the one variable of interest. This would mean taking a sample of 100 children and assigning half of them to the condition of spending one hour alone per day and assigning the others to a second condition of spending three hours alone per day, and then measuring their vocabulary at some later date. Obviously, this is not an ethical solution to our research dilemma. If this sort of experimental manipulation is unethical, it should be clear that we cannot ethically conduct true experiments that explore the consequences of child maltreatment.

This may be a bit confusing to those who do not have a background in research methods, so I want to provide a crazy example to help you remember the limitations of correlational data. I can tell you (quite truthfully) that there is a positive correlation between Coca-Cola sales and murder. As the number of Cokes sold increases, so does the murder rate. If I try to make a causal statement based on this data, you will find that I sound a bit ridiculous. I could say that buying Coca-Cola makes you murder people. After all, there is a lot of sugar and caffeine in soda, so maybe it leads to murder! Or, maybe committing murder causes an increase in cola sales. Committing murder is hot, thirsty work, and you need a cool drink to refresh yourself! Either way, I look crazy. Can you figure out what causes this correlation? If you guessed heat or summertime, you are correct. This third variable explains the relationship between the other two; they are not causally linked to each other.

Lack of Clear Definitions

Another issue in child maltreatment that impacts research is the lack of clear, consistent definitions for terms. As I mentioned earlier, this is a field that is plagued with definitional ambiguity. One place to look for definitions is in the law. However, since each state has its own laws, you will find 50 definitions for child maltreatment instead of one! Also, the definitions all include terms that are not operational. For a term to be operationally defined, it must have a precise meaning that can be measured by way of observable operations. It is ideal in research situations for all variables to have **operational definitions**; this is the only way the exact meaning of a term can be clear. For example, "fails to meet child's emotional needs" is a vague phrase. It is likely that multiple observers would disagree if they were rating the interaction of a mother and her infant over a period of time according to this criterion. A possible operational definition would be "the parent fails to respond to the child's cry within 5 minutes." While we would have better interrater reliability with this second measure, we also lose something. After all, meeting a child's emotional needs surely entails more than responding to cries. We could add to this by measuring the amount of time a parent makes eye contact with the child, the number of times a child is praised, and so forth. By all of these ratings we are trying to precisely measure a complex phenomenon. We are using these behavioral observations to measure, in a consistent way, how well a parent is meeting a child's emotional needs. Even though there is no perfect solution to this problem, researchers can work on using the same or similar measures, and we can all be attentive to how researchers operationally define their variables. (This information is generally included in the Methods section of a research report.)

The Secrecy Surrounding Child Maltreatment

Finally, abuse is by definition a private event. We are talking about behavior that occurs within the privacy of the home. This is an arena that is typically not open to intense examination. Also, parents and often children are motivated to keep abuse secret. While it may seem obvious for parents not to want anyone to know because they fear punishment and loss of their children, why would children remain silent? Some children are threatened into silence. They are told explicitly not to let anyone know what is happening or something terrible will happen. Parents may even coach children to tell stories to account for injuries they have suffered. Other children have more complex reasons for not telling about abuse, reasons that range from a deep sense of shame to a lack of knowledge that what is happening is wrong or different from what goes on in other families. Because so many children will never self-identify, we need to be as observant as possible in order to figure out which children are being maltreated.

CONCLUSION

Although the mistreatment of children is not new, the formal, public study of it has a relatively short history, as does the consistent, legal response. Furthermore, even though a number of issues make research on child maltreatment a challenge, none of them stop researchers from trying. Although progress may seem frustratingly slow at times, a historical context can help us maintain perspective. We know more today about child maltreatment than we ever have, and the research literature continues to grow at an amazing rate.

DISCUSSION QUESTIONS

1. You may have heard newscasters making statements such as, "Our children are at a greater risk today than ever. There is an epidemic of child abuse. Something must be done." Based on the information presented in this chapter, would you agree or disagree with the points made by the newscaster? Why or why not?
2. Which is worse: child abuse or child neglect? (Return to this question at the end of the course to see if your opinion has changed.)
3. Over time, there has been a trend toward more governmental intervention to protect children. Is this a good thing or a bad thing?
4. Some of the research limitations seen in this field can be overcome, but others cannot (for ethical reasons). Does this mean we should stop attempting to study child maltreatment empirically? Why or why not?
5. Find a recent article that deals with either physical abuse or neglect. Does the researcher clearly define the maltreatment term? Compare the operational definition you find with those found by your classmates. Did all of the researchers use the same definitions? Discuss how the use of different definitions impacts progress in the field.

DEFINITIONS

Child Maltreatment: the abuse and/or neglect of children. Specific definitions vary by state and purpose (legal, research, etc.).

Child Abuse: an act, generally deliberate, by a parent or caregiver that results in harm or death to a child.

Child Neglect: the failure of a parent or caregiver to meet the minimal physical and psychological needs of a child.

Infanticide: the killing of an infant, particularly a newborn.

Tabula Rasa: a blank slate; a mind that has not yet been affected by experiences or impressions.

Society for the Prevention of Cruelty to Children (SPCC): a nonprofit organization that was founded in 1875 to protect children and strengthen families. The SPCC offers mental health, legal, and educational services.

Juvenile Court: a court established in 1899 to hear cases of dependency and juvenile delinquency.

Parens Patriae: a Latin term meaning that the State acts on behalf of a child or mentally ill person. The State is the guardian of those who cannot protect themselves.

PsycINFO: an electronic database produced by the American Psychological Association that indexes the psychology literature.

Children's Bureau: the oldest federal agency for children. This agency is charged with providing for the safety, permanence, and well-being of children.

National Clearinghouse on Child Abuse and Neglect (NCCAN): a national resource for professionals that provides information regarding child maltreatment including prevalence, incidence, treatment, statistics, and statutes.

Retrospective Design: a research design that uses data based on recollections of past events. This type of design is limited because of concerns about memory degradation over time.

Child Protective Services (CPS): a government agency charged with protecting children and preserving families. This is the agency that responds to charges of child maltreatment. Not all states use the title CPS; variations include Department of Family Services (DFS) and Department of Social Services (DSS).

Longitudinal Research: a research design that involves repeated observations of a group of participants at regular intervals over a relatively long period of time.

Poverty: a situation in which income and resources are inadequate to obtain and maintain an acceptable standard of living. Official poverty levels are set by the Social Security Administration.

Socioeconomic Status (SES): a measure of a person's standing within a social group based on factors such as income and education.

Correlational Research: a study in which two or more variables are measured so that the degree of relationship between them can be measured.

Experiment: a form of scientific research in which a researcher manipulates one or more variables in order to see the effects on another variable or variables.

Operational Definition: a precise definition of a variable in terms of observable procedures or measurements.

CHAPTER 2

Risk Factors for Child Maltreatment

There are many factors to consider when attempting to figure out why child maltreatment occurs. We are not able to simply say, "If x is true, then abuse will occur." If it were determined that x caused child maltreatment, child protective services (CPS) would have a much easier job. First, professionals could work to prevent or fix x. Second, if x was present, CPS would know a child was at risk; and if x was absent, they would know the child was safe from maltreatment. Sadly, the picture that has emerged from research is not nearly so clear-cut. There does not seem to be any one factor that will cause maltreatment or prevent it from occurring. Instead, there are a multitude of factors that increase the likelihood that a particular child will be the victim of maltreatment. In trying to understand the complex phenomenon of child abuse, many researchers have found it helpful to keep the work of Bronfenbrenner in mind. This well-known psychologist says that in any attempt to understand human behavior, we must consider many levels of influence. We cannot look only at the child or even only at the family if we want to truly understand the problem. We must consider the broader social contexts in which these families exist. Researchers must examine the roles played by communities, local and federal government, the media, and even the time in which we live (Bronfenbrenner, 2000). Factors that increase the risk for child maltreatment have been identified in all of these contexts. While none of the factors discussed in this chapter means that a child will definitely be maltreated, each increases the likelihood that maltreatment will occur.

CHILD FACTORS

Certainly, we can start at the most narrow level and look at the individual child. We should never blame child victims for the maltreatment they suffer; however, there are things about children that may increase the chances that they will be the victims of maltreatment. For instance, female children are at a greater risk for sexual abuse than are male children; younger children are more likely to be victims of maltreatment than are older children. Neither of these factors can be changed, but they point to populations that may need more protection. Young children are vulnerable for a number of reasons, including the fact that they are more dependent on caregivers than are older children, it is more normative to use physical force against them, they are in greater danger of sustaining an injury due to their smaller size and strength, and they

19

may have greater problems with regulating their emotions (Belsky, 1993). Children with difficult temperaments, disabilities, psychiatric illness, or retardation are also at a greater risk for physical abuse (Brown, Cohen, Johnson, & Salzinger, 1998). Again, this does not mean that abuse is the child's fault, only that some child characteristics are risk factors for maltreatment. However, knowing what the child is like is not enough to predict maltreatment status. After all, most female children are not sexually abused, and most difficult children are not physically abused. We need to consider much more than the individual child if we want to fully determine the risk level for maltreatment.

PARENTAL FACTORS

While most parents will not maltreat their children, no matter what challenges those children pose, other parents are more likely to succumb to abusive behavior. For instance, parents who struggle with issues such as depression, low self-esteem, substance abuse, emotional instability, or poor impulse control are more likely to maltreat, as are parents who were themselves the victims of child abuse.

Parental Gender

Males and females are not equally likely to be perpetrators of child maltreatment. When it comes to child neglect, female caregivers are more likely to be guilty. Eighty-seven percent of all neglect charges are made against females, and if you focus exclusively on physical neglect, 93% of charges are made against females. This is largely accounted for by the fact that, in our culture, women are far more likely to be the primary caregivers for children than are men. On the other hand, 67% of all abuse charges are made against men. Men account for 89% of the charges of sexual abuse, 63% of the cases of emotional abuse, and 58% of all charges of physical abuse (Sedlak & Broadhurst, 1996).

Parental Substance Abuse

Parental substance abuse is frequently associated with all types of maltreatment; almost 80% of the families who come to the attention of CPS have some sort of substance abuse problem (Winton & Mara, 2001). However, the relationship between parental substance abuse and child neglect is stronger than the relationship between parental substance abuse and other types of maltreatment (Smith & Fong, 2004). When states were asked to report which problems were most likely to lead to child maltreatment, 85% listed substance abuse as one of the top two (poverty was the other leading cause). Substance abuse has also been noted in approximately two thirds of all cases involving child maltreatment fatalities. The relationship between substance abuse and maltreatment has been found among samples taken from CPS and also in community samples. Another depressing finding has been that a history of substance abuse on the part of the parent increases the chance that he or she will maltreat a child (see Focus on Research 2.1). Therefore, even if the parent is currently not using drugs, a history of drug use still increases the likelihood that he or she will maltreat children (Kelley, 2002). Not only does the abuse of drugs or alcohol inhibit the parents' ability to be fully present for the child, the child may have access to the substances or be endangered by riding in a car with an impaired parent.

There are a number of mechanisms whereby substance abuse may lead to child maltreatment. First, the direct effects of the drugs, or withdrawal from those drugs, may cause the parents to act out in anger or frustration. Many drugs are noted for their **disinhibition** of aggressive impulses. In an unimpaired state, an adult may well be able to resist the temptation to strike a child who is pestering him or her. However, while under the influence of drugs, this inhibition mechanism is compromised. Even if adults do not become aggressive when under the influence,

---

FOCUS ON RESEARCH 2.1

Ammerman, Kolko, Kirisci, Blackson, and Dawes (1999) conducted a research study aimed at exploring the link between substance use disorders and child abuse. They recruited the biological parents of 290 boys who were between 10 and 12 years of age. All of the children came from intact families. Clinical interviews were conducted with the parents to assess whether they currently suffered from a substance use disorder or had a history of previous substance use disorders. For the purpose of this research study, the authors excluded parents who used only nicotine, caffeine, or alcohol. After the parents were diagnosed with regard to substance use problems, they were asked to fill out the Child Abuse Potential Inventory (CAPI). This instrument is designed to measure how likely the parent is to engage in physically abusive behavior. They found that parents who currently had substance use disorders and those who had previously had a substance use disorder were at an increased risk for abusing their children, based on their Child Abuse Potential Inventory scores. There was no difference in risk between parents who currently had a substance use disorder and those who had a substance use problem at an earlier time. The authors concluded that for mothers and fathers, both past and present substance use disorders are strongly linked to an increased risk for child maltreatment.

---

they are likely to show impaired judgment in other ways. You have probably noted, in yourself or others, the tendency to make particularly poor decisions when a substance like alcohol is involved. Parents who are addicts may also focus on the drug to the point that they cannot meet their children's need (Kelley, 2002). Finally, if a pregnant woman uses drugs, she may have a direct impact on the fetus (see chapter 8, Fetal Abuse).

Although women who use drugs may value motherhood, they are likely to struggle with fulfilling that role. Kearney, Murphy, and Rosenbaum (1994) interviewed 68 cocaine-using mothers who were not in treatment. Most of these women were heavy drug users; 85% had used cocaine more than 1,000 times. The women reported that they placed a high value on motherhood, they had high standards for raising children, and they tried to protect their children from their drug habit (e.g., they would not use in front of their children, but they would hire sitters or wait until the children were in bed). However, even though they did not want their drug use to interfere with their parenting, they did note that the cocaine use interfered with their paying attention to their children. Furthermore, their use of cocaine took money that could have gone to the children, and it decreased their ability to be a good role model for their children. Sixty-nine percent of the women in this study had, at some point, either lost custody of their children or voluntarily placed their children with family members.

Parental Mental Illness/Problematic Personality Traits

As a group, people who abuse children are more likely to suffer from mental illness than are nonabusers. Maternal sociopathy and serious mental illness are both associated with an increased risk for child maltreatment (Brown et al., 1998). However, the vast majority of people who maltreat their children do not meet the criteria for a major mental illness. The strongest relationship between mental illness and child maltreatment is depression, particularly maternal depression.

Depression.   Depression is the most common mental disorder. Between 10% and 25% of women, and between 5% and 12% of men, will struggle with depression at some point during their lives. People who suffer from a major depressive episode experience a host of symptoms including a depressed mood, lack of interest in most activities, weight loss without dieting, sleeping problems, fatigue, problems concentrating, and thoughts of death. By definition, these symptoms impair the person's social functioning (American Psychiatric Association, 1994). Given these symptoms, it is not difficult to imagine that people who suffer from depression are at an increased risk for maltreating their children. Zuravin, Bliss, and Cohen-Callow (2005) reviewed the literature on the link between maternal depression and child maltreatment and concluded that there is a positive correlation between the two. The relationship was particularly strong for mothers of young children. Across studies, it was noted that depressed mothers were less emotionally involved with their children and showed less affection than did nondepressed mothers. Not only were depressed mothers lacking in positive interactions with their children, they were also more likely to be overtly hostile and to use harsh punishment than were other mothers.

Postpartum Depression.   If the onset of symptoms for depression occurs within four weeks of delivery, the descriptor *postpartum* is added to the diagnosis. Postpartum depression can be either nonpsychotic or **psychotic**. While psychotic postpartum depression is rare (only one in 500 to 1,000 births), it is more likely if the mother has suffered from a previous mood disorder, including postpartum depression following an earlier birth (American Psychiatric Association, 1994). In either case, it interferes with the relationship between the mother and her infant. Researchers have found that even mild maternal depression during the first months of a child's life has a significant, negative impact on bonding between the mother and infant (Moehler, Brunner, Wiebel, Reck, & Resch, 2006). With regard to psychotic depression, one study of 108 women who suffered from severe mental illness during the postpartum period found that 53% of the mothers reported delusions about their infants. The nature of the delusions greatly impacted the mother's interaction with her child. If the mother's delusions were of persecution, she tended to provide competent, affectionate care. These mothers did differ, however, from normal mothers in that they were overly anxious if separated from their children. On the other hand, a mother who had delusions that her child was evil (e.g., a devil) or that the baby was not hers was significantly more likely to be abusive (Chandra, Bhargavaraman, Raghunandan, & Shaligram, 2006). We should take special precautions with mothers experiencing psychotic depression because it is associated with abuse and infanticide; however, the *Diagnostic and Statistical Manual of Mental Disorders* notes that any maternal mood disorder increases the risk for infanticide (American Psychiatric Association, 1994).

While most abusers do not have a mental illness, they are more likely than nonabusers to have the following personality traits: feelings of inadequacy, impulsivity, violent tendencies, low self-esteem, immaturity, low frustration tolerance, and anxiety (Dorne, 2002). Raising children is a challenge for even the most even-tempered, well-balanced parents. People who are hampered by these types of personality traits are often not able to adequately meet the needs of their children.

Lack of Preparation

It seems that many maltreating parents are simply not prepared to adequately fulfill the parental role. It has been reported, for example, that neglecting parents tend to lack basic caregiving skills such as food preparation and housecleaning, which are important in meeting a child's physical needs. Neglectful parents also know less about children and child development than do nonneglecting parents. This lack of knowledge can lead to unrealistic expectations about what children should be able to do for themselves (Burke, Chandy, Dannerbeck & Watt, 1998; Dubowitz, Black, Starr, & Zuravin, 1993). A mother may fail to provide adequate food or supervision simply because she is unaware that her child needs such care. It is also possible that some neglectful mothers are not likely to learn the necessary parenting skills because they lack maternal motivation and they have less empathy for their children than do nonmaltreating mothers (Slack, Holl, McDaniel, Yoo, & Bolger, 2004).

Lack of knowledge can also lead to an over-reliance on physical punishment. If a parent does not know any alternatives to corporal punishment to control a child's behavior, they may resort to harsh, physical punishment for all infractions (Dorne, 2002). Because adults in the U.S. generally do not receive any formal instruction on parenting techniques, it is not uncommon to see adults who are bad parents simply due to ignorance. One has only to watch a few episodes of *The Super Nanny* to recognize that some parents have no idea how to control their children in appropriate ways.

Closely related to a lack of preparation is the finding that both maternal age and education level are risk factors for child maltreatment. Younger mothers and women with lower educational levels are more likely to maltreat their children than are older, better educated women (Brown et al., 1998). One study of 4,851 cases of child maltreatment found that over 30% of the children involved were born to teenage mothers (Bolton, Laner, & Kane, 1980). Furthermore, Lee and Goerge (1999) found that even when they controlled for other sociodemographic variables (e.g., race, birth year, sex of child, birth order), there was still a significant relationship between maternal age and all types of child maltreatment. By the time children were 5 years old, those born to mothers who were 17 or younger at the time they gave birth were 3.5 times more likely to be maltreated than were children born to mothers who were at least 22 at the time they gave birth.

Intergenerational Transmission

The idea that being maltreated as a child would increase the likelihood that you would maltreat your child is not new. Beginning in the 1970s this connection was highlighted in the literature. However, many of these early reports were based on the recollections of adults who had already been identified as abusers, and a lot of them relied on clinical samples with poor control groups. As studies with stronger designs began to appear, a rate of **intergenerational transmission** of approximately 30% was reported. If this number is accurate, it would suggest that being maltreated does increase the risk that you would abuse your children, but that the majority of maltreated children do not go on to become abusers. There are still, however, some significant limitations that should be noted about much of this work. For instance, the majority of studies do not account for the developmental status of the children studied. If the children (born to the previously abused mother) are young at the time of the study, it is not clear that they will not be abused later, or that a later-born child would not be abused (Belsky, 1993). In addition, if previous victims are maltreating their children, and this is not known, they would be counted as nonabusive. Furthermore, it may be that certain types of maltreatment are more likely to be handed down than are others. Ney (1989) reported that the highest intergenerational transmission rate was for verbal abuse, while the lowest rate was for physical neglect. Finally, others have reported that parents who suffered from one form of maltreatment may be at an increased risk for perpetrating a different form of maltreatment. For instance, DiLillo, Tremblay, and Peterson (2000) found that women who were sexually abused as children were more likely to physically abuse their own children than were women who were not sexually abused. This relationship was particularly strong for women who were still angry about their own victimization.

There are a number of reasons to explain why a maltreated child may grow up to be an abusive parent. First, the parent is simply doing what he or she knows. Most of what we learn about how to parent is from watching how our parents reared us. Researchers have noted that children as young as 3 years of age will interact with infant siblings in a manner that is similar to that used by their mothers. In other words, as early as the preschool years, children learn to parent by observing their own mothers (Ney, 1989). Even if we say we will not do what our parents have done, that can be difficult, especially during times of frustration or stress. Second, being the victim of maltreatment can lead to problems such as poor **attachment** skills, lack of empathy, and social isolation. All of these can, in turn, make a person fail at parenting. Another possible effect of being victimized as a child is becoming a substance abuser as an adult. Victims report turning to drugs to escape from problems or to help them deal with painful emotions. As reported above, substance abuse increases the chance that a person will abuse his or her child (Kelley, 2002). In this cycle, the effects of child maltreatment become risk factors for the next generation.

But, just as not all difficult children or all children with disabilities will be abused, not all depressed parents or all parents with a history of being maltreated will abuse their children. Will the depressed parent who was abused as a child, and who is now the parent of a disabled child, definitely maltreat that child? No. These are three risk factors, but the parent and the child are just two pieces of the maltreatment puzzle. We also need to look at the entire family.

FAMILY FACTORS

Families in which maltreatment occurs tend to score lower on a host of measures related to family functioning. In other words, child maltreatment is not the only problem seen within the family. Members of maltreating families report less togetherness and less communication within the family than do nonabusive families. Persons living in families that maltreat the children also report fewer positive interactions and a lower level of verbal exchange within the family (Paavilainen, Åstedt-Kurki, Paunonen-Ilmonen, & Laippala, 2001). There are also specific familial factors including single parenting, domestic violence, and large family size that increase the risk for child maltreatment.

Single Parents

A familial risk factor for child maltreatment is being raised by a single parent. The National Incidence Study-3 (see Focus on Research 2.2) revealed that children living with a single father were at the greatest risk, followed by those being raised by a single mother. The risk associated with single parenting is startling. Children who live with a single parent have a risk factor for physical neglect that is 87% higher than that of children who live with married parents. They are 77% more likely to be physically abused, and 165% more likely to be physically neglected. Children being raised by single parents are also at a greater risk of being emotionally neglected (74% greater) and educationally neglected (220% greater). Children being raised by a single parent are not only more likely to be abused, but they are also 80% more likely to be seriously injured by that abuse (Sedlak & Broadhurst, 1996). The association between single parenting and maltreatment was also evident in the data from the National Center for Child Abuse and Neglect (NCCAN). Paxson and Waldfogel (1999) examined this data from 1990 to 1996 and concluded that states with a greater percentage of absent fathers had higher rates of child maltreatment. This connection was particularly strong for families with absent fathers and working mothers. Brown et al. (1998) noted that both low involvement on the part of the father and low paternal warmth were associated with an increased risk for child physical abuse.

Domestic Violence

Sadly, having two parents does not guarantee safety from child maltreatment. Too often, intimate relationships are marked by violence. It is estimated that as many as 10 million children between the ages of 3 and 17 witness **domestic violence** each year in the U.S. Children who grow up in homes where one parent is beating the other can be harmed directly or indirectly by this type of behavior. In some cases, children are physically harmed by being in the wrong place at the wrong time. In other cases, children are hurt when they attempt to protect the parent who is being beaten. Even if a child is not physically harmed by domestic violence, he or she may be

---

FOCUS ON RESEARCH 2.2: THE NATIONAL INCIDENCE STUDIES

Congress mandates a periodic study of the incidence of child abuse and neglect in the U.S. So far, three National Incidence Study (NIS) reports have been written. The first, NIS-1, was conducted in 1979–80 and published in 1981; NIS-2 was conducted in 1986–87 and published in 1988; and the most recent report, NIS-3, was conducted in 1993–1995 and published in 1996. Although NIS-4 is currently under way, it is not yet available; therefore, information from NIS-3 (Sedlak & Broadhurst, 1996) will be used throughout this textbook. Work on NIS-4 began in April 2004, and the completion date is scheduled for the end of December 2008. The NIS reports are considered to be the best source of national information on the incidence of child abuse and neglect. The data that the report is based on comes from a sample of more than 5,600 professionals who represent 842 agencies and 42 counties. The participants surveyed were selected to accurately represent the population of the U.S.

The 1996 study defined child abuse and neglect in two ways. First, the authors used the Harm Standard to label children as maltreated if they had already been harmed by some type of abuse or neglect. Second, they used the Endangerment Standard to include already harmed children and children who were at risk of being harmed by maltreatment.

NIS-3 had four main objectives:

1. The authors' first goal was to assess the incidence of child abuse and neglect in the U.S. as accurately as possible. To this end, they wanted to include all cases of maltreatment, even if they had not come to the attention of CPS. Therefore, data was collected not only from CPS, but also from a host of other professionals who are likely to be aware of maltreatment cases in their communities (law enforcement, public health workers, school personnel, day-care providers, etc.).
2. The second objective was to identify factors that are commonly associated with maltreatment. They examined characteristics of the abused children, their families, and their circumstances.
3. Thirdly, the authors examined data on the incidence of civil and criminal proceedings in cases of maltreatment.
4. The final objective of NIS-3 was to probe the relationship among incidents of maltreatment, their detection, and what actions, if any, were taken to aid the children.

---

psychologically harmed by seeing this sort of violence. Children who are exposed to domestic violence exhibit a range of symptoms including aggression, anxiety, low self-esteem, academic difficulties, and stress (Graham-Bermann, 2002).

Large Family Size

Large family size also increases the risk of child maltreatment. In the National Incidence Study-3, children from the largest families (defined as families with four or more children) were at an increased risk for maltreatment when compared with children in families with fewer children. Interestingly, the lowest risk was associated with two to three children, and only children were at medium risk. While it may be easy to speculate why families with four or more children were more likely to maltreat, it is less easy to explain why only children are at a greater risk than those with one or two siblings. In families with many children, there are simply more responsibilities and stressors. Because the parent(s) have more to do, it is more likely that the demands of child rearing will overwhelm their available resources. On the other hand, only children may be at risk because they are the firstborn children and may have young, inexperienced parents (Sedlak & Broadhurst, 1996).

EXTRA-FAMILIAL FACTORS

In addition to examining the child, the parents, and the family, we also need to consider what type of support the family is or is not receiving. What sort of communities are these families living in? Are support services available? Are families linked with the available services and with families who could provide support? Anyone who has spent considerable time with children knows that they can be challenging. Can parents get a break? Programs like Mother's Morning Out or informal programs that trade child care can provide a much-needed break for stressed parents.

Lack of Support

Maltreating parents often have very little social support from either family or friends. Many times, maltreating families are best described as **socially isolated**. Abusive parents report less involvement with their communities and churches than do nonabusive parents (Brown et al., 1998). Maltreating mothers report that they have fewer friends who are available to offer them support, and they report less frequent contact with the friends they do have than do nonmaltreating mothers. Maltreating mothers also rate the support they do receive from friends as low quality (Bishop & Leadbeater, 1999). A number of explanations have been proposed to account for why maltreating parents are socially isolated. Some of this isolation may be due the tendency of maltreating families to be more transient than are other families. In one study, families who were neglecting their children were significantly more likely to have lived at their current address for less than one year than were control families (Zuravin, 1989). Others have argued that maltreating parents may avoid contact with other people in an attempt to hide their inadequate parenting. On the other hand, it may be that the peers of maltreating mothers see them as abusive and actively avoid them. Finally, it may be that maltreating mothers reach out to other parents who are attempting to deal with similarly stressful life situations themselves. If an impoverished, substance-using mother attempts to rely on other drug-using women who are living in poverty to provide parenting assistance, it is not surprising that these attempts will fail (Bishop & Leadbeater, 1999).

It has also been reported that the relationships that abusive parents do have tend to be of poorer quality than those enjoyed by nonabusive parents (Belsky, 1993). Williamson and Borduin (1991) reported that neglectful mothers seem unable to deal with the demands in their life, and they feel overwhelmed by the responsibility of raising children. Although all people experience moments when there seems to be too much to handle, one reason these mothers struggle more, and are more likely to fail, is that they have no one to turn to in times of need.

In addition to a lack of child care services or support, understanding the impact of a community requires looking at what is offered physically. Are there safe places to play? Does the community have parks where families can gather to play, socialize, and support each other? It has likely already occurred to you that many of these community factors will be dramatically affected by the socioeconomic status (SES) of the area.

Poverty

Poverty is strongly correlated with many types of maltreatment. The authors of the National Incidence Study reported that family income was related to all categories of child maltreatment except for emotional neglect and child fatalities. In all cases, lower income was correlated with a higher incidence of abuse. Even in the nonsignificant cases of emotional neglect and child fatalities, the differences were in the expected direction (Sedlak & Broadhurst, 1996). Other researchers agree that poverty is associated with increased risk for physical abuse and neglect but not for sexual abuse (Brown et al., 1998). One of the most consistent findings is that neglect, especially physical neglect, is clearly associated with poverty. Although most poor families do not neglect their children, being poor is a definite risk factor. According to National Incidence Study-3, the incidence of child neglect in families who earn less than $15,000 a year is 27 per 1,000 children, while the rate of neglect in families earning over $30,000 is only 1 per 1,000. Children from poor families are 44 times more likely to be neglected, 40 times more likely to be harmed by physical neglect, and 56 times more likely to be educationally neglected than their peers from wealthier families. Similar findings have been published by Lee and Goerge (1999), who reported that children from impoverished neighborhoods were 6 times more likely to be neglected than were children from neighborhoods with a higher socioeconomic status. The authors of this type of research assert that these differences are not due simply to the fact that poor children are more likely to come to the attention of professionals. Although it is possible that the higher rates of reported child maltreatment among those with lower socioeconomic status can be accounted for by the fact that poor children are more likely to be in contact with service providers (who would detect and report maltreatment), it is not the whole picture. Even when contact with agencies is controlled for, low socioeconomic status is still a significant risk factor for child maltreatment. Sedlak and Broadhurst (1996) noted that the National Incidence Study is based on information from CPS and other professionals who are likely to see a broader range of clients. In addition, the report uses information from public schools, and 89% of the children in the U.S. do attend public schools. (See Focus on Research 2.2 for a review of the National Incidence Study procedures.) In other words, the relationship between poverty and child neglect is well established.

Not only were poor children found to be at a greater risk for maltreatment, according to the National Incidence Study-3, but they were also more likely to be seriously injured by that abuse than were children from families with higher incomes (Sedlak & Broadhurst, 1996). Lack of money contributes directly to neglect by interfering with a family's ability to provide for the children, and it also contributes indirectly to other types of maltreatment by increasing stress and frustration while decreasing opportunities for relaxation and breaks from the demands of parenting.

Closely related to poverty is the problem of unemployment. In addition to decreasing income, unemployment increases stress and decreases self-esteem while often putting the unemployed parents in constant contact with their children. Other factors that are associated with poverty may also lead to child maltreatment. Many researchers have noted that there is a relationship between socioeconomic status and authoritarian parenting (demanding with low warmth), lack of parental involvement, and less emphasis on creating independence in children (Trickett, Aber, Carlson, & Cicchetti, 1991).

There are several reasons why an association might exist between poverty and child neglect. Dubowitz (1999) points out that families who are poor are more likely to be faced with a host of factors that are less common among the more affluent, such as extreme stress, unemployment, unstable housing, poor community support, dangerous environments, and minimal access to health care. In many cases it is the parents' inability to cope with all of these things that makes them unable to adequately provide for their children. Pelton (1994) further pointed out that because poor families tend to live in dangerous surroundings, there is less room for parental error. If a middle-class mother is distracted by a problem with her job and does not notice that her child has left the home, it is likely that the child will not be seriously harmed by wandering about a suburban area (lower in crime and traffic) without supervision. A poor mother, living in the inner city, would need to be more vigilant to keep her child safe.

CULTURAL FACTORS

Looking beyond the community, one also needs to consider the broader society. For instance, how accepting is a given **culture** of violence? When we listen to the music of the times, watch the movies being released, and tune in to the daily television shows, what messages are we receiving about violent behavior? Are children portrayed as innocent or as sexual beings? What messages are being sent about the importance of patient, nurturing parenting? What is the level of acceptance for **corporal punishment** by parents; how far can parents go before their behavior is considered inappropriate? What is the political climate with regard to parenting? The U.S. government has historically been reluctant to interfere with the sanctity of the family, and this cautious approach is seen in the traditionally low legal costs associated with violence within the family (Gelles & Straus, 1988). Consider how much more likely you are to be prosecuted for hitting my child than for hitting your own! We don't often consider these "big picture" questions, but it seems clear that they can impact the likelihood of maltreatment.

America is a country that tolerates a high level of violence. The rates of violent crime are shocking. During 2006 there were 1,417,745 violent crimes reported. Among these were 17,034 murders, 862,947 aggravated assaults, and 92,455 forcible rapes (The Disaster Center, 2007). It has been argued that this violent setting provides a background for the acceptance of violence within families.

Americans are also generally accepting of corporal punishment. Interestingly, the only people you can legally hit in the U.S. are children. This attitude probably grows out of the prevalent societal thought that children are the property of their parents. Even though corporal punishment is not considered abusive in the U.S., it has been noted that abusive parents are more likely to make frequent use of physical punishment and power assertion than are nonmaltreating parents (Brown et al., 1998). Although some laws and court decisions have called this into question, many still assert that parents should be allowed to raise their children as they see fit (Belsky, 1993).

CONCLUSION

Even if we consider all of these levels of influence, we still do not have a simple additive model for maltreatment. For instance, imagine you hear about a young, disabled boy being raised by his single, unemployed mother in a poor, dangerous community where messages of violence are prevalent in the entertainment that surrounds them and severe physical punishment is an accepted community norm. Do you know that he will definitely be abused? Although this is certainly not an ideal child-rearing scenario, it is not the case that there will *definitely* be maltreatment. All of these things are risk factors; none of them, alone or in combination, causes abuse. Surely, it would be appropriate to be concerned about a family facing so many hardships, but we cannot assume the boy is being maltreated. In one longitudinal study of risk factors for child maltreatment (Brown et al., 1998), the authors found that children who faced no recognized risk factors for child maltreatment had only a 3% chance of experiencing any form of maltreatment during their life (0% for physical abuse, 2% for neglect, and 1% for sexual abuse). At the other end of the risk spectrum, children who had four or more risk factors had a prevalence rate of 24% for child maltreatment (16% for physical abuse, 15% for neglect, and 33% for sexual abuse). Based on this information, the authors recommended that a large number of risk factors should be assessed in order to determine the level of risk the child is facing.

Just as there are risk factors for abuse, there are also protective factors that can prevent abuse, even when multiple risk factors are present. Diverse factors ranging from good health to a supportive extended family to good schools can all serve as compensatory factors. All of these factors make abuse more or less likely; none of them guarantees either abuse or safety. In assessing a particular situation, we should attempt to measure both the risk factors and the protective factors in the child's environment. It is when the risk factors outweigh the supportive factors that maltreatment is more likely to occur.

DISCUSSION QUESTIONS

1. Think about your own upbringing. What risk factors and what protective factors were present in your family?
2. Which risk factors do you think are more serious (more predictive of maltreatment), and which are less serious?
3. Based on the information presented in this chapter, if you were given $1 million to prevent child abuse in your community, how would you spend your funds?
4. Does research on child factors related to child maltreatment amount to blaming the victim? Why or why not?
5. Are there risk factors that would be unethical to attempt to eliminate? For instance, should family size be limited, or should adults who suffer from depression be prevented from having children?
6. While watching the news, you hear a local politician say, "Only married people should have children because single parenting causes child maltreatment." How would you respond?

DEFINITIONS

Disinhibition: a loss of the ability to restrain from or suppress behaviors or impulses.

Psychotic: mental disorders marked by the loss of contact with reality; generally marked by delusions, hallucinations, or serious thought disturbance.

Intergenerational Transmission: the passing down of a trait or behavior from one generation to the next.

Attachment: a strong, affectionate bond between two people. Infants typically form an attachment to their primary caregiver between 6 and 12 months.

Domestic Violence: violence, abuse, or intimidation that takes place in the context of an intimate relationship.

Socially Isolated: lacking sufficient social ties or support.

Culture: the socially transmitted behaviors, arts, beliefs, and institutions that characterize a group of people.

Corporal Punishment: physical punishment such as spanking or slapping.

CHAPTER 3

Mandated Reporting

It has been my experience that many students who elect to take a child abuse and neglect course do so because they are, or know they will become, **mandated reporters**. This is a role that can be intimidating, and the best way to address these insecurities and to better serve maltreated children is to learn more about abuse and neglect, as well as what exactly one is obligated to do as a mandated reporter. As you will see, it is a complex role that will place you in situations with no easy answers.

HISTORY OF MANDATED REPORTING

States adopted mandated reporting laws in the 1960s as part of the child abuse prevention movement. This movement was spurred by the publication of "The Battered-Child Syndrome" in 1962 (Kempe, Sivlerman, Steele, Droegemueller, & Silver) and by a conference addressing child abuse that was sponsored by the federal government in that same year. Once child abuse was recognized as a problem that the government should take a role in addressing, it was clear that there would need to be some way to bring these abused children to the attention of authorities. Given that there is a general reluctance to interfere with families and parenting practices, there needed to be some way to push people to make referrals. Professionals at this conference recommended laws requiring physicians to report possible physical abuse. This recommendation was quickly endorsed by the American Medical Association, the American Humane Association, and the Children's Bureau of the U.S. Department of Health (Myers, 1998). Although all states and the District of Columbia had mandated reporting laws by 1967, it wasn't until the Child Abuse Prevention and Treatment Act of 1974 that states were required to list mandated reporters as well as to provide **immunity** for them in this role, and to ensure confidentiality of records in order to be eligible for federal aid (Kalichman, 1999). States are required to have such laws; however, it is up to each state to decide exactly who is a mandated reporter, what type of penalty will be imposed for failure to report suspected maltreatment, and what safeguards will be in place to protect reporters from criminal or civil action (e.g., being sued). While all states grant immunity from civil and criminal liability to mandated reporters, this does not hold if one self-reports. In other words, if you report that you are abusing a child, you cannot claim immunity under the reporting laws; and yes, people have tried (Small, Lyons & Guy, 2002).

Impact of Reporting Laws

There is no doubt that the mandated reporting laws have been successful in increasing the number of reports made to child protective services (CPS). There were approximately 10,000 reports of child maltreatment made in 1962, and there were almost 3 million made in 1992 (Lindsey, 1994). So, if the goal of the mandated reporting laws was simply to increase the number of cases brought to the attention of CPS, it is clear that they fulfilled that role. The question of whether they have improved the situation for maltreated children will be addressed later.

PERSONS REQUIRED TO REPORT

Originally, states only included physicians as mandated reporters. Because the focus in the 1960s was on physical child abuse, it made sense to target those professionals who were most likely to see a physical injury. Over time, the understanding of child maltreatment grew to include nonphysical injury and physical injury that may not require a physician's care (e.g., bruising). In order to detect these cases, the lists of mandated reporters have grown to include many classes of people who come into contact with children as part of their professional duties. Today, states typically include all medical personnel, teachers, day care providers, religious personnel (with the exception of communication between priest and penitent), counselors (privileged communication is **abrogated** to allow for disclosure of child maltreatment), social service personnel, police, and others. Some states have more expansive lists that include such occupations as undertakers, Christian Science practitioners, and even film developers (who may become aware of abuse, particularly sexual abuse, when they develop pictures). You may find it interesting to note that lawyers are not listed as mandated reporters in any state. Some states (e.g., Kentucky, Mississippi, North Carolina) simply require that anyone with knowledge of maltreatment is mandated to report that information. It is important that you be aware of the state law where you live so that you know if you are required to report suspicions of child maltreatment (see Search the Web 3.1).

Permissive Reporters

What if you suspect child abuse and you are not a mandated reporter? You are still allowed, and even encouraged, to report. Nonmandated reporters are referred to as **permissive reporters.**

SEARCH THE WEB 3.1

With the Internet, it has become easy to search for relevant state statutes. To find the statute that lists mandated reporters for your state, you can log on to the site entitled the Child Welfare Information Gateway, which now includes the information previously included on the page for the National Clearinghouse on Child Abuse and Neglect Information at http://www.childwelfare.gov/systemwide/laws_policies/state/. At this site you need to complete three steps:

1. First, select the state you are interested in knowing about.
2. Second, choose an issue or issues. The relevant issues would be Immunity for Reporters of Child Abuse and Neglect, Making and Screening Reports of Child Abuse and Neglect, Mandatory Reporters of Child Abuse and Neglect, and Penalties for Failure to Report and False Reporting of Child Abuse and Neglect.
3. The final step is to submit your request by selecting "Go." You will then see a copy of the mandated reporting statute for the state you selected.

There is no legal consequence if a permissive reporter fails to report suspicions, yet many people feel a moral obligation to protect children they believe are at risk.

Conducting Research and Reporting Obligations

One recent controversy has developed around the role of research and mandated reporting. Are people who research child maltreatment obligated to report suspicions of maltreatment? Researchers are not generally listed as mandated reporters, so for the most part, they fall under the category of permissive reporters. However, their role is complicated by **informed consent**. Before people agree to participate in a research study, they are asked to give their informed consent. In addition to telling participants what will be expected of them during the experiment, researchers guarantee them confidentiality. While it is clear that the mandate to report trumps confidentiality for a mandated reporter, it is not clear how these two issues are balanced for a permissive reporter. In order to avoid such situations, some researchers limit questions that might lead to allegations of abuse. Others may include a notice of this limitation to confidentiality on their informed consent sheet. These approaches may keep the question from arising, but they also mean that data is incomplete and some children may continue to be at risk when they could have been identified and referred to CPS (Farberman, & Finch, 1997). Again, there are no easy answers, but this is a question that should be discussed with an **institutional review board** (IRB) before data collection begins. (Every institution where research occurs must have a board comprised of individuals charged with the task of ensuring the ethical treatment of research participants. Before any research project is conducted, the researchers submit a proposal to the IRB for approval. In this proposal, all risks and benefits are explored, and plans to ensure participants' safety are laid out. If the IRB does not approve the proposal, the research may not be conducted.)

WHEN TO REPORT

Determining whether you are required to report is actually the easy part. A much more difficult decision is deciding when to report. The typical standard is that you should report when you have "reasonable cause" to believe that a child has been, or may be, maltreated. This, of course, requires you to know the legal definitions of maltreatment (subsequent chapters in this book will be devoted to providing you with that information) and what "reasonable cause" means. How sure do you have to be before you report? As you may guess, there is no black-and-white answer to this question. One possibility is to err on the side of caution and report even the smallest suspicion. While this certainly covers you as mandated reporter, it overwhelms CPS and takes time that could be devoted to more serious cases. On the other hand, waiting until you have solid proof may leave a child in a dangerous situation when he or she should have received help. Most professionals recommend that you discuss your suspicions with senior colleagues whose opinions you trust. Let them guide you in your early decisions about which cases should be referred as you develop a feel for what is "reasonable cause." Also, by seeking the input of other reasonable people, you are fulfilling the requirement of the law; you are checking to see if the present situation would cause a reasonable person to make a report. Another way to begin to develop a feel for reasonable cause is to examine case studies that include a discussion of reporting issues. Seth Kalichman's (1999) book entitled *Mandated Reporting of Suspected Child Abuse: Ethics, Law, and Policy* is an excellent resource. He provides 12 case studies where suspected abuse was not reported and 7 cases where a report was made. Each of the case studies is followed by commentary and a list of "lessons learned." Exercises like this will help you to bridge the gap between the law and practical experience.

It may be helpful to keep in mind that you are not necessarily making an accusation when you call CPS; you are expressing concern for a child's well-being. It is not your job to investigate the claim or provide proof. Finally, if you wait until you are sure abuse has occurred, you have violated the law. The law requires that you report suspicion, and leaves the determination of abuse to CPS. Research reveals that several factors increase the likelihood that professionals will report. These factors include more serious maltreatment, suspicion of sexual abuse (as compared to physical abuse or neglect), and alleged victims who are younger. Furthermore, most mandated reporters will call CPS anytime a child discloses abuse (Myers, 1998).

There is some concern that the threshold for considering a situation abusive enough to report may be relatively high. Ashton (1999) had 86 graduate students in social work evaluate vignettes in terms of their "seriousness" and then indicate whether they would report in that situation. Participants were asked to rate the seriousness of the incident on a scale from 1 to 7, where 7 represented *very serious*. She found that a rating of 6.5 on this 7-point scale was needed before two thirds of the sample would report. Several scenarios described in this study did not meet this threshold. For example, readers assigned an average rating of less than 6.5 to the following situations: (1) a 9-year-old is left alone most of the day and night, parent is working; (2) parents make child kneel in closet; (3) father punches drunk teen. This means that less than one third of the sample would have reported these situations to CPS.

HOW TO REPORT

If you decide to report a case of suspected child maltreatment, you may call your local CPS, your state child abuse hotline, or the police. If you are not sure of how to contact your local or state services, you can call the **National Child Abuse Hotline** for assistance (1-800-4-A-CHILD).

When you call, be prepared to offer as much complete and detailed information as possible (making notes of suspicious behavior, markings, etc., is recommended). The first thing you will be asked to do is to provide the name of the child and where that child can be located. If CPS cannot locate a child, it is not going to be able to intervene. While this may seem obvious, CPS workers can tell stories of receiving calls with virtually no information, for example, about what some woman was doing to her child in a rest area, but with no other details provided! You will also be asked to supply the name and location of the alleged **perpetrator**, as well as his or her relationship to the victim, if you have this knowledge. After CPS has this basic information, staff will want to know specifically what you have seen or heard that has led to your suspicion of maltreatment. Be as accurate as possible, and resist the temptation to exaggerate the situation to get faster service, or to downplay the situation so that nobody will get into trouble. You may then be asked for the names of any other people who may have knowledge of the abuse. Finally, you will be asked to provide your own name and a contact number where you can be reached (Children's Bureau, 2005).

Many reporters, mandated and permissive, are reluctant to leave their name with CPS. Anonymous reporting is permissible, but it is not recommended for several reasons. First, reports are generally considered to be more credible if the reporter is willing to leave his or her name. CPS workers who are pressed for time may allot more resources to investigating those calls they think are most likely to be true. Second, if CPS needs to ask you a follow-up question, it is necessary for them to know who you are and how to reach you. Third, if you are a mandated reporter, this provides a clear record that you have performed your duty. If you are required to report and opt for an anonymous call, be sure to keep a record for yourself of when you called and whom you spoke to so that you can prove you reported. Finally, reporters are protected in that the family is never told who made the report to CPS. This does not, of course, mean that families would not figure out that you were the reporter. For instance, imagine that you are a daycare provider who asks a mother about suspicious bruising on her infant, and gets vague or defensive answers. Being unconvinced by the mother's account, you make a report, and then CPS contacts the mother. It is likely that she will assume you made the call, and she may decide to confront you about it. What you know, because of CPS policies, is that she is only guessing; she does not know for a fact that you made the report. While situations like this can be intimidating and even frightening, the law requires reports even if you are concerned for your own safety. There is no discretion for mandatory reporters: "Professionals who have attained a level of reasonable suspicion of child abuse are not afforded professional judgment and legal flexibility in reporting" (Kalichman, 1999, p. 153).

FAILURE TO REPORT

What happens if a mandated reporter fails to report suspected maltreatment? Failure to report is considered a **misdemeanor** and may result in fines (typically around $1,000, with a range of $25 in Pennsylvania to $5,000 in Michigan and Washington) and/or jail terms of 10 days to one year (Small, Lyons, & Guy, 2002). Professionals who fail to report can also be sued for **malpractice** in all states. In addition, several states (Arkansas, Colorado, Iowa, Michigan, New York, and Rhode Island) have laws that specifically target the willful failure to report abuse (Myers, 1998).

The landmark case for failure to report in America is *Landeros v. Flood*. In this 1976 case, the Supreme Court of California held that a child could sue a physician who had examined her, seen injuries consistent with abuse, failed to report that abuse, and allowed the child to be returned home where she suffered further injury. The facts of this case indicated that when the plaintiff was 11 months old, she was treated by Dr. Flood at the San Jose Hospital. At that time she suffered from a spiral fracture of the right tibia and fibula, her entire back was bruised, and she had assorted abrasions on her body. In addition, the doctor noted that she had a nondepressed linear fracture of the skull that was partially healed. The plaintiff's mother was not able to provide a sufficient explanation for these injuries. Because Dr. Flood failed to properly diagnose battered-child syndrome and report to authorities, the child was returned home. She subsequently suffered additional injuries including puncture wounds, burns, bites, and traumatic blows to her eye and back. When the plaintiff was brought to a different hospital just two months later, she was immediately diagnosed with battered-child syndrome, her case was reported to authorities, and she was taken into protective custody. Although the trial court originally ruled that Dr. Flood owed no duty to the child, the California Supreme Court said that the malpractice laws required a certain level of knowledge in both diagnosis and treatment. The court further held that it was reasonable to expect a medical doctor to be able to diagnose and treat battered-child syndrome (Sagatun & Edwards, 1995).

Despite these penalties, it is clear that many professionals do not report as mandated by law. For example, many researchers have found that approximately one third of therapists were not willing to break confidentiality by reporting suspected abuse (Kalichman, Craig, & Follingstad, 1989; see section titled Confidentiality and Mandated Reporting for further discussion of this issue).

There are several reasons why a professional may opt not to make a report when he or she suspects maltreatment. Some professionals say that they are not confident that making a report will help the child. These professionals frequently cite previous contact with CPS that they did not find helpful. Other professionals, particularly therapists, say that their decision not to report was motivated by a desire to protect the **therapeutic relationship** they had established with their client. They believe that they are better able to treat their client than CPS, and that disrupting the therapeutic relationship would be counterproductive. If a report would lead to distrust of the therapist, then that therapist would be less likely to be helpful to the client. Given that a

likely result to an investigation by CPS would be that the parent would be ordered to seek counseling, therapists note that they are back where they started, but with a less cooperative client.
These therapists want to focus on what is best for a specific family instead of following blanket
reporting laws that may not be best in every situation (Crenshaw & Bartell, 1994).

There is some evidence that therapists' concerns are well-founded. Brown and Strozier
(2004) examined three studies looking at the impact of reporting and found that in 25% of
the cases a report has a negative impact on the therapeutic relationship (termination, missed
appointments, late arrival for sessions, and/or anger at therapist). Of course, the flip side of this
investigation is that 75% of the time, the impact of reporting was either neutral or positive.
Regardless of therapists' concerns, they are still mandated reporters. If they fail to report suspected abuse, they can be fined, jailed, or sued per the mandated reporting laws of their state,
no matter what justification they offer.

EDUCATION REGARDING MANDATED REPORTING

While it is likely that the above-mentioned dilemmas will never be fully resolved, there are
other impediments to reporting that can be reduced or eliminated through education. A study
by Kenny (2001) revealed that many of the doctors and teachers surveyed lacked knowledge
about the reporting process. In this study, 75% of physicians and 62% of teachers indicated
that their preservice training in child abuse was either minimal or inadequate. Significantly,
these mandated reporters did not know that they were immune from prosecution if they made
a report that turned out to be unfounded. Knowing that one cannot be sued for reporting in
good faith may increase the likelihood of reporting. Kenny also found that mandated reporters
preferred to report to their colleagues and/or supervisors than to CPS and that, in some cases,
this was the policy at their hospital or school. All mandated reporters need to know that state
policy is clear on this issue: the person who suspects the abuse is the one who is mandated to
report to protective services; a report to your supervisor does not fulfill this obligation. Finally,
many of the professionals surveyed said they were not aware of the signs of maltreatment. All
of these concerns can be addressed with preservice and in-service training on abuse and the
reporting laws.

CONFIDENTIALITY AND MANDATED REPORTING

All mental health professionals are exposed to the rules of confidentiality during their training.
Both legal and ethical guidelines make it abundantly clear that communication between a client
and helping professional is to be kept confidential. However, as should be clear by now, there
are limits to this confidentiality that have been established by law. Professionals are obligated
to break confidentiality if their client threatens violence toward themselves or others, and if the
professional suspects child abuse. How can a mental health professional make peace with these
two competing, and mutually exclusive, demands?

One possible solution is the forewarning of clients. Before mental health professionals
begin to work with a client, they should inform the client of the limits of confidentiality. Clients should be told that anything they say will be held in confidence unless they
threaten violence or admit to child abuse. This then allows the client to decide what to
confide in the therapist (Crenshaw & Lichtenberg, 1993). Even though this is one way to
avoid the ethical/legal dilemma, it is obvious that it is not a perfect solution. Imagine, for
instance, a woman who seeks out a therapist because she knows she is maltreating her child
and wants help to be a better parent. When she shows up for her first appointment, she is
told that if she tells her therapist that she has abused her child, the therapist will call CPS.

What is this mother to do? Will this sort of forewarning prevent her from discussing this issue with her therapist? Will forewarning prevent her from getting the help she needs to be a better parent?

Another possible approach to this dilemma is informing. In this case, the therapist does not forewarn the client, but if the mental health professional begins to suspect abuse, he tells the client he is going to make the report before he makes the call. The hope is that this will maintain the therapeutic relationship (Crenshaw & Lichtenberg, 1993). Clearly, this option is also not a perfect solution. As long as the current laws regarding mandated reporting exist, therapists will need to struggle with this issue.

A third alternative would be for the therapist to encourage the client to self-report. If the client is willing to make the call to CPS, it could fulfill the reporting requirement and preserve the therapeutic relationship (the therapist would need to witness the call). While the parent would be admitting maltreatment, he or she would also be showing willingness both to take responsibility and to take initiative in seeking help to keep the child safe.

One possible change that has been suggested is to modify the existing laws so that mental health professionals (MHPs) are not required to report less serious instances of child maltreatment if the family is in therapy (Emery & Laumann-Billings, 1998). Of course, defining "less serious" will have its challenges, but advocates argue that this could reduce the caseload for CPS and offer better, uninterrupted service to clients.

IS MANDATED REPORTING A GOOD THING?

Now that reporting laws have been in existence for around 40 years, it may be time to ask whether or not they are a good thing. Interestingly, few people seem to raise this question. The reasoning seems to be that if the laws increase reporting, they are working and effective. As previously mentioned, the laws do increase reporting, but do they help children? In 1994, Lindsay and Duncan examined U.S. statistics to determine if mandatory reporting led to a decrease in the most serious form of maltreatment, child fatalities. Unfortunately, they found that there had been little change in fatality rates over 30 years of mandated reporting.

Some have questioned whether the costs of mandated reporting outweigh the potential benefits. Although not much attention has been devoted to the costs of mandatory reporting, some researchers are trying to address this complex question. The U.S. and Australia have led the way in legislating mandated reporting. Because all states in the U.S. require reporting, it makes comparison within the country impossible. However, New South Wales has mandated reporting laws, but Western Australia does not, so a comparison can be made there. Like any study done outside of the laboratory, it will not be perfect, because New South Wales and Western Australia will obviously differ in more ways than just reporting laws. With that limitation in mind, consider the following information that was published in 2002 after New South Wales had mandated reporting laws for 25 years. Of the reports made to protective services in New South Wales, 59.6% were investigated, and those had a substantiation rate (maltreatment was found) of 21.3%. Conversely, 97.4% of the calls to protective services in Western Australia were investigated, and 44.2% of them were substantiated. (Note: According to Emery and Laumann-Billings, 1998, the substantiation rate in the U.S. is less than 33%, and 40% of those cases receive no services.) The concern is that mandatory reporting is increasing the number of reports and investigations, but not the number of children helped. In fact, investigating unfounded claims may be wasting resources that could be better used to aid children in families in other ways.

The decision of whether to mandate reporting does not have to be simply "yes" or "no." There is precedent for modification of the mandatory reporting laws in the U.S. to address these concerns. For example, in 1995, Missouri incorporated a system where reporters could select "assessment" for less severe situations or "investigation" for more serious incidents. After two years, Missouri saw a decrease in reports and an increase in substantiation rates (Delaronde, King, Bendel, & Reece, 2000). This may be a way to get the best of both worlds.

As the debate over how to most effectively help children rages on, professionals will continue to do their best under the current guidelines. The advice that is easiest to agree on at this time is to be aware of the relevant laws and to learn as much as possible about maltreatment and its effects on children.

CONCLUSION

If you enter a profession where you become a mandated reporter of child maltreatment, you will have to make difficult decisions about when to make reports. You are already on your way to preparing yourself for this role by reading the information in this text and familiarizing yourself with your state laws. Even though there are many controversial issues related to mandated reporting, the current laws require mandated reporters to provide reasonable suspicions to the proper authorities. To build your skills, you can discuss hypothetical cases with your colleagues and work out what you should do if you were in such a situation. Similarly, when confronted with a real case, turn to your more experienced colleagues for advice.

DISCUSSION QUESTIONS

1. Read the following scenarios and decide whether you would make a call to CPS based on the information you have. In cases where you are unsure, what further information would you seek to help you make your decision? Write your answers down now and return to these scenarios at the end of the course to see if your responses have changed.

   a. Imagine you are second-grade teacher and you have a student, Nathan, about whom you are concerned. When 7-year-old Nathan arrives at school, he is very dirty and frequently says that he is hungry. You have taken to giving him cereal bars in the morning and he seems grateful for them. Although Nathan does not appear to be malnourished, he is small for his age. Academically, Nathan is not a strong student and he almost never completes his homework assignments. He says there is nobody at home to help him with his school work. Although you have asked Nathan's mother to come in for a conference, she says that because she works full-time and is a single mother, she cannot make it to school. When you ask her about breakfast, she says that Nathan is hard to get up in the morning and, therefore, does not have time for breakfast.

   b. Ten-year-old Jocelyn has really changed this year. She used to be very outgoing, but over the past few months she has become withdrawn. She almost never makes eye contact, and she pulls away if you touch her. When you talk to her about her feelings, she tells you that she is sad, but she will not say why. Jocelyn's mother says that Jocelyn is having a difficult time adjusting to her new stepfather because she is used to having her mother all to herself. When you ask Jocelyn about her stepfather, she says she used to like him, but now she doesn't. When you press for more information, she says she does not want to talk about him. Later she admits that she does not like her stepfather because he makes her keep secrets. She will not tell you what the secrets are, and she begins to cry.

c. In your role as a kindergarten aide, you frequently have to reprimand 5-year-old Zachary because he bullies his peers. He seems especially vicious toward the youngest and smallest children. One day you are leading Zachary away from the playground by placing your hand on his back. When he winces, you lift his shirt and notice a bruise on his back. Zachary says that he fell down the stairs at home and hurt his back. When Zachary's mother picks him up, you mention the bruise and she says that Zachary is a bit wild and hurt himself when he fell from a tree in their yard over the weekend. Two weeks later, you notice some bruising on Zachary's ear. He says he hurt himself playing and his mother supports his story. Neither provides any details about how this new injury occurred. It is now April, and when you look over Zachary's school record, you notice that he has missed about five days of school each month this year.

d. As a worker at a daycare facility, you are in charge of the room for the 4-year-olds. One day you see Sally kissing one of the boys in the pretend kitchen. When you ask what they are doing, Sally informs you that they are "TV kissing with open mouths." You gently explain that this is not appropriate behavior and direct the children to another activity. However, two weeks later, you find Sally and a different boy showing each other their private parts. Sally also tells you that it feels good when she touches her "front privates." When you talk to Sally's mom, she says that recently Sally has become very interested in the difference between boys and girls. She apologizes for Sally's behavior in class and says she will talk to her. Although Sally's mother seems a bit embarrassed, she does not seem very concerned.

2. How do you think you would feel if you had to make a report of suspected child maltreatment? How might a colleague or other professional help you cope with any negative feelings?

DEFINITIONS

Mandated Reporters: people required by law because of their occupation to report suspected cases of child maltreatment to the proper authorities.

Immunity (legal): exception from civil or criminal liability or prosecution.

Abrogated: cancelled or annulled by official means or authority.

Permissive Reporter: a person who is allowed, but not required, to report suspected child maltreatment.

Informed Consent: the ethical requirement that participants voluntarily agree to take part in an experiment only after they have been told what their participation will entail.

Institutional Review Board (IRB): a group of professionals charged with determining whether the benefits of a proposed research project outweigh the potential costs to participants.

National Child Abuse Hotline: 1-800-4-A-CHILD; a phone line that is staffed 24 hours a day, 7 days a week, by professional counselors who can answer questions about child maltreatment. The counselors have access to a very large database of resources including emergency, social services, and support services.

Perpetrator: a person who commits an offense or crime.

Misdemeanor: a crime that is less serious than a felony and is usually punished with a lesser penalty (a fine, forfeiture, or less than one year in prison).

Malpractice: professional negligence; failure to exercise the minimum degree of care expected by professional standards.

Therapeutic Relationship: the working alliance between a counselor and patient.

PART II

Types of Abuse

CHAPTER 4

Physical Abuse

When someone hears the term *child abuse*, what most often comes to mind is a picture of a child who has been physically abused. This makes sense because **child physical abuse** (CPA) was the first type of child maltreatment to be identified by professionals, and it makes the most visible marks on its victims. While growing media attention to other types of maltreatment (like sexual and emotional abuse) may eventually change this, for many people, the image of a bruised and battered child is the one that is most closely tied to the concept of child maltreatment.

DEFINITION

The definitions of physical abuse vary, but a general way of thinking about this type of maltreatment is to label any act by a caregiver that results in a nonaccidental physical injury to a child as physical abuse. This provides a starting point, but it does not fully define the concept. For example, driving under the influence of alcohol with a child in the car can be labeled physical abuse, even though any injury to the child would be accidental. Most people are comfortable seeing driving under the influence as child abuse, but a nonaccidental injury that occurs when a parent is engaging in corporal punishment to correct their child's behavior is more controversial. In this scenario, any injury to the child is nonaccidental, but the parent's behavior was intended to teach the child, not to harm him. Another complicating factor is that physical abuse at one age may not be physical abuse at another age. For example, a slap to the face of a newborn is considered to be child physical abuse, while slapping the face of an adolescent is not necessarily labeled as maltreatment. Finally, in some descriptions of physical abuse, the risk of injury can also be part of the definition. For instance, Alabama defines physical abuse as including "harm or threatened harm to the health or welfare of a child" [§26-14-1(1)-(3)]. Other states only include harm that has already occurred. For example, Connecticut's law reads, "Abused means that a child or youth has been inflicted with physical injury or injuries by other than accidental means" (§46b-120). (See Case Example 4.1.)

CASE EXAMPLE 4.1

Consider the father's behavior in the following case that took place in Baltimore, Maryland, in 2004. A 12-year-old girl was having trouble with her computer while her father napped on the couch. When she first approached him, he asked her to wait until after his nap. The second time the girl interrupted his sleep, he yelled at her. The third time she woke him, he kicked a step stool in anger. The stool ended up flying over the couch and hitting his daughter in the face. He immediately took her to the hospital, where she received three stitches in her nose and was treated for other abrasions to her face (Parks, 2004).

In this case, the Department of Social Services felt that the father's acts constituted physical child abuse. The Hartford County Circuit Court agreed with the Department of Social Services, saying, "It was certainly foreseeable that when he kicked the stool in her direction, the stool could have struck her" (Parks, 2004, p. 1). The Court of Appeals, however, was not convinced. They noted that under Maryland law, the court could not find someone guilty of child abuse if the injury was "accidental or unintentional and not reckless or deliberate" (Parks, 2004, p.1).

DISCUSSION QUESTIONS

1. Is kicking a step stool when a child is in the room reckless?
2. Was the injury to the child the result of a deliberate act on the part of the father?
3. Which court's decision do you agree with?

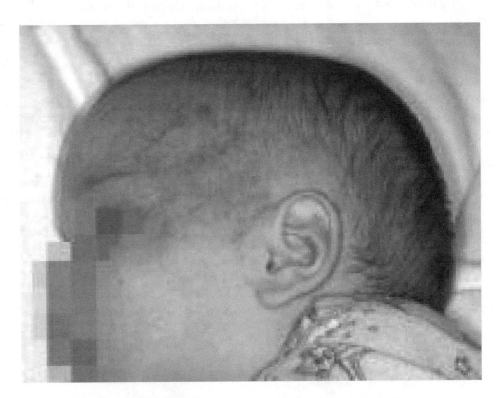

Figure 4.1   An infant with a slap mark on the face. Photo credit: Lawrence Ricci, MD.

The authors of the Third National Incidence Study, or NIS-3 (see Focus on Research 2.2 for a description of this study), wrote that, "Acts constituting physical abuse include hitting with a hand, stick, strap, or other object; punching; kicking; shaking; throwing; burning; stabbing; or choking a child" (Sedlak & Broadhurst, 1996, p. 2-10). The National Clearinghouse on Child Abuse and Neglect Information (2005) provides a similar definition, "All states and territories provide definitions for physical abuse. The term is generally defined as any nonaccidental physical injury to the child, and can include striking, kicking, burning, or biting the child, or any action that results in physical impairment of the child." This provides a general definition, while also reminding the reader that small differences will occur between states.

Definitions in State Laws

To find the statute that defines physical abuse for your state, you can log on to the site entitled "The Child Welfare Information Gateway," which now includes the information previously found on the page for the National Clearinghouse on Child Abuse and Neglect Information (see Search the Web 4.1).

There are some specific issues you should consider when reading state law. For instance, does the **statute** deal specifically with bruising, and if so, does it include severity of bruising? Some states, like Colorado and Idaho (§ 19-1-103 and § 16-1602, respectively), list "skin bruising" from nonaccidental injury as evidence of abuse, yet in other places, like Hawaii, the description of abusive bruising reads, "substantial or multiple skin bruising" (§350-1). A second issue of interest is the overlap between abuse and neglect statutes seen in some states. For instance, Arizona statute 8-201; 13-3623 includes the following in its definition of physical abuse: "permitting a child to enter or remain in any structure in which chemicals or equipment used for the manufacture of a dangerous drug is found." Even though this behavior would certainly increase the child's risk of injury, it also describes neglect (lack of supervision). Another issue is that of *harmed*, which all states include, versus *threaten to harm* or *put at risk for harm*, which only some states include. In terms of protecting children, it seems like a good idea to remove them from risky situations before they are actually harmed by their parents. On the other hand, it is extremely difficult to prove that a parent has placed a child in a situation with an unacceptable level of risk.

Some states have unique behaviors included in their statutes describing physical abuse. For example, Illinois specifically notes that female genital mutilation is considered abusive (Ch. 325, §5/3), and the District of Columbia includes "interfering with a child's breathing" and "threatening a child with a dangerous weapon" in its statute (§16-2301). Minnesota law specifies that shaking a child under three years of age constitutes physical abuse (§626.556). While these behaviors would likely be considered abusive in all states, it is interesting to see what behaviors

SEARCH THE WEB 4.1

Go to the following Web site: http://www.childwelfare.gov/systemwide/laws_policies/state/. At this site you need to complete three steps in order to find the statute for a specific state.

1. First, select the state you are interested in knowing about.
2. Second, choose an issue or issues. The relevant issue for finding a state's definition of physical abuse would be Definitions of Child Abuse and Neglect.
3. The final step is to submit your request by clicking Go. You will then see a copy of the statute for the state you selected.

The sad situation that has become known as the "Baby Haley" case illustrates many of the concepts dealt with in this text: physical abuse, mandated reporting, investigation by child protective services (CPS), criminal court, and civil court. In June of 2004, officers arrested Tommy Joe Owens, 31, and his girlfriend, Charlotte Kay Claiborne, also 31, at their mobile home in eastern Tennessee (Balloch, 2005, June 12). Although the couple was originally arrested on charges of forgery (Claiborne) and failure to appear in court (Owens), more serious charges were filed once the condition of the children living in the home was discovered (Balloch, 2005, June 29). The couple was subsequently charged with aggravated child abuse, reckless endangerment, and felony child neglect regarding Mr. Owens's 3-year-old daughter, Haley. They were also charged with the neglect of two other children in the home. In addition, both Owens and Claiborne tested positive for methamphetamines (Balloch, 2005, June 12). At the time that Haley was removed from their care, she had numerous serious injuries. She had multiple burns and bruises on her arms, legs, eyes, and buttocks. The burn to her eyes was believed to be chemical in nature, and it was so severe that it required surgery. Furthermore, her ears and nose were damaged, and she was suffering from a fever (Balloch, 2005, June 29).

In addition to the charges filed against Owens and Claiborne, Haley's babysitter, Teresa Draughn, was charged with failure to report suspected child abuse (Balloch, 2005, June 12). Although nonprofessional babysitters are not mandated reporters in most states, Tennessee law states that "any person who has knowledge that a child has been harmed by abuse or neglect must report" (§§37-1-403; 37-1-605). Witnesses suggested that not only did Draughn fail to report the abuse, she may have actively tried to conceal some injuries (Balloch, 2005, June 29).

Only Mr. Owens's case went to trial; both of the women pled no contest to the charges against them. The babysitter, Draughn, was sentenced to 11 months of probation for failure to report child abuse. The judge's order required that she receive counseling and that she enroll in either a GED program or a vocational training program. In addition, she was not allowed to have any contact with Haley, and she had to pay $400 in court costs (Alapo, 2005, November 11). The girlfriend, Claiborne, was sentenced to 20 years, of which she must serve at least 15 years, for three counts of aggravated child abuse (Balloch, 2005, June 29).

At the trial of Mr. Owens, Haley's 10-year-old stepsister testified that she and the other children had caused most of Haley's injuries. However, upon cross-examination, the child appeared confused and was not able to provide believable responses to questions about the abuse (Balloch, 2005, June 30). A medical doctor, Mary Campbell, testified that Haley had suffered significant nonaccidental injuries. She noted that Haley had been burned, possibly with hot water, but more likely by chemicals. Other burns were determined to be consistent with cigarette burns. She stated that an ear injury was likely the result of a direct blow to the organ. Finally, one bruise was described as possibly being inflicted by a coat hanger (Balloch, 2005, June 29). Mr. Owens testified on his own behalf at his trial. Although he admitted using methamphetamines and shoplifting, he maintained that he was not guilty of abusing Haley. Owens's lawyer argued that even though the evidence showed that Haley had been injured, it did not prove that Owens had inflicted those injuries (Balloch, 2005, June 30). At the conclusion of the trial, the jury deliberated for less than 1 hour before finding Mr. Owens guilty of three counts of aggravated child abuse and one count of aggravated neglect (East Tennessee, 2005, June 30). Mr. Owens was subsequently sentenced to 95 years in prison (Balloch, 2005, October 12).

After Haley was released from the hospital, she was placed with her mother, Rosemary Spicer. According to Ms. Spicer, Haley has more surgeries ahead of her, and she still suffers from nightmares. Although Ms. Spicer had been in a custody dispute with Mr. Owens prior to the arrest, she said she never thought he would harm Haley. Ms. Spicer has filed an $11.5 million civil suit against Owens and Claiborne. In addition, a $600,000 claim has been filed against the Department of Children's Services (DCS) on her behalf (Satterfield, 2005, June 25). The claim against the Department of Children's Services asserts that initial reports to investigate Haley's situation were ignored. After the arrests, three employees at the Department of Children's Services were disciplined internally for the oversight (Balloch, 2005, June 12).

DISCUSSION QUESTIONS

1. Do you think appropriate verdicts and sentences were rendered in this case? Were the punishments too mild, too severe, or adequate?
   a. For Draughn?
   b. For Claiborne?
   c. For Owens?
2. In this case, was it appropriate for Ms. Spicer to sue Owens and Claiborne for damages?
3. Was it appropriate for Ms. Spicer to sue the Department of Children's Services?

each state's legislature decides to list in its statute. The specific behaviors listed may indicate that professionals in that state are especially sensitive to that particular form of maltreatment. Often a high-profile case involving a specific form of abuse leads to changes in the wording of the state law (see Case Example 4.2).

PREVALENCE/INCIDENCE

Throughout this text the rate of maltreatment will be discussed in terms of **incidence** and **prevalence**. *Incidence* is the term used to refer to the number of new cases that occur or are diagnosed each year. In terms of physical abuse, the incidence may be described as the number of cases **substantiated** by child protective services (CPS) in a given year. *Prevalence* is defined as the total number of cases in a specified population at a given point in time. In other words, prevalence tells you how many people in a population have ever suffered from that problem. For physical abuse, prevalence data tells you how many people in the population of interest have ever been victims of substantiated cases of physical abuse.

Although it is not as common as child neglect, which will be covered in the next chapter, child physical abuse accounts for 22.7% of all calls to the Department of Social Services and is associated with nearly two thirds of child fatalities (Kolko, 2002). According to National Incidence Study-3 (see Focus on Research 2.2), the incidence of physical abuse in 1993 was 381,700, or 5.7 per 1,000 children. This study measured the incidence of abuse according to the harm standard, which means the children were already hurt, not only at risk of being harmed.

Sedlack and Broadhurst (1996) broke the 1993 incidence of maltreatment down into subcategories of severity. Unfortunately, this information was not reported separately for physical abuse, as the Third National Incidence Study was, but instead the authors summarized injury from all maltreatment. Fatal maltreatment occurred at a rate of 1,500 children per year, or 0.02 per 1,000. Serious maltreatment included such things as life-threatening injuries (e.g., something that stopped the child's breathing), injuries leading to long-term impairment (e.g., third-degree burns), and injuries that required professional intervention in order to prevent long-term impairment (e.g., broken bones). During 1993, there were 565,000 cases, or 8.4 per 1,000, that were classified as serious. The third category, moderate, included cases where some observable sign of injury persisted for at least two days, even if it did not require medical care. Sedlack and Broadhurst reported 822,000 cases of moderate maltreatment, or 12.2 per 1,000. When you consider the incidence of abuse using the endangerment standard, you will find higher numbers. For 1993, the incidence of physical abuse under the endangerment standard was 614,000, or 9.1 per 1,000 children (Sedlack & Broadhurst, 1996).

CORPORAL PUNISHMENT

One important question that arises when you discuss physical abuse concerns differentiating between child physical abuse and appropriate physical punishment. In some countries (e.g., Austria, Denmark, Finland, Germany, Iceland, Israel, Italy, Norway, Sweden), such a distinction is not needed because their laws forbid any corporal punishment and label all such behavior as abusive.

Because corporal punishment is legal in the U.S., one must try to establish guidelines for what is and what is not abusive. This can be a tricky business. Let us take, for example, the state law of South Carolina. According to §20-7-490, the state's definition of child physical abuse includes injury in cases of *excessive* corporal punishment, but allows *appropriate* corporal punishment if the following conditions are met (emphasis added):

1. the punishment must be administered by parents or the person in loco parentis (a person acting as a temporary guardian for the child);
2. the sole purpose of the physical act is to restrain or correct the child;
3. the force of the physical act is both reasonable in manner and moderate in degree;
4. the degree of force used in disciplining the child must not bring about permanent or lasting damage;
5. the behavior of the parent administering the punishment must not be reckless or grossly negligent.

As you can see, even this careful list has terms that are open to interpretation or difficult to know. For instance, consider "reasonable in manner and moderate in degree". Can you imagine that rational, educated persons may disagree about what types of physical punishment meet these criteria? As mentioned earlier, some countries have passed laws saying that any physical punishment is unreasonable. Therefore, U.S. legislators clearly disagree with them by allowing corporal punishment at all. Even within the U.S., attitudes vary greatly about what is reasonable. For instance, Southerners tend to be more accepting of harsh physical punishment than are Northerners. Many times, when college classes attempt to define physically abusive punishment, much debate erupts over spanking a child with an object (from a wooden spoon to a belt). In these informal discussions, while many Northerners are shocked by the very idea that a parent would use a belt in disciplining, many Southerners accept it as normative. Not only do interpretations vary by region, they also vary by time. What was once accepted as appropriate parenting (say, by our grandparents), is now considered abusive. So, even though many young adults report that their parents were punished with a belt, they have no intention of using a belt to spank their own children. As we hear more and more stories of permissive parents and out-of-control children, it is possible that the pendulum will swing back toward a greater acceptance of harsher physical punishment. Or, more optimistically, a greater concern for the rights and dignity of children may push parents to learn about, and adopt, effective, nonphysical means of behavior modification.

In addition, how can we know whether the sole purpose of the physical act is to restrain or correct the child? Does this mean that if I spank my child out of anger or frustration, I am guilty of child abuse? Further, are parents always fully aware of the motivations behind their behaviors? While these questions do not have black and white answers, they are important to think about. As professionals working with children, you will not only need to familiarize yourself with state and federal laws, but you will also need to understand how the terms used in those laws are interpreted by your community.

Do Laws Against Corporal Punishment Protect Children?

Would children be safer if corporal punishment was not permitted at all? Certainly, this would address the problem of trying to define appropriate corporal punishment. Because some countries have enacted bans on spanking, there is data that speaks to this question. Larzelere and Johnson (1999) attempted to assess the impact of the ban on spanking that was enacted in Sweden in 1979. Their first discovery was that shockingly little research had been done to assess the impact of the spanking ban on child abuse rates. They found only seven articles with pertinent information, and many of them were weak in terms of empirical evidence. Still, they were able to draw several conclusions. First, the spanking ban did not eliminate spanking. A year after the ban, 28% of parents admitted to either spanking or slapping their children during the previous year. In addition, the rate of spanking, as assessed by retrospective design, was barely changed by the ban. Second, the rate of physical child abuse was at best unchanged in the 20 years following the ban. Some evidence points to a small increase in physical evidence after the ban. It may be that banning spanking without educating parents about alternative types of discipline could actually increase physical abuse. In these cases, parents may become so frustrated by their inability to enforce their rules that they lose control with their children. It is possible that any increase due to this type of problem would resolve itself after parents became more adept with alternative means of discipline. As for now, the relationship between spanking and child physical abuse is not clear. The one thing that is known at this time is that a law prohibiting corporal punishment does not eliminate either spanking or child physical abuse.

CONSEQUENCES OF PHYSICAL ABUSE

Bruises

The most obvious effects of physical abuse are the immediate medical or health problems caused by abuse. The most common physical injury associated with child physical abuse is **bruising**. All children will occasionally be bruised as the result of normal play or accidental injury, but there are characteristics of abusive bruising that arouse suspicion. When assessing a bruise, one must first consider the age of the child. Prior to being able to move around without help, it is rare that a child will suffer an accidental bruise. Given that children do not begin to crawl until approximately six months of age, any bruising prior to this age should raise questions. This does not, of course, mean that all young infants with bruises have been abused. Certainly, young children can be accidentally dropped or allowed to roll off a bed or changing table. As children begin to crawl and walk, it is common to see bruises on certain parts of their body. Accidental bruises tend to be on areas of the body where the bone is close

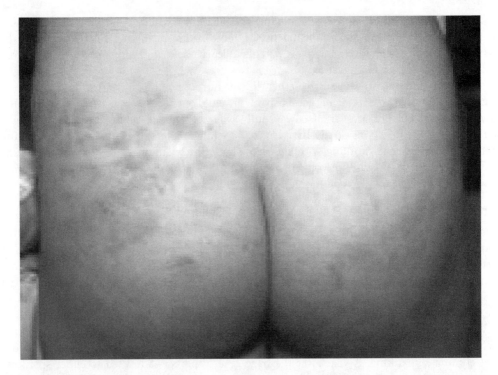

Figure 4.2   A child with bruises that resulted from being hit with a belt. Photo credit: Lawrence Ricci, MD.

to the surface and on the parts of the body the child leads with. For instance, areas on the front of a child like the forehead, chin, knees, and shins are low-suspicion areas for bruising, as are the back of the head and the back of the arm from the elbow down. As you think about a child playing and exploring his or her environment, it is easy to imagine an accidental bruise occurring in these places. New crawlers can bang their forehead against objects, and new walkers frequently run into things with their shins. On the other hand, bruising on the ears, trunk, genitals or the back of the hands is suspicious (Johnson, 2002). Not only are these places where an accidental bruise is unlikely, they are also common locations for abusive injuries.

In addition to considering the location of the bruise on the body, the pattern of the bruise provides information about its cause. An examination of bruising may reveal that the bruise is the mark left by a palm or an object such as a hanger, a belt, a spoon, or a cord. In these cases, you can see the shape of the object on the child's skin. If the story the parent or child provides to explain the mark is not consistent with the pattern you see, there is cause for suspicion.

Certainly, seeing a child with many bruises may cause concern. One way to assess whether the injuries occurred at one time, as could be the case in a serious accidental injury like falling from a tree, or over time, is to pay attention to the coloring of the bruises. The color cannot tell you exactly how long ago an injury occurred, but it does give some indication. New bruises tend to be red, but within 6 to 12 hours, they begin to turn blue. Approximately 12 to 24 hours after an injury, bruises are blackish purple in color. By 4 to 6 days after an injury, a dark, greenish tint appears, and within 5 to 10 days, the bruise fades to a pale green or yellow. All of these color changes are much more obvious on lighter skinned children, so special attention will be necessary to notice the same degree of bruising on a child with darker skin. A child who has many suspicious bruises at various stages of healing may be the victim of child physical abuse.

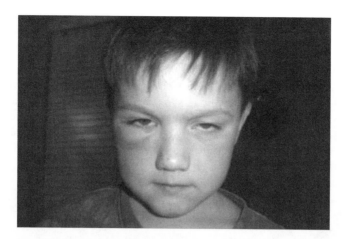

Figure 4.3 Although this may look bad, it is the result of an accidental injury. This 8-year-old boy was hit in the eye while playing baseball. When you see an injured child, you should not assume the worst.

A special case of bruising in abused children is the human bite. Bites leave a distinct pattern that makes them fairly easy to identify. Furthermore, it is difficult to argue that a bite was accidental. In some cases, forensic dentists have even been able to identify perpetrators by analyzing bite marks (Brodeur & Monteleone, 1994). If you notice a bite mark on a child, it is a good idea to ask the child what caused the mark.

As you think more about child physical abuse, it is important that you keep in mind that children do suffer accidental injuries. Even a bruise that looks bad can be the result of normal childhood play. It is appropriate to ask a child or their parent how an injury happened. Generally, children who have suffered an accidental injury do not mind telling you about it; they may even enjoy the attention.

Fractures

Most mandated reporters other than medical doctors would not be expected to assess **fractures**, because this type of evaluation requires expert training in radiology. Also, if you thought a child had an untreated fracture, you would immediately refer the child to a medical doctor. Still, there are some basic facts about fractures that a nonmedical professional can know that might help in assessing a child's history.

The greatest incidence of abusive fractures is seen in young children. Most children who suffer fractures from physical abuse are under 2 years of age, and between 55% and 70% of them are less than 1 year old. Compare this to the fact that less than 2% of all accidental fractures are seen in children who are less than 18 months old. Given these numbers, fractures in infants are always worth noting carefully. The biggest red flag is when the history provided by the caregiver does not adequately correlate with the injury seen on an x-ray. In other words, what the parent says occurred would not have caused an injury of this severity. (For examples, see the section Injuries From Falls in this chapter.) Other suspicious fractures are those found during an exam for an unrelated problem. For instance, if a child is presented as suffering from pneumonia and the doctor discovers a rib fracture, there is cause to be concerned about a possible abusive injury. Nonabusive parents are almost always aware when their child has suffered a trauma that could break a bone, and they readily describe it to physicians. Another potential indicator of abusive fractures is when multiple fractures are noted on different parts of the body, and the reported history did not include a major trauma (such as a car accident). Finally, a fracture becomes more suspicious when the child has other injuries such as burns or bruises. If a doctor is suspicious, a complete skeletal survey should be done. A "baby gram," which x-rays the entire body with just one or two pictures, is not considered to be a sufficient investigation (Moore & Smith, 2006).

There are also certain bones that are more likely to be broken in abusive situations. Breaks of the long bones of the arms and legs are seen frequently in abuse cases, yet abusive fractures to the hands and feet are not common. Long bone breaks are often spiral breaks, which means they were caused by twisting the limb. This can happen accidentally, especially in an older child, but this type of break is suspicious in young children. Rib fractures are also often the result of abuse. Because a child's ribs are somewhat pliant, a significant amount of force is required before they will break. Ribs can be broken by direct blows or by extreme squeezing. Finally, skull fractures in infants (that were not caused by the birth process) are suspicious. These can result from a direct blow to the head or from a child being hit against something (Moore & Smith, 2006).

Head Injuries

In addition to assessing for fractures and bruising, doctors need to assess potentially abused children for head injuries. This type of injury is common in abuse situations, and it can have dire consequences. Hekmatpanah, Pannaraj, and Callans (2002) reviewed the records of 190 abused children who had been treated at the University of Chicago Medical Center between 1965 and 1995, and whose primary trauma was a head injury that required hospitalization. All of the children were under 48 months of age (4 years), 89% were under 3 years, and 63% were under 1 year. The most common symptom at admittance was depressed level of consciousness (64%), which was followed by respiratory distress (32%), seizures (32%), and vomiting (23%). Frequent signs included retinal hemorrhage (41%), bulging fontanel (44%) and capillary change (22.5%). The outcomes for this type of injury were quite serious. Twenty-two (12%) of the children died as a result of their injuries. Others suffered delayed physical development (15%), delayed mental development (8%), or both (2%).

Shaken Baby Syndrome

Abusive head injury may be the result of **shaken baby syndrome** (SBS) or shaken impact syndrome (SIS). These terms were first used in the 1970s when doctors began to notice a set of injuries that results when a young child has been violently shaken. In these cases, an adult grasps a child by the arms or trunk and shakes the child forcefully. This sharp shaking causes the brain to collide with the skull. In addition to the violent shaking, the child's head may also make contact with a hard surface such as a wall or the floor. Like many of the injuries we have been discussing, shaken baby syndrome is seen almost entirely in children under 2 years of age, and frequently the child is under 6 months. In most cases, there are no externally observable signs of shaken baby syndrome; however, some children may have bruises where they were held. This lack of obvious, visible symptoms does not mean they are not injured. Shaking can cause serious injury, including subdural hematomas (blood pools between the dura and the brain) and retinal hemorrhage (bleeding on the surface of the retina). While you cannot see these injuries with the naked eye, there are symptoms you can note. Victims of shaken baby syndrome are often extremely irritable, they have problems feeding (including a decreased appetite or vomiting for no apparent reason), and they are lethargic, which may include poor muscle tone (Wells, 2006). Because shaking a baby can cause serious injury, some hospitals now send newborns home in onesies that say "Don't Shake Me" and include a toll-free phone number for parents who feel out of control. The thinking behind this campaign is that even though parents know not to hit a child, they may not realize that shaking a child can be just as harmful. Although educating caregivers about the dangers of shaking is an important first step, it is also necessary to provide assistance to parents who may be overwhelmed by the caregiving role. It seems that parents who shake their children are frequently frustrated by their inability to soothe a crying child.

Injuries From Falls

When presenting a child for treatment, many parents report that the child was injured by falling. What researchers have found, however, is that falls from short distances generally do not cause significant harm to children. A common situation is for a child to fall from a bed or a sofa. Helfer, Slovis, and Black (1977) studied the hospital incident reports for 85 children under the age of 5 years who had fallen a distance of approximately 3 feet (generally from a bed or a sofa). Of these children, 57 were not injured, 17 had very minor injuries (small cuts or scrapes and/or bloody noses), 20 ended up with a bump or a bruise, and only 1 had a skull fracture (which did not include any soft-tissue damage). In 40 of these cases x-rays were taken, and the only fracture revealed was the one already noted. Because parents only seek medical help when they think a fall may have resulted in an injury, Helfer et al. also surveyed parents at a pediatric clinic. They asked parents to complete a survey indicating any instances where their children fell from a bed or couch, and what the consequences of the fall were. While it is probable that parents were more likely to recall falls that resulted in injury, the results still indicated that short falls do not result in traumatic injury. In 176 of these incidents (80%), there were no observable injuries at all. In 37 cases (17%), the child sustained a minor injury such as a bruise or a scratch. In only 6 falls (3%) did the child suffer a serious injury (a fracture). Three children fractured their clavicles, two had skull fractures with no serious head injury (both of whom were under 6 months), and one had a fractured humerus. None of the children suffered life-threatening injuries. The authors concluded that serious injury from a short fall is extremely unlikely. Therefore, if a parent reports that a child has fallen a short distance and suffered an extreme injury, it should make the professional consider that the parent is not providing an accurate history.

Others have since replicated the finding that serious injuries are not likely to result from short falls. Even falls from greater distances are generally not fatal. One study by Chadwick, Chin, Salerno, Landsverk, and Kitchen (1991) found that of 65 children who had fallen from 5 to 9 feet, none died: Further, only 1 of 118 children who fell from 10 to 45 feet was fatally injured (see Focus on Research 4.1). Along these same lines, Barlow, Niemirska, Gandhi, and Leblanc (1983) reported that only 14 of 61 infants and children who fell four or more stories were killed, and 47 survived with few permanent injuries.

Burns

The most likely victims of abusive **burns** are infants and young children. Although many children suffer accidental burns, it is often possible to determine from the characteristics of the burn whether it was the result of abuse or an accident. Because abuse has been found to be the cause of between 10% and 25% of burn injuries in children, it is good to assess for possible abuse when presented with a burned child (Feldman, 1997).

A common burning agent is tap water. Once water exceeds 130 °F, it will cause seconddegree burns on a child in approximately ten seconds. This is why some parents who have young children will have the temperature on their water heater lowered to 120–125 °F. Although this is a good safety measure, especially once children can turn on faucets (about 24 months), it is not necessary to prevent burns when a child is supervised. A parent would not accidentally leave a child in 130°F water long enough for the child to burn because the threshold for a pain response is 114–118°F (Feldman, 1997). A parent may accidentally place a child in water that is hot enough to burn them, but they will remove the child immediately once they hear the child's cry of pain.

FOCUS ON RESEARCH 4.1

In 1991, Chadwick, Chin, Salerno, Landsverk, and Kitchen published an article entitled, "Deaths From Falls in Children: How Far is Fatal?" in *The Journal of Trauma*. The setting for their study was the trauma center at the Children's Hospital in San Diego, California. The authors examined records for cases that had occurred between August of 1984 and March of 1988. They identified 317 cases where children had allegedly been injured by a fall. Of these, 283 indicated the estimated distance of the fall, so these became the focus of the study.

The children who had fallen were generally young. Thirty were under 1 year of age, 145 were between 1 and 3 years old, 61 were between 4 and 6 years, 65 were from 7 to 12 years, and 16 were older than 13 years at the time of the injury. There were more male children (199) who had fallen than female children (118).

The authors then looked at how far the parent or caregiver reported that the child had fallen. The most common report was of a short fall. One hundred of the falls were estimated to be between 1 and 4 feet. Sixty-five reported falls were from a distance of 5 to 9 feet. Seventy-five of the children were said to have fallen between 10 and 14 feet. Twenty-four falls were from a distance of 15 to 19 feet. Seventeen falls were from heights of 20 to 29 feet, and two falls were from distances between 30 and 45 feet.

The next information gathered from the file was whether the falls resulted in a fatality. Only eight of the children died of their injuries. What was striking, however, was the relationship between the reported distance of the fall and fatality. Seven of the fatalities were from children who had reportedly fallen a distance of four feet or less. None of the children who had fallen between five and nine feet died, and only one of the children who had fallen between 10 and 45 feet had died. Based on these results, the authors said you would end up with the absurd conclusion that the risk of death from short falls is eight times greater than the risk of falls from 10 to 45 feet. Because this seemed unlikely to them, they focused more extensively on the cases where children had died, hoping to determine whether the caregivers had provided an accurate report of how the injury had occurred.

Of the seven children who died following an allegedly short fall, one 11-month-old was reported to have fallen down the stairs, because the child was found at the bottom of the stairs by a babysitter; nobody observed the fall. (A fall down stairs is considered to be a series of short falls, not a long fall). In addition to massive head injuries, this baby had small, round bruises on both arms, inner thighs and on the labia major. Two infants were reported to have died after suffering a fall while in an adult's arms. In one case, a babysitter said she fell while carrying a 13-month-old child upstairs. In addition to the current injuries, this child had an older, healing fracture of the tibia. In the other case, a father reported that he had fallen against the crib with his then 6-week-old child in his arms. He did not take the child for treatment until six days later, at which time the child was unconscious. The final four children who died as the result of a short fall were said to have either suffered a standing fall (two) or fallen from a bed or table (two). The authors found these accounts to be problematic because of the work done by Helfer, Slovis, and Black (1977), who reported that of 180 falls by small children that took place in a hospital, there were no fatalities. Children suffered minor injuries, if any. The authors then concluded that all of the deaths that allegedly occurred following short falls may have been false reports. The authors hypothesized that abusive parents may not realize that short falls are unlikely to cause serious injury in children, so they use the short fall as an excuse for what may, in fact, be abusive injuries.

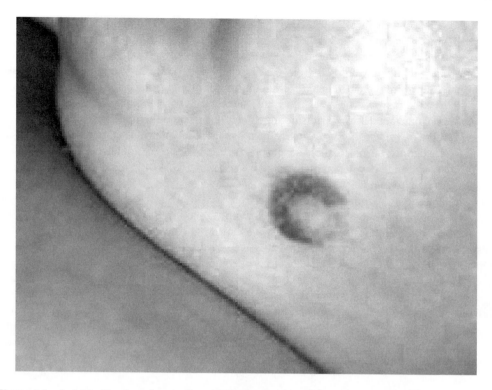

Figure 4.4 A child with a burn from a cigarette lighter. Photo credit: Lawrence Ricci, MD.

If you see a child with a tap water burn, there are some features you can look for to determine the origin of the burn. First, consider burns to the hands and feet. If a child accidentally places one of his extremities in hot water, he will immediately remove it. This results in a burn with an irregular contour and splash marks above the burn. By contrast, a child whose hand or foot has been forcibly immersed in hot water will have a burn with a relatively even edge and few splash marks. These burns have been described as "glove" or "sock" burns because the area of burnt skin looks like one of those objects. Because the child was not free to kick his feet or flail his arms, there will not be as many splash marks. Another telling pattern from a tap water burn results when a child is held in a hot tub. These victims show burns over much of the torso, but a patch of skin on the buttocks will be spared. This happens because the part of the bottom that was pressed against the tub did not burn due to the fact that the tub surface was cooler than the water (Feldman, 1997; Johnson, 2002).

Another suspicious type of burn is the pattern burn. In other words, the burn clearly resembles a common hot object. These burns may indicate that a hot object was placed on the child or that the child was held against the hot object. A frequent source of pattern burns is cigarettes. The result of a cigarette burn is a clear, circular imprint that, after healing, resembles a small pox vaccination. Accidental cigarette burns are likely to occur on the fingers or the mouth (when the child mimics smoking with the wrong end); abusive burns are usually seen on body parts that are generally covered by clothing (abdomen, genitals, etc.) Also, in abuse cases you frequently see multiple burns; accidents most often result in only one cigarette burn (Feldman, 1997).

Other abusive pattern burns result from objects that are easily available in a home—heating grates, heated silverware, clothing irons, curling irons, and the like. At this point, many female readers are probably recalling an instance when their mother accidentally brushed their forehead with a curling iron while trying to make them look good for picture day. This is clearly not the type or placement of a pattern burn that would concern a mandated reporter. More suspicious curling iron burns would be found on the trunk of the body, and they would reflect a deeper burn than you would get from grazing the forehead. For instance, in an abusive situation, the imprint of the entire length of the curing iron might be visible on the child's back. Likewise, a child may step on a heating grate that is located on the floor and accidentally burn the bottom of one foot. However, it is not likely that they would then put their other foot on the grate as well. So, a single, blurred, surface burn is more likely to be accidental, while multiple, deep, clearly defined burns are more suspicious (Feldman, 1997). And, of course, you still need to consider the child's developmental level. If a child is not yet walking, he or she should not be able to burn the bottom of even one foot.

Although many mandated reporters are frustrated by the language of "likely" or "suspicious" instead of more concrete rules for determining the origin of injuries, it is not possible to give black-and-white answers. The best we can do is to consider the injury, and then, if suspicious, compare what we see to the parent's and/or child's report of what happened. If one remains skeptical, call CPS. Ultimately, it is the job of CPS to determine whether a child has been abused.

Finally, the abused child may try to hide these injuries. These children may wear inappropriate clothing such as long sleeves and pants during the summer months or be wary of physical contact. Contrast this to the showing-off behavior that is often seen in children with accidental injuries. The reluctance to let others see an injury can provide one more reason to be concerned about a mark on a child.

CAUTION: NOT ALL MARKS ARE SIGNS OF ABUSE

As we learn to recognize signs of child abuse, we must be careful not to assume that all suspicious-looking marks are evidence of child abuse. There are some conditions that may be easily mistaken for abuse. For instance, both chicken pox and **impetigo** (a bacterial skin infection that causes blisters that will eventually burst and form a crust; Medline Plus, 2006) can look like cigarette burns, and **Mongolian spots** can look like bruises. Mongolian spots are congenital and are present at birth or within the first few weeks of life. The spots are bluish gray in appearance, so they look similar to bruises. However, unlike bruises, they do not change color over time. Most children do experience a disappearance of the marks by the age of four years. Mandated reporters want to be especially careful when assessing marks on children of certain ethnic groups such as Asians, Hispanics, and children from East Africa, who experience high rates of Mongolian spots (Tannous & Abdul-Ghani, 2005). In addition, a child may suffer from a condition such as **osteogenesis imperfecta** (OI) or a **platelet aggregation disorder** that can mimic child physical abuse. Children who suffer from osteogenesis imperfecta have a genetic disorder that causes their bones to break easily. This gives rise to the more commonly used name of the disorder, "brittle bone disease." A child with osteogenesis imperfecta can break a bone doing something as innocent as rolling over during sleep (Osteogenesis Imperfecta Foundation, 2006). Children who have a platelet aggregation disorder have platelets that do not form plugs at injury sites. This means that the child will bruise easily and also suffer from nosebleeds as well as bleeding of the gums (Canadian Hemophilia Society, 2006). If you have a child in your care at a daycare or school, you should be made aware of any condition the child has that may be confused with signs of child abuse or that should impact your dealings with them. If you are not sure about a particular child, ask a nurse or supervisor to review the child's record and inform you of anything you need to know to assess marks on the child.

MARKS FROM FOLK MEDICINE PRACTICES

A problem that requires sensitivity to cultural diversity is dealing with children who have been treated with **folk medicine** practices. The term "folk medicine" encompasses all health practices that have grown from cultural traditions. The roots of these practices can be anything from the empirical use of natural food remedies to superstition. It is when these practices conflict with accepted Western treatment that problems arise. If a parent does something he or she believes will help their child, and Western medical knowledge suggests the practice hurts the child, is the parent abusive?

Cao Gio

Some Southeast Asians practice *Cao Gio*. In this form of treatment, the practitioner massages a heated ointment or oil on an ill child's neck, spine, and ribs. Next, a coin or spoon is run along the child's skin with firm, downward strokes. This results in red, linear marks (burns or abrasions) on the child's skin (Brodeur & Monteleone, 1994). The parents are not doing this because they are angry at the child, and they are generally willing to readily discuss what was done to the child (Johnson, 2002). Therefore, we see some similarities to physical abuse (child suffers a nonaccidental injury at the hands of a caregiver), but other differences (parents are not angry or secretive, and believe they are helping). To make this situation even more confusing, there is disagreement among Western professionals as to whether *Cao Gio* is a harmful practice. Some (e.g., Davis, 2000) argue that "there is no need to discourage the use of *Cao Gio* in conjunction with the use of Western health treatments" (p. 94). Davis states that this practice, which has been handed down for generations, is not harmful and is believed by the people using it to be helpful. Yeatman and Van Dang (1980) interviewed 46 Vietnamese living in the U.S. about *Cao Gio* and found support for this position. Ninety-four percent of the participants they interviewed said they had practiced *Cao Gio*, and they all said they felt better after the treatments. In addition, none of the participants knew of anyone who had been hurt by *Cao Gio*. Based on these results, the authors recommend that U.S. doctors should not discourage *Cao Gio* because that may make Vietnamese patients distrust them. Unfortunately, not all doctors agree that *Cao Gio* is harmless. A research letter published in the *Journal of the American Medical Association* in 2002 stated that possible complications of *Cao Gio* include burns, cerebral hemorrhage, and camphor intoxication from a balm used in coining (Rampini, Schneemann, Rentsch, & Bachli, 2002).

If some doctors believe a procedure to cause unnecessary pain and/or suffering, should it be considered abusive? Galanti (1997) makes the following thought-provoking statement in her book *Caring for Patients from Different Cultures: Case Studies from American Hospitals, 2nd ed.*: "It is not that Asians never abuse their children, but rubbing them with coins is not the way they do it, any more than Americans abuse their children by having thin pieces of metal wrapped around their teeth and tightened until their teeth move out of place. Braces are often applied for primarily aesthetic reasons. Coin rubbing, at least, is an attempt to heal. Apparently, it often works. Only the failures show up in the medical system" (p. 123). If this example does not engage you, consider the common practice of male circumcision in the U.S. While this painful and unnecessary medical procedure is accepted by most Americans, is it possible that people from other cultural backgrounds would consider it to be abusive?

Caida de Mollera

Another example of folk medicine that some consider child abuse is found in the remedies used to treat *Caida de Mollera* (fallen fontanello). Children with *Caida de Mollera* have a sunken anterior fontanel (space between the bones in an infant's skull). This can be the result of severe illness, significant weight loss, or dehydration. Folk treatments include holding children upside down and perhaps shaking them (in an up-and-down motion) or slapping their feet. The impact of this treatment is debated. Some researchers clearly feel that it is dangerous and note that the procedure does not cure dehydration and it may cause retinal hemorrhages or other symptoms that mimic shaken baby syndrome (Brodeur & Monteleone, 1994; Johnson, 2002). Conversely, Hansen (1997) argues that significant force is required to cause shaken baby syndrome, but the folk treatment of *Caida de Mollera* is neither violent nor forceful. So, if a baby presents with symptoms of shaken baby syndrome and the parents admit to *Caida de Mollera*, this folk treatment is not necessarily the cause of the observed injury.

What should be done in cases such as these? Perhaps the best advice for professionals is to be knowledgeable about local folk medicine practices and then attempt to provide education about other, more accepted, medical treatments (Brodeur & Monteleone, 1994). The purpose behind the reporting laws is to help children. You must ask yourself whether this child would be better served by a referral to CPS or by parental education.

NONPHYSICAL CONSEQUENCES OF PHYSICAL ABUSE

Intellectual/Academic Problems

Not only does physical abuse hurt a child's body, but we also see problems that are not necessarily physical in nature. For instance, most, although not all, studies show that victims of childhood physical abuse suffer from intellectual and academic problems. These problems can be seen in academic performance and in school behavior. Victims of childhood physical abuse have lower test scores on measures of overall intellectual ability and on specific tests in math and reading. In addition, they are more likely to receive special education services, and they are diagnosed with learning disabilities more often than their nonabused peers. Most of these documented differences remain even when socioeconomic status is controlled for by researchers (Miller-Perrin & Perrin, 1999). Physically abused children are also more likely to be disciplined in school, and they are more likely to be suspended than nonabused children. Researchers have also noted that victims of child physical abuse are 2.5 times more likely to repeat a grade than are nonabused children. Failure to pass a grade can be related to academic and/or behavior problems. While some children may suffer from intellectual problems due to brain injury that resulted from abuse, others do not perform well in school because they are too distracted by their home situation to concentrate. Still others struggle because they miss a lot of school. Students may be kept home when their parents are attempting to hide an abusive injury, or the child may be too hurt to attend. In either case, their sporadic attendance is, at least partially, to blame for their school failure. Finally, abusive families frequently move around a great deal, which leads to discontinuity in the educational process. All of these factors can negatively impact school performance (Kolko, 2002).

Changes in Cognitive Processing

It has also been noted that, as a group, victims of child physical abuse may think differently than do nonabused children. For instance, physically abused children are more likely to assume that others have hostile intentions. If a classmate accidentally bumps into a child who has been the victim of physical abuse, the abused child will generally assume that the child who bumped him or her did it on purpose. This, of course, is likely to provoke a hostile response in return. The tendency to attribute hostile intent to others may be related to abused children's more general problem with perspective; they are not good at examining a situation from another person's perspective (Kolko, 2002). In nonabusive households, children learn to consider other's perspectives through interactions with their parents. When parents gently and rationally encourage children to think about what others were thinking or feeling, they develop the child's ability to take on another's perspective. When lacking this type of interaction, children do not spontaneously develop this ability.

Issues with Interpersonal Relationships

Not surprisingly, these victims have difficulties in forming strong **interpersonal relationships**. They are often insecurely attached to their parents and are frequently categorized as having a resistant or avoidant attachment to their caregivers. This poor attachment relationship lays a weak foundation for future relationships. As a result, physically abused children have a great deal of trouble making friends because they have not developed the appropriate social skills. Researchers have found that victims of physical abuse are deficient in certain prosocial behaviors such as smiling when they are with their peers, and their interactive play skills are below age level (Miller-Perrin & Perrin, 1999). These social deficits can lead children to being rejected by their peers.

Aggression

One of the most extensively documented effects of physical abuse is **aggression**. In a physically abusive household, aggression is modeled as a way to solve problems and as an appropriate behavior. Aggressive behavior in physically abused children is a robust finding that is seen over a variety of settings (Miller-Perrin & Perrin, 1999). Victims of physical abuse indicate a greater willingness to use physical punishment than do their nonabused peers. No matter how much some people want to deny that they are shaped by their parents, parents are children's first, and most profound models. A number of studies have demonstrated a link between early child abuse and later delinquent behavior. For instance, Widom (1989) reported that children who were physically abused prior to the age of 11 were significantly more likely than their peers to have a juvenile delinquency record (26% vs. 16.8%), to have an adult criminal record (28.6% vs. 21.1%), and to have a violent criminal record (11.2% vs. 7.9%). A literature review by Malinosky-Rummell and Hansen (1993) found evidence supporting a strong link between physical abuse during childhood and subsequent violent behavior in adulthood. People who had suffered physical abuse as children were more likely to engage in aggressive behavior including fighting and violent criminal activity. They were also more likely to report violence toward dating partners, spouses, and their own children. While the estimated range for the rate of intergenerational transmission of abuse stretches from 7% to 70%, most researchers suggest that approximately 30% of abused children will become abusive parents.

Substance Abuse

Physical abuse during childhood has also been linked with subsequent substance abuse. These children are at an increased risk for using legal drugs like alcohol and tobacco and illegal drugs (Pelcovitz, Kaplan, DeRosa, Mandel, & Salzinger, 2000). The use of alcohol and other drugs can be seen as a form of delinquent behavior, but it may be mediated by a child's internal pain that results from abuse. In other words, the substance abuse is less about acting out and more about self-medicating to deal with issues of depression and low self-esteem.

Internalizing Symptoms

Abused children show externalizing symptoms like aggression, and they also show internalizing symptoms. Child victims of physical abuse generally have lower self-esteem than do their nonabused peers. They tend to show evidence of hopelessness and depression at a higher rate than do their nonabused peers (Kolko, 2002, Miller-Perrin, & Perrin, 1999). Physically abused children in psychiatric (Kazdin, Moser, Colbus, & Bell, 1985) and nonpsychiatric (Allen &

Tarnowski, 1989) settings have significantly higher scores on measures of depression and self-concept than do nonabused comparison children. This is true even when samples are matched for age, sex, race, and socioeconomic status. It is important to note, however, that just because physically abused children are receiving higher scores than nonabused children, they are not necessarily scoring within the impaired range when compared with standardized norms (Allen & Tarnowski, 1989).

Post-Traumatic Stress Disorder

Being physically abused as a child also increases the likelihood that the individual develops **post-traumatic stress disorder** (PTSD), a disorder that may arise after someone has experienced an intense, negative event. The *Diagnostic and Statistical Manual of Mental Disorders* (DSM), Fourth Edition, indicates that this episode must be something that involved "actual or threatened death or serious injury, or a threat to the physical integrity of self or others," and that the person responded to this event with "intense fear, helplessness or horror" (p. 467). A person suffering from post-traumatic stress disorder will persistently re-experience the event (e.g., intrusive thoughts, dreams), avoid reminders of the event, and show increased forms of arousal. These symptoms must persist for over a month before a diagnosis would be made (American Psychiatric Association, 2000). Furthermore, females who are physically abused as children are at increased risk for being raped and/or assaulted as adults. This further injury can increase the post-traumatic stress disorder symptoms shown by these revictimized females (Schumm, Hobfoll, & Keogh, 2004). So, not only does physical abuse lead to post-traumatic stress disorder in some children, but in others it also makes them more vulnerable to future violence, which may make the existing post-traumatic stress disorder more severe.

Other Consequences

Finally, children who are the victims of childhood physical abuse are at an increased risk of suffering from a range of other psychiatric disorders including major depression, **dysthymia**, **attention deficit hyperactivity disorder** (ADHD), **conduct disorder**, and **oppositional defiant disorder** (Pelcovitz et al., 2000). Clearly, these victims suffer not only external, physical injuries, but internal damage as well. As a mandated reporter, you should be attentive to both forms of damage when you are assessing a child for potential physical abuse.

CONCLUSION

Nearly 23% of all calls to CPS involve allegations of child physical abuse. Although definitions vary by state, there is a general agreement about the types of acts that constitute this type of maltreatment, especially at the more severe end of the spectrum. Over time, physicians and mental health professionals have become more adept at noticing the signs of child physical abuse. Due in large part to the mandated reporting laws, these professionals are now more likely than ever to report their suspicious findings to the authorities. Although all forms of maltreatment are a challenge to prove in court, the physical marks left by this type of maltreatment can aid investigators in proving their case, and securing safety for the child.

DISCUSSION QUESTIONS

1. Over time the definition of child physical abuse has changed. The trend has been to classify more behaviors as abusive. Is this a good thing or a bad thing?
2. Should people who engage in folk medicine practices be prosecuted for child physical abuse? Why or why not?

3. If you read in the newspaper that a father told doctors that his 2-year-old son had fallen off the couch and broken his arm and fractured three ribs, what would you think about his account?

4. How important are parental intentions in the assessment of child physical abuse? Should acts that were not meant to harm the child, but did cause harm, be considered abusive?

5. Do you think that laws regarding child physical abuse should cover only harm, or both harm and threatened harm? Why?

DEFINITIONS

Child Physical Abuse: an act by a caregiver that results in a nonaccidental injury to a child.

Statute: a law passed by a legislative body.

Incidence: the number of new cases occurring or being diagnosed in a year.

Prevalence: the number of cases that exist in a specified population at a given point in time.

Substantiated: a report of child maltreatment that has been confirmed by child protective services.

Bruising: injury in which capillaries are damaged, allowing blood to seep into the surrounding tissue; generally caused by striking or pressing that does not break the skin.

Fractures: the partial or complete breaking of bone or cartilage.

Shaken Baby Syndrome (SBS): a condition of severe internal bleeding, particularly around the brain or eyes, that is caused by violently shaking an infant or young child.

Burns: injuries caused by fire, heat, or acid; first-degree burns cause red skin, second-degree burns result in blisters, and third-degree burns cause deep skin destruction.

Impetigo: a contagious skin infection that is marked by blisters that erupt and form crusts.

Mongolian Spot: a birthmark that is a smooth, flat, bluish gray spot that looks like a bruise.

Osteogenesis Imperfecta: a genetic disorder in which bones fracture easily.

Platelet Aggregation Disorder: a medical condition that occurs when platelets do not form plugs at injury sites.

Folk Medicine: health practices that come from cultural traditions; native remedies.

Cao Gio: a Southeast Asian practice in which a practitioner massages a heated ointment or oil on an ill child's neck, spine, and ribs, and then runs a coin or spoon along the child's skin with firm, downward strokes.

Caida de Mollera: a sunken anterior fontanel (space between the bones in an infant's skull) that can be the result of severe illness, significant weight loss, or dehydration.

Interpersonal Relationship: social association, connection, and involvement between two people.

Aggression: behavior that is intended to cause harm or pain; a disposition to behave in a violent way even when not provoked.

Post-Traumatic Stress Disorder (PTSD): an anxiety disorder that occurs in response to experiencing extreme stress (generally involving actual or threatened death or serious injury). The person experiences symptoms including re-experiencing the event, avoiding stimuli reminiscent of the event, and increased arousal for at least one month.

Diagnostic and Statistical Manual of Mental Disorders **(DSM):** a manual published by the American Psychiatric Association that lists the criteria for diagnosing mental disorders as well as providing information on causes, age of onset, gender differences, and prognosis.

Dysthymia: a chronic, mild depression that persists for more than 2 years.

Attention Deficit Hyperactivity Disorder (ADHD): a mental disorder characterized by a limited attention span, overactivity, restlessness, and impulsiveness.

Conduct Disorder: a personality disorder of childhood marked by persistent disruptive behavior and repeated violation of the rights of others and societal norms.

Oppositional Defiant Disorder: a disruptive pattern of behavior in childhood that is characterized by defiance and disobedience as well as hostile behavior. These behaviors persist for at least 6 months and interfere with everyday functioning.

CHAPTER 5

Child Neglect

DEFINITION

Child neglect is an act of omission. Parents or caregivers are not doing something that they should be doing for their children. Neglect can be thought of as the failure to meet the *minimum* requirements for care; it is not the failure to provide ideal care. The federal government identifies abuse and neglect together as follows:

> Any recent act or failure to act on the part of a parent or caretaker, which results in death, serious injury or emotional harm, sexual abuse, or exploitation, or an act or failure to act which presents an imminent risk of serious harm (42 U.S.C.A. §5106g(2)).

As you can see, this definition does not provide much guidance about what, exactly, constitutes child neglect. One of the common complaints heard from people who work in child protection is that the language used to define maltreatment is not precise. To further complicate matters, each state and the District of Columbia has its own definition of child neglect. What the definitions have in common is that neglect entails the failure of parents or caregivers to meet needs for food, clothing, shelter, protection, and medical care. There are, however, substantial differences among the states' statutes.

Differences in State Definitions of Child Neglect

States differ in whether they take into consideration the parents' ability to provide for their children. Consider the following statutes:

> Arizona: "Neglect or neglected means the inability or unwillingness of a parent, guardian or custodian to provide for that child…" (§8-201)
> Nevada: "…because of the faults or habits of the person responsible for his welfare or his neglect or refusal to provide them when able to do so" (§432B.140)
> Wisconsin: "Neglect means failure, refusal, or inability…for reasons other than poverty, to provide…" (§48.981)

In these three examples, you see three different ways of determining neglect. Arizona considers failure to provide for the child to be neglect, whether or not that failure is due to the parents being unwilling or unable to provide. Parents who are incapable of providing because of poverty or mental illness are considered neglecting, as are parents who fail their children due to their disinterest in them. Nevada has a softer approach by only labeling parents as neglectful if they don't provide for their children when they are able to do so. Finally, Wisconsin exempts parents who can't provide due to poverty, but does not exclude those who are unable to provide for other reasons.

Fetal Neglect.   States also differ in their inclusion or exclusion of fetuses in their neglect statutes. Recent years have seen a dramatic increase in the legal penalties for women who use drugs while they are pregnant. By 2005, five states (Illinois, Indiana, Massachusetts, Minnesota, and North Dakota) had neglect statutes that dealt explicitly with exposing fetuses to drugs or alcohol. For example, Illinois defines a neglected child in part as, "A newborn whose blood, urine or **meconium** contains any amount of a controlled substance or a **metabolite** thereof" (Ch. 325 §5/3). Minnesota includes the following statement in its definition of neglect, "Prenatal exposure to a controlled substance, used by the mother for a nonmedical purpose, as evidenced by withdrawal symptoms in the child at birth, results of a **toxicology** test performed on the mother at delivery or the child at birth, or medical effects or developmental delays during the child's first year of life that medically indicate prenatal exposure to a controlled substance" (§626.556). Drug use during pregnancy may seem more like an act of abuse than an act of omission; however, legislators have chosen to see this behavior as the failure to provide an adequate prenatal environment. For an in-depth exploration of this topic, see the chapter entitled Fetal Abuse.

Postnatal Exposure to Drugs.   As states are beginning to address prenatal exposure to drugs, others are adding **postnatal** exposure to drugs (or at least the manufacturing of drugs) to their definitions of neglect. Two states have listed exposure to drug production as a specific way in which parents may fail to provide a safe environment for their children. Iowa's legal definition of child neglect includes the sentence, "The person responsible for the care of a child has, in the presence of the child, manufactured a dangerous substance, possesses a product containing ephedrine, its salts, optical isomers, salts of optical isomers, or pseudoephedrine, its salts, with the intent to use the product as a precursor or an intermediary to a dangerous substance" (§232.68). Similarly, South Dakota law defines a neglected child in part as one "whose parent, guardian or custodian knowingly exposes the child to an environment that is being used for the manufacturing of methamphetamine" (§26-8A-2).

Unique Aspects of State Laws.   There are many other states that have fairly unique entries in their neglect statutes. Nebraska's law includes leaving a child under age 7 in a car unsupervised (§28-710); the law in Montana mentions failure to provide cleanliness (§41-3-102); both Connecticut and Tennessee mention threats to the child's moral development (§46b-120; §37-1-102); and California differentiates between neglect and serious neglect (§11165.2). Some states (Idaho, New Mexico, North Carolina, North Dakota, and Ohio) include improper adoption as part of neglect, while most do not. For instance, North Carolina includes in its definition of a neglected child one "who has been placed for care or adoption in violation of law" (§7B-101).

Finding Your State Law.   Once again, it should be clear that you need to know what the law is in the state(s) where you live and work. This information can be found on the website for the National Clearinghouse on Child Abuse and Neglect Information (see Search the Web 5.1).

SUBTYPES OF NEGLECT

Although many state laws provide only a minimal definition of child neglect, child protective services (CPS) has developed a more complete and complex definition that is based on the state

---

SEARCH THE WEB 5.1

The definitions of child abuse established by each state can be found at http://www.childwelfare.gov/systemwide/laws_policies/state/index.cfm.

1. Under number one, select the state or states you are interested in learning about.
2. For number two, check Definitions of Child Abuse and Neglect.
3. For number three, click Go.

---

laws. The broad concept of child neglect is broken down into different subtypes and these are all defined separately.

Physical Neglect

First, there is **physical neglect**, which is the type of situation most commonly associated with the term "neglect." This type of neglect is defined as the failure to meet the minimal physical needs of the child. These physical needs include food, shelter, and clothing as well as protection from harm or danger. Certainly, there is much debate over what constitutes the minimal level of acceptable care and what should be labeled as maltreatment.

On the extreme ends of the continuum, you can imagine a family in which the child is starved to the point of being **malnourished** (obvious physical neglect; see Case Example 5.1: Extreme Neglect) and a family where the child receives three nutritious, well-balanced meals per day along with two healthy snacks (food needs are met exceptionally well). We could all probably agree that the first family is not meeting their child's minimal needs and the second family is providing adequately. But, where do you cross the line from inadequate to adequate? Consider a family in which the children are given donuts for breakfast every day because it is their favorite food and because it is easy. For lunch and dinner they eat fast food, and a frequent treat is a trip to the ice-cream store. Are the physical needs of these children being met? Assume they are of normal weight and generally healthy; does that impact your decision? If this sort of diet seems neglectful to you, how much of this sort of food can a child be served by parents who are not neglectful? If a 5-year-old child has never been served a vegetable, are his parents neglectful?

The Chronic Nature of Neglect. One of the problems with defining neglect is that we are often talking about a pattern of behavior, not just one or two instances. Nearly all parents will occasionally feed their children food with questionable nutritional value, and we do not call this neglect. However, a parent who breaks his or her child's arm once will be labeled as physically abusive. Therefore, with neglect, we need to know not only that something is not being done, but that it is not being done on such a consistent basis that the child's minimal needs are not being met. We also need to keep in mind that we are not requiring that parents provide optimal care, only the minimal level of acceptable care. There are many parents who are not doing a great job of meeting their children's needs but do not fall to the level of neglect. One yardstick that is used is whether the child is maintaining normal growth. If a child is at a normal height and weight and relatively healthy, it is generally presumed that his or her food needs are being met adequately.

Appropriate Shelter. Shelter needs are similarly complex. The law generally requires that parents provide a "suitable place of abode," without specifying exactly what that would be. Is a car a suitable place of abode? Is a tent acceptable? Would raising a child in a tepee be appropriate? Must a home have electricity and running water to be considered suitable? If you live in a state where you cannot be labeled as neglectful simply because you are poor, will this change

CASE EXAMPLE 5.1:   Extreme Neglect

In September of 2002 a couple was arrested in Tampa, Florida, and charged with maltreating a 7-year-old child. The mother, Connie Warrington, and her boyfriend, David LaPointe, had locked the girl, Mandy,[1] in her room for months and given her only minimal food and water. The child, who should have weighed between 50 and 55 pounds, weighed only 29 pounds when the police found her. The room where she was kept had no furniture other than a bare mattress; the child was forced to use a small closet as a bathroom, and she did not attend school (Humphrey, 2002). Apparently, Warrington occasionally tried to sneak food to Mandy when LaPointe was not around, but she said she could not leave LaPointe because she had nowhere else to go (Morelli, 2002a).

The police learned of the case from Mandy's biological father, who saw the conditions she was living in when he arrived from New York with a court order to take the child. Investigation revealed that this was not the first time the authorities had been contacted about Mandy. In January of 2001, Warrington, LaPointe, and Mandy had been living in New York when they came to the attention of child protective services (CPS). The allegations at that time were that Mandy had been absent from school, was not adequately supervised, and that she was medically neglected. The determination at that time was that Mandy was not in imminent danger (Morelli, 2002b).

Then, in May of 2002, the family was again reported to CPS. Warrington and LaPointe had admitted Mandy to a psychiatric hospital because she was having problems with incontinence. The staff at the hospital began to suspect that Mandy was being maltreated. When Warrington and LaPointe realized that the hospital staff was going to report them to the state authorities, they took Mandy from the hospital against the doctor's orders and they fled to Florida (Morelli, 2002a). New York social services did not contact Florida authorities to report the move because at the conclusion of their investigation in 2001, they did not think Mandy was at high risk, and they were not able to investigate in 2002 because the family had left the state.

When Mandy's biological father learned of her location in Florida, he obtained the court order and went to get her. Warrington handed her daughter over without conflict, and Mandy went back to New York with her father. Once in New York, Mandy was treated for malnutrition and dehydration. It was also noted that she was bruised and had a human bite mark on her back. In addition, the doctors had to surgically remove a bead that Mandy said LaPointe had shoved into her ear because she was bad. Mandy also reported that LaPointe said he locked her up and refused to feed her because he hated her (Couple accused, 2002). Detective John Yaratch who investigated the case reported that LaPointe was jealous of the affection his girlfriend had for Mandy (Morelli, 2002a).

When the police arrested Warrington and LaPointe, the state took custody of the couple's young children, a 1-year-old boy and a 3-year-old girl. Both children were healthy, and it appeared that they had not been maltreated (Humphrey, 2002).

Because Mandy was too traumatized to testify in court, prosecutors settled for a plea bargain with LaPointe. He was sentenced to 6 years and 4 months in prison for aggravated child abuse and child neglect. After his release, he will serve 10 years of probation. Warrington pled guilty to child neglect and to failure to report child abuse (Good, 2004).

In 2004, Mandy was healthy and living with her biological father (Good, 2004).

CASE POINTS

1. Many cases involve more than one type of maltreatment. Mandy suffered from several forms of neglect (physical, emotional, medical, and educational) and was also physically and psychologically abused.
2. It is possible that only one child in a family may be maltreated. Despite the horrific treatment of Mandy, her siblings were not maltreated. In this case, Mandy was targeted because she was not the biological child of the father figure in the home. In other cases it is not clear why one child is singled out for maltreatment.
3. Mandy's sad story also points to a problem in the system. Although this family had been reported to CPS, it took years for her to be removed from the family. Certainly, technology has made it easier to track children, but we still see break-downs in communication when families relocate—especially across state lines.

DISCUSSION QUESTIONS

1. Should CPS be held responsible for failing to protect Mandy? If so, what sort of penalty would be appropriate?
2. Should Warrington and LaPointe retain custody of their two young, nonmal-treated children?
3. Should Warrington be allowed contact with Mandy? If so, under what conditions?

Endnote

1. The child's name was changed to protect her privacy.

---

who is and who is not a neglected child? While no state law lists precisely what is required, unwritten norms that vary from one community to the next develop among social workers. On a case-by-case basis, CPS workers determine whether a home is suitable, and if they feel it is not, they present the case to a judge.

Adequate Supervision. CPS also requires that parents adequately supervise their children in order to protect them from harm. State laws vary, but all require that children attain a certain age (usually 12 years) before they can be left at home alone. This sort of neglect includes not only lack of supervision, but also inadequate supervision. It is not enough for parents to be physically present; they must be somewhat attentive to the child or children present. As you may guess, this leads to another gray area. A parent who has passed out after drinking is clearly not providing adequate supervision, but what about the parent who is on the phone or in the bathtub? Once again, one needs to consider the age and immediate circumstances of the child. Being distracted by an important phone call while an infant is safe in the playpen is different from being distracted while the infant is in a pool (see Case Example 5.2).

Being present and attentive is the first part of not being a neglectful parent, but this alone is not sufficient to keep children safe. Parents are also expected to provide a safe atmosphere for their children. Unnecessarily exposing a child to possible harm is considered **child endanger-ment** — a form of physical neglect. Even though it is impossible to protect children from all possible harm, caregivers are expected to use good judgment to keep the children in their care safe from unnecessary risks. For instance, exposing children to inappropriate sexual material can be considered a failure to provide a safe atmosphere. There is a great deal of discussion about what is too sexual for a child of a certain age to see, but there is general agreement that it

CASE #1

Amber Johnson was charged with child neglect after a neighbor spotted Johnson's 2-year-old son playing in the parking lot and in his mother's car unsupervised. When the neighbor went to Johnson's apartment, she found her asleep and could not wake her. At that point, the neighbor called the police. Johnson told the police that she had taken both prescription and nonprescription drugs in the last 24 hours. The police also noted that the contents of Johnson's purse had spilled and that 15 Soma pills and 3 diazepam pills were on the floor in easy reach of the child (Mother faces neglect, 2005).

Case Points

1. A parent can be charged with neglect even if the child is not harmed. The fact that the child was exposed to unacceptable risk is sufficient for a charge of neglect. In this case, the child could have been harmed by playing unsupervised in an unsafe area or by ingesting drugs.
2. This case also highlights the frequent connection between parental substance use and child maltreatment charges.

DISCUSSION QUESTIONS

1. Do you think Ms. Johnson was guilty of child neglect? If so, what action(s) should be taken (e.g., removal of the child from her care, mandatory counseling, jail)?
2. In this case the child was not harmed. Does that affect your analysis of the situation?

CASE #2

Three children, ages 8 years, 2 years, and 17 months, were left in a car for over 30 minutes while their babysitter shopped for groceries. The outside temperature that day was 93 degrees. Store employees noticed the children and they brought them water. The employees also called the police. The babysitter was ticketed on suspicion of child neglect (Safranek, 2005).

Case Points

1. Although neglect is often defined as a chronic pattern of behavior, one severe incident can also be labeled as neglect.
2. It is not only parents who can be charged with child neglect. Anyone who is acting *in loco parentis* can be charged with child maltreatment.

DISCUSSION QUESTIONS

1. Was the babysitter guilty of child neglect?
2. Does the age of the children left in the car affect your decision? How old is "old enough" to be left alone in a car?

CASE #3

A woman called the sheriff's office to report that two toddlers (both 3 years old) were walking barefoot and unsupervised along a highway. Their diapers were dirty and their clothes were stained with the juice of poisonous berries. The adults who were responsible for the children were asleep at the time that the children wandered away (2 wandering toddlers, 2005).

Case Point

This case illustrates the importance of considering a child's developmental age when assessing level of supervision. Older children may be safe when playing outside alone, but this is not true for toddlers.

DISCUSSION QUESTIONS

1. Were these caregivers guilty of child neglect? If so, what penalty would be appropriate for them?
2. Would your answer to the first question change if the children had been harmed?

CASE #4

A 26-year-old-woman, Sandra Davis, was charged with child neglect after leaving her four children alone at home on a Saturday night. All four children died in a fire caused by a candle that was being used to light the apartment, which had no electricity or heat. Davis told firefighters that she had been gone for only minutes, but other witnesses said she had been away for hours (Mother is charged, 1984).

Case Point

This tragic case illustrates the fact that child neglect can lead to fatalities. The consequences of neglect can be as severe as the consequences of abuse.

DISCUSSION QUESTIONS

1. Was Ms. Davis guilty of child neglect? If so, what would be an appropriate punishment?
2. If nothing had happened to the children that night, would Ms. Davis be guilty of child neglect?
3. The children's ages were not provided in this case. How would your responses change based on the ages of the children involved?

not appropriate to expose young children to graphic sexual material. Failure to provide a safe environment can result in charges of child neglect (see Case Example 5.3).

Domestic Violence. Recently, attention has been paid to children who are exposed to domestic violence. Chapter 2 noted that domestic violence is a *risk factor* for child maltreatment. The question at hand is whether it is also a *form* of child maltreatment. While it is obvious that living in a home where there is violence is not an ideal situation for children, it has been difficult to say what form of child maltreatment it should be considered. If the child is physically hurt, perhaps by attempting to intervene, it could be considered physical abuse. However, even if the child is not harmed physically, he or she may be harmed psychologically by witnessing the abuse or by knowing that is happening in the home. In such cases, domestic violence may best be labeled a form of psychological maltreatment. In all cases, it can be seen as a form of child endangerment, because it places the child in a dangerous environment. There has been

CASE EXAMPLE 5.3:   CHILD NEGLECT—ENDANGERMENT

In April of 2005, Donald Poplick was charged with child neglect for furnishing a firearm to a minor. Poplick was arrested after a 3-year-old child in his care was seen playing with an unloaded gun. Poplick denied giving the gun to the child, but said he had shown the child how to load, unload, and operate his shotgun (Man accused, 2005).

CASE POINTS

1. It is important to consider a child's developmental level when assessing caregiver behavior. Even though it may have been acceptable to teach a child of 12 to operate a shotgun, giving this information to a 3-year-old shows a striking lack of good judgment.
2. This case also shows that caregivers and police may have radically different ideas about what is safe or appropriate behavior. Poplick freely admitted to behavior that the police thought constituted child endangerment.
3. Finally, even if a parent does not expose the child to harm deliberately, they are still neglectful if they allow the child to be in a potentially harmful environment. In this case, the 3-year-old should not have had access to a gun.

DISCUSSION QUESTIONS

1. Was Mr. Poplick guilty of child neglect? If so, what would an appropriate punishment be?
2. Would your response change if the child had accidentally injured or killed himself?

a push recently to say that exposing a child to domestic violence is a crime, or to increase the penalty for domestic violence if it happens in the presence of a child. For instance, Georgia's law reads as follows:

> Any person commits the offense of cruelty to children in the second degree when such a person, who is the primary aggressor, intentionally allows a child under the age of 18 to witness the commission of a forcible felony, battery, or family violence battery; or having knowledge that a child under the age of 18 is present and sees or hears the act, commits forcible felony, battery, or family battery (Georgia Code Ann. §16-5-70).

Idaho law states that penalties for domestic violence are doubled if they are committed in the presence of a child under the age of 16 (Idaho Code §18-918). Because it is estimated that as many as 10 million children are exposed to domestic violence each year (Straus, 1992), this represents an area of study that desperately needs more attention from researchers and legislators.

Indicators of Possible Physical Neglect. Because each family situation is unique, it is difficult to say what exactly constitutes neglect. Frequently professionals put together lists of things a CPS worker can look for in determining whether a child is being neglected. Consider the following list that was provided by Sagatun and Edwards (1995, p. 28) in the book *Child Abuse and the Legal System*:

Neglect may be suspected if the following physical indicators are present:

1. Lack of adequate medical or dental care
2. Chronic sleepiness or hunger
3. Poor personal hygiene; dirty clothing; inadequate dress for weather conditions

4. Evidence of poor supervision; child is left alone in the home or unsupervised under circumstances when he or she should have been supervised
5. Conditions in the home constitute a health hazard
6. Home lacks heating or plumbing
7. Fire hazards or other unsafe conditions in the home
8. Inadequate sleeping arrangements
9. Nutritional quality of food in the home is poor
10. Spoiled food in refrigerator or cupboards

As is often the case with neglect, some of the items (1, 4, 5, and 7) on the list seem clearly harmful, while others are occasionally true of almost every home. Who among us has not come upon some scary, moldy thing growing in our refrigerator or hasn't let a child get extremely dirty? These items require us to consider not just one instance, but a pattern of behavior that interferes with the child's welfare. A child who comes in from a hard day at play and is filthy until his parent gets him bathed is not neglected. A child who shows up for school day after day in dirty, smelly clothing that elicits teasing and taunts from his classmates may be neglected.

Harder still are the items on the list that are open to interpretation. Take number 8, for example, "Inadequate sleeping arrangements." What does this mean? Is it possible that what it means to me may be quite different from what it means to you? Often this item is interpreted to mean that after a certain age children should have a room that is separate from rooms of the opposite sex (parents and siblings). This leads to two questions: (1) At what age does room sharing among family members of the opposite sex become inadequate? and (2) Regarding impoverished families, if a family can only afford a one-bedroom apartment and they have male and female children, what are they to do?

Questions like this exemplify the point that decisions about child maltreatment are often more art than science. Case workers can be given things to look for and be aware of, but there are no easy answers. The case worker assesses each situation and brings the case before the court. Ultimately, family court judges decide on a case-by-case basis if the child's physical needs are being met or if the parents are guilty of neglect.

Emotional Neglect

A second subtype of neglect is **emotional neglect**. This type of neglect is defined as the failure to meet the child's emotional needs. As you might imagine, this is even more difficult to quantify than is physical neglect. The National Incidence Study-3 provides the following definition for emotional neglect: "the failure to provide adequate affection and emotional support and permitting a child to be exposed to domestic violence" (Stowman & Donohue, 2005, p. 496). Emotional neglect is rarely charged as the sole type of maltreatment because it is so difficult to operationally define and to prove. Even though extreme cases of emotional neglect may be clear, it is much more difficult to say how much emotional attention is enough or how many moments of neglect constitute likely harm. This aspect of maltreatment is explored in-depth in the chapter entitled Psychological Maltreatment.

Medical Neglect

A third, and often controversial, type of neglect is **medical neglect**: the failure to provide prescribed medical treatment. This type of neglect has proved to be a particularly sensitive area when parents' religious beliefs conflict with the advice of medical doctors, often in life-or-death situations. For instance, the beliefs of Jehovah's Witnesses prohibit blood transfusions, and some Buddhists believe that a body cannot go into the next life if any of the organs have been removed (Cantwell, 1997). These beliefs can result in parents refusing to permit their child to receive life-saving medical interventions. Some medical cases are serious enough that the child's life is at risk or it is likely that there will be a significant negative impact on the child's health if he or she does not receive treatment. In such situations, the courts have been called on to force the parents to allow treatment even if the treatment conflicted with their religious beliefs.

Legal Precedents.   The legal rulings have been complex in this area. In 1944 in *Prince v. Massachusetts* (see chapter 1 for a full description of this case), the U.S. Supreme Court ruled that "the right to practice religion freely does not include the liberty to expose the community or child to communicable disease, or the latter to ill health or death." However, in 1974, the federal government said that states must provide religious exemptions to child abuse and neglect charges if they wanted to receive federal funds. Because states are largely dependent on federal funds, the vast majority of them quickly added this exemption and did not charge parents with medical neglect if they withheld treatment for religious reasons. Nine years later, in 1983, this federal mandate was repealed and states were allowed to remove religious exemptions from their statutes without risking the loss of federal funds. However, due to well-organized lobbying on the part of supporters of religious exemption, the process of repealing the exemptions has been slow (Asser & Swan, 1998). The federal government took another step back toward protecting children, regardless of their parent's beliefs, in 1984. The Child Abuse Prevention and Treatment Act of 1984 (PL 98-457) stated explicitly that the failure to secure medical treatment for a seriously ill newborn is medical neglect unless such treatments would serve only to prolong dying. This is a battle that is not likely to be resolved quickly because people on both sides of the issue have strong feelings about what is right. On the one hand, advocates of religious exemptions cite their constitutional guarantee to practice religion, yet others believe that failure to provide medical treatment for seriously ill children is neglect no matter what the parental motivation. The **American Academy of Pediatrics**' Committee on Bioethics released a strong statement in 1988 recommending that all pediatricians work to increase the public's awareness of the dangers to children inherent in religious exemptions and to work to legislate protections for all children from medical neglect(see Focus on Research 5.1).

The Age of the Child.   Much of the focus on medical neglect is on infants and young children, but older children can also be medically neglected. However, as children age, they are more able to speak for themselves and say whether or not they want a specific treatment. Teenagers have generally been allowed to refuse medical treatment for serious conditions based on their religious beliefs because they are seen as mature enough to make such decisions even if they are not yet legal adults (Dubowitz, Black, Starr, & Zuravin, 1993). Even allowing only older children to make medical decisions that involve refusal of treatment does not sit well with everyone. An adolescent may have a better understanding of his or her medical condition and the possible consequences of not getting medical treatment; however, many argue that adolescents are not truly free to opt for treatment that their families are adamantly opposed to and/or that they are not mature enough to make such important decisions on their own (see Legal Example 5.1).

In trying to make decisions about complex issues, it is helpful to have as much information as possible. A question for researchers is to determine how many children are harmed by religious exemptions and to assess whether this harm could have been prevented (see Focus on Research 5.1).

Delay in Seeking Treatment.   Medical neglect also includes the failure to seek help for a medical condition in a timely manner when a reasonable person would have realized that the child needed professional medical attention (Winton & Mara, 2001). This does not mean that a parent who waits a day to seek treatment for an injury that is not clearly traumatic is guilty of medical neglect. Many attentive parents (mine included) have waited a day before a trip to

FOCUS ON RESEARCH 5.1:   RELIGION-MOTIVATED MEDICAL NEGLECT AND CHILD FATALITIES

In 1998, Asser and Swan published a paper in *Pediatrics* that presented their review of 172 child deaths that occurred between 1975 and 1995 where there was clear evidence that the parents had withheld medical treatment because of religious convictions. The cases they reviewed were collected from the nonprofit organization Children's Healthcare is a Legal Duty (CHILD), which gathers information on cases of religiously motivated child medical neglect. Doctors reviewed the cases and determined the likely outcome if the child had received the standard medical care that had been available at the time of the child's illness.

They found that in 81% of the cases, the child's chance of survival if treated with conventional medical care would have been greater than 90%. In an additional 10% of the cases the survival rate would have been over 50% with medical treatment, and in all but 2% of the cases it was determined that the child would have benefited in some way from medical treatment. Not only would medical care have dramatically reduced child fatalities, it also would have prevented a great deal of pain and suffering.

There were five religious groups that accounted for 83% of the fatalities in this study:

Faith Assembly	64 deaths
First Church of Christ, Scientist (Christian Science)	28 deaths
Church of the First Born	23 deaths
Faith Tabernacle	16 deaths
Endtime Ministries	12 deaths

The researchers concluded that a great deal of child pain, suffering, and death is directly attributable to the failure to seek medical treatment motivated by religious beliefs. They also proposed that the actual numbers are likely much higher than those they reported because it is suspected that many cases of religiously motivated medical neglect go undocumented. Finally, the authors stressed that many of the deaths they explored were from conditions that are easily cured in a medical center, such as dehydration, appendicitis, and antibiotic-sensitive bacterial infections.

LEGAL EXAMPLE 5.1:   RELIGION-MOTIVATED MEDICAL NEGLECT AND THE MATURE MINOR

In 1987, a young girl identified in court records as "E.G." was diagnosed with acute nonlymphatic leukemia. When the girl and her mother, Rosie Denton, learned that the treatment would involve blood transfusions, they declined based on their convictions as Jehovah's Witnesses that the "eating" of blood is prohibited. Mrs. Denton did agree to permit any other medical treatments, and she signed a release form saying that the medical facility was not liable for failure to conduct the blood transfusions.

Because Mrs. Denton refused to give parental consent for the blood transfusions, the State of Illinois filed a child neglect petition in juvenile court. At the initial hearing on February 25, 1987, Dr. Stanley Yachnin testified that if E.G. did not receive the transfusions, it was likely that she would die within one month. He further testified that treatment with blood transfusions and chemotherapy had an 80% chance of achieving remission. However, Dr. Yachnin did note that the long-term prognosis was still poor, with only 20–25% of patients having a long-term survival rate even with full treatment.

Dr. Yachnin went on to testify that E.G. was a mature minor who appeared to understand the consequences of her decision to refuse treatment. He also testified that she seemed sincere in her religious beliefs. The associate general counsel for the University of Chicago Hospital, Jane McAtee, corroborated Dr. Yachnin's testimony.

After hearing the testimony, the juvenile court judge appointed Ms. McAtee as E.G.'s temporary guardian and gave her the authority to consent to blood transfusions on E.G.'s behalf. Following several blood transfusions, E.G. was well enough to testify in further hearings held on April 8, 1987. E.G. testified that she did not wish to die, but that based on her deeply held religious convictions she did not want to receive transfusions. She said she felt her wants and beliefs were being completely disregarded by the courts. Dr. Littner, a psychiatrist, testified that E.G. had the maturity level of an 18- to 21-year-old and was competent to make her own medical decisions.

Again, the judge ruled that E.G. was medically neglected and that a State-appointed guardian should continue to assent to treatment on her behalf. The court ruled that the State's interest in the case was greater than that of E.G. or her mother.

The case was appealed, and the appellate court ruled that as a mature minor who was nearly 18, E.G. was partially emancipated and could, therefore, refuse medical treatment. The appellate court did, however, uphold the medical neglect charge against Rosie Denton.

Finally, the case was brought before the Illinois State Supreme Court. Although the case was technically moot by this time because E.G. had reached the age of 18, the court agreed to hear the case because it presented an issue of substantial public interest. The court found that the age of 18 is not an "impenetrable barrier." The justices noted that in many specific situations minors were treated as adults by the court (e.g., a 12-year-old may seek medical care if he or she may suspect a sexually transmitted disease, is addicted to drugs or alcohol, and is pregnant; at 16, a child may be declared emancipated; children under 18 may be charged criminally as adults; females under the age of 18 may undergo an abortion without parental consent).

Based on this reasoning, if a trial judge finds a minor to be mature, they should allow that minor to refuse medical treatment. This should be done on a case-by-case basis in order to balance the rights of the minor with the State's duty to protect those who cannot protect themselves. The court also noted that the interests of third parties should be considered (i.e., if the parents disagree with the child and want the child to receive medical treatment, their opinions should be weighed heavily). The Illinois State Supreme Court ruled that in this case E.G. should have been allowed to refuse medical treatment, and they ordered the lower court to expunge the finding of medical neglect against Rosie Denton (*In re E.G.*, 1989).

DISCUSSION QUESTIONS

1. Should E.G. have been forced to have the blood transfusions?
2. If you think E.G. was old enough to make this type of medical decision, what should the "cut-off" age be (16 years? 14 years? 12 years? 10 years?) ?
3. Given that the experts in the first trial testified that E.G. was very mature, were you surprised that the judge ruled against her?

the hospital only to find out that a bone was broken! In order for a caregiver to be charged with delay of treatment, the injury must be serious and the delay obvious (see Case Example 5.4).

Mental Health Neglect

A fourth subtype of neglect is **mental health neglect**, which is defined as the failure to comply with recommended psychological treatment. In these situations, parents have not sought or followed through with the mental health services that were recommended to them by professionals (e.g., school psychologists, medical doctors). Hart and Brassard (1987) suggested that in order to make a diagnosis of mental health neglect, the following criteria should be met: (1) a team of two or more appropriately accredited mental health professionals must conclude that the child has a serious emotional or behavioral problem, and (2) the child's caregiver refuses to provide or maintain the suggested treatment. Hart and Brassard further argue that the caregiver should be notified of treatment options in writing, and that the mental health professionals should ensure that scheduling and paying for the treatments are within the caregiver's ability.

Mental health neglect also includes unacceptable delay in seeking or providing treatment that the child needs when a reasonable lay person would have realized that mental health treatment was necessary (e.g., after a suicide attempt). Currently, the issue of mental health neglect is not widely addressed by CPS, and correspondingly, little research exists on this subtype of neglect.

Educational Neglect

The fifth subtype of neglect, **educational neglect**, is often the easiest to document. This type of neglect is defined generally as the failure to meet legal requirements for school attendance. The National Incidence Study-3 (Sedlak & Broadhurst, 1996) defined educational neglect as any of the following three situations:

1. Permitted chronic truancy—the child is absent for an average of at least five days per month after the parent has been notified, and the parent has not done anything to address the situation.
2. Failure to enroll/other truancy—the parent has failed to enroll a school-aged child in school, allowing the child to miss at least one month of school, or the parent keeps the child at home for inappropriate reasons (e.g., to work or to watch younger siblings) at least three days per month. (Note: Parents are exempt from enrolling their children in school if they document according to state law that the child is receiving adequate home schooling and attaining academic achievement that is appropriate to the child's developmental level.)
3. Inattention to special education needs—the parent fails to follow recommended interventions for remedial education without a reasonable cause.

Because schools keep excellent attendance records, this is often the simplest way to demonstrate neglect. Also, educational neglect often co-occurs with other types of maltreatment that may be harder to prove. For instance, physically abusive parents may keep their children at home so that others will not see bruises and ask the children what has occurred. Even if you cannot provide evidence of other maltreatment, educational neglect is enough to get CPS involved. Some teachers and CPS workers also consider educationally neglectful parents to include those who are not involved with their child's education or who don't cooperate with suggested programs to aid in their child's learning, but this sort of definition has not had legal success. Of course, a child in an approved home school situation is not required to meet the state attendance requirement, but home schooling parents can still be charged with educational neglect if they fail to keep up with age-appropriate work or to foster peer interaction. It is, however, important to note

CASE EXAMPLE 5.4:   MEDICAL NEGLECT

In August of 2005, a 13-year-old girl was found near death in her home. The girl was ema-ciated, having lost between 30 and 40 pounds as she battled an infection for weeks with-out medical attention. The infection, which had become life-threatening, began when the girl attempted to pierce her own belly button. Despite the dramatic weight loss, extreme pain, lethargy, pus around the wound, and loss of control of the bowels, her mother did not seek medical help. Instead, the mother wrapped her 13-year-old in diapers (Slack, 2005). Although the family did ultimately call 911, the police notified child protective services (CPS) on suspicion of delay of treatment. Denise Montero, the spokeswoman for CPS said it was the worst case of medical neglect she had ever seen. CPS also took custody of the girl's 15-year-old brother (Smalley, & Slack, 2005a).

An investigation revealed that the mother, Debora Robinson, had been investigated twice before for child neglect. Although CPS would not reveal details of the previous investigations, they did say they were not as serious as the current situation. The first case was closed after CPS determined that the mother was providing adequate care and the second case was closed by a judge. CPS is not required to monitor cases after they have been closed.

Ms. Robinson maintains that she did not realize the severity of her daughter's illness. When she was confronted by the police, she threatened to harm herself, so she was sent to the hospital for psychiatric evaluation (Smalley & Slack, 2005b). After Ms. Robinson was released from the hospital, she was charged with "wanton and reckless behavior creating a risk of serious bodily injury to a child" (a felony charge). She was also charged with child endangerment, which is a misdemeanor (Levenon & Jadhav, 2005).

At the time of her arrest, Ms. Robinson was a single mother with no health insurance and was suspicious of doctors.She had a history of mental illness. She told a psychologist that she feared a doctor would sexually abuse her daughter if she took her for treatment. Despite these issues, she was indicted by the Suffolk County Grand Jury on September 28, 2005 (Associated Press, 2005).

CASE POINTS

1. In this case you see how problematic a delay in seeking medical treatment can be for a child; a simple infection can turn into a life-threatening illness.
2. The complex causes of medical neglect are clear in this case. This family was confronted with poverty, single parenting, maternal mental illness, and a lack of health insurance. It is difficult to say what precisely caused the medical neglect.
3. Finally, this case shows how difficult it is to substantiate neglect before children are seriously harmed. Despite two previous investigations by CPS, this tragic story was not prevented.

DISCUSSION QUESTIONS

1. Was Ms. Robinson guilty of child neglect? If so, what punishment would be appropriate?
2. Does the fact that Ms. Robinson had a history of mental illness impact your deci-sion in this case?
3. Should CPS be held responsible for not doing something to protect this child earlier?

that this is truer in theory than in practice. Cases like this are not likely to come to the attention of CPS, and even if they did, they would have low priority.

Abandonment

Perhaps the most extreme act of neglect is **abandonment**. Rates of abandonment in the U.S. are relatively low but range across the nation from a low of 0.4% in San Francisco to a high of nearly 2% in Washington, D.C. The term *abandonment* covers a range of behaviors, from leaving a newborn anywhere from a hospital to a trash bin, to kicking an older child out of the home. In the most severe cases, when infants are left in unsafe places with a low chance of being discovered alive, the labels of attempted infanticide or child abuse may be more appropriate than neglect (Giardino & Giardino, 2002).

Incidence. The National Clearinghouse on Child Abuse and Neglect Information (2004) reported that of the 906,000 children who were maltreated in 2002, more than 60% of them were neglected. This is much greater than the percentages associated with other types of maltreatment (19% were physically abused, 10% were sexually abused, 5% were emotionally abused, and 17% were classified as "other," reflecting specific state laws). Even though this is a very high number, it most likely underestimates the problem because it includes only those cases that have been brought to the attention of professionals and identified as neglect. Because neglect is often difficult to see, the authors of the National Incidence Study-3 estimated that the incidence of neglect is actually much higher. They suggested that as many as two million children may have been neglected in 1993 in the U.S.

In cases of neglect, the perpetrators are almost always the birth parents. In 91% of all neglect cases, the perpetrator is one or both of the child's birth parents. It is more likely that children will be neglected by females (87%) than by males (43%). (Many children are neglected by both females and males, so the combined percentages are over 100.) This difference is due to the fact that female caregivers are generally the primary caretakers and are therefore more likely to be held accountable for any shortcomings in child care.

CONSEQUENCES OF NEGLECT

Although child neglect has not received nearly the attention that has been garnered by physical abuse, recent researchers have begun to address the "neglect of neglect" in their work. The common consensus seems to be that this type of maltreatment is simply less obvious and less dramatic than physical or sexual abuse, so it is not given as much attention. There is also a consistent belief that neglect is not as bad as abuse. Despite this belief, the statistics indicate that it is not a true conclusion. Not only is neglect the most commonly reported and substantiated type of maltreatment (49% of cases are neglect), it is also a leading cause of fatalities from child maltreatment (42%) and can cause lifetime impairment (Cantwell, 1997). In 1996, 502 children died as the result of child neglect in the U.S. (NCCAN, 2001). Furthermore, researchers assert that emotional neglect leads to more severe outcomes than any other type of maltreatment (Bath & Haapala, 1992; Eckenrode, Laird, & Doris, 1993; Rohner, 1986). Rohner (1986) reported that as many as 74% of emotionally neglected children suffer grave consequences including such things as serious failure to thrive and suicide attempts.

Resilient Children

Not all children will be negatively affected by being neglected. The consequences to the child are dependent on numerous factors including the severity and duration of the neglect along with many child factors. The age and developmental level of the child at the time of the neglect will have a major influence on how the neglect impacts the child. A parent who is too drunk to feed an infant for a few days will see dire effects, but a parent who fails to feed a 12-year-old for the same period of time may see no effects. As children become more capable of caring for themselves, they are less likely to be seriously physically impacted by neglect. This is not to say that they may not be harmed emotionally by their parents' indifference towards them. There are other child factors that may protect the child such as intelligence, creativity, a good sense of humor, or a strong tendency toward independence. Children who survive less-than-ideal child rearing with minimal negative effects are often referred to as **resilient** children. This resilience can come from within, as mentioned, or from outside of the child. For instance, children who find support from a caregiver or mentor beyond the family may not suffer the ill effects of neglect seen in children without these resources (NCCAN, 2001).

Consequences of Neglect in Infancy

The impact of neglect will vary with the age of the child. Young children are at risk for some of the most serious, physical effects of neglect. Some severely neglected infants will be diagnosed with **nonorganic failure to thrive** (NFTT). These infants, who were once in the normal range, now fall below the fifth percentile for height and weight in the absence of any organic explanation (Wallace, 1996). They are also likely to display **psychomotor** delays during infancy, and they are at risk for continued growth problems, school failure, and mental retardation. In many cases these infants are malnourished due to inadequate feeding. In some cases this may be intentional on the part of the parent who is not interested in meeting the demands of an infant. In other situations, this neglect may be the result of parental inexperience. Some parents have no idea how much or how often a newborn should eat. I once worked with parents who were feeding their newborn when they ate: three times per day. They did not realize that this was insufficient feeding for a newborn. Still other parents underfeed their child to save money or to prevent the child from becoming overweight. Finally, even parents who meet their child's physical needs may have an infant with nonorganic failure to thrive. It appears that some infants who are deprived of emotional attachment may lose weight and withdraw even if their physical needs are being met. Researchers have reported that frequent touch from caregivers is absolutely necessary for both physical and psychological growth (Black, 1998).

   Poor Attachment.   Another possible consequence of neglect is poor attachment. Normally developing children form a close attachment with a primary caregiver by the time they are six to eight months old. This relationship is characterized by close physical contact, separation anxiety, and pleasure upon reunion. In an experimental setting, attachment is assessed using the **strange situation task** when the child is approximately one year old. This test involves the parent, generally the mother, entering a play room with their infant. A child who is securely attached to a parent should explore this new environment while using the parent as a base. In other words, the child will bring new toys to the parent's attention or try to engage the parent in play in addition to exploring on their own. The next step in this task is the entry of a stranger. At this point, the securely attached child will move to the parent and examine the parent's facial expression for cues about the stranger. This behavior, termed **social referencing**, allows a parent to guide a child by expression alone. For instance, a parent who looks fearful or tense will communicate to the child to stay close. Conversely, a relaxed, smiling parent lets the child know that this new person is safe and that the child should feel free to return to play. Next, the parent leaves the room and the child is alone with the stranger. The typical response in a securely attached child is crying or other signs of being upset. They suffer separation anxiety when the adult they are attached to leaves them. Finally, the parent returns and researchers observe the reunion between parent and child. The baby with a **secure attachment** will eagerly approach the parent, and have a joyful reunion. It is clear that the infant prefers a parent to a stranger. When researchers observe this pattern or behavior, they say that the infant has a secure attachment. This sort of relationship is believed to be the result of consistent, warm, and loving parenting. The child has learned to trust this adult and to look to this adult for guidance (Bowlby, 1982).

As you might expect, we see disrupted attachment in infants who have been neglected. Researchers suspect that as many as two thirds of neglected children may be poorly attached to their mothers by one year of age. These infants are especially likely to show avoidant or resistant styles of attachment. Children who have an **avoidant attachment** seem generally unresponsive to their parent in the strange situation task. In addition, they are not distressed when their parent leaves, and may not show any observable reaction at all. When the parent returns, they do not rush for a joyous reunion, but instead are slow to react and may fail to cling if picked up by the parent. These infants do not show a clear preference for the parent or the stranger. Infants who are described as having a **resistant attachment** are often clingy prior to the time the parent leaves the room. They will stay very close to the parent and fail to explore the play room. Like the securely attached baby, they are distressed at separation, but unlike the securely attached infant, they are not happy when the parent returns. At reunion, these infants appear angry, and they may resist the parent by pushing or hitting. They are not easily calmed down by their parent.

Beyond odd behavior in the strange situation task, what does it mean to have an insecure attachment? Psychologists now believe that the first relationship a child has forms the basis for all of their future relationships. As we grow, we use our first relationship as a model for subsequent relationships. Therefore, a good early relationship will make it more likely that we will be able to form satisfying relationships throughout our lives. Poor attachment in infancy has also been linked to aggression in elementary school and lower levels of cognitive development (Cantwell, 1997).

Other Signs of Possible Infant Neglect. There are a number of other signs that may indicate an infant is being neglected. If an infant shows a number of the symptoms listed below in the absence of other psychopathology that would explain them, it may point toward a problem of neglect.

Poor muscle tone. A child who is not moved about and encouraged to move and reach will have less developed muscle tone than a child who is engaged in frequent movement by caregivers. These babies also have difficulty supporting their own weight (Crosson-Tower, 2005).

Flat, bald spot on the back of the head. A child who is left lying in a crib most of the time will have a skull that is flat in the back, and hair is unlikely to grow or will be rubbed off if the child is rarely upright (Crosson-Tower, 2005). As a note of caution, with the "Back to Sleep" movement to decrease sudden infant death syndrome by always placing children on their backs to sleep, we may see more of this symptom in nonneglected children.

Lack of smiling, babbling. Normal children will begin to smile by six weeks in response to other people. At one to two months of age, children begin to make vowel sounds that we label as cooing, and consonant/vowel combinations that make up babbling appear between three and six months. In children who are neglected, we see few smiles and hear very little cooing or babbling. This happens because infants do not persist in smiling or vocalizing if they are not reinforced for doing so.

Rashes, infections. Infants who are not changed and bathed consistently will develop diaper rashes and infections.

Lower intelligence. Physically neglected children have lower overall IQ scores at 24 and 36 months than nonmaltreated children. Emotionally neglected children show the same IQ deficits at 12, 18, 24, and 36 months (Gowan, 1993).

Consequences of Neglect in Childhood

Language Delays. One of the most consistent findings regarding neglected children is that they suffer from **language delays** (Allen & Oliver, 1982; Crosson-Tower, 2005; Fox, Long,

FOCUS ON RESEARCH 5.2:   CHILD NEGLECT AND DELAYS IN LANGUAGE DEVELOPMENT

Allen and Oliver (1982) studied language development in 79 children with an average age of 47 months (3 years and 11 months). Their participants included 13 abused children, 7 neglected children, 31 abused and neglected children, and 28 nonmaltreated children. The maltreated children were selected from cases handled by the Family Resources Center in St. Louis, Missouri. This is a center that provides services to maltreating families. The nonmaltreated children were selected from a local daycare and did not differ significantly from the maltreated children in terms of age, family income, maternal education, race, or the presence of a father figure in the home.

The researchers measured language development with the Preschool Language Scale (PLS). This test assesses language competence in two ways: it measures both receptive (auditory comprehension) and expressive (verbal production) language ability. Items assessing receptive language require nonverbal responses to verbal questions. For instance, a child may be asked to point to a specific object. To assess expressive language ability, children are asked questions that require a spoken response. The Preschool Language Scale is considered to be a well-constructed test of verbal ability in preschool children.

The researchers found that neglect was the only variable that was significantly related to either receptive or expressive language ability. In both cases, neglect was associated with lower scores of language ability. Children who were only physically abused (and not neglected) did not differ significantly from their nonmaltreated peers in this study.

The authors conclude that their data supports the theoretical explanation that the language development of neglected children is hindered by a lack of stimulation. However, they acknowledge that a correlation study cannot be used to establish cause and effect (see chapter 1). What this study does show is that neglect is correlated with poor language development in the preschool years. The researchers suggest that the treatment of neglected children should include speech therapy and/or intensive language stimulation in addition to addressing emotional issues.

& Langlois, 1988). Children whose parents do not engage them in conversation or pay attention to them do not learn to listen to and comprehend complex sentences. If a teacher tells the class to go in, put their coats away, pick up their reading books, and sit down, a neglected child's linguistic capabilities may be overwhelmed. Being more familiar with only hearing short commands like "shut up" or "go away," these children may focus on only one aspect of the teacher's instructions (Crosson-Tower, 2005; see Focus on Research 5.2).

Intellectual/Academic Problems. Not surprisingly, given their significant language delays, neglected children have documented cognitive deficits and underachieve academically (Pianta, Egeland, & Erickson, 1989). Researchers examined the academic performance of 47 neglected children and compared them to a control group of matched socioeconomic status. The children who were neglected scored significantly lower than their nonmaltreated peers on a composite index of school performance, on the mathematics and language portions of the Iowa Basic Skills Test, and on the reading portion of the Georgia Criterion Reference Test.

There are several possible explanations for these academic deficits. First, it may be that neglected children are less successful because they are less persistent and less enthusiastic than their peers when engaged in learning tasks (Egeland, Sroufe, & Erickson, 1983). Nonneglectful parents help their children to develop persistence by encouraging their early efforts, even if they are not perfect. Second, some of these academic deficits may be attributable to poor attendance. In one study, the neglected children had missed significantly more days of school during the past year than had their nonmaltreated peers. While the children in the comparison group had missed an average of only 4.52 days, the neglected children had been absent an average of 21.35 days (Wodarski, Kurtz, Gaudin, & Howing, 1990).

Another explanation for poor academic performance is that the lower IQ scores seen in negelcted infants persist into childhood. Neglected children have lower IQ scores than their classmates. Rogeness, Amrung, Macedo, Harris, and Fisher (1986) studied a large group of children (539) who had been admitted to a private, psychiatric hospital for children. The ages of their participants ranged from 4 to 16 years. Their sample included 99 children who had experienced physical abuse, 128 who had been neglected but not abused, and 313 who were not maltreated. They compared Wechsler Intelligence Scale for Children (WISC) scores for all children. The Wechsler test provides an overall IQ score as well as scores on verbal and nonverbal subtests. The subtests that make up the verbal scale involve questions that are posed verbally to a child and require a verbal response. The nonverbal tests make up the performance scale and do not require a verbal response (e.g., children are asked to put pictures in order, to construct puzzles, or to match a block design). The neglected boys in their sample had significantly lower full-scale IQ scores than either the physically abused boys or the nonmaltreated boys. This difference was attributable to low subtest scores on two verbal tests, information (responding to questions about information that a child of a certain age should know) and vocabulary (word definition). That neglected boys struggled with these areas is consistent with the lack of environmental stimulation they receive. The neglected girls did not differ from the physically abused girls in terms of IQ, but both maltreated groups had significantly lower full-score IQ scores, verbal scores, and performance scores than did the nonmaltreated girls.

Impaired Socialization.   Neglected children are also impaired socially; they do not have many friends (Erickson & Egeland, 2002). Researchers have found that neglected children tend to be passive socially, and they are less likely than their nonmaltreated peers to display affection or initiate playful interactions (Crouch & Milner, 1993).

To assess socialization skills, researchers utilize a technique called "peer rating." Children are asked to list three children in their class whom they would most like to play with and three children whom they would least like to play with. Researchers use these ratings to classify children in one of the following categories:

Popular: frequently listed as preferred playmates and rarely listed as someone a child does not want to play with

Peer Rejected: frequently listed as someone a child wishes to avoid, but rarely listed as a preferred playmate

Peer Neglected: a child who does not show up on either set of lists

Controversial: a child who appears frequently on both the positive and the negative list

Average: a child with an average number of appearances on the preferred lists and a small number of appearances on the least preferred list

Neglected children are frequently neglected or rejected by their peers. Why would peers neglect a neglected child? One explanation may tie back to language delays. A child who is not proficient in language may find that it is difficult to communicate with the other children. Also, a child who has not learned from loving, attentive parents how to approach others and engage them in play will not have the skills to approach peers. Bousha and Twentyman (1984) observed maltreated and nonmaltreated children interacting with their mothers in their home environment. They found that the neglectful mothers interacted significantly less with their children than did physically abusive or nonmaltreating mothers. They also noted a depressed rate of positive social behavior on the part of the neglected children (e.g., they were less likely to initiate social interaction, and they showed less inquisitive or exploratory behavior). Many neglected children also suffer from low self-esteem, which may prevent them from seeking out attention from others and cause them to be simply more withdrawn than other children. Taken together, these factors may make the child who is neglected at home the same one who is overlooked at school.

While it may seem intuitive to expect that neglected children would be peer neglected, what causes some of these children to be rejected by their peers? First, as a group, neglected children are more aggressive than are other children, and this is frequently linked to peer rejection. Rogeness et al. (1986) reported that neglected boys, but not girls, had higher levels of conduct disorder than did a nonmaltreated control group. Bousha and Twentyman (1984) suggested that the increased rate of aggressive behavior among neglected children may be the result of the child doing whatever is necessary to get his or her mother's attention. Neglected children tend to engage in a high number of both positive and negative attention seeking behaviors at school. As we all know, young children are very competitive when it comes to getting the teacher's attention. A child who demands a disproportionate share of this attention is going to meet with hostility from peers. Children who are physically neglected also tend to be unappealing in more direct ways. These children are not dressed well; they often appear dirty and may have an unpleasant smell. If you have spent any time around young children, you will know that diplomacy is not their strong suit; they may very well tell the neglected child, "You stink!" Finally, children whose needs are not met at home may be more likely to steal or act impulsively to get what they want (Winton & Mara, 2001). Any of these behaviors will increase the chance that the child will be rejected by peers.

Consequences of Neglect in Adolescence

Certainly adolescents are more capable of caring for themselves than are younger children. However, this does not mean that neglect does not harm older children. Also, because neglect is generally a chronic condition, children who are neglected as adolescents often have a long history of being neglected.

Runaways.   One risk associated with neglect in adolescence is leaving home early. It makes sense that a child would be more willing to leave a home if his or her needs were not being met there. However, life on the street is dangerous, especially for adolescents. These young runaways may end up engaged in crime or as the victims of crime.

Social Isolation.   Not only are their needs not being met at home, neglected adolescents also have trouble developing a network of support outside of their family. Many neglected children are socially isolated during adolescence. Their poor social skills continue to inhibit them in making and maintaining friendships. Some neglected children may be drawn to gangs in order to meet their need to belong (Cantwell, 1997).

Intellectual/Academic Problems.   Neglected children have a higher rate of school expulsion and dropout than do their nonneglected peers, and those who remain in school are more likely to have low achievement scores. Perez and Widom (1994) followed 413 children who had been maltreated and found that neglect as a child still predicted lower IQ and lower reading ability at the age of 28. In other words, the children do not outgrow the intellectual deficits first noted in infancy.

Delinquency.   Researchers have noted a positive correlation between neglect and later criminal conduct. When McCord (1983) reviewed the cases of 48 men who had been neglected between 1939 and 1945, she found that 73% of them had been convicted for criminal behavior, as compared to only 23% of the control group. While 31% had been convicted only as juveniles, 17% had both juvenile and adult records, and 27% had only adult records for criminal behavior. It may be that the relationship between neglect and delinquency is mediated by IQ.

If, as noted above, neglected children have lower IQs, this may be what contributes to higher rates of delinquency. A number of studies have demonstrated that adolescents with lower IQs are more likely to engage in delinquent behavior than are their more intelligent peers (Perez & Widom, 1994).

Psychiatric Disorders.   Finally, neglected children have a higher rate of psychiatric disorders, and they are more likely to attempt suicide than are their peers. Williamson and Borduin (1991) had mothers and adolescents complete the Global Severity Index of the Symptom Checklist-90-Revised. This test measures symptoms of several psychological problems including **somatization**, **obsessive-compulsions**, interpersonal sensitivity, depression, anxiety, hostility, **phobic anxiety**, **paranoid ideation**, and **psychoticism**. They found that the neglected adolescents had significantly higher scores than did those in the nonmaltreated control group. In addition, mothers completed the Revised Behavior Problems Checklist (RBPC), which is used to screen for behavior disorders in children and adolescents. Maternal ratings on the Revised Behavior Problems Checklist revealed that neglectful mothers rated their adolescents as having higher levels of conduct disorder and socialized aggression than were seen in the nonneglectful mothers' ratings of their teenagers.

INTERGENERATIONAL TRANSMISSION OF NEGLECT

As part of the Minnesota Parent-Child Project, Pianta, Egeland, and Erickson (1989) studied the relationship between child maltreatment and the care the mother had received as a child. They found that seven of the nine mothers who had been neglected as children went on to maltreat their own children, most often by neglecting them (three of the mothers were rated as seriously maltreating, and four were labeled as questionable caregivers). This not only highlights the fact that being neglected may start a cycle of maltreatment, but it also illustrates that this is not inevitable; not all of the neglected mothers went on to be poor parents.

Other researchers have looked at what factors may help to break the cycle of abuse. Four things have been identified that may help prevent abused children from becoming maltreating parents. First, the presence of a supportive adult during childhood can help a child to be resilient. This person models appropriate behavior for the child and also gives the child positive feedback and attention that partially compensates for the lack of attention from parents. Second, having a supportive, competent partner to help raise children can protect the next generation. This person can reduce the stress of parenting and also serve as a positive model. Third, mothers who engage in therapy that helps them come to terms with their past are better able to parent appropriately. Fourth, mothers who incorporate their own maltreatment into their life story are less likely to maltreat their children. Women who dissociate themselves from the abuse they experienced are less likely to move beyond their past and be good mothers (Erickson & Egeland, 2002).

CONCLUSION

In cases of child neglect, caregivers fail to meet the minimum acceptable level of care necessary to ensure the child's physical and psychological health. Instead of actively doing something to hurt the child, the parents are failing to do what is needed. Although certain subtypes of neglect have been well researched, others, such as mental health neglect, are only beginning to receive attention.

Not only is child neglect the most common type of child maltreatment, researchers have carefully documented its negative impact on child development.

Clearly, this form of maltreatment, which is too often seen as "not as bad as physical abuse," has very real, very negative consequences for many children. Being the victim of child neglect increases the chances that a child will suffer social, emotional, and cognitive deficits that persist throughout his or her lifetime.

DISCUSSION QUESTIONS

1. Were you surprised by the number and variety of behaviors that fall under the category of "child neglect"? Do you think it would be helpful to have a more narrow definition?
2. Which type of neglect do you think you would most be comfortable reporting to CPS? Which type would you be least comfortable reporting?
3. If a parent is not providing for his or her child(ren) because the family is impoverished, is the parent guilty of child neglect?
4. How would you compare the consequences of child neglect to the consequences of child physical abuse?
5. Discuss "adequate supervision" with your classmates. Can you come up with specific rules? For instance, at what age should a child be permitted to play in her own yard unsupervised? At what age should she be allowed to cross a street in a subdivision on her own? Is it permissible to take a nap while your toddler plays in the family room?
6. Should the government be allowed to order parents to let their children receive medical treatment that the parents do not believe in for religious reasons?

DEFINITIONS

Meconium: dark greenish-brown material that builds up in the digestive tract before birth; excreted as fecal matter shortly after birth.

Metabolite: a product of metabolism.

Toxicology: the study of poisons and drugs and their effects.

Postnatal: occurring after birth.

Physical Neglect: the failure to meet the minimal physical needs of the child.

Malnourished: having a medical condition caused by an improper or insufficient diet.

Child Endangerment: placing a child in a situation that is potentially harmful.

Emotional Neglect: the failure to meet a child's emotional needs.

Medical Neglect: the failure to seek medical treatment or to provide treatment that has been prescribed.

American Academy of Pediatrics: an organization of approximately 60,000 pediatricians dedicated to the health of all children.

Mental Health Neglect: the failure to seek help for a child's severe psychological problems or to comply with recommended therapeutic procedures.

Educational Neglect: the failure to meet legal requirements for school enrollment or attendance, or the lack of attention to special educational needs.

Abandonment: desertion; severing ties with and failing to support one's own child.

Resilient: having the ability to recover from adversity.

Nonorganic Failure to Thrive: a child's failing to reach normal milestones for physical growth (falling below the third percentile) when the child has no known organic disease.

Psychomotor: pertaining to the function of voluntary muscles.

Strange Situation Task: a laboratory task designed to measure an infant's attachment to a caregiver.

Social Referencing: reading another person's facial expressions in order to decide on an appropriate response.

Secure Attachment: an infant's using a caregiver as a secure base from which to explore his or her surroundings.

Avoidant Attachment: an insecure attachment style in which the infants tend to avoid or ignore their caregivers.

Resistant Attachment: an insecure attachment style in which infants cling to their caregivers at times and resist closeness at other times.

Language Delays: the failure to develop language skills according to the usual timetable resulting in development that is significantly below the norm for a child of a given age.

Somatization: the expression of psychological distress as physical symptoms.

Obsessive Compulsions: the persistent intrusion of unwanted thoughts accompanied by ritualistic actions.

Phobic Anxiety: worry about irrational fears.

Paranoid Ideation: abnormal suspicion that is not based on fact.

Psychoticism: impaired contact with reality.

CHAPTER 6

Psychological Maltreatment

DEFINITION

Psychological, or emotional, maltreatment includes both **psychological neglect** and **psychological abuse**. In cases of psychological neglect, the parents fail to meet the emotional needs of their children. Parents who ignore their children or who fail to make emotional contact with their children may be guilty of psychological neglect. In psychological abuse, the parents are engaging in behaviors that actively harm a child's mental health. For instance, a parent who yells at a child, calling the child stupid, lazy, and no good, or a parent who threatens the life of a child may be considered psychologically abusive. What is difficult about this type of maltreatment is evident in my use of the phrase "*may* be considered." There is probably no such thing as a parent who never ignores the emotional needs of a child. There are times when even the best caregiver is distracted, tired, or too angry to provide the perfect emotional response to a child. We do not, however, say that all parents are psychologically neglectful. Likewise, nearly all parents occasionally speak more harshly to a child than is ideal, and we do not label them psychologically abusive. Contrast this with physical abuse. If a parent intentionally burns a child once, he or she is guilty of physical abuse, but how many times does a parent have to say something negative to a child before he or she is guilty of psychological abuse? Does it matter if the parent is saying something that happens to be true? In other words, if you call your lazy child "lazy," is that abusive? To complicate things further, tone of voice and intent may be as important as what is said. Have your parents ever threatened your physical well-being, or even your life? Before you say, "Not mine!" see if any of the following statements sound at all familiar:

> Stop crying or I will give you something to cry about.
> I brought you into this world, and I darn well can take you out of it.
> If you want to live to see your next birthday…

Hearing phrases like the ones above is a fairly normative part of growing up in the U.S. (As an interesting side note, this is not true in all cultures. While I was lecturing at the University of Iceland, I mentioned these phrases, and my students were appalled that any parent would ever say such a thing to a child!) Is a statement like this psychologically abusive if the child knows the parent does not mean it? Is it sufficient to make the statement nonabusive if the person voicing the threat does not mean it, even if the child is unsure?

Despite these very real difficulties in pinpointing exactly what psychological maltreatment is, psychologists know that children's mental health can be endangered by how they are treated emotionally. As you will see later in this chapter, psychological maltreatment has very real, negative consequences for its victims. Therefore, extensive attempts have been made to define psychological maltreatment. First, I will cover legal definitions, then psychological definitions.

Legal Definitions

Every state and territory in the U.S., with the exceptions of Georgia and Washington, mentions emotional *abuse* in its child abuse statutes, and nearly half of these provide some type of definition that is generally based on child outcomes (National Clearinghouse on Child Abuse and Neglect, 2005). Psychological, or emotional, *neglect* is less well covered in the statutes.

Some state's statutes provide only minimal coverage of psychological abuse. They mention that it is against the law but provide no further information. For instance, Alabama statute 26-14-1 (1) – (3) reads, "Abuse includes nonaccidental mental injury." Similarly, in Connecticut the law (§46b-120) reads, "Abuse includes emotional maltreatment," and in Michigan (§722.622), "Child abuse includes mental injury."

Other states provide more information about how one would know if psychological abuse had occurred. For instance, Arizona's statute (§8-201) reads, "Abuse means the infliction of or allowing another person to cause serious emotional damage to the child, as evidenced by severe anxiety, depression, withdrawal, or untoward aggressive behavior, and such emotional damage is diagnosed by a medical doctor or psychologist, and the damage has been caused by the acts of an individual having care, custody, and control of a child." In Nevada, the relevant statute (§432B.070) states, "Mental injury means an injury to the intellectual or psychological capacity or the emotional condition of a child as evidenced by an observable and substantial impairment of his ability to function within his normal range of performance or behavior." As a final example in this category, the statute in Iowa (§232.68) says, "Mental injury is defined as any mental injury to a child's intellectual or psychological capacity as evidenced by an observable and substantial impairment in the child's ability to function within the child's normal range of performance and behavior as the result of the acts or omissions of a person responsible for the care of the child, if the impairment is diagnosed and confirmed by a licensed physician or qualified mental health professional." Even with this added detail, it is still not obvious what marks a child as a victim of psychological maltreatment. It is for this reason that several states, including Alabama and Indiana as mentioned above, say that such a finding must be supported by the diagnosis of a medical or mental health professional. This presumes, of course, that such professionals have a clear definition to work from. You can also see from the statutes above that some states focus on mental harm caused by the parents, while others include instances where a parent allows others to harm their children psychologically.

While most states explicitly mention psychological abuse, the same cannot be said for psychological neglect. In many states, psychological neglect must be inferred from the more general statutes that describe neglect more broadly. Consider South Dakota's statute 26-8A-2, which defines a neglected child as one "whose parent, guardian, or custodian fails or refuses to provide proper or necessary subsistence, supervision, education, medical care, *or any other care necessary* for the child's health, guidance, or well-being" (emphasis added). In cases like this, emotional responsiveness would fall under other necessary care. There are a few states that directly describe emotional neglect in their child abuse statutes. For example, Montana statute 41-3-102 directly addresses psychological neglect by stating, "Psychological abuse or neglect means severe maltreatment through acts *or omissions* that are injurious to the child's emotional, intellectual, or psychological capacity to function, including acts of violence against another person residing in the child's home" (emphasis added).

Even in the laws that include more detail, it is still not perfectly clear what behaviors constitute psychological maltreatment. When professionals are asked to assess this sort of maltreatment, what are they looking for? Is psychological maltreatment defined as the acts of adults or the effects on children? For answers to these questions, we turn to examining how psychologists define psychological maltreatment.

Psychological Definitions

Most of the research on psychological maltreatment is very new. This form of child maltreatment was not addressed by professionals until the 1980s, and it was not included in policy and research on a consistent basis until the 1990s. The *Diagnostic and Statistical Manual of Mental Disorders* lists diagnostic codes for physical abuse, sexual abuse, and neglect, but it does not do so for psychological maltreatment. The closest diagnostic code is probably **parent-child relational problem** (V61.20), which is appropriate when clinical intervention is geared toward the relationship between the parent and the child and that interaction is characterized by a pattern of behavior that impairs the child or the family. While this sounds as if it may cover psychological maltreatment, the examples of inappropriate interactions included in the *Diagnostic and Statistical Manual* are impaired communication, overprotection, and inadequate discipline, which do not seem necessarily reflective of emotional maltreatment. In addition, it would not be appropriate if the focus of the treatment was on the child alone (American Psychiatric Association, 1994).

The problem of defining psychological maltreatment was highlighted in 1991 when the editors of the journal *Development and Psychopathology* devoted an entire issue to assessing the progress on defining this type of maltreatment (Cicchetti, 1991). Because the study of psychological maltreatment has such a short history, it should not be surprising that there are many ongoing debates.

First, despite the fact that it is done consistently, not all psychologists agree with using *psychological* and *emotional* as synonyms in this context. As O'Hagan (1993) points out, *emotional* means feeling, and emotional development entails learning to express and interpret emotions. *Psychological*, on the other hand, means pertaining to the mind, and psychological development is related to improving mental processing through more advanced cognitive skills. While different, these terms are related and are frequently used to refer to the same types of behavior, even if the terms are not used perfectly. Although I am aware of these differences, I will use the terms interchangeably in this chapter, as do most authors in the field.

Child Outcome Versus Parental Behavior. Another primary source of contention is whether the focus of the definition should be based on child outcomes (as is the case with most legal statutes), or on parental behavior. Hamarman and Bernet (2000) argue that psychological maltreatment should be defined as ill treatment by adults. First, this type of definition would allow for the possibility of prevention or intervention before harm has occurred. If this type of maltreatment is only recognized after a child has been harmed, there is no hope for prevention. Second, it is very difficult to establish that any particular emotional outcome was caused by one specific antecedent. For instance, just because a child is anxious, it does not follow that the anxiety was caused by verbally abusive parents. Even if it is known that the child's parents were verbally abusive, it is still possible that something else led to, or contributed to, the child's anxiety (dangerous neighborhood, overly critical teacher, bully at school, etc.). A third possibility is to define psychological maltreatment as the interaction between an adult's behavior and a child's vulnerabilities. This allows one to consider the developmental level of the child at the time of the behavior, as well as his or her individual sensitivity. Furthermore, interactions are observable, whereas things like parental motivation and the negative impact on the child's psychological development are not. Because negative interactions can be observed, they can be quantified in terms of frequency and content. This allows researchers to establish norms against which psychological maltreatment can be specifically defined (McGee & Wolfe, 1991).

The Meaning of Psychological.   Another obstacle to understanding psychological mal-treatment is knowing precisely what is meant by *psychological*. Does this mean that the parent's behavior was nonphysical, or does it mean that the child was harmed in a nonphysical or emotional way by the behavior? McGee and Wolfe (1991) point out that if you classify nega-tive parental acts as either physical or psychological, and child outcomes as either physical or psychological, you have four possible pairings. If a parent hits a child and the child develops a bruise, you have a physical parental act and a physical child outcome. The classification in this situation is straightforward: child physical abuse. On the other hand, if a parent continually showers a child with insults and the child becomes depressed, you have a nonphysical act and a nonphysical outcome. This would clearly fall under the rubric of psychological abuse. This leaves two pairings that are not as obvious. Consider a parent who is not emotionally respon-sive to a child, and the child develops asthma. In the case of a nonphysical parental act with a physical child outcome, the authors argue that the label of psychological maltreatment is still appropriate. However, in cases where a physical act (like sexual abuse) leads to a psychological consequence (such as anxiety), McGee and Wolfe do not think psychological maltreatment is the appropriate label. In this scenario, the interaction is already labeled and defined as a differ-ent sort of maltreatment (sexual abuse in my example). In order to avoid overlap among defini-tions, this should not be considered psychological maltreatment.

Parental Intention.   Most psychologists do agree that parental intention is not an issue in defining psychological maltreatment (Glaser, 2002). It does not matter whether the parent deliberately ignored the child, intended to harm the child with harsh words, or behaved out of ignorance. In any case, maltreatment has occurred.

A Professional Definition.   One of the premier professional groups in the area of child maltreatment is the **American Professional Society on the Abuse of Children** (APSAC). In 1995, the society published a definition of psychological maltreatment that included six sub-types. The general definition is that "psychological maltreatment means a repeated pattern of caregiver behavior or extreme incident(s) that convey to children that they are worthless, flawed, unloved, unwanted, endangered, or only of value in meeting another's needs" (APSAC, 1995, p. 2). Furthermore, there are six major subtypes: (1) spurning, (2) terrorizing, (3) isolating, (4) exploiting/corrupting, (5) denying emotional responsiveness, and (6) mental health, medical, and educational neglect.

Spurning captures what first comes to mind when most of us think of psychological abuse. This category consists of verbal and nonverbal caregiver behaviors that are hostile and reject-ing toward the child. It includes belittling, degrading, shaming, ridiculing, publicly humiliat-ing, and repeatedly singling out one child for punishment (scapegoating) or failing to reward one child. Other researchers simply use the term *rejecting* to refer to this type of behavior. If authors use rejecting instead of spurning, they often add degrading as a separate category (Hart, Germain, & Brassard, 1987). The second subtype, **terrorizing**, is the label given to caregivers who threaten a child or a child's loved ones or possessions with violence or abandonment. Less obviously, it includes placing a child in unpredictable, chaotic, or recognizably dangerous situ-ations. **Isolating** includes confining a child within a space and failing to allow the child appro-priate opportunities to socialize with others. **Exploiting/corrupting** is the subtype used to describe instances where parents encourage their children to develop inappropriate behaviors. This encouragement may take the form of modeling some negative behavior, permitting it, or actively encouraging the child to take part in it. The types of activities covered by this category range from criminal acts (e.g., teaching a child to steal) to acts that are developmentally inappropriate (e.g., parentification of the child, or refusing to allow the child to become autonomous). Acts that restrict or interfere with a child's cognitive development also fall under this category. The next subtype, **denying emotional responsiveness**, refers to parents who ignore their child or who show no emotional reactions when interacting with the child. Parents whose behavior is classified as denying emotional responsiveness interact with their child infrequently and do not express affection for the child. The final type of psychological maltreatment is **mental health, medical, and educational neglect**. Parents who ignore their child's needs in any of these areas, or who fail to provide them with necessary services, are guilty of this type of psychological maltreatment (APSAC, 2005).

Glaser's Definition. While the criteria established by the American Professional Society on the Abuse of Children is commonly taught and well recognized, it is not without its critics. Glaser (2002) has argued that its framework does not have a theoretical basis and that there is overlap among the subtypes. In addition, some of the subtypes are not cohesive. For instance, Glaser argues that "restricting or interfering with cognitive development" is not clearly related to the category of exploiting/corrupting, even though it is listed there.

Glaser (2002) proposed an alternative understanding of psychological maltreatment based on a conceptual framework of a child's needs. Glaser stated that in order for a child to be psychologically healthy, their needs must be recognized and respected by those who care for them. The definition proposed by Glaser has five subtypes (Glaser, 2002, pp. 703–704):

1. "Emotional unavailability, unresponsiveness, and neglect." This first category is used to describe parents who are insensitive as well as those who are not available or responsive to their children. This includes caregivers who are preoccupied by things ranging from drug addiction to demanding jobs. These parents can be physically or psychologically unavailable, and they do not arrange for sufficient alternative care.

2. "Negative attributions and misattributions to child." Attributions are the explanations we make for another person's behavior. They can be positive, neutral, or negative. Say, for instance, that a young child brought a flower to his mother. The mother could make a positive attribution by thinking, "My son is a sweet, caring boy who wants to show me his love," or a neutral attribution such as, "He must have seen this flower on his way home and decided to pick it for me." It is in psychologically abusive cases that we see mothers making a negative attribution like, "He must have done something really bad, and he is trying to distract me with this stupid flower. He has always been a sneaky child." In each case, the child's behavior is identical; what varies is how that behavior is interpreted. If a parent consistently makes negative attributions, then he or she is likely to become hostile toward the child and ultimately reject the child. Because such parents think the child is driven by bad things, they also think this rejection is what the child deserves. Sadly, over time, children may come to believe these things about themselves.

3. "Developmentally inappropriate or inconsistent interactions with child." This type of behavior is seen among parents who do not seem to know what sort of behavior is appropriate for children of a given age. As a result, they may have inappropriate expectations of their child. For example, a mother may tell her toddler to come inside after 15 minutes and then punish her when she fails to do so, without understanding that young children have a very poor perception of time. Parents may also expose children to situations they are not old enough to handle. A parent's asking a young child for advice on dating would be considered age-inappropriate. Although the term is not used by Glaser, others talk about *overpressuring*. When overpressuring a child, a parent

expects too much, too soon, from the child (academically, physically, or socially) and makes the child feel that he or she is not meeting expectations (Hamarman & Bernet, 2000). On the opposite end of the spectrum, instead of expecting too much, some parents will be extremely overprotective and not allow their children to explore in age-appropriate ways. These children are then deprived of the experiences that they should be having.

4. "Failure to recognize or acknowledge the child's individuality and psychological boundaries." This category captures parents who use their child to fulfill their own needs. An extreme example is seen in factitious disorder by proxy (see chapter 8), where a parent makes a child ill to attract attention. More commonly, this may be seen when children are used as weapons in difficult divorce situations.

5. "Failing to promote the child's social adaptation." A parent could maltreat a child through neglect by simply failing to provide age-appropriate experiences, or could deliberately missocialize the child by teaching the child to behave in ways that are inappropriate.

While Glaser (2002) admits that rigorous work needs to be done to validate these subtypes, she does say that agreement among her multidisciplinary team has been high with a sample of 60 cases.

As you may have noted, the criteria of the American Professional Society on the Abuse of Children and those proposed by Glaser are not radically different. The similarity between these definitions indicates that some consensus may be developing about how to define psychological maltreatment. The areas of discrepancy should be the targets of future research.

As you think about the definition of psychological maltreatment, it may be helpful to consider some scenario. Read the cases presented in Case Examples 6.1 and discuss them with colleagues to see if you reached similar conclusions.

DEFINING A LINE ON A CONTINUUM OF BEHAVIOR

Regardless of which specific definition of psychological maltreatment one adopts, everyone must deal with where on the continuum of parental behavior an act becomes abusive. Consider, for example, the isolating subcategory. When does confining a child move from good parenting to poor parenting to abuse? If a father punishes his teenage son for curfew violation by grounding him for the weekend, how would you label his behavior? If I told you that the son had never been late before, had called this time to report a flat tire, and was less than ten minutes late, would it change your decision? What if the punishment was for a week, a month, or three months?

Hamarman and Bernet (2000) suggest that two things should be considered when determining the severity of psychological maltreatment: parental intent and degree of harm. If intent and harm are both present, the maltreatment is severe. Conversely, if there is no intent to harm and the child is not harmed, the inappropriate behavior is labeled as mild maltreatment. Having only intent or only harm puts the behavior into the moderate category. This, of course, presumes that both intent and harm can be measured.

Areas of Agreement

Despite this dizzying array of definitional concerns, there is some hope that agreement can be reached, at least in some cases. Schaefer (1997) asked 151 participants who were either parents or mental health professionals to consider 18 categories of parental verbalizations. Ten of the 18 were rated by 80% of the participants as never being acceptable (rejection/withdrawal of love, verbal put-downs, perfectionism, negative prediction, negative comparison, scapegoating, shaming, cursing, threatening, and guilt-tripping). While this falls 20% shy of perfect

CASE EXAMPLE 6.1

DISCUSSION QUESTIONS

For each of the cases below, answer the following questions:

1. Are the parents guilty of psychological maltreatment?
2. If so, what type of psychological maltreatment is present?
3. What sort of intervention, if any, is necessary to help this family?

Beth, age 17, was concerned that her boyfriend, Bob, was going to leave her. In an attempt to keep him, she stopped taking her birth control pills without Bob's knowledge and became pregnant. Although Bob stayed around during the pregnancy, he left shortly after their son, Sean, was born. Beth continually tells Sean that he is a failure because he was not good enough to keep his father around. When a friend tells Beth that she should not say things like that, Beth says it doesn't matter because Sean is only 22 months old and does not understand what she is saying. Although Beth does her best to take care of Sean, she does not seem to enjoy being with him, and she seldom plays with him.

Barbara desperately wanted to be a ballerina when she was a little girl, but her mother refused to pay for the necessary lessons. Now, as a mother, Barbara is determined that her little girl, Ashley, will be a professional dancer. She started taking Ashley to dance lessons when she was 18 months old, and now that Ashley is 6 years old, she has lessons six days per week and practices two hours per day. Lately, Ashley has begun to complain about dancing and asks to spend more time with her friends. Her mother explains that the practice is necessary to meet her goals, and that Ashley can play when her practice and homework are complete. When Ashley asked if she could try out for the soccer team with her friend, her mother explained that she could not risk an injury that would interfere with dance. Whenever Ashley says she wants to quit dancing, her mother sends her to her room.

Brandon was raised by extremely strict parents and turned out to be a very successful businessman. In return, he is very strict with his own three children, who are currently 8, 10, and 13 years old. When the children do not perform to his expectations, he lets them know that they have left the family down and that they should be ashamed of themselves. After being sent to his room, the offending child has to report to the family at dinnertime about his failure and apologize. The child is not allowed to join the family for the meal until Brandon is assured that the child is contrite. The children have been punished in this manner for offenses such as coming in late for dinner, for making poor grades (less than an A), for accidentally breaking a vase, and for fidgeting during church services.

Realizing that few people are suspicious of a young child, Tony and Linda encourage their 4-year-old daughter to take things from stores. Their daughter, Sara, thinks of this behavior as a fun game and is not at all distressed about it. Tony and Linda justify their behavior by saying that money is really tight and that it is appropriate for Sara to help out. They also point out that if Sara was caught, nothing bad would happen to her because of her young age.

Christina is raising two young children on her own. Unfortunately, she is having a great deal of difficulty trying to make ends meet. In order to provide for her children, she takes a second job working night shift as a waitress. She knows her children are too young to be left alone at only 6 and 8 years of age, so she leaves them with her boyfriend, Alan. Alan has always been good to Christina and her children, but he does earn extra money by selling drugs from his home. He assures Christina that the buyers who come to his home are safe and that the children are not in any danger while they are with him.

Kelly and Chris have a 10-year-old son and a 5-year-old daughter. While most of their parenting techniques seem to be appropriate, family members have noted that both parents are much harder on their son than they are on their daughter. Anytime the children fight, it is automatically assumed that their son is at fault. He is punished, normally by being sent to his room, and he is required to apologize to his little sister. When questioned about this treatment, the parents assert that their son is older, so more is expected of him. Extended family members have also commented that it is the girl's preferences for places to eat, vacation destinations, and outings that seem to be followed.

agreement, it does mean that there is some consensus about what sort of parental behaviors are inappropriate. An even higher level of agreement about what constitutes maltreatment was reported by Burnett (1993) when he asked professionals and nonprofessionals to rate vignettes for psychological maltreatment. Both groups identified the same nine parental behaviors as abusive (see Focus on Research 6.1).

INCIDENCE

Determining how common psychological maltreatment is depends on how it is defined and how it is measured. Variations in definition and methodology lead to vastly different estimates.

National Incidence Study-3 Data

Let us first consider the information provided by the third National Incidence Study (see chapter 2 for a review of the methodology). This study lists three types of emotional abuse and seven types of emotional neglect. With regard to emotional abuse, it considers the following behaviors to be abusive:

1. *Close confinement (tying or binding)*. This category includes any extreme restriction of the child's ability to move. In addition to tying, enclosing a child in a small space for the sake of punishment also counts as close confinement.
2. *Verbal or emotional assault*. This subtype of emotional abuse consists of habitual, nonphysical hostile or rejecting treatment. It includes acts of belittling, denigrating (defaming or disparaging), and scapegoating, as well as threatening the child.
3. *Other or unknown abuse*. This final category refers to parents who are overly punitive or emotionally abusive in ways that are not included in the other definitions of abuse used by the researchers.

Emotional neglect is defined by the National Incidence Study-3 as one of the following seven subtypes:

1. *Inadequate nurturance/affection*. In these cases, caregivers are not sufficiently nurturing in their interactions with the child.

FOCUS ON RESEARCH 6.1

Burnett (1993) mailed 1,413 packets to citizens and social workers asking them to rate vignettes in terms of psychological maltreatment. Based on 10 definitions that existed in the literature at the time, the author devised 20 vignettes with the input of professionals, two for each definition. For each type of abuse, one vignette described a single incident, and one described chronic behavior that had already had a documented impact on the child. All of the children described in the vignettes were either 8 or 9 years old; half were male, and half were female. The 10 types of abuse evident in the vignettes were: confining a child to a small space, severe public humiliation, "Cinderella syndrome" (making one child in the family the target of rejection or exploitation), severe verbal abuse, encouraging or coercing a child into delinquency, threatening a child, denial of psychological treatment, not allowing social and emotional growth, not providing a loving and supportive atmosphere, and immoral parental behavior.

For instance, following are two vignettes Burnett used. The first is the vignette designed to describe a chronic, harm-causing failure to provide a loving, nurturing home. The second vignette was to illustrate a single episode of singling out a child for rejection.

> Since his wife died, a father lost interest in his 9-year-old son who now had to get his own meals, wash his own clothes, and spent long hours alone at home. The father spent long periods of time locked in his room. The boy's grades dropped in school, he became more aggressive and was caught recently with drugs.
>
> Mrs. G. and Mr. R., her boyfriend, and two of her three children went on a weekend trip. They told their other child, Donna, age 8 (their second child), that they did not want her to accompany them. Donna was told they were ashamed of her, and that she would have to find a neighbor to house her for the weekend.

Burnett, 1993, p. 444

After reading the vignettes, the participants were asked to indicate if the behavior was abuse, to note how serious it was on a 6-point scale from *not serious* to *extremely serious*, and to select an intervention on a 4-point scale from *no major problem* to *child should be removed from the family*.

If participants did not respond to the original mailing, a reminder was sent out three weeks later. Participants who still failed to reply were sent the full packet again six weeks after the original mailing. After all three prompts, 833 (59%) of the surveys were returned. The response rate was higher for social workers (74%) than it was for citizens (47%).

Both social workers and citizens considered vignettes of 9 out of the 10 presented definitions to be abusive. The only vignette not seen as abusive by either group was immoral parental behaviors. With regard to seriousness, the two groups did not differ on half of the vignettes, and there was not a consistent difference on the remaining 10 (in 5 cases, the citizens gave higher ratings of seriousness, and on the other 5 the reverse was true). Overall, citizens gave a mean serious rating to 3.54, and social workers had a mean response of 3.51. There was a larger difference when it came to intervention recommendations. Although there was no difference on 9 vignettes, there were 10 cases in which citizens wanted a more drastic intervention than was recommended by social workers. The authors further reported that responses did not differ by respondent age, parental status, or experience with child abuse. There was, however, a significant effect for respondent sex. Female participants rated more acts as abusive, serious, and requiring intervention than did male participants.

2. *Chronic/extreme spouse abuse.* This is an interesting subtype because the negative behavior is directed at an adult in the household, not at the child directly. However, because research shows that being in the presence of violence is detrimental to children's well-being, this type of abuse is included here.

3. *Permitted drug/alcohol abuse.* If parents either encourage their children to use drugs or fail to intervene if they know their children are using drugs, they are guilty of this type of emotional neglect.

4. *Permitted other maladaptive behavior.* Parents who are aware of their child's involvement in maladaptive behavior, other than drug use, and do not attempt to stop the behavior are also guilty of emotional neglect.

5. *Refusal of psychological care.* This subtype includes cases where a competent professional has said that the child needs care, yet the parents have not secured services.

6. *Delay in psychological care.* If it should be obvious to a lay person that a child needed help but such help was not sought, parents are guilty of delay in psychological care.

7. *Other emotional neglect.* This final, miscellaneous category covers a general inattention to the child's needs that does not fit any of the above categories.

Using these definitions, Sedlak and Broadhurst (1996) reported that the incidence of emotional abuse according to the harm standard was 204,500 (3.0 per 1,000) children in 1993. This is significantly higher than the rate of 155,200 (2.5 per 1,000) that was reported in 1986. According to the harm standard, the rate of emotional neglect was 212,800 (3.2 per 1,000). This was also higher than the 1986 rate of 49,200 (0.8 per 1,000) children. If we look to the incidence under the endangerment standard, we find that the rate of emotional abuse was 532,200 (7.9 per 1,000) children, as compared to 188,100 (3.0 per 1,000) in 1986. For emotional neglect, Sedlak and Broadhurst (1996) reported an incidence rate of 584,100 (8.7 per 1,000) for 1993, and 203,000 (3.2 per 1,000) for 1986. While it is possible that these dramatic increases represent a true increase in this type of maltreatment, it is much more likely that they reflect a growing awareness of emotional abuse and neglect.

National Child Abuse and Neglect Data System

A different sort of data is compiled each year by the **National Child Abuse and Neglect Data System** (NCANDS). Each year, data is gathered on a voluntary basis from each U.S. state and territory. The states are asked to provide case-level data that includes all cases that were investigated by child protective services (CPS) that year, to indicate what type of abuse was alleged in each instance, and to specify what the findings were for each case. If this information is not available, the states submit summary data. After compiling this data, the National Child Abuse and Neglect Data System reported that there were 63,497 cases of psychological maltreatment in 2005. Based on this report, it was calculated that 7.1% of all reports of maltreatment dealt with emotional maltreatment (U.S. Department of Health and Human Services, 2007).

The national rates of emotional maltreatment need to be interpreted with care because there are dramatic variations among states. Hamarman, Pope, and Czaja (2002) examined the National Child Abuse and Neglect Data System data for 1998 and found a 300-fold variation in the rates of emotional abuse reported by states. Pennsylvania reported the lowest rate of only 0.37 cases per 10,000 children, while Connecticut reported a high of 113.02 per 10,000 children. Overall, 7% of responding states had extremely high rates (greater than 34 per 10,000), and 47% of states had very low rates (less than 3 per 10,000). This radical variation in reported incidence underscores the impact of the various legal and psychological definitions addressed earlier. For the purpose of comparison, the authors noted that these large differences among states were not evident for the more clearly defined types of maltreatment (the variation for sexual abuse was only 13-fold, and the variation for the reporting of physical abuse was 12-fold). Neglect, which is also difficult to define, had the largest variation in reporting among states (510-fold).

National Society for the Prevention of Cruelty to Children Data

Rates of psychological maltreatment as determined by examining reports to CPS pale in comparison to rates obtained by community samples of adults who are asked to report on their childhood. Although this sort of retrospective data is subject to the whims of memory and is not substantiated, the numbers are still staggering. Researchers at the National Society for the Prevention of Cruelty to Children (NSPCC) interviewed nearly 2,000 adults in 2006 and found that one third of them reported having been the victims of emotional abuse during their childhoods. Respondents reported being terrified of their parents, being habitually screamed at, and being called lazy or worthless. Among the adults reporting such treatment, 33% said it went on throughout their entire childhood (Doward, 2006). Even if these claims are exaggerated, this sort of finding still provides evidence that the emotional abuse of children is not a rare event.

CONSEQUENCES OF PSYCHOLOGICAL MALTREATMENT

Maslow's Theory

A number of theoretical explanations have been put forth to explain why psychological maltreatment is likely to be damaging to children. First, one can look to the hierarchy of needs proposed by **Maslow**. According to Maslow, the goal that humans are striving to achieve is to reach **self-actualization**. This state is defined as one in which a person achieves his or her full potential. In order to reach this pinnacle, Maslow argued that one must first meet lower-level needs. In his pyramid of needs, with self-actualization at the peak, Maslow put basic needs at the base. Basic needs include physical needs for food and shelter and the need to feel safe and secure. Once these needs are met, one can focus on meeting the psychological needs of belongingness, love, and esteem. What happens in cases of psychological maltreatment is that some basic and most psychological needs are not met. With these deficits, it is difficult if not impossible to reach one's full potential (Maslow, 1962).

Erikson's Theory

A second explanatory theory is that proposed by **Erikson** in his psychosocial theory of development. Erikson suggested that humans develop by facing a series of psychological crises, or conflicts, as they go through life. For instance, Erikson said that the first conflict faced by a human is to develop a sense of trust or mistrust during the first year of life. If the child's needs are met on a consistent basis, she will learn to have faith in the world and trust that she is safe. This sense of safety will provide an advantage when facing the next crises. On the other hand, if the child learns that the world cannot be trusted, she will not have a confidence basis for facing future conflicts. Moving into the next stage of life, from 1 to 3 years of age, Erikson said that children either develop a sense of autonomy or they begin to doubt themselves. If parents allow the child to make age-appropriate decisions and to feel proud of herself, the child will become autonomous. Conversely, parents who cause a child to feel ashamed will lead their child toward doubt. It is obvious how psychological maltreatment can derail a child's ability to conquer these early social conflicts. If this basis is not stable, it will impact a child's ability to face the conflicts that will mark the rest of the life span: initiative versus guilt, industry versus inferiority, identity versus role confusion, intimacy versus isolation, generativity versus stagnation, and integrity versus despair (Erikson, 1963).

Attachment Theory

A third theory that has been used to explain the mechanism by which psychological mal-treatment interferes with normal development is attachment theory. According to this theory, humans between 6 and 12 months of age should develop a strong, affectionate tie to a primary caregiver. If the caregiver is physically and emotionally available to the child, this tie develops naturally. Once a child has a secure attachment, he or she can use this relationship as a basis from which to explore the world. Hence, a well-attached infant has the confidence to explore the world while keeping their caregiver in sight. Securely attached children share their new discoveries with the person they are attached to and turn constantly to that person for advice. For instance, if a stranger enters a room where a mother and infant are playing, the baby will immediately move toward the mother and look closely at her face and then determine whether or not there is cause for alarm. This first attachment relationship also establishes a basis for all future relationships. Therefore, it is expected that securely attached infants will be more likely to have secure relationships as adults than will children who formed an insecure relationship with their primary caregiver (Hart, Brassard, Binggeli, & Davidson, 2002).

Findings from the Minnesota Mother/Child Interaction Project

Whether one, none, or all of these theories accurately explains the mechanism by which psy-chological maltreatment harms children, more and more evidence is accumulating that this type of maltreatment has a significant negative impact on development. The researchers behind the **Minnesota Mother/Child Interaction Project** followed children born to high-risk mothers from the time of their birth into adulthood. They concluded that children who had been exposed to hostile, verbal abuse suffered a host of negative consequences including poor attachment, act-ing out in anger, showing poor impulse control, and learning problems related to being easily distracted and having low enthusiasm. These negative effects were every bit as strong as those seen in children who had been physically abused. Even more startling, children with parents who denied emotional responsiveness suffered from all of the symptoms listed above and also had lower self-esteem, a tendency to engage in self-abusive behavior, and a greater likelihood of having serious psychopathology than their nonmaltreated peers. As a group, the children who had been denied emotional responsiveness were worse off than any other group of maltreated children (Erickson, Egeland, & Pianta, 1989).

Similar to the other forms of maltreatment we have covered, psychological maltreatment will produce different responses in different children. These responses will be partly dependent on their age, sex, and developmental level at the time that the maltreatment occurs. The impact of the abuse on its victims will also be related to the severity and chronicity of the maltreatment (Sirotnak, 2006). So, while victims are more likely to show the effects covered here, no one symptom is true of every victim, and no victim is going to have all the symptoms listed below.

Five Areas of Concern

In 1998, Hart, Binggeli, and Brassard reviewed the extant literature on the effects of emo-tional maltreatment on children. They divided the noted effects into five different categories: (1) intrapersonal thoughts, feelings, and behavior; (2) emotional problems; (3) social and antisocial functioning; (4) learning problems; and (5) physical health. Additional research conducted after Hart et al.'s examination has added support to many of their findings.

Interpersonal Thoughts, Feelings, and Behavior. With regard to intrapersonal thoughts, feelings, and behavior, Hart et al. (1998) reported that researchers had found evidence that child victims of psychological maltreatment had low self-esteem, created negative life reviews, and were more likely to suffer from depression and anxiety than were other children. Infants who are emotionally abused are likely to have a negative affect, to be apathetic, or to cry and be irritable. Generally, they are difficult to calm, and they do not make good eye contact. Related to the depression, emotionally abused children were also more likely to have suicidal ideation (thoughts or fantasies about dying) and engage in suicidal behaviors. Mullen, Martin, Anderson, Romans, and Herbison (1996) reported that a history of psychological abuse was correlated with a significant increase in suicidal attempts. The rate of attempts was 12 times higher for victims of emotional maltreatment than it was for nonabused controls, and it was also considerably higher than the rate seen in children with a history of physical abuse (5 times the nonabused rate). The negative life reviews formed by these children can include themselves and the world around them. Not only do they view themselves as unworthy, the see the world as a hostile place (Pearl, 1994).

Among the studies reviewed by Hart et al. (1998), some provide evidence that the negative impact of psychological maltreatment on its victims persisted beyond childhood, even in non-clinical populations. Briere and Runtz (1990) had female college students fill out surveys about their family experience (including sexual, physical, and emotional abuse) and about their current functioning in terms of self-esteem, sexual behavior, and aggression. To measure the participants' experience with psychological maltreatment, they were asked to indicate how often they had experienced the following parental behaviors in an average year prior to their 15th birthday: yells at you, insults you, criticizes you, tries to make you feel guilty, ridicules or humiliates you, embarrasses you in front of others, and makes you feel like you were a bad person. Self-esteem was measured by having the women rate seven statements such as, "Sometimes I feel that I don't deserve to live," and, "I like myself most of the time," on a scale of 1 (not at all true) to 5 (very often true). After controlling for physical and sexual abuse experiences and other negative outcomes, the authors found a significant relationship between psychological maltreatment in childhood and decreased self-esteem in college-age women. This result was replicated by Mullen et al. (1996) using a community sample of females in New Zealand, 57 of whom were the victims of self-reported emotional abuse. Mullen et al. used different measures to identify emotional abuse (parental bonding instrument) and self-esteem (Robson's self-esteem questionnaire), but they still found a significant correlation between emotional abuse in childhood and lower self-esteem. Complementary results such as these make us more confident about a finding.

Emotional Problems. When they examined emotional problems, Hart et al. (1998) found that reports of emotional instability, poor impulse control, substance abuse, unresponsiveness, **borderline personality disorder**, and eating disorders were higher among victims of psychological maltreatment than they were for matched controls. Rorty, Yager, and Rossotto (1994) studied 80 women who suffered from bulimia nervosa (an eating disorder marked by cycles of bingeing and purging), and reported that the most common type of abuse history among bulimics was psychological maltreatment. Reports of past experiences with emotional maltreatment were four times more common than reports of physical abuse.

Social and Antisocial Functioning. As predicted by the theories above, particularly Erikson's theory and attachment theory, these victims also suffered from a host of social problems. Reported issues ranged from attachment problems and poor social competence to non-compliance, aggression, violence, and delinquency. Researchers also found evidence of social isolation, poor empathy skills, and sexual maladjustment in victims of emotional maltreatment (Hart et al., 1998). With regard to aggression, it has been reported that this is a generalized aggression. The child is not necessarily reacting to a specific external event. Loeber and Strouthamer-Loeber's (1986) review of the literature on juvenile delinquency revealed that the best predictors of delinquency were parental rejection and lack of involvement. Related to social problems, some victims of emotional maltreatment are very hesitant socially, while others approach even unfamiliar adults indiscriminately (Pearl, 1994). In my work at a local children's shelter, it is not uncommon for children I have never met to cling to me within moments of my arrival. They will say they love me and fight when I try to leave. While this may be good for my ego, it is not appropriate behavior for a child!

Learning Problems. The children who were participants in the research reviewed by Hart et al. (1998) also struggled in school. On average, these children had lower mental competency, had more academic and intellectual problems, and scored lower on tests of achievement and IQ than did children in control groups. In addition, they showed significant delays in the development of moral reasoning. Doyle (1997) reported that a full 62% of the adults in her study who had been the victims of emotional abuse suffered from school problems. Furthermore, 21% of the victims were kept out of school by their parents, and their parents had not arranged for alternative home schooling.

Physical Health. Finally, and perhaps most surprisingly, Hart et al. (1998) noted that researchers had found evidence that psychological maltreatment had a negative impact on some children's physical health. If parents were found to be rejecting, their children were more likely to have allergies, asthma, respiratory problems, and hypertension (abnormally high blood pressure) than were other children. Children of parents who used spurning or who denied emotional responsiveness to their children had more somatic complaints and an increased risk for mortality. In cases of severe emotional maltreatment of infants, you may see nonorganic failure to thrive. This is a child's failing to grow as expected when there is no known organic disease (Pearl, 1994). Some of the earliest work in this area was conducted even before professionals used the term *psychological neglect*. Rene Spitz (1956) spent the 1950s studying infant development in nonideal situations. He observed children being raised in penal nurseries and in foundling homes (orphanages). The babies in the penal nurseries were cared for by their incarcerated mothers under the supervision of a nurse. The infants in the foundling homes were cared for by professional caregivers, but the infants did not have contact with their mothers. While the foundling homes were cleaner and the children there received regular medical attention (a doctor visited daily), they did not fare nearly as well as the children in the penal nursery.

During the five years of observation, not one child in the penal nursery died, and there were no major infectious epidemics. In addition, most of the children met physical and psychological developmental milestones on time. Conversely, 37.5% of the infants from the foundling homes died during the observation period. The surviving infants were significantly underweight, and all but one was delayed in cognitive and physical development. Interestingly, the one child that was developing appropriately was described as an "angelic beauty." Spitz (1956) noted that everyone was charmed by the child, and nobody entered the nursery without stopping to speak with or cuddle this beautiful child. The other children received only enough attention to meet their physical needs. The difference between the children who did well and those who struggled and even died seemed to be whether they received loving attention. This work was shocking in the 1950s and continues to be so today. It certainly underscores how potentially damaging psychological neglect can be for young children.

There is also evidence that children who are emotionally abused outside of their home may suffer psychological and physical consequences. In a unique study of emotional abuse, Krugman and Krugman (1984) examined children who were allegedly being emotionally abused by their classroom teacher. The investigation began after 17 of 27 children assigned to one male teacher began to show noticeable symptoms of distress. The children also reported that the teacher engaged in emotionally abusive behaviors such as belittling, inducing fear, negative labeling, and yelling. Parents also observed some of these behaviors. In addition to the expected psychological problems such as excessive worry about school performance, fear, and the development of a negative self-image, the children also began to manifest physical symptoms. Six of the children suffered from headaches and five reported stomachaches. This demonstrates that not only can emotional abuse lead to physical distress, but it also can occur outside of the home.

Factors Related to Resiliency or Greater Harm

In attempting to assess the impact of parental behavior on child development, it is important to keep in mind that the relationship between parent and child does not occur in a vacuum. Other things going on in and around the family may mediate or exacerbate the possible effects of maltreatment. For instance, much research has found that children are more likely to be resilient in the face of maltreatment if there is an adult in their life whom they can trust and turn to for support. On the other hand, living in a family where domestic violence is present can result in children suffering greater effects than would be expected from psychological maltreatment alone. Moore and Pepler (2006) studied 110 children whose mothers were in shelters for battered women and 100 children whose mothers were living in nonviolent relationships. They measured the interactions between mothers and children with the **Conflict Tactics Scale** (CTS), and they measured children's behavior with the **Child Behavior Checklist** (CBCL). While mothers from both groups who used insults and threats had children with more problematic behaviors, there was also a significant effect related to the mother's relationship status. Children whose mothers were in a violent relationship and insulted or threatened the children had worse Child Behavior Checklist scores than children whose mothers were insulting or threatening but lived with nonviolent partners.

Overlap With Other Forms of Maltreatment

It is well established that different types of maltreatment are likely to coexist. This is particularly true of psychological maltreatment. Claussen and Crittenden (1991) compared families who had been reported for child abuse or neglect (excluding cases of sexual abuse) with a community sample of families who were labeled as normative and a sample of families in the community who had a child in a mental health treatment. Based on two to four home visits and multiple assessments, the authors concluded that among families who had been reported for physical abuse, 91% were also guilty of psychological maltreatment. The relationship was not as strong in the other direction; only 45% of families engaging in emotional abuse were also found to be physically abusive. While the same pattern was seen in community families, there was also a significant difference in the degree of overlap. As was true in the reported sample, most (93%) cases of physical abuse included psychological maltreatment. However, only 18% of the psychological maltreatment cases included physical abuse. While most cases of physical abuse or neglect include psychological maltreatment, the reverse is not necessarily true, especially in a community sample. Many children may be the victims of psychological maltreatment alone.

CONCLUSION

In many ways, research on psychological maltreatment is in its infancy. Unfortunately, what we have learned is starting to paint a bleak picture. Psychological maltreatment seems to have a high incidence rate, is extremely difficult to prove, and is associated with significant negative developmental outcomes. At the same time, psychological maltreatment cases are underreported to CPS. Taken together, is seems likely that many children continue to suffer from this sort of maltreatment with little hope of prompt relief. This is the type of maltreatment that might be most appropriately targeted by prevention efforts. While most parents realize that it is hurtful to rape or beat a child, many do not realize that words can be equally damaging.

DISCUSSION QUESTIONS

1. After reading the information in this chapter, do you think parents should be charged with psychological maltreatment alone (i.e., no other form of maltreatment is evident)? If so, what would be an appropriate punishment for this type of behavior?
2. Would you be more or less comfortable reporting a case of alleged psychological maltreatment to CPS as compared with a case of alleged physical abuse or neglect?
3. Which of the six subtypes of psychological maltreatment specified by the American Professional Society on the Abuse of Children would be the easiest to prove? Which would be the most difficult to prove?
4. Which description of psychological maltreatment did you prefer, the one from the American Professional Society on the Abuse of Children or the one from Glaser? Why?
5. Different data sources provide varying estimates of the incidence of psychological maltreatment. Which do you think is closest to the truth?

DEFINITIONS

Psychological Neglect: a parent's failing to meet the emotional needs of his or her child.

Psychological Abuse: parental behaviors that actively harm their child's mental health.

Parent-Child Relational Problem: a mental disorder marked by clinically significant impairment in the interaction between parent and child that impacts family functioning or leads to the development of negative psychological symptoms in the parent or child.

American Professional Society on the Abuse of Children (APSAC): a national nonprofit organization that is committed to preventing child maltreatment, promoting research, informing American public policy, and educating the public about maltreatment.

Spurning: caregiver behaviors that are hostile and rejecting toward a child.

Terrorizing: a caregiver's threatening his or her child or the child's loved ones or possessions with violence or abandonment, or placing the child in a dangerous situation.

Isolating: confining a child or not allowing a child to have the opportunity to socialize with others.

Exploiting/Corrupting: encouraging children to develop and engage in inappropriate behaviors.

Denying Emotional Responsiveness: a caregiver's ignoring his or her child or showing no emotional reactions while interacting with the child.

Mental Health, Medical, and Educational Neglect: caregivers' failing to meet their children's psychological, medical, or educational needs.

National Child Abuse and Neglect Data System (NCAND): a voluntary, national data collection and analysis system that gathers and maintains data relevant to child maltreatment.

Maslow: considered to be the father of humanistic psychology, Maslow studied healthy people and classified human needs into a hierarchy.

Self-Actualization: according to Maslow, the highest level of psychological development; a person's reaching his or her full potential.

Erikson: a psychologist who proposed a theory of psychosocial development in which people develop across their entire life span by confronting various social issues.

Minnesota Mother/Child Interaction Project: a longitudinal study of 267 children who were born to high-risk mothers.

Borderline Personality Disorder: a mental disorder marked by significant impairment in interpersonal relationships, problems with self-esteem and self-image, and impulsivity.

Child Behavior Checklist (CBCL): a 118-item scale designed to measure a child's behavioral problems and social competencies based on parental report.

Conflict Tactics Scale (CTS): a scale that measures psychological and physical maltreatment as well as nonviolent discipline. The parent/child version was designed to gather information about how parents have disciplined their children over the past year. The child fills out one form, and a parent fills out another.

CHAPTER 7

Sexual Abuse

The sexual abuse of children is, unfortunately, not new. In *The History of Childhood*, Lloyd deMause (1974) presents evidence that sexual behavior between adults and children was prevalent in antiquity. Sexual activity between adult males and boys was particularly common with boy brothels, and services that rented boys to men were commonplace. There is evidence in literature and art from ancient times that young girls were also used sexually by adults. Though some laws were eventually passed to attempt to restrict sexual behavior with children in ancient times, it appears that they were not well enforced. Although the sexual abuse of children has its roots in ancient time, only recently has it become the focus of scientific research within the psychological literature (see Focus on Research 7.1). **Case studies** began to appear in the professional literature in the 1970s. These studies described victims and sometimes their families. While these studies were not experiments, they did lay the groundwork for later research studies. Even though the first published articles were mostly anecdotal, they did give information on the symptoms that might be seen in victims of childhood sexual abuse. However, these early reports were flawed because they did not include **control groups**, they did not use standardized methods of assessment, and they failed to determine whether the problems seen followed the abuse or predated it. It was not until the 1980s that a body of literature based on rigorous, empirical studies began to emerge (Green, 1993).

DEFINITION

Haugaard (2000) asserts that defining **child sexual abuse** (CSA) is an ongoing struggle, with debate raging over the proper operational definition of each word in the phrase *child sexual abuse*. *Child* has been defined as any person under the age of 18 years by many professionals, but others use less than 17 years, while still others choose less than 16 years. While there is agreement that certain acts are *sexual*, such as sexual intercourse, other acts are not so easily categorized. Expert opinions differ when it comes to acts such as being nude in front of a child, bathing or sleeping with a child, and massaging a child. Many of these acts fall along a continuum between sexual and nonsexual that is related to a child's age and the parent's motivation. For instance, few would argue that a father should not bathe his 4-month-old daughter. However, what if the child is 4, or 10, or 12, or 14 years old? At what point does the act move from being nonsexual to sexual? Does

FOCUS ON RESEARCH 7.1

In 1994, I examined the publications that were referenced in PsycLit and Psychological Abstracts for the years 1974 to 1992 (McCoy, 1994). For each year, I noted the number of articles published and what aspect(s) of sexual abuse the articles dealt with (interrater reliability for the categorization of articles into 1 of 11 categories was 80%).

Prior to 1981, very little research on sexual abuse appeared in the psychological literature (less than 15 articles per year). From 1982 until 1988, the research increased steadily. After this point, the increase in articles was dramatic. By 1989, more than 400 articles were published each year. The aspect of sexual abuse that has consistently been given the most attention is victim characteristics. Each year, on average, 31% of all articles published on sexual abuse dealt with impact on the victim. The second most popular topics for research were treatment and perpetrator characteristics, each accounting for approximately 18% of the articles published.

During this time, only two categories of research showed large changes in the percentage of attention that they received. First, between 1991 and 1992, the proportion of articles about the assessment of allegations increased significantly (from 6% to 16%). Second, articles on prevention peaked in 1988 and then decreased between then and 1992 (from a high of 13% to a low of 4%). Articles about victim characteristics and treatment were consistently highly frequent (31% and 18% respectively). The other categories were less common, and stable: legal issues, 9%; exploitation, 1%; definition, 1%; incidence, 3%; and anatomical dolls, 2%.

It is possible that the dramatic increase in research seen in the late 1980s was spurred by the intense media coverage of high-profile abuse cases such as the McMartin day care case in California. The initial complaint in the McMartin case was filed in August 1983 (see Case Example 10.1). By March 22, 1984, Ray Buckey and six others were indicted on 115 counts, and in January 1985, the first child testified during the preliminary hearings. The McMartin case became the longest and most expensive trial in the history of the U.S. legal system, costing over $12 million. The case raised a plethora of questions about the sexual abuse of children that researchers have been struggling to answer ever since (McCoy, 1994).

it depend only on the age of the child, or is the father's motivation relevant? If a father bathes his 2-year-old daughter because he finds it sexually arousing, it is a different situation from a father who bathes his daughter because she needs to be cleaned and the task falls to him. The problem is that in most cases we cannot determine the father's motivation (see Case Examples 7.1). Not only do experts debate what is meant by *child* and *sexual*, but there is also discussion about the word *abuse*. Some argue that the definition of abuse includes only cases where there is observable harm. Therefore, if there is no observable harm, there has not been abuse. Others propose that acts can be abusive even if no harm is detected. Some of the confusion and conflict that is evident in the literature on child sexual abuse may well stem from these definitional problems. Researchers are aware of the problem, and authors do attempt to find workable definitions.

One broad definition of sexual abuse is that it includes "any sexual activity with a child where consent is not or cannot be given" (Berliner & Elliott, 2002, p. 55). Acts ranging from the forcible rape of a 5-year-old by her father to a 14-year-old being flashed by a stranger in a park would be included in this broad definition as *any* sexual activity. The second part of the definition includes not only acts where threats or force are used to gain compliance, but also acts where a child is a seemingly willing participant. These acts are included as abusive because

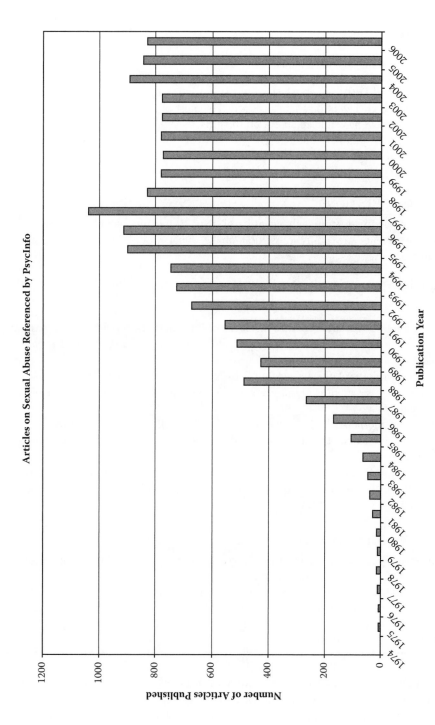

Figure 7.1   Articles on sexual abuse referenced by PsycInfo.

CASE EXAMPLE 7.1

Consider the scenarios described below. Are the actions described examples of appropriate parenting, inappropriate parenting, or sexual abuse? You do not, of course, know the motivation behind the parent's actions. Assume that the parents in each case assure you that their motivation was not sexual.

1. A single dad hosts a sleepover for his 13-year-old daughter. He brings the girls snacks and checks in on them regularly. For most of the evening, he sits in the kitchen where he can keep an eye on the girls.
2. Mr. and Mrs. Jones are nudists. They never wear clothing in their own home (if they do not have company). This has been the case even as they raised their two children.

DISCUSSION QUESTIONS

1. Are the parents described above guilty of sexually abusing their children?
2. If the parents are guilty of sexual abuse, what would be an appropriate intervention?

For the next scenarios, consider the gender of the parent and the child, and the age of the child.

1. A parent (mother/father) bathes his or her child (son/daughter) who is 6 months old, 12 months old, 2 years old, 5 years old, 10 years old, 13 years old, 15 years old.
2. A parent (mother/father) sleeps with his or her child (son/daughter) who is 6 months old, 12 months old, 2 years old, 5 years old, 10 years old, 13 years old, 15 years old.
3. A parent (mother/father) showers with his or her child (son/daughter) who is 6 months old, 12 months old, 2 years old, 5 years old, 10 years old, 13 years old, 15 years old.
4. A parent (mother/father) massages (full body, nongenital) his or her child (son/daughter) who is 6 months old, 12 months old, 2 years old, 5 years old, 10 years old, 13 years old, 15 years old.

DISCUSSION QUESTIONS

1. Were your decisions impacted by the gender of the parent and the child? If so, does this amount to a double standard?
2. Most students change their responses to several of the scenarios above based on the age of the child. Compare your cut-off age with those of your colleagues. Can you come to an agreement about when it is no longer appropriate to engage in the behaviors described above?

children cannot legally consent to sexual activity. (In the U.S., the age of consent for sexual intercourse ranges from 14 to 18 years.) Finally, because this definition does not state that the perpetrator must be an adult, it also includes situations involving an older and a younger child if there is a significant difference in age, size, or power. With regard to age differences, most experts consider a 5-year difference to be abusive. Some find this definition a bit too broad for the purposes of maltreatment and limit the term to acts where the perpetrator is a caregiver, thereby eliminating stranger assault. To deal with the range of seriousness, other professionals differentiate between contact and noncontact abuse. Acts such as flashing or talking sexually to a child would be categorized as noncontact sexual abuse. Contact abuse can be further broken down into penetration (oral, anal, or vaginal) and nonpenetration, but all contact abuse involves touch.

Working with a broad definition for child sexual abuse has had a number of consequences. First, it has led to high estimates of incidence and prevalence (see Incidence/Prevalence section, this chapter). Second, the range of severity in cases labeled child sexual abuse is extremely broad. Instances range from very minor events to horrifically invasive acts. Third, this broad definition makes it difficult to determine the effects of sexual abuse. If the children labeled as sexually abused have had radically different experiences, it makes sense that it would be difficult to find evidence that any specific developmental outcomes result from these experiences. Finally, broad definitions do not deal with the context in which the act occurred. Haugaard (2000) provides an excellent example to illustrate this point. Imagine that you are told that a father massaged the thighs of his 10-year-old daughter, and you were asked if it was an abusive act. Now, consider that you are given the additional information that the daughter had just played an intense soccer game, and the father massaged her thighs on the field in full view of spectators. Is this different from a father massaging the thighs of his 10-year-old in bed at night? Are both abusive?

One possible solution to the problem of a broad definition is to adopt a more narrow definition. However, if this is done, some children who were exposed to sexual acts will be left out. Advocates worry that this sends the message that the excluded acts are not really abuses (Haugaard, 2000). As a consumer of research, you need to be very attentive to how child sexual abuse is defined in each research article you read, so that you can appropriately interpret the results. When reading about child sexual abuse, pay careful attention to the method section of the report, and note to yourself what definition they used for their study.

Legal Definitions

All states in the U.S. include sexual abuse in their definitions of child maltreatment. As we saw with other types of abuse, some states refer to sexual abuse in general terms in their child maltreatment statutes, while others refer to specific acts. In addition, most states also address the **sexual exploitation** of children. Exploitation involves allowing, encouraging, or forcing a child to engage in prostitution or pornography (National Clearinghouse on Child Abuse and Neglect, 2005). As an example, consider Arkansas statute §12-12-503, which defines sexual abuse as "sexual intercourse, deviate sexual activity, or sexual contact by forcible compulsion; attempted sexual intercourse, deviate sexual activity, or sexual contact; indecent exposure; forcing, permitting, or encouraging the watching of pornography of live sexual activity," and which defines sexual exploitation as "allowing, permitting, or encouraging participation or depiction of the juvenile in prostitution, obscene photographing, filming, or obscenely depicting a juvenile for any use or purpose." An example of a more general approach to defining sexual abuse is Delaware Statutes Title 16, §902, which simply states, "Abuse includes sexual abuse and exploitation." On the other extreme, some states get very specific in their statutes. Consider Florida statute §39.01, which specifies that the "sexual abuse of a child means one or more of the following acts: (1) any penetration, however slight, of the vagina or anal opening of one person by the penis of another person whether there is the emission of semen, (2) any sexual contact or intentional touching between the genitals or anal opening of one person and the mouth or tongue of another person, (3) the intentional masturbation of the perpetrator's genitals in the presence of a child, (4) the intentional exposure of the perpetrator's genitals in the presence of a child, or any other sexual act intentionally perpetrated in the presence of a child, if such exposure or sexual act is for the purpose of sexual arousal or gratification, aggression, degradation, or similar other purpose, (5) the sexual exploitation of a child, that includes allowing, encouraging, or forcing a child to solicit for or engage in prostitution, or engage in a sexual performance." Sadly, even with this degree of detail, questions will remain. For instance, in section (4), the act is only illegal if the perpetrator's motive was tied to the child's presence. How do we measure another's motive for engaging in a particular sexual act? Finally, some states like Nevada (§432B.100) highlight age of consent by stating that sexual abuse includes statutory sexual seduction (unlawful sexual intercourse with a person under the age of consent).

INCIDENCE/PREVALENCE

It should not surprise you to know that it is extremely difficult to assess the incidence or prevalence of childhood sexual abuse. Not only do definitions vary widely, but this type of maltreatment, even more than others, occurs in secret. Frequently, only the perpetrator and the victim know what is occurring. Because there are seldom any outward, physical signs of sexual abuse, it is feared that many cases go unrecorded. Based on interviews with adults, researchers conclude that fewer than half of child victims disclose sexual abuse at the time it occurs, and many never tell (Berliner & Elliott, 2002). The evidence to support this secrecy is compelling. For instance, Lawson and Chaffin (1992) interviewed children who had **sexually transmitted diseases** (STDs) and reported that 43% of them did not acknowledge sexual contact. Children may not tell about being abused for a host of reasons. In some cases the perpetrator threatens the child or the child's loved ones with harm if the child tells of the abuse. In other cases, children stay quiet in order to protect the perpetrator, whom they may have strong feelings for. Some victims will stay silent in order to keep the family intact. They may fear that they will be blamed for tearing the family apart by removing the perpetrator, who may be loved and respected by other members of the family. Children who are very young or mentally delayed may lack the necessary language skills to convey to someone what has happened, and some may not even realize that what is happening is wrong. Still others may fear that they would not be believed if they told anyone. As a result of all of these factors, it is normal that children will not tell someone when they are being sexually abused.

Incidence

The National Incidence Study-3 (see chapter 2 for a description of the methods used in this national survey) defines sexual abuse as any one of the following three categories of behavior. First, acts of intrusion are considered sexual abuse. This means that any penetration of the child's mouth, anus, or genitals with a penis or penetration of the anus or genitals with fingers constitutes abuse. The second category, **molestation** with genital contact, includes all acts where genital contact occurred without penetration. The third category, other or unknown sexual abuse, includes acts that did not include genital contact. Included in this category were acts of exposure, touching of the breasts or buttocks, and inadequate supervision of sexual acts that the child engaged in willingly. Based on the harm standard, the National Incidence Study-3 report indicated that 217,700 (3.2 per 10,000) children were sexually abused in 1993. This was significantly higher than the numbers reported for 1986 (119,200; 1.9 per 10,000) and 1980 (42,900; 0.7 per 10,000). Under the endangerment standard, the number of sexual abuse victims was 300,200 (4.5 per 10,000), which was also significantly higher than the number reported in 1986 (133,600; 2.1 per 10,000; Sedlak & Broadhurst, 1996).

Although the National Incidence Study data is generally considered the official estimate of child sexual abuse, there are a number other reports dealing with the incidence of sexual abuse, and many of those provide much higher estimates. For example, a poll conducted by Gallup, Moore, and Schussel in 1995 reported a rate of child sexual abuse that was significantly higher than the incidence reported by the National Incidence Study. The Gallup researchers surveyed 1,000 parents who were selected as a representative national sample. In addition to many other questions on childrearing, the parents were asked about their child's experiences with sexual abuse in the past year. They were asked whether their child had been forcibly touched in a sexual manner or had been forced to touch in a sexual manner an adult or an older child in the past year. If they said "no," they were asked whether their child had ever had such an experience. The Gallup Poll reported an incidence rate of 19 per 1,000 children and a prevalence rate of 57 per 1,000. Interestingly, the Gallup Poll found similar rates of reported sexual abuse for boys and girls. They also found two peaks with regard to victim age. Children seemed especially vulnerable from 5 to 8 years and from 13 to 17 years. When parents were asked to report on their own experiences with child sexual abuse, 30% of mothers and 9% of fathers said that they were victims.

Prevalence

Another way to assess how frequently child sexual abuse occurs is to focus on adults rather than children. Instead of determining how many children are currently being abused, researchers ask how many adults were abused when they were children. This shifts the measure from one of incidence (cases per year) to one of prevalence (proportion of people in a population who have ever been victims). These retrospective studies ask adults to report on their own childhood experiences. Finkelhor (1994) summarized the results from 19 such studies and reported that between 2% and 62% of females reported a history of child sexual abuse, as did 3% to 16% of males. This wide discrepancy reflects a variation in definition (contact versus noncontact, age at which childhood ended, etc.) as well as different sampling techniques. Focusing on the studies with better methodologies, Finkelhor (1994) suggests that the rate for women is likely at least 20%, and the best estimate for men is between 5% and 10%. If the rates of abuse that are reported by adults are accurate, it would mean that there are approximately 500,000 new cases per year. If child protective services (CPS) is aware of 150,000 cases, and some unknown number is handled exclusively by law enforcement (if the abuser is not a family member, the accusations would be handled by law enforcement, not CPS), then how many are going undetected? It seems that many cases, at least half (and probably more), are not being addressed.

While it is possible that people may overreport past experiences with child sexual abuse to gain attention or to see themselves as a "survivor," there is no evidence suggesting that fabrication is a significant problem with this type of research. In fact, underreporting due to shame, embarrassment, or forgetting is considered the more likely problem. One researcher (Williams, 1994) did a follow-up study of 129 females who had been treated for sexual abuse as young children at an emergency room. When Williams interviewed the victims 17 years later (without telling them why they were contacted), 38% of the women did not disclose the abuse. Therefore, the rates of child sexual abuse may be even higher than those reported in retrospective studies.

Clinical Populations

Rates of child sexual abuse among **clinical populations** are generally found to be significantly higher than rates for the general population. Estimates of between 44% and 50% are reported among female psychiatric inpatients and outpatients. However, this is not always the case, because others have reported rates among clinical populations that are similar to rates in the general population (16% to 22%). Briere and Zaidi (1989) speculated that this wide range of results might be attributable to how carefully the patients were assessed for a history of child sexual abuse. They noted that patients might not spontaneously tell about child sexual abuse if they were not asked directly about it. Further, clinicians may not make note of child sexual abuse even if the patient had mentioned it. To test the impact of direct inquiry on rates of child sexual abuse in a female clinical population, they compared the charts for 50 nonpsychotic women from a psychiatric emergency room that were pulled at random with 50 charts written by clinicians who were told to ask specifically about child sexual abuse. The two samples did not differ significantly with regard to age, race, marital or employment status, education level, or income. Among the random sample of charts the documented rate of child sexual abuse was 6%, and among the queried group it was 70%. Therefore, when assessing the incidence literature, it is clearly important to pay particular attention to how child sexual abuse was assessed.

Change in Rates Over Time

It should also be noted that the reporting of child sexual abuse has changed over time. We saw a sharp increase in reports of child sexual abuse in the late 1980s and early 1990s. This increase, probably in response to media attention at that time, was followed by a decline. Between 1994 and 2001, the majority of states saw a decrease in reports of child sexual abuse of almost 30%. There are several ways to interpret this change. First, it may reflect a tendency to overreport child sexual abuse in the late 1980s that corrected itself by the mid-1990s. Second, it may be that there has been a true decline in cases of child sexual abuse in the last decade. While this may seem overly optimistic, it is true that this time period saw a decrease in other crime rates as well. It could also be that the prevention efforts that began in the late 1980s were successful. Thirdly, it could be that more stringent criteria were adopted for investigation, and as a result it only appears that there are fewer cases of child sexual abuse (Berliner & Elliott, 2002). However, evidence is beginning to accumulate that this pessimistic interpretation is not true. Self-reports of abuse by adults and children in community samples have also started to reflect a trend toward a decrease in the incidence of child sexual abuse. Although the research in this area is still limited (e.g., only a small number of studies have been conducted, and they have limited samples), the preliminary results are promising (Jones & Finkelhor, 2003).

PERPETRATORS

Only a minority of perpetrators (10% to 30%) are strangers (Finkelhor, 1994). Despite the fact that we are careful to warn our children about strangers who may attempt to hurt them, the far greater risk comes from family and friends or acquaintances. Approximately 10.4% of perpetrators are close family members (parent, stepparent, or sibling). In this close family group, the most likely perpetrator is a stepparent, usually the stepfather. It is estimated that stepparents are 10 times more likely to offend than are natural parents. When the victim is female, the abuser is a family member in one third to one half of all cases. Intrafamily abuse is less common when the victim is male. Only one tenth to one fifth of male victims are abused by family members. Acquaintances are the most frequent perpetrators of sexual abuse for boys and girls. Across studies, about 47.8% of perpetrators are known to the victim but are not close family members. While familial abuse is less common than abuse by other perpetrators, it is more likely to involve severe and recurrent abuse than is abuse at the hands of other perpetrators (Fergusson & Mullen, 1999).

The age of perpetrators can range from quite young (even younger than their victims in some extreme cases) to old age. About one third of all perpetrators are under the age of 18 at the time they abuse. The majority of perpetrators are between the ages of 15 and 45, with a peak between 18 and 25 years (Fergusson & Mullen, 1999).

Most perpetrators (as many as 90%) are male. While most agree that males are far more likely to be perpetrators, it is also believed that abuse by female perpetrators is less likely to be reported

Case Example 7.2

One of the best known female perpetrators of child sexual abuse is Mary Kay LeTourneau. Ms. LeTourneau was a 36-year-old teacher when she admitted to having sex with one of her former students, a boy who had just turned 13 years old at the time the affair started. Although both the boy, Vili Fualaau, and LeTourneau maintained that the sex was consensual, children cannot legally consent to sex in the state of Washington until they are 17 years old. Prior to their relationship becoming sexual, Vili had been a student in LeTourneau's class for both second and sixth grades. The two had become close, with Vili frequently confiding in LeTourneau. Vili even spent the night with his teacher when his mother had to work late. During this time, LeTourneau was experiencing marital and financial difficulties, and her father was suffering from cancer. Toward the end of his sixth-grade year, Vili began to write love letters to LeTourneau and asked her to have sex with him. Although she originally refused, after having a fight with her husband one night, LeTourneau began an 8-month sexual relationship with Vili that was revealed when she became pregnant by him. LeTourneau gave birth to a daughter, her fifth child, Vili's first, and named her Audrey (Olsen, 1999; Robinson, 2001).

LeTourneau pleaded guilty to second-degree child rape (Washington's term for statutory rape) and was sentenced to 7 1/2 years in prison. However, the judge in the case was lenient in the face of testimony that LeTourneau was suffering from manic depression and that she showed remorse and promised that it would not happen again. Not even Vili's mother pushed for serious punishment. In the end, all but 6 months of LeTourneau's sentence was suspended. After early release for good behavior, LeTourneau served only 3 months in prison. She was required to take part in a 3-year sexual deviancy treatment program, and she was forbidden to see Fualaau. What makes this case even more shocking is that just 4 weeks after her release, LeTourneau was found with Vili. At that time she was sent back to prison to serve her entire 7 1/2-year sentence. It was also at that time that the public learned she was pregnant again (Miller-Perrin & Perrin, 1999). While in prison, LeTourneau gave birth to her second child with Vili, a daughter named Alexis. Her husband, Steve, also divorced her while she was in prison. LeTourneau did not follow court orders while in prison, continuing to attempt to contact Vili. At one point she spent 6 months in solitary confinement for this offense (Montaldo, 2005).

In the meantime, Vili's family sued the school district for failure to protect him, but the jury found in favor of the school. Fualaau was not awarded any damages. LeTourneau was paroled in 2004, and just 2 days later, Vili, who was then 21, asked the court to remove the no-contact rule. The court did this, and Mary Kay and Vili were married on May 20, 2005 (Montaldo, 2005).

DISCUSSION QUESTIONS

1. Was LeTourneau's original punishment sufficient?
2. Would the legal response have been different if LeTourneau was a male teacher and Vili was a female student?
3. Is it possible for a child of 13 and an adult woman to be in love?
4. Does the fact that Mary Kay and Vili are now married mean that their prior relationship was not abusive?

than abuse by a male perpetrator (Finkelhor, 1994). Fergusson and Mullen (1999) report that when the victim is female, nearly all (92% to 99%) of the perpetrators are male. When the victims are male, between 63% and 86% of the perpetrators are male. Lately, the media has been giving a great deal of attention to sexual abuse between female teachers and male students (see Case Example 7.2). It will be interesting to see if this has any impact on reporting practices.

VICTIMS

Victims of child sexual abuse are more likely to be female than male. Only 20% of child sexual abuse cases that are reported to CPS involve males (Finkelhor, 1994). After reviewing the literature, Fergusson and Mullen (1999) concluded that depending on how child sexual abuse is defined, the rate of abuse for females is between 1.8 and 3.4 times higher than the rate for males. This rate is smallest (1.8 times higher for females than for males) when abuse is defined as intercourse, the most severe type of child sexual abuse.

Berliner and Elliott (2002) found that the peak age of vulnerability to child sexual abuse seems to be between the ages of 7 and 13, with the age of onset being later for male victims than for female victims. The median age at the onset of sexual abuse is between 10 and 11 years of age. Prior to this peak, there is also evidence for a sharp increase between the ages of 4 and 8 years. Fergusson and Mullen (1999) also found evidence that rates generally increase from the age of 4 to 11 and then level out before decreasing around the age of 14, and increasing again around the age of 17. However, the sexual abuse of children under the age of 6 years is probably reported at a lower rate than abuse at other ages (Finkelhor, 1994). Young children may not have the ability to tell (they do not have contact with adults beyond their family, they do not know the necessary words, etc.), or they may not even realize that what is happening to them is wrong or unusual.

Socioeconomic status does not seem to be a risk factor for child sexual abuse, as it is for other forms of maltreatment. While slightly more cases of child sexual abuse from lower classes come to the attention of CPS, this difference is not seen in retrospective studies (Finkelhor, 1994). It is likely that abuse among lower-class families is simply more commonly detected and reported because the families have more contact with social service agencies.

Lack of parental supervision and parental involvement does seem to increase the risk that a child will become the victim of sexual abuse. If parents are emotionally unavailable for their children, the children may look for attention elsewhere (Finkelhor, 1994). Pedophiles may also actively search for such needy children. In addition, children who live without one of their biological parents are at an increased risk for being the victims of sexual abuse (Berliner & Elliott, 2002). This risk comes both from being raised by a single parent who may not be able to be as attentive as parents in a two-parent household and from being exposed to parental dating partners who enter the child's world.

Some researchers have also proposed a link between physical and/or cognitive disability and child sexual abuse. Children with a disability have an incidence rate that is 1.75 times greater than the rate for nondisabled children (Berliner & Elliott, 2002). However, some feel that the evidence for this link is not sufficiently strong to establish disability as a risk factor. It may be that disabled children are at a greater risk because they are needier or because they are less able to defend themselves or seek help, but it is also possible that disabled children have more contact with service providers who are, in turn, more likely to detect and report abuse.

CONSEQUENCES OF SEXUAL ABUSE

Despite a good deal of attention and research paid to the problem in the last 20 years, there is still little to no evidence to suggest that there is a set of symptoms unique to victims of sexual abuse (Finklehor, 1990). Instead of sexual abuse leading to a particular set of negative consequences, it seems to put victims at risk for developing any of a large number of negative outcomes. However, no one symptom is seen in the majority of victims.

Meta-Analyses

A number of **meta-analyses** have been done to summarize the research on sexual abuse and the possible consequences for victims. In 1993, Arthur Green, a medical doctor, published an article detailing the short- and long-term effects of child sexual abuse. He found evidence to suggest that sexual abuse victims are more likely to suffer from a range of problems including anxiety disorders, dissociation, hysterical symptoms, depression, low self-esteem, and disturbances in sexual behavior than are their nonabused peers when they are children. As adults, these victims continue to be at risk for anxiety disorders, depression, low self-esteem, suicidal behavior, substance abuse, borderline personality disorder, multiple personality disorder, sexual dysfunction, revictimization, and sexual offending. Green does, however, caution that many of these research studies are still plagued by significant methodological flaws including imprecise definitions for sexual abuse, insufficient information about the severity of abuse suffered by the participants in the study, a failure to identify the perpetrator, the use of assessment instruments that are not specific to sexual abuse, insufficient validation of sexual abuse history (e.g., relying solely on self-report in some cases), and poorly constructed control groups in some cases. Finally, all data must be interpreted in terms of where the sample for the study came from. If participants are selected from a treatment facility, they are likely to have more negative symptoms than would victims who are not seeking treatment. Keep these cautions in mind as you read about the research on the consequences of sexual abuse.

Paolucci, Genuis, and Violato (2001) conducted a more focused meta-analysis on the effects of child sexual abuse. They opted to focus on only six specific outcomes: post-traumatic stress disorder, depression, suicide, sexual promiscuity, victim-perpetrator cycle, and poor academic performance. Looking only for studies that included empirical data, had control groups, used standardized psychometric measures, and had a sample size of at least 12, Paolucci et al. identified 37 studies that had been published between 1981 and 1995 dealing with the impact of child sexual abuse on at least one of their six measures of interest. The definition of child sexual abuse used by the authors was any unwanted sexual contact (not limited to penetration) that occurred while the victim was legally a child and the perpetrator was in a position of relative power as compared to the victim. Taken together, the studies they reviewed covered 25,367 participants, 9,230 of whom had a history of child sexual abuse. As is common in meta-analyses, the authors calculated a measure of effect size for each variable. (If you are not familiar with effect sizes, see Focus on Research 7.2 for a brief overview.) The authors found that a history of child sexual abuse significantly increased a child's risk for all six of the variables studied. The effect sizes were as follows: post-traumatic stress disorder, $d = .40$; depression, $d = .44$; suicide, $d = .44$; sexual promiscuity, $d = .29$; victim-perpetrator cycle, $d = .16$; and poor academic performance, $d = .19$. Surprisingly, the authors did not find any significant differences in outcome based on the victim's gender, socioeconomic status, or age at the time of abuse; the number of incidents; or the relationship between the perpetrator and the victim. This is different from what others have reported.

For instance, Roland, Zelhart, and Dubes (1989) found that for female college students, those who were victimized by a father or stepfather showed significantly more elevations on the **Minnesota Multiphasic Personality Inventory** (MMPI) than did those who were not abused and those who were abused by someone in a different role. The Minnesota Multiphasic Personality Inventory is one of the most widely used personality tests. It consists of 567 true/false questions and 10 clinical scales: hypochondria, depression, hysteria, psychopathic deviance, masculinity/femininity, paranoia, obsessive-compulsive behavior, schizophrenia, hypomania, and social

An effect size is a measure of the magnitude of an effect. It tells you how big an effect is. There are a number of different measures of effect size, but they are similar. Generally, you calculate the mean difference between the two groups you are comparing. In a meta-analysis on child sexual abuse, you take the mean (or average) score for the abused group, and then subtract the mean score for the control (nonabused) group. This mean difference is then divided by the standard deviation (*SD*) of either group. The standard deviation of a group of scores measures the average deviation of scores around the group's mean. Therefore, the *SD* reflects how much variation there is among scores in a group. A small *SD* means that that scores are similar to each other, while a large *SD* means that the scores vary widely. Two common measures of effect size are Cohen's *d* and Glasser's delta. Cohen's **delta** allows you to use the *SD* from either the control group or the experimental group; Glasser's delta requires division by the *SD* of the control group.

In order to understand a meta-analysis, you need to know not only what an effect size is but also how to interpret it. There are, as you might have guessed, numerous ways to do this. The most straightforward to is follow Cohen's (1988) guidelines. He suggested that *d* = .2 constituted a small effect, *d* = .5 indicated a medium effect, and *d* = .8 meant a large effect. Another way to interpret *d* scores is to think of them as indicating the percent of nonoverlap between the groups. For instance, if the distribution of depression scores for the abused group completely overlapped the distribution of scores for the nonabused group, the *d* would be 0, indicating that there is no difference in the scores of the two groups—percent of nonoverlap = 0. A *d* of .2 (a small effect) means that 14.7% of the distribution of one group does not overlap the distribution of the second group. A *d* of .4 (a medium effect) means that 33% of the distribution of the one group does not overlap the other distribution of scores. A *d* of .8 (a large effect) means that the percentage of nonoverlap is 47.4%.

Other researchers opt to report *r* as a measure of effect size. This statistic tells you how much of the variance in what you are measuring is accounted for by your independent variable. According to Cohen (1988), an *r* = .1 is a small effect, an *r* = .3 is a medium effect, and an *r* = .5 is a large effect.

At this point, it may be obvious to you why most psychology students are required to take at least one course in statistics!

introversion. In addition, it has a scale designed to measure whether or not the respondent is being honest. Even when the relationship to the perpetrator is not considered, a number of studies have shown that both males and females with a history of child sexual abuse have elevated Minnesota Multiphasic Personality Inventory scores. This is evidence of a general level of psychological distress among victims (Polusny & Follette, 1995). Wind and Silvern (1992) replicated Roland et al.'s finding that child sexual abuse was particularly damaging if the perpetrator was a father figure, and they found evidence that victims' depression levels were also related to both the frequency and the duration of the abuse. Therefore, for any specific symptom it is important to consider whether it is related more strongly to a subset of child sexual abuse victims than it is to all victims.

Depression

Among adult victims of child sexual abuse, the most commonly reported symptom is depression (Briere & Runtz, 1993). Evidence from both clinical and community samples supports a relationship between child sexual abuse and subsequent depression. This connection is evident across a variety of measures for depression including the **Beck Depression Inventory** (BDI), the depression scale of the Minnesota Multiphasic Personality Inventory, and clinical interviews leading to a diagnosis of major depression according to criteria of the *Diagnostic and Statistical Manual of Mental Disorders*. While nearly all studies report that being sexually abused increases the risk for the development of depression, the degree of risk varies widely. Studies find that between 13% and 88% of child sexual abuse victims experience depression, as compared with between 4% and 66% of nonabused control participants (Polusny & Follette, 1995).

While this is a common finding, it is not a universal one. For instance, Fromuth and Burkhart (1989) studied 582 college males (253 from a midwestern university and 329 from a southeastern university). They did not find a correlation between child sexual abuse and depression among their southeastern sample, and only a small correlation for their midwestern sample. The nonsignificant finding for their southeastern sample and the small effect found in the other sample may be attributable to the fact that Fromuth and Burkhart included noncontact abuse in their definition of child sexual abuse. Because this is generally a less damaging type of abuse, it may have masked the effects of contact abuse. In addition, the exclusion of females, who are more likely to suffer from depression, may also account for their findings. However, the difference between no effect and a small one seen in two similar samples (both male college students) speaks to the need for multiple studies on diverse samples before making strong conclusions.

Self-Destructive Thinking and Behavior

Given the apparent relationship between child sexual abuse and depression, it makes sense to explore whether child sexual abuse victims are at greater risk for suicidal behavior. Not surprisingly, evidence exists to show that in both community and clinical samples, victims of child sexual abuse are at an increased risk for **suicidal ideation** and suicidal behavior. While actual suicide attempts or suicides are labeled as suicidal behavior, suicidal ideation consists of thoughts or fantasies about suicide or wanting to take one's life. Among community samples, the rate of suicidal ideation has been reported to be 32% among victims of contact sexual abuse and 36% among victims of childhood rape. This compares to a rate of 20% among nonabused peers. This same pattern holds true for suicide attempts. Sixteen percent of victims of contact abuse attempted suicide, as did 18% of childhood rape victims and 6% of nonabused control participants (Polusny & Follette, 1995). This finding holds true among clinical populations as well. At a crisis counseling center, Briere and Runtz (1988) found that 51% of patients who reported a history of child sexual abuse also made a previous suicide attempt, as compared to 34% of patients who were not the victims of child sexual abuse. These results were replicated by Briere and Zaidi (1989) when they examined the charts of 50 nonpsychotic female patients at a psychiatric emergency room. The rate of suicidal ideation was 77% for child sexual abuse victims and 33% for nonvictims. Likewise, 66% of the child sexual abuse victims had previously attempted suicide, as compared with 33% of patients who were not victims of child sexual abuse.

In addition to an increase in suicidal ideation and suicide attempts, a link between child sexual abuse and self-mutilation has also been demonstrated. Self-mutilation includes acts, such as cutting or burning, that are not intended to be life-threatening but involve deliberate physical harm to one's body. Research dealing with clinical samples has shown that child sexual abuse, especially if it has an early onset, will increase the risk that a child will engage in self-mutilating behavior (Polusny & Follette, 1995). In the Briere and Zaidi (1989) study mentioned above, the rate of self-mutilation was 17% among women with a history of child sexual abuse and 0% among those with no history of child sexual abuse.

Anxiety

Most of the published literature shows that victims of child sexual abuse are more likely to be anxious than are their nonabused peers. This increase has been noted across a variety of measures including structured clinical interviews, the **Beck Anxiety Inventory**, and the psychasthenia scale of the Minnesota Multiphasic Personality Inventory, which is associated with anxiety. Victims of child sexual abuse are up to five times more likely to be diagnosed with some type of anxiety disorder than are nonvictims (Berliner & Elliott, 2002). This anxiety may stem from **hypervigilance**. A victim who sees the world as a dangerous place may be constantly on guard, expecting that something bad will happen and interpreting things that are neutral, or even positive, as evidence of danger. Living in a world that is consistently perceived as threatening increases anxiety levels to a maladaptive level. While vigilance is appropriate and adaptive when walking alone at night in a strange city, it is not a productive response if it is chronic. Constant vigilance wears a person out and makes his or her miss out on enjoying what is going on in the world. Victims may also experience anxiety because they are preoccupied with control. With a history of being victims with no control, they continually worry about how much control they have (Briere & Runtz, 1993). While general anxiety seems to be high among child sexual abuse victims, it has been noted that this is true only of chronic anxiety, not acute anxiety, and that victims are not more likely, as a group, to show more specific fears as measured by the Fear Survey Schedule (Polusny & Follette, 1995).

Post-Traumatic Stress Disorder

A history of child sexual abuse seems to be associated with an increased risk for developing post-traumatic stress disorder, especially if the abuse included contact (see chapter 4 for a description of post-traumatic stress disorder). Reports in the literature indicate that the rate of post-traumatic stress disorder among child sexual abuse victims is between 33% and 86%. Much of this variation is likely due to how child sexual abuse is defined. Saunders et al. (1992) studied a community sample of 391 women, 131 of whom had suffered some sort of childhood sexual assault. They found that rates of post-traumatic stress disorder varied significantly with the type of sexual abuse that had occurred. None of their nonvictims had post-traumatic stress disorder, as compared with 11.4% of the noncontact victims having a history of post-traumatic stress disorder, 33.3% of molestation victims, and 64.1% of the rape victims. The rate of post-traumatic stress disorder is also much higher among clinical samples (72%) than it is among community samples (8.8% to 17.9%), according to Polusney and Follette's (1995) review of the literature. The rate of post-traumatic stress disorder among sexually abused children is higher than the rate seen among children who suffer from other types of maltreatment (Berliner & Elliott, 2002).

For victims of child sexual abuse, flashbacks seem to be especially prominent. The person suffering from flashbacks has recurring, intrusive thoughts about the event. These memories may be very vivid and include visual, auditory, and tactile sensations. The memories can be triggered by a variety of stimuli including sexual situations (personal or in the media), abusive behavior, or even disclosing their own abuse (Briere & Runtz, 1993). Because these recollections are painful for victims, they may go out of their way to avoid possible triggers. In doing this, they place limitations on their daily life.

Substance Abuse

Victims of child sexual abuse are also at an increased risk for the abuse of substances, both legal and illegal. Again, this outcome is especially likely if the abuse included contact. Among community samples, between 15% and 22% of sexual abuse victims have a problem with substance abuse or dependence, as compared with 4% to 7% of control participants. Drug-related problems are even higher among clinical samples. Between 21% and 57% of sexual abuse victims in clinical settings are reported to have substance abuse problems, as compared with between 2% and 27% of patients who have not experienced child sexual abuse (Finkelhor, 1994). Based on the results of numerous studies, it can be concluded that the relationship between child sexual abuse and adult substance abuse is between moderate and strong (Fergusson & Mullen, 1999). It has been theorized that victims may be using substances as way of dealing with the memories of the abuse.

Personality Disorders

Victims of child sexual abuse are more commonly diagnosed with personality disorders, particularly borderline personality disorder, than are nonabused children. Borderline personality disorder is marked by instability in a range of personality areas including interpersonal relationships, mood, behavior, and self-image. According to the *Diagnostic and Statistical Manual of Mental Disorders*, Fourth Edition, a person must have at least five of the following symptoms to be diagnosed with borderline personality disorder: a pattern of unstable and intense relationships; impulsiveness that is potentially self-damaging; affective (emotional) instability; inappropriate, intense anger; recurrent suicidal or self-mutilating threats or behaviors; identity disturbance; feelings of emptiness or boredom; and frantic efforts to avoid abandonment (American Psychiatric Association, 1994). Among clinical populations, between 67% and 93% of patients diagnosed with borderline personality disorder or noted to have borderline traits have a history of child sexual abuse (Briere & Runtz, 1993).

Eating Disorders

There is some conflict in the literature regarding the relationship between child sexual abuse and the development of eating disorders. Many researchers report that approximately one third of people with eating disorders (between 24% and 69% across studies) have a history of child sexual abuse, and others argue that the rate of child sexual abuse among patients with eating disorders is not higher than the rates seen in well-constructed control groups. Many authors assert that a history of child sexual abuse is more strongly associated with **bulimia** (bingeing and purging) than it is with **anorexia** (Briere & Runtz, 1993), and others question whether there is any connection at all. Pope and Hudson (1992) reviewed the literature on the relationship between child sexual abuse and bulimia and concluded that the "current evidence does not support the hypothesis that childhood sexual abuse is a risk factor for bulimia nervosa" (p. 455). Pope and Hudson began their report by noting that a prospective study is lacking in this area. An ideal way to answer the question of whether child sexual abuse increases the risk of developing bulimia would be to identify a large group of child sexual abuse victims and follow them across their life span, periodically assessing them for eating disorders and also measuring for other factors that may contribute to eating disorders. Lacking this sort of evidence, Pope and Hudson reviewed six retrospective studies that made use of control groups. Four of these six studies found no difference between the rate of child sexual abuse among bulimic patients and the rate seen in their control groups. One of the two studies that reported a significant difference (Hall, Tice, Beresford, Wooley, & Hall, 1989) did not control for the gender of participants in their groups. While 98% of their eating-disorder group was female, only 85% of their control group was female. Because sexual abuse is more common among females, this is a significant confound. When participant gender was controlled for, there was no difference in child sexual abuse rates between the groups. In the other study that showed significant differences (Steiger & Zanko, 1990), the rate of child sexual abuse was similar in patients with eating disorders and those with other psychiatric problems (21% of anorexics, 36% of bulimics, and 33% of psychiatric comparisons had a history of child sexual abuse), but the rate was significantly higher than that of the nonpsychiatric control group (9%). Pope and Hudson question this finding, because 9% is a very low rate of child sexual abuse according to nearly all incidence studies. Because some of the participants in the control group were hospital staff, and therefore known to the authors, Pope and Hudson suggest that underreporting of abuse may have occurred for this group.

In reviewing retrospective studies without control groups, Pope and Hudson find that the rates of child sexual abuse among bulimics do not differ from overall rates of child sexual abuse among the general population. Pope and Hudson speculate that the relationship between child sexual abuse and bulimia may be an illusory correlation. Because both are relatively common, especially among females, they will frequently co-occur. However, it is not true that one of them is causally linked to the other.

Dissociation and Memory Impairment

Dissociation, or a separation of specific mental structures from the mainstream of consciousness, is also seen in some child sexual abuse victims. Participants who have a history of child sexual abuse have higher scores on the **Dissociative Experiences Survey** than do nonabused children (Briere & Runtz, 1993). Psychologists theorize that this may be a way for the mind to defend against full awareness of the abuse. By avoiding a full realization of one's victimization, the survivor is able to reduce the negative feelings associated with the trauma. The forms of dissociation that may be seen include psychic numbing, depersonalization, disengagement ("spacing out"), and amnesia (Berliner & Elliott, 2002). The dissociation is especially likely to occur during times of stress.

Repressed Memory.   At the extreme end of memory impairment is the controversial topic of memory **repression**. Repression is one of the mind's defense mechanisms proposed by Sigmund **Freud**. Freud stated that the mind, in order to protect itself, could reject unacceptable thoughts, desires, or memories by forcing them into the unconscious. The mind is able to bury the traumatic experience so completely that the person is no longer consciously aware of the memory. Freud did speculate that it required significant psychic energy to keep a buried memory hidden. A good analogy is to imagine the effort it takes to keep a beach ball under water: one can do it, but it takes a great deal of work. In addition, while a victim may not recall the event, aspects of it may "leak" into the conscious mind. So, theoretically, a woman who was repressing memories of child sexual abuse may be afraid of men, anxious, or unable to enjoy a normal sexual relationship. The goal of psychotherapy would then be to help such persons recall the memory and deal with it directly so they could move forward with their lives. Freud himself was somewhat conflicted in his writings about repression. He first wrote that his patients were recovering true memories of abuse, but he later wrote that the patients were recalling childhood fantasies.

The debate about the possibility of the mind to repress, and later recover, memories is a fierce one. Entire books have been written on the topic, and passions run high on both sides. I will present just a brief overview of the debate here. I would encourage the interested reader to consider exploring *The Myth of Repressed Memory: False Memories and Allegations of Sexual Abuse*, by Elizabeth Loftus and Katherine Ketcham, and *Trauma and Recovery: The Aftermath of Violence From Domestic Abuse to Political Terror*, by Judith Herman.

It would be ethically impossible to test the theory of repression empirically. In order to do so, we would need to randomly assign a group of children to sexual abuse and a group to nonabuse. After videotaping the abuse for appropriate documentation, we would threaten the abused children to maintain secrecy and never speak to them about what happened. Then, the children from both groups would need to be interviewed carefully over their life spans to see if they recalled the event. Even this is not perfect because some may recall the abuse but refuse to admit it. Still, if it turned out that some of the abused children went through a period of time when they apparently had no memory of the abuse and were later able to recover an accurate memory of it, then the theory would be supported with strong evidence. Because research like this will not and should not be conducted, we have to make generalizations from research that is ethically permissible. Unfortunately, there is much disagreement about how the available information should be interpreted.

Many practicing clinicians express a belief in the construct of repressed memory. When Dammeyer, Nightingale, and McCoy (1997) asked clinicians, "Do you believe that repressed memory exists?" the average response among clinicians holding a Ph.D. in clinical psychology was 7.28 on a scale from 1 (*definitely no*) to 10 (*definitely yes*). While these Ph.D. clinicians indicated a moderate preference for belief, other clinicians were even more accepting of repression. The average response of participants with a Psy.D. (doctorate of psychology) was 8.13, and the average response among therapists with an M.S.W. (master of social work) was 7.85.

Certainly, clinical examples of recovered memory cases are prevalent. Clients, generally women, enter therapy for a range of problems including depression, low self-esteem, and sexual dysfunction and deny any history of child sexual abuse. However, over the course of therapy, the client recalls memories of past sexual abuse. The memories cause a great deal of distress, and the therapists, who are trained in interpreting human behavior, believe that their clients are genuine. In addition, many cite Williams's (1994) study as good evidence for repressed memory. Williams obtained the emergency room records for girls who had been treated for sexual abuse between 1973 and 1975. In 1990 and 1991 she was able to contact and interview 129 of these women. When the women were contacted, they were told only that the study was about the lives of women who had received medical care at the city hospital. Each woman was interviewed in person for approximately three hours. Thirty-eight percent of the women did not report the abuse that had been documented between 1973 and 1975. Because the women were willing to report other negative events, the researchers felt confident that it was a lack of recall, not an unwillingness to tell that led to this failure to report. The women who did not recall the abuse were, on average, younger at the time of abuse than those who did recall the abuse. This, of course, is not evidence for recovered memory. It is simply evidence that abuse can be forgotten, or that it can be repressed. Williams goes on to report that 16% of the women who did recall the abuse said there was a time in their life when they had not remembered the abuse. This, if the self-report is accurate, is evidence for the repression and recovery of memories.

Other psychologists remain skeptical about repressed and recovered memories. Dammeyer et al. (1997) found that experimental Ph.D.s were close to the middle of the scale when it came to belief in repressed memory (6.01), indicating neither strong belief nor strong disbelief. In other words, many psychologists argue that we simply do not know if this is possible. Further, there is strong evidence that it is possible to create false memories for negative childhood events, even among healthy adults. Researchers have found that by asking repeated, leading questions, false memories can be created in children and adults (see chapter 10). In addition, techniques such as imaging, journaling, dream work, and hypnosis that are used by some therapists are especially likely to lead to the recovery of false memories. Skeptics also point out that the so-called recovered memories are odd in that they do not fit with what we know about how memory works. The recovered memories tend to be overly detailed, to include memories from very young ages, and to be bizarre (memories of satanic cults, animal sacrifice, etc.). Real memories tend to get blurry with age, and humans do not have memories from their infancy (we all suffer from **infantile amnesia**). The extreme memories of murder or torture that are recovered are not supported by physical evidence. If children were being murdered, scarred, or mutilated, then there should be missing children that fit the descriptions of the murdered children, and there should be adults who carry the marks of this sort of abuse. Despite years of investigation, the

FBI has not been able to find such physical evidence. Finally, skeptics point out that patients who recover a memory of abuse do not get better as the theory would predict (e.g., by addressing the "buried" problem, they should be able to move on). In fact, many patients get much worse (Loftus & Ketcham, 1994). For these reasons, many argue that therapists should be extremely careful in pursuing repressed memories. In court cases across the country, both sides of this debate have been argued repeatedly. On the one hand, there have been convictions based on recovered memory testimony, and on the other hand, therapists have been successfully sued for implanting false memories.

Cognitive Distortions

Everyone makes assumptions about themselves and the world around them. Many of these assumptions are based on experiences during childhood, when one is first learning about themselves and others. Being the victim of child sexual abuse can change a child's thought processes. Being victimized leads some children to overestimate the amount of danger in the world and to underestimate their **self-efficacy**. Because they were abused at a time when they were not able to resist, many victims have low self-esteem and see themselves as helpless in the face of chronic danger (Briere & Runtz, 1993). While some victims suffer from self-blame, it appears that most victims do not; they place blame appropriately on the perpetrator (Berliner & Elliott, 2002).

Another important aspect of cognition is the sort of **attributions** a person makes to explain events. Among victims of child sexual abuse it is common to see internal/stable attributions of negative events. In other words, if something bad happens, victims are likely to think that they caused of the bad thing (internal) because of something that is always true of them (stable). Conversely, they attribute positive events to external and nonstable causes such as luck (Briere & Runtz, 1993). This is the reverse of the type of thinking that most nonvictims engage in as they interpret the world around them. Most people take credit for positive events and blame negative events on things beyond their control (e.g., "I got a good grade on my psychology test because I am smart. I got a bad grade on my biology test because my professor is crazy and nit-picky.")

Social Functioning

Victims of child sexual abuse are, as a group, less socially competent than their nonabused peers. They are less able to trust than are nonvictims and are therefore less able to form secure relationships. Children who have been victimized may also see themselves as being different from their peers, and this difference makes them feel that they do not fit in with other children. They are likely to have difficulty forming and maintaining intimate relationships. As adults, female victims are more likely to remain single, and if they do marry, they are more likely to separate or divorce than are their nonabused peers. Female victims of child sexual abuse report that they do not have many friends, and they are less likely to find the relationships they do have to be satisfying than are nonabused women (Finkelhor, 1994).

Sexualized Behavior

Children who are victims of child sexual abuse are more likely to have sexual behavior problems than are their nonabused peers or children who are the victims of other types of maltreatment. Although sexual curiosity and sex play are common among children, victims of child sexual abuse are more likely to engage in behaviors associated with genital sexual activity such as simulating intercourse or inserting objects into the vagina or the anus. Sexual play and exploration in nonabused children typically appears between the ages of 4 and 7 years, but it may be evident as early as 2 years. Normal sexual play includes masturbation, some looking at and touching of others' genitals, and drawings of genitals. What is not generally seen in nonabused children is insertion of objects, insertion of the finger or the penis, or oral-genital contact. High levels of abnormally sexualized behavior are associated with abuse that is more intrusive, abuse committed by a greater number of perpetrators, and abuse that is accomplished with threats of harm. However, this does not mean that all children who act out sexually have been abused. Children who suffer from behavior disorders such as oppositional defiant disorder or conduct disorder may also engage in developmentally inappropriate sexual acts such as performing fellatio or cunnilingus. Other experiences, such as visual exposure to sexual material or acts, have also been associated with inappropriate childhood sexual behavior (Kuehnle & Sparta, 2006). So, although children with a history of child sexual abuse are more likely than others to act out sexually, you cannot assume that sexual abuse is at the root of all inappropriate sexual behavior in childhood.

Among seriously mentally ill children, female child sexual abuse victims are more likely than others to be **hypersexual**, and male victims are more likely to expose their genitals to others or use sexual coercion than are children who were not abused (Adams, McClellan, Douglass, McCurry, & Storck, 1995). Adams et al. (1995) reviewed the charts of 499 children from a psychiatric hospital. The children were categorized as having no inappropriate sexual behaviors or being hypersexual, exposing, or victimizing. Forty-one percent of the children had shown some type of inappropriate sexual behavior, and 16% had victimized others. A history of sexual abuse was related to inappropriate sexual behavior. Eighty-two percent of the children with a history of sexual abuse behaved inappropriately, as compared with 36% of children who were not sexually abused. So, while child sexual abuse is associated with sexual misbehavior, it is neither a necessary (36% of nonabused were inappropriate) or a sufficient (18% of children with a history of child sexual abuse were not inappropriate) link. The children who victimized others were likely to have been the victim of chronic abuse by a greater number of abusers. They were also more likely to be male; only slightly over a quarter were female. On the other hand, children in the hypersexual group were more likely to be female. The authors conclude by saying that children in psychiatric settings should be carefully screened for sexually inappropriate behaviors, especially if they have a history of sexual abuse.

As adults, victims of child sexual abuse are more likely to suffer from **sexual dysfunction** or to be preoccupied with sex. Victims are also at a greater risk for engaging in unsafe sexual behaviors and of being revictimized as adults (Berliner & Elliott, 2002). Senn, Carey, Vanable, Coury-Doniger, and Urban (2006) assessed child sexual abuse and risky sexual behavior among adults attending a sexually transmitted disease clinic. They reported that child sexual abuse victims had a higher number of sexual partners in the previous three months and over their lifetime. They also found that patients with a history of child sexual abuse were more likely to have exchanged sex for money or drugs. These behaviors were even riskier in light of the finding that participants with a child sexual abuse history reported more episodes of unprotected vaginal and anal intercourse. Not surprisingly then, adults with no history of child sexual abuse had a lower lifetime incidence of sexually transmitted diseases (69%) as compared to those who had a history of child sexual abuse (83%). Females with a history of child sexual abuse are also at a slightly higher risk for teenage pregnancy than are nonvictims (Tyler, 2002). Victims of child sexual abuse may engage in numerous, short-term sexual relationships in order to meet their needs for closeness and intimacy.

Controversy in the Professional Literature Regarding the Impact of Child Sexual Abuse

Like most aspects of sexual abuse, there is disagreement among professionals about the effects of child sexual abuse on later development. Despite the research reviewed here, there are researchers who argue that the effects of child sexual abuse are not typically intense or pervasive. In fact

In 1998, Rind, Tromovitch, and Bauserman published an article entitled, "A Meta-analytic Examination of Assumed Properties of Child Sexual Abuse Using College Samples," in the prestigious journal *Psychological Bulletin*. Rind et al. stated that past reviews of the literature in this area had been flawed. They criticized qualitative literature reviews for relying largely on clinical and legal samples. Their argument was that these samples represented the worst case scenarios. They further stated that people suffering from a clinical disorder are searching for an explanation for their current problems and may, therefore, be predisposed to blaming them on past child sexual abuse experiences. Further, if a therapist believes that child sexual abuse generally leads to negative outcomes, this idea may be transmitted to patients. Further, these studies do not examine other factors, such as family environment, that may lead to negative outcomes. In other words, even if the person is suffering, it is not clear that the child sexual abuse was the cause. Rind et al. are more supportive of past quantitative reviews that rely on more nonclinical samples and use meta-analysis to determine effect sizes. They point out that the quantitative reviews show fairly low effect sizes for negative outcomes following child sexual abuse. However, even these studies did not examine gender or family environment as carefully as Rind et al. thought was necessary.

Rind et al. (1988) therefore opted to conduct their own meta-analysis. They chose to focus on studies that examined the functioning of child sexual abuse victims who were college students at the time of the study. They made this decision because the largest number of nonclinical, nonlegal samples was from college populations. In addition, they noted that more than half of all people in the U.S. have some college experience. Finally, it was the work with college students that was most likely to include data on other variables that might explain negative outcomes (e.g., issues related to their family environment). While they acknowledge that college samples might be criticized because symptoms may have yet to appear or because persons able to attend college may be better able to cope than nonstudents, they defended their choice with past research. They noted that other researchers had found no age differences in symptoms among adult victims, and that past studies had reported that college samples were similar to other nonclinical populations.

Rind et al. (1988) went on to identify 59 studies that reported data for college samples. The studies had to have a control group, a distinct child sexual abuse group (i.e., sexual abuse victims could not be grouped with victims of other types of abuse), and enough data provided so that an effect size could be calculated, and they had to report on at least 1 of 18 dependent measures of interest (alcohol problems, anxiety, depression, dissociation, eating disorders, hostility, interpersonal sensitivity, locus of control, obsessive-compulsive symptomatology, paranoia, phobia, psychotic symptoms, self-esteem, sexual adjustment, social adjustment, somatization, suicidal ideation and behavior, and general psychological adjustment). Of the 59 studies identified, 36 were published, 21 were unpublished dissertations, and 2 were unpublished master's theses. The definition of child sexual abuse varied across studies, but most used an age discrepancy of at least 5 years to denote abuse, while only 20% focused on unwanted contact as the definition of abusive acts. Seventy-three percent of the studies included both contact and noncontact abuse, while the others used only contact abuse. For most studies, "child" was defined as 16 and under.

They found that child sexual abuse victims were more likely to report psychological problems than were nonabused students. The overall effect size, however, was small

(r = .09, 95% *CI*: .08 to .11). In other words, less than 1% of the variation in adjustment was accounted for by sexual abuse history. The effect sizes for the 18 specific symptoms ranged from .04 to .13. While all but one, locus of control, were significantly different (child sexual abuse victims had higher rates than nonvictims), all of the effects were small. The authors also noted that female victims tended to report more symptoms than did male victims.

The authors went on to examine whether these symptoms resulted from sexual abuse or from other factors. As expected, they found that participants who had suffered sexual abuse were also more likely to come from nonideal family environments (FE). After controlling for nonsexual abuse or neglect, adaptability, conflict and pathology, family structure, support/bonding, and traditionalism, they concluded that even the slight difference seen between child sexual abuse victims and nonvictims disappeared when family environment was controlled for statistically.

Finally, Rind et al. (1988) summarized by saying that these results can be explained by the definition of child sexual abuse used by most researchers. They argue that not all sexual experiences between adults and children should be labeled as sexual abuse. Their suggestion was that children and adolescents should be dealt with separately, and that willingness (or lack thereof) and positive versus negative reactions should also be considered. So, if a child willingly has a sexual experience with an adult, and has a positive reaction to it, it should be labeled with the value-neutral term "adult-child sex." If the child is unwilling or reacts negatively, then "child sexual abuse" is appropriate. The same pattern would hold true for "adult-adolescent sex" and "adolescent sexual abuse." They argued for the separation of children and adolescents because adolescents have more sexual interests, they are more likely to know whether they want to engage in a particular act, and they are better able to resist encounters they don't want, plus adult-adolescent sex has been common and even sanctioned in many cultures historically.

This article caused a storm of controversy after it was picked up by the popular press. Although it originally had little impact beyond the scientific community, this changed when it was referenced on the Web page of North American Man/Boy Love Association (NAMBLA, a pedophilia advocacy group) as scientific support for its views. In 1999, Dr. Laura attacked the American Psychological Association on her radio show for daring to publish the article (Ondersma et al. 2001).

In 2001, two articles were published in *Psychological Bulletin* responding to Rind et al.'s article. The first was by Ondersma et al., who raised some concerns about the methodology used by Rind et al. and major concerns about how the data was presented and interpreted. Regarding the methodology, Ondersma et al. criticized the definition of child sexual abuse used by Rind et al. By using definitions that included both contact and noncontact abuse, Rind et al. may have obscured consequences of contact abuse. Secondly, they objected to Rind et al.'s partialization of family environment based solely on self-reported, retrospective, quasi-experimental data. They noted that this type of analysis does not take into account the fact that the experience of child sexual abuse may be what led to the more negative reports regarding family environment.

Ondersma et al. (2001) are clear, however, that the methodological problems pale in comparison to the way the data was presented and interpreted. The first problem was in how narrowly the authors defined "harm." They looked only at long-term psychological effects. While this may be an appropriate definition for a study, one cannot conclude from this type of definition that there is no harm. They did not consider short-term harm, medical harm (e.g., sexually transmitted disease, injuries), rate of revictimization, how much time abused children spent in therapy, and so on. Also, just because something does not cause long-term harm, it does not follow that it is not abusive. As a point of comparison, Ondersma et al. propose this question: If a rape victim has no measurable negative effects a year after the event, should we call the event "unilaterally consenting adult-adult sex" instead of rape? Second, Ondersma et al. note that just because effect sizes are small, it does not mean that they are clinically insignificant. As a means of comparison, Ondersma et al. noted that the relationship between taking an aspirin each day and the prevention of future heart attacks is smaller than the effect sizes reported by Rind et al. ($r = .03$), yet given that second heart attacks are relatively common (as is child sexual abuse), this translated into patients who take aspirin having only half as many heart attacks as patients who were not on aspirin therapy. Third, despite Rind et al.'s claim that symptom rates between college students and members of community samples are similar, Ondersma et al. caution generalizing from this high-functioning group to all child sexual abuse victims. Fourth, in asking whether or not the sex was wanted implies that a child is capable of consenting to sex with an adult. In order to give consent a child would need to be fully aware of what was being asked, and fully free to say no to the request. It has been argued by many that children are not capable of this with regard to sexual decisions. In conclusion, Ondersma et al. argue that Rind et al. went beyond scientific findings to questioning moral values about child sexual abuse.

A second response to Rind et al. was published in the same issue of *Psychological Bulletin*. Dallam et al. (2001) seconded many of the arguments presented by Ondersma et al. (2001), including the use of a college sample and the inclusion of noncontact abuse, and backed up their statements with considerable research. Dallem et al. went on to question the statistics used by Rind et al. While the level of statistical analysis used by Dallem et al. is advanced, the conclusion was that Rind et al. used very conservative statistical methods and failed to make necessary statistical corrections. As a result, the data presented by Rind et al. underestimated the effects of child sexual abuse. Dallem et al. were especially critical of the analysis based on gender. They argued that if base rates (e.g., how common something is in a given population) were incorporated properly, the global effect sizes for males and females were nearly identical.

Perhaps it is not surprising to know that Rind et al. (2001) published an article in the same issue of *Psychological Bulletin* defending their original article and addressing the criticisms from Ondersma et al. and Dallem et al. In addition to being instructive about the possible effects, or lack thereof, of child sexual abuse, this series of articles points to many of the difficulties inherent in this type of research. I would urge the interested student to read all of the original works with an eye toward understanding the scientific method, the relationship of science to morality and the law, and how difficult it is to conduct objective work in a field that is as emotionally charged as childhood sexual abuse.

DISCUSSION QUESTIONS

1. In what ways is it easier to determine that sexual abuse has occurred as compared to other types of maltreatment? In what ways is it more difficult?
2. Compared to the other types of maltreatment covered so far, would you be more or less comfortable reporting suspicions of child sexual abuse to child protective services?
3. Do you favor a broad or a narrow definition of sexual abuse? Why?

> 4. The estimates of sexual abuse vary, depending on the method used to collect data. Which estimates to you think professionals should put the most faith in?
> 5. Do you think that the estimated rate of sexual abuse for boys may be low because of underreporting? If so, do you think this is related to the fact that sex between a young boy and a woman is not considered as problematic as sex between a young girl and a man?
> 6. Given the controversy surrounding some research findings in this area, should researchers be limited to presenting only their data and no commentary on it?

a meta-analysis conducted by Rind, Tromovitch, and Bauserman (1998) made this claim and triggered a storm of controversy (see Focus on Research 7.3).

The Impact of Abuse on Boys as Compared to Girls

Although most researchers acknowledge that boys make up between one quarter and one third of abuse victims, much less research has been devoted to them. While boys have r‌ ‌ attention in recent decades, the literature is still lacking. From what is known, it boys, like girls, suffer both short- and long-term consequences as a result of child se‌ experiences. What may surprise you is to know that researchers have found more ties than differences between male and female responses to child sexual abuse. Boys s‌ same stress-related responses after **disclosure** as do girls. They are fearful, they have pr‌ sleeping, and they are distracted. Boys also seem to self-report the same number of symp‌ that girls report. It had been expected that boys might show less negative outcomes beca‌ they were more likely to be abused by people outside of their families than were girls. Perha‌ because the majority of perpetrators are male, the added stigma regarding issues of homosexu‌ ality serves to increase symptoms in boys (Finkelhor, 1990).

While male and female responses to sexual abuse are similar, they are not identical. Boys are more likely to have externalizing symptoms like aggression, while girls are more likely to have internalizing problems such as depression. Men who were victims of child sexual abuse are also more likely to report a sexual interest in children (25%) than female victims (3%) or men who were not victims (9%). Finally, both male and female victims are at risk for developing some type of psychopathology, but male victims are most likely to develop substance abuse problems, while female victims suffer from affective disorders, anxiety disorders, and substance abuse (Finkelhor, 1990).

Consequences Over Time

The good news is that many sexually abused children do recover over time. Most longitudinal research shows that symptoms decrease in number and severity over time for many children. Unfortunately, however, a minority of child victims show a worsening of symptoms with time. One factor that has been associated with worsening symptoms is the involvement in a long, drawn-out criminal trial. On the other hand, family support is consistently associated with more positive outcomes. Also necessary for healing is the protection from further abuse. The good news is that victims of child sexual abuse are less likely to be reabused than are victims of other types of maltreatment. The bad news is that some, between 15% and 19%, are likely to be reabused, and that those who are not abused again are often safe from abuse because they were removed from the presence of the abuser (Finkelhor, 1990). While this ends the abuse, if it disrupts the family, it introduces a new set of conflicts that the child must face (being blamed for tearing the family apart, a decrease in family income, missing the abusive parent, etc.).

Victims with No Symptoms

One of the puzzling realities of the sexual abuse research is that almost all studies find a substantial group of victims who appear not to have any symptoms. Generally between one quarter and one third of victims do not seem to experience any negative impact from their experiences. While some have argued that this reflects a lack of sufficiently sensitive measures (they have symptoms, but we cannot detect them), even very thorough clinical assessments have failed to find symptoms in all victims. Another explanation is that victims may be asymptomatic at the time of assessment, perhaps because they are in denial, but they may suffer negative effects at some later date. However, it is also possible that some victims will not have any negative effects. These resilient victims do seem to be those who have suffered less serious forms of abuse and who have the resources and support necessary to cope with the situation (Finkelhor, 1990).

CONCLUSION

What seems to be lacking is "sexually abused child syndrome." Evidence does not exist to indicate that a sexually abused child will show a certain list of symptoms. Instead, child sexual abuse seems to increase the chances that a child will suffer from any of a large variety of symptoms as addressed above. The problem with this is that the symptoms described above can also be seen in children who have not been sexually abused. So, even though sexually abused children are more likely to be depressed than are nonabused children, if we look at the entire population of children who are depressed, the majority of them will not have a history of child sexual abuse. Also, a substantial minority of children will not show any symptoms at all (Fergusson & Mullen, 1999). Because of this, it is often extremely difficult to determine whether a particular child is the victim of sexual abuse. In a small number of cases, a child will have a sexually transmitted infection or a pregnancy that can provide evidence of abuse. In most cases, however, either there is no medical evidence or the medical evidence that is available is controversial. Experts for the prosecution testify that the findings are evidence for abuse, and experts for the defense say that physical findings can be explained by a nonabusive past experience (see Case Example 7.3). In the vast majority of cases, the determination is based largely on the child's report. For this reason, professionals must be very careful in interviewing children about suspected abuse. If the result of the interview will form the basis for a diagnosis and/or legal action, it is imperative that the information gleaned be as accurate as possible. Getting accurate information from children, without suggesting erroneous information, is more complex than one might expect, especially with young children. (See chapter 10 for more information on interviewing children.)

CASE EXAMPLE 7.3

In 1989, K.V. was 10 years old. Both she and her brother lived with their father and step-mother and had overnight visitation with their mother, who lived with her boyfriend, D.R.H. On May 2, 1989, both K.V. and her brother told their father that D.R.H. had physically abused their mother. K.V. also said that D.R.H. had touched her breasts and that he had put his finger in her vagina, and warned her not to tell. K.V.'s father called the police, and the prosecutor sent K.V. for a medical exam. Dr. Smith conducted the exam and noted that K.V. was sad and cried, but she did not appear to be in any acute stress. There were no abnormal scars or scratches on her skin; there was no scarring in the vaginal, anal, or breast area; and her general physical exam was normal. Dr. Smith did note that K.V.'s hymenal ring appeared to be broken. Smith concluded that this injury was consistent with digital penetration. Dr. Smith testified to his findings at trial. K.V.'s previously recorded statements about the alleged abuse were also presented, along with corroborating testimony from K.V.'s mother. K.V.'s mother stated that D.R.H. had admitted to her that he had fondled K.V. and that he wanted to rape her. Based on this testimony, D.R.H. was found guilty and sent to prison.

D.R.H. appealed his conviction. After visiting D.R.H. in jail, K.V.'s mother recanted her statements, as did K.V. D.R.H.'s lawyer requested a second genital exam to be conducted by a doctor selected by the defense. K.V. refused a second exam and stated that she did not need to be examined because nothing had happened to her. The appeals court agreed with D.R.H., and the conviction was overturned pending a second exam.

The Supreme Court of New Jersey reviewed the case and concluded that the courts could not compel a second exam. They argued that the court had an interest in protecting a child witness and that the exam could be traumatic for her. The supreme court argued that D.R.H. was not challenging Dr. Smith's finding, only his interpretation of those findings. The court said that the defense expert was free to offer a different interpretation of the findings from the existing exam. The court ruled that any harm done to the defendant because his expert had not personally conducted the exam was not sufficient to override the court's desire to protect the witness. Previous rulings had protected children from multiple psychological examinations, and the court felt that similar reasoning applied to physical exams (*State v. D.R.H., 1992*).

DISCUSSION QUESTIONS

1. Do you think K.V. was sexually abused by D.R.H.? If so, why did she recant?
2. Was the appeals court right to order a second medical exam, or was the state supreme court right to say it was more important to protect K.V.?
3. Should K.V.'s mother be charged with anything? Should she have visitation with K.V. and her brother?

DEFINITIONS

Case Study: an in-depth analysis of one person or event. This research method provides significant detail about one case, but the findings cannot be generalized to other persons or events.

Control Group: participants in a study who are not exposed to the variable being explored.

Child Sexual Abuse (CSA): the involvement of a child in any sexual activity where consent is not or cannot be given.

Sexual Exploitation: use of a child (under the age of 18 years) for the purpose of prostitution or pornography.

Sexually Transmitted Diseases (STDs): diseases that are most commonly spread via sexual contact; also called venereal disease (VD) or sexually transmitted infections (STIs).

Molestation: the act of subjecting someone to unwanted or improper sexual activity.

Clinical Population: a group of people defined by their association as patients within a treatment facility.

Meta-analysis: a statistical technique that allows researchers to combine the results of several different studies.

Minnesota Multiphasic Personality Inventory (MMPI): a 576-item, true/false questionnaire that provides scores on 10 clinical scales and 1 scale designed to assess whether the participant was truthful.

Beck Anxiety Inventory: a 21-item scale designed to measure anxiety and to discriminate between anxiety and depression.

Hypervigilance: excessive watchfulness or wariness; constant scanning of the environment for signs of danger.

Bulimia: an eating disorder characterized by cycles of bingeing and purging.

Anorexia: an eating disorder characterized by the relentless pursuit of thinness through starvation.

Dissociation: the separation of some mental processes from conscious awareness.

Dissociative Experience Survey: a 28-item self-report measure designed to be a screening test for Dissociative Identity Disorder (DID), formerly called Multiple Personality Disorder (MPD).

Repression: a defense mechanism in which painful or unacceptable memories or fears are rejected by the conscious mind and buried in the unconscious.

Freud: a Viennese physician who developed the psychoanalytic theory that stresses the importance of the unconscious mind and the constant conflict within each person's personality.

Infantile Amnesia: the inability of adults to remember much, if anything, about the first 3 years of their life.

Self-Efficacy: a person's belief that he or she is capable of doing what is necessary to produce the desired result in a given situation.

Attributions: determinations about what caused an even or condition; explanations for one's own behavior or the behavior of others.

Hypersexual: excessively or unusually interested in sexual matters.

Sexual Dysfunction: any problem during the sexual response cycle from desire to arousal to orgasm that prevents the achievement of sexual satisfaction.

Disclosure: the act of revealing; telling someone else or making known what has previously been hidden.

CHAPTER 8

Fetal Abuse

DEFINITION

Fetal abuse is an umbrella term that has been used to describe a wide variety of behaviors. What the behaviors have in common is that they cause harm, usually accidental harm, to a fetus. Mothers can be guilty of fetal abuse by ingesting chemicals, such as drugs or alcohol, that harm their fetus, or by the much less common means of direct physical assault (see Case Example 8.1). People other than the mother can also be guilty of fetal abuse via physical assault. Although the term *fetal abuse* is controversial, and a concise definition is elusive, some term is needed to describe these types of behavior. If professionals are to become aware of and vigilant about a problem, it needs to be named (Condon, 1986). Therefore, despite the debate over the validity of the term *fetal abuse*, I will use it here to describe behaviors engaged in by pregnant women that put their fetuses at risk.

INCIDENCE

It has proven extremely difficult to determine the incidence of drug use during pregnancy. Focusing on illegal drugs, Chasnoff (1989) reported that approximately 375,000 newborns are affected each year, while Gomby and Shiono (1991) stated that 739,200 women use at least one illegal drug while pregnant. Fetuses can also be harmed by legal substances such as alcohol. In 1987, Balisy reported that between 5% and 10% of pregnant women drink heavily. Using data from the **National Institute on Drug Abuse** (NIDA), Chasnoff and Lowder (1999) estimated that more than 1 million children are prenatally exposed to drugs (legal and/or illegal) each year. Other studies have attempted to determine incidence by testing all patients at selected hospitals or clinics. Researchers in Detroit screened 3,010 newborns at one hospital and found that 44% of them had been exposed to drugs prenatally (Ostrea, Brady, Gause, Raymundo, & Stevens, 1992). Chasnoff, Landress, and Barrett (1990) tested pregnant mothers during their first prenatal visit and found that 13.8% tested positive for drugs. Clearly, the estimates vary dramatically based on the sample tested and the method of assessment. Although we do not have a clear understanding of the number of children exposed to drugs prenatally, there is sufficient data to consider it a significant problem.

CASE EXAMPLE 8.1

D.R. had a difficult childhood. She was shuffled around to various foster homes and occasionally sent back to attempt living with her biological parents. Her father had physically and sexually abused her, and her mother told her that she had tried to induce an abortion when she was carrying her by doing things like jumping off furniture and drinking to excess. When D.R. was 15 years old, she was impregnated by her 18-year-old boyfriend. D.R. declined terminating the pregnancy at 18 weeks because the boyfriend wanted the baby. However, the boyfriend quickly grew disillusioned with the idea of becoming a father. The couple requested an abortion at 25 weeks, but the request was denied. Hours later, D.R. was taken to the doctor's office due to atypical bleeding. Upon questioning, D.R. revealed that she had been punching the fetus through the abdominal wall whenever she felt it moving. She denied that she was trying to cause an abortion, but admitted feeling angry at the fetus because it was purposely destroying her life (Condon, 1986).

CASE POINT

Although very rare, there are documented cases of direct assault on the fetus by the mother.

DISCUSSION QUESTIONS

1. Should D.R. have been found guilty of fetal abuse? If so, what sort of punishment would have been appropriate?
2. If D.R.'s child was born alive, should child protective services do anything to protect the child, or should they wait until allegations of child maltreatment were brought to their attention?

CAUSES OF FETAL ABUSE

Very little research has been done to determine what factors cause women to use substances while pregnant. Certainly, addiction is the most likely explanation. Although women may wish to protect their fetuses, they may not be able to control their substance use during their pregnancy. The causes of addiction vary and are beyond the scope of this book, but what is relevant to the current discussion is that use of drugs by pregnant women is not believed to be directed toward the child. In other words, the mothers are not trying to harm their fetuses when they ingest drugs.

In many cases there may be additional contributing factors when it comes to drug use during pregnancy. Kent, Laidlaw, and Brockington (1997) studied five women who were referred because of fetal abuse. Although the sample was very small, they did note several similarities that may be contributing factors for fetal abuse. All five of the women suffered from depression, and three of them had previously struggled with **postpartum depression**. All five women had mixed feelings about their pregnancies, and four had considered terminating the pregnancy. Two of the women actually denied the pregnancy for some time. Finally, three of the five women had significant difficulties in their personal relationships. Although one cannot generalize from such a small sample, this research suggests that future work should examine factors beyond addiction when attempting to understand what causes fetal abuse.

A different causal mechanism may be in play when dealing with the rare cases of direct physical assault on the fetus by punching the anterior abdominal wall. While this is not a common cause of fetal abuse, Condon (1987) argues that this sort of behavior may be caused by the perception that the fetus is attacking or depriving the mother. To research this question, Condon had 112 pregnant women and their partners fill out a survey that included questions about feelings toward the fetus. In response to the phrase, "Over the past 2 weeks, when I think about my developing baby, my thoughts…," 21% of women and 8% of men chose the answer "are a mixture of tenderness and irritation" versus answers that described feelings as either always or mostly tender and loving. More directly, 8% of women and 4% of men said they had occasionally wanted to hurt or punish the developing baby. It is important to note, however, that none of these participants was believed to have actually attempted any sort of assault on their fetuses.

EFFECTS OF DRUGS ON PRENATAL DEVELOPMENT

There is little doubt that the use of certain substances during pregnancy is not ideal for the developing fetus. When pregnant women ingest drugs or alcohol, they pass these substances on to the fetus. Medical research has shown that the substances remain active for a longer period of time in the fetus than they do in the mother, thereby increasing the risk posed to the fetus (Merrick, 1993). It is very difficult, however, to determine empirically exactly what impact a specific drug has on a developing organism. The research in this field is plagued by methodological problems. First, many women are **polydrug** users. If a mother is ingesting more than one drug and her baby is born with a problem, it is impossible to know which drug, if any of them, caused the problem. In addition to drug use, many of these mothers have poor nutritional habits, may live in poverty, may be homeless, and often receive little or no prenatal care. If a negative fetal outcome is noted, it could have been caused by any of these things, a combination of them, or something else that is unknown. One study done in New York City reported that 58% of substance-abusing mothers received no prenatal care at all (Merrick, 1993). Because the use of one drug alone during an otherwise optimal pregnancy is a rare (or nonexistent) occurrence, it is difficult to make strong causal statements about the impact of a drug on fetal development. This question is further complicated by the fact that a drug will likely impact the developing organism differently, depending on how far along the mother is in her pregnancy when she ingests the drug. Many drugs have a dramatic negative impact early in pregnancy, but minor or no effects if ingested in the third trimester (Niccols, 1994). Research that is conducted on prenatally drug-exposed children when they are not newborns to determine long-term effects is further confounded by mixing prenatal exposure to drugs with postnatal experiences in a drug-using household. Even with these significant limitations, there is evidence that some drugs, especially alcohol, have a definite long-term negative impact on children who are exposed prenatally (Merrick, 1993).

Although nowhere near an exhaustive list, the research on the impact of selected drugs on prenatal development is presented below.

Alcohol

It is well established that prenatal exposure to **alcohol** can harm a fetus. While professionals do not know how much alcohol can be consumed before harming a fetus, it is known that some infants born to mothers who consume alcohol during pregnancy will have **fetal alcohol syndrome** (FAS). It is a challenge to know how much alcohol was consumed, because the data is always an estimate and relies on self-report measures. To make matters more complicated, some children born to alcoholics do not have fetal alcohol syndrome, so experts cannot know when a baby will be born with fetal alcohol syndrome. It is estimated that as many as 1 in 750 live births in the U.S. involves fetal alcohol syndrome (Little & Streissguth, 1981). This disorder is marked by pre- and postnatal growth deficiencies, dysfunction in the central nervous system,

dysmorphic features including a flat nasal bridge, withdrawal symptoms at birth, heart problems, and mental retardation (Merrick, 1993). In 1981, researchers estimated that fetal alcohol syndrome was the third most common cause of mental retardation in the U.S.; **Down syndrome** was first and **spina bifida** was second (Little & Streissguth, 1981). By 1994, fetal alcohol syndrome had moved into first place as the most common known cause of mental retardation. The retardation seen in children with fetal alcohol syndrome generally involves IQs in the range of 60–65 (Niccols, 1994).

Some children who are exposed to alcohol prenatally do not show full-blown fetal alcohol syndrome but still suffer from **fetal alcohol effects** (FAE). Children with fetal alcohol effects have a higher than normal rate of **perinatal** mortality, low birth weight, and a lower than average IQ (Little & Streissguth, 1981). The prevalence of fetal alcohol effects is thought to be three to four times higher than the rate of full-blown fetal alcohol syndrome (Niccols, 1994).

Cocaine

While there is general agreement about the effects of alcohol on fetuses, the impact of **cocaine** on development is far more controversial. Despite the fact that women who use cocaine have been the ones most likely to be prosecuted for fetal abuse, it is not clear exactly what cocaine does to a fetus. For instance, there is no agreement as to whether cocaine causes **congenital** abnormalities (Merrick, 1993). In the late 1980s, the popular media inundated the public with dire messages about "crack babies," children prenatally exposed to cocaine. The media exaggerated preliminary research reports that were based on small samples and studies that did not include control groups. It was reported extensively that these children were at significant risk for spontaneous abortion, **sudden infant death syndrome**, growth problems, and a host of serious **neurobehavioral** abnormalities. Both the public and policymakers responded swiftly to these fears by creating policies and passing new laws, yet more careful research that followed did not support these early, dire predictions. In fact, a special section in the journal *Neurotoxicology and Teratology* that was published in 1993 concluded that the existing data proved few, if any, negative effects from prenatal exposure to cocaine (Ondersman, Simpson, Brestan, & Ward, 2000). A meta-analysis of well-designed studies that was published in the *Journal of the American Medical Association* in 2001 reported similar findings. The authors concluded that "after controlling for confounders [other variables such as poverty that might account for negative outcomes], there was no consistent negative association between prenatal cocaine exposure and physical growth, developmental test scores, or receptive or expressive language. Less optimal motor scores have been found up to age 7 months but not thereafter, and may reflect heavy tobacco exposure" (Frank, Augustyn, Knight, Pell, & Zuckerman, 2001, p. 1613, parenthetical added).

This does not, however, mean that other researchers have not found evidence of negative effects of prenatal cocaine exposure. There does seem to be some consensus that use of cocaine during pregnancy is linked to smaller head circumference at birth and through the age of 24 months (although the difference in head circumference between cocaine-exposed and nonexposed infants decreases by 18 months of age), a higher rate of miscarriage, a greater likelihood of prenatal strokes, problems with self-regulation particularly when stressed, difficulties with habituation, kidney disorders, and breathing disorders (Merrick, 1993). Long-term studies are still lacking, but those that exist point to small or nonexistent differences between children exposed to cocaine prenatally and those who were not. For instance, some research shows no IQ differences by 4 to 6 years of age, while other work points to very small deficits (3.26 points). However, even small impairments can be problematic if they persist. Researchers at the National Institute on Drug Abuse (NIDA) have documented deficits in arousal, emotional regulation, and the ability to sustain attention in children prenatally exposed to cocaine. They have also found that these problems are impacting school performance; children who were exposed to cocaine before birth were more likely to repeat a grade and to require special education classes than were their nonexposed peers. Of course, it is not clear whether long-term effects are the result of prenatal exposure or postnatal factors (such as being raised in a home where drugs were used). Overall, the current consensus seems to be that cocaine can negatively impact fetal development, but not all children are harmed, and the problems that may occur are not generally devastating (Ondersman, Simpson, Brestan, & Ward, 2000). Perhaps the current state of knowledge about the effect of prenatal exposure to cocaine is best summed up by the title of an article written by Dr. Alan I. Leshner (1999), director of the National Institute on Drug Abuse: "Research Shows Effects of Prenatal Cocaine Exposure Are Subtle but Significant."

Methamphetamine

The highly addictive drug **methamphetamine** (MA) is the most commonly abused amphetamine. The use of methamphetamine increased substantially between 1992 and 1998 and has remained steady since then. By 2002, it was estimated that 5.3% of the population in the U.S. (over the age of 12) had used methamphetamine at least once. With regard to pregnancy, a study of 1,632 mothers by Arria et al. (2006) found that 5.2% had used methamphetamine during their pregnancy (as determined by self-report and/or a positive meconium screen).

In animal studies, a number of negative fetal outcomes have been linked with prenatal exposure to methamphetamine, including "offspring mortality, retinal eye defects, **cleft palate**, rib malformations, decreased rate of physical growth, and delayed motor development" (Arria et al, 2006, p. 294). However, one must be careful in generalizing from animal studies in order to understand human outcomes. Unfortunately, little research exists with human participants, and what does exist is limited by poor methodology including small samples, lack of control groups, and problems with confounding variables. With this is mind, the extant literature does suggest that human fetuses exposed to methamphetamine are at increased risk for "clefting, cardiac anomalies, fetal growth retardation, behavioral problems, and cranial abnormalities" (Arria et al., 2006, p. 294). These infants are also at a greater risk for postnatal death, and they are more likely to have a low birth weight than are nonexposed infants (Santrock, 2007).

Marijuana

Despite the fact that **marijuana** is the most commonly used illicit drug by women of child-bearing age (Kuczkowski, 2005), little research has examined the impact of this drug on fetal development. Work that does exist links prenatal exposure to marijuana with premature birth, small birth size, poor habituation to visual stimuli at birth, and an increased startle response at birth. Despite early deficits, by 12 months, no differences were seen in visual or motor performance when babies who were prenatally exposed to marijuana were compared to non-exposed infants (Brick, 2005). One must interpret this result carefully though, because in other domains, problems have not been detected at a given age and then did appear later. For instance, deficits in verbal skills and lower memory scores were evident at 48 months of age in children prenatally exposed to marijuana, even though no shortcomings in these areas had been noted at 36 months (Chasnoff & Lowder, 1999). Other long-term effects have also been documented. For instance preschool children who had been exposed to marijuana prenatally made more information-processing errors due to problems with sustained attention than did their nonexposed peers. In addition, both memory and learning difficulties have been noted at 11 years in children who were exposed to marijuana prenatally. Researchers do note that these results should be viewed with caution because very little work has been done in this area (Santrock, 2007).

Nicotine

Over 30% of women who are of childbearing age smoke cigarettes (Kuczkowski, 2005), and approximately 18% to 25% of pregnant women continue to smoke (Huizink & Mulder, 2006; Jones, 2006). The women who smoke while pregnant tend to be young, single, and poor (Huizink & Mulder, 2006). Pregnant women are advised to avoid cigarettes because exposure to **nicotine** has been linked with low birth weight, premature delivery, respiratory problems, and sudden infant death syndrome (Brick, 2005; Santrock, 2007). Newborns who were prenatally exposed to nicotine also showed heightened tremors and startles, and they were more excitable than nonexposed infants (Huizink & Mulder, 2006). In addition, children whose mothers smoked during pregnancy had poorer language skills and lower cognitive functioning at both 36 and 48 months when compared with nonexposed peers (Chasnoff & Lowder, 1999). These findings may be linked to a heightened rate of attention deficit hyperactivity disorder (ADHD) in children who were exposed to nicotine before birth (Santrock, 2007). A number of well-designed studies have shown a dose-response relationship between cigarette smoking and attention deficit hyperactivity disorder (Huizink & Mulder, 2006). This means that the greater the prenatal exposure, the more likely it is that the child will show symptoms of attention deficit hyperactivity disorder. As a caution, when long-term consequences of nicotine exposure are assessed, it is important to note that damage may be due, in part or whole, to postnatal exposure if the child is raised in a smoking environment.

Heroin

Use of **heroin** during pregnancy may lead to smaller body size and head circumference at birth, premature birth, or even prenatal or perinatal death (Brick, 2005; Nichtern, 1973). Some infants born to mothers who use heroin (25% in one sample) will go through withdrawal symptoms after birth. The common symptoms seen include tremors, irritability, disturbed sleep cycles, and abnormal crying (Nichtern, 1973; Santrock, 2007). Effects documented later include behavioral problems at 12 months of age and deficits in attention during preschool years (Santrock, 2007).

Even treatment for heroin can be problematic for fetuses. **Methadone** is commonly used to treat heroin addiction, but it is also an opiate narcotic. Fetuses exposed to methadone have problems with both fine and gross motor skills at birth, and the fine motor problems are still evident at 5 years of age. In addition, at age 5, methadone-exposed infants are more active, and that activity is frequently off-task (Brick, 2005). A new treatment for heroin, **buprenorphine**, may be a safer option for pregnant women. Newborns who were exposed to buprenorphine before birth had shorter hospital stays and needed less morphine to deal with withdrawal symptoms than did newborns who had been exposed to methadone (Jones, 2006). In order to better protect fetuses, more research is needed to develop treatment options that are safe for mother and baby.

RESPONDING TO FETAL ABUSE

While there is debate about how serious the effects of some drugs, such as cocaine, can be for a fetus, there is agreement that many drugs, both legal and illegal, can have a negative impact on fetal development. The next question is, What, if anything, should be done to protect children from prenatal exposure to drugs? Should the response to substance use/abuse during pregnancy be therapeutic or punitive?

Treatment

In the late 1980s, when the media began to pay close attention to the effects of drugs on fetal development, treatment programs were not readily available for pregnant women. The initial response of the federal government was generally therapeutic. States were mandated to increase the proportion of their drug treatment funding that was designated to aid pregnant women and women with children (from 5% to 10%). Congress also ruled that pregnant females should have priority access to a range of services. Shortly after these guidelines were established, budget cuts made them nearly impossible to implement. For instance, if a larger percentage of a shrinking budget was earmarked for pregnant women, it meant that other populations, like people on probation, would be underserved. From 1992 to 1995, this therapeutic approach shifted to a more punitive approach. In one study, 45% of responding states (responses were gathered from 46 states) mandated criminal prosecution for substance abuse by a pregnant woman in 1992, and by 1995 that number had jumped to 71%. In addition, the identification of a positive neonatal toxicology test was defined legally as abuse or neglect by 14% of states in 1992, and by 35% in 1995 (Chavkin, Breitbart, Elman, & Wise, 1998).

Mandated Reporting

The first step in punishing a behavior is to bring it to the attention of the authorities. To this end, states began to mandate the reporting of drug use during pregnancy. Doctors who knew, via self-report or positive toxicology reports, that their patients were using substances while pregnant were mandated to report this to authorities. There is some evidence that mandatory reporting practices with regard to fetal abuse are not being enforced equally across racial groups. Chasnoff, Landress, and Barrett (1990) examined the reporting practices for 5 public health clinics and 12 private obstetrical offices in Pinellas County, Florida. During the study, they screened all of the women seeking care (380 women from the public clinics and 335 women from the private offices) for alcohol, opiates, cocaine (and its metabolites), and **cannabinoids**. Of the 715 women, 14.8% had a positive toxicology report. There was no significant difference between the percentage of positive tests from the public clinics (16.3%) and the percentage (13.1%) from the private clinics. Broken down by specific drug type, only cocaine use varied by setting; it was significantly more common among women using the public clinics. The overall drug use by Caucasian women was 15.4%, and the overall use by African American women was 14.1%. However, there were racial differences with regard to the use of specific drugs. Cocaine use was more common among African American women (7.5% versus 1.8% for Caucasian women), and the use of cannabinoids was more common among Caucasian women (14.4% versus 6.0% for African American women). What was most interesting about the study is that even though Florida had a law that required reporting all women who used illicit drugs during pregnancy, this is not what occurred. African American women were far more likely to be reported for positive toxicology tests than were Caucasian females. During the 6 months of the study, 48 Caucasian women were reported for drug use and 85 African American women were reported. Despite the fact that analysis of all urine samples revealed equal rates of drug use by women of both races, African American women were significantly more likely to be reported than were Caucasian women. One possible explanation was that African American women were more likely to use the public clinics. However, even when the setting was controlled for, the **racial bias** was still evident. The study also found that poor women were more likely to be reported for drug use than were more affluent women. Because doctors (unlike these researchers) do not test every woman who comes to them for care, the bias may be in the doctors' expectations of who is likely to use drugs. This would, in turn, impact whom they would test. It is important to keep the potential of racial bias in mind when implementing strategies to intervene in cases of alleged fetal abuse.

Criminal Prosecution

Shortly after the implementation of mandatory reporting laws for fetal abuse, prosecutors began to arrest women and charge them with crimes related to pregnancy. By 1992, 167 women from 24 different states had been charged criminally for behaviors ranging from the ingesting of illegal drugs to taking legal drugs to failure to follow doctor's orders while pregnant (Merrick, 1993). The outcomes of these cases varied widely. The cases presented here, and the legal issues related to their prosecution, are some of the most well-known. These charges are fundamentally different from other child maltreatment charges because the rights of a fetus are not clear. Because fetuses are generally not considered legal persons or children, it is not obvious that harming a fetus or putting a fetus at risk is a violation of the child maltreatment laws. Further, even if fetuses have legal rights in some arenas (e.g. a person can be charged with harming a fetus after assaulting a pregnant woman), it is controversial as to whether a fetus can have rights hostile to the mother. Due to the unique relationship between a fetus and the woman carrying the fetus, the Illinois Supreme Court ruled in 1988 that a child could not sue its mother for prenatal injury. In this case (*Stallman v. Youngquist*), the mother was charged with negligent driving while pregnant, not drug use, but the principle is similar. When fetuses have been granted rights, it was generally when they were harmed near the end of pregnancy, after the age of viability. Therefore, even though drug use is more likely to cause harm early in the pregnancy, laws focus on drug use at the end of pregnancy.

State v. Johnson. Because it is problematic to charge women with harming their fetuses, a Florida court attempted to charge a woman with hurting her child in the moments after birth, before the umbilical cord was cut.

In October of 1987, an African American woman, Ms. Jennifer Johnson, gave birth to a baby boy in Florida. Because Johnson told her doctor that she had consumed cocaine the night before delivering her son, she and the baby were given toxicology tests. Both mother and baby tested positive for cocaine metabolites. Ms. Johnson was not prosecuted at this time, and she went on to become pregnant again. In December of 1988, Johnson gave birth to a second child, a daughter. Again, she admitted to using cocaine during the pregnancy and on the day of delivery (Merrick, 1993). Johnson had previously tried to get treatment for her drug addiction but was turned away (Pollitt, 1990).

During the deliveries of both children, between 60 and 90 seconds elapsed between the child emerging from the birth canal and the umbilical cord being cut. Based on this, Ms. Johnson was charged with delivering a controlled substance to her minor children. Expert testimony as to whether drugs could have passed via the umbilical cord, after birth, conflicted. While experts for the prosecution argued that this was possible, the defense's experts contested this opinion. In addition, neither child showed signs of cocaine addiction, and both were considered to be healthy newborns. Regardless, Johnson was convicted, and her conviction was upheld by the appellate court. However, the Supreme Court of Florida unanimously reversed the ruling of the lower courts. The justices ruled that the legislature had not intended the statute regarding the delivery of drugs to minors to include the passing of drugs via the umbilical cord. They further argued that this sort of prosecution violated Florida's policy of keeping families together (Merrick, 1993, Sagatun & Edwards, 1995).

Discussion Questions

1. What criteria were used to try to establish maltreatment in this case? Do you think the criteria were influenced by political or cultural forces?
2. Was this prosecution an appropriate use of the law prohibiting the passing of drugs to minors?
3. If this was not a good use of existing law, should a new law be written to cover this sort of circumstance?

People v. Stewart.   Other states also tried to bend existing laws to make them cover fetal abuse.

One of the more creative uses of law to punish women who use drugs while pregnant was seen in the case of Pamela Rae Stewart in California. Ms. Stewart was receiving prenatal care and was told by her obstetrician to avoid street drugs and sexual intercourse during her pregnancy and to stay off her feet because of a misaligned placenta. She did not follow this advice, and subsequently gave birth to a brain-damaged son, who died 6 weeks after his birth. Stewart was charged with failure to deliver support to her child based on a criminal statute that had not been used in years but was originally intended to punish men who failed to provide for children they had fathered. In the end, the judge did dismiss the case, and Stewart spent only a week in jail (Bhargava 2004; Pollitt, 1990). An interesting side note to this case is the role played by Stewart's husband. He was present when the doctor told her of the restrictions, yet he used drugs with her, had sex with her, and even beat her while she was pregnant. He was never charged with anything, not even domestic violence (Pollitt, 1990).

Discussion Questions

1. What criteria were used to try to establish maltreatment in this case? Do you think they were influenced by political or cultural forces?
2. Was the judge right to dismiss the charges in this case?
3. Do cases like this worry people about a possible "slippery slope"? (If failing to follow doctor's orders can be prosecuted, where will it end? Could a woman be prosecuted for gaining too much weight or failing to take folic acid as prescribed?)
4. Should Stewart's husband have been charged with a crime? If so, what charges would have been appropriate?

Whitner v. State.   Other women have been prosecuted under existing child abuse laws, with the prosecution's argument being that the term "child" includes fetuses.

On April 20, 1992, Cornelia Whitner pled guilty to criminal child neglect for causing her infant son to be born with cocaine metabolites in his system. Even though her son was born healthy, Whitner pled guilty and was sentenced to 8 years in prison. Although Whitner did not immediately appeal this verdict, she later filed an appeal claiming ineffective counsel. At the time of her plea, Whitner did not realize that the statute under which she was being prosecuted might not apply to drug use during pregnancy. At the time of her conviction, the South Carolina law included only the term "child," with no references to fetuses. The appeals court upheld the conviction and maintained that the term "child" included viable fetuses. They referred to an earlier case, *State v. Horne* (1984), in which a male defendant was convicted of manslaughter after he stabbed his pregnant wife in the stomach, causing the death of a 9-month fetus. The dissenting justices argued that the use of the word "child" was ambiguous, and that previous bills to make fetal abuse illegal had failed in the state legislature. Whitner served her full 8-year sentence before being released.

Discussion Questions

1. Do you agree with the courts that Whitner was guilty of child abuse?
2. What criteria were used to establish maltreatment in this case? Do you think the criteria were influenced by political or cultural forces?
3. If Whitner is guilty, was her sentence appropriate? If not, what sort of punishment or intervention would you suggest?
4. Was the South Carolina appellate court right to say that a fetus is included in the term "child"?

State v. McKnight.   Once the Whitner case established that the child maltreatment laws in South Carolina covered fetuses, prosecutors were set to move ahead with further prosecutions.

Regina McKnight of Conway, South Carolina, was the first woman in the U.S. to be convicted of homicide for using crack cocaine during her pregnancy. Ms. McKnight gave birth on May 15, 1999, to a stillborn baby girl at 8½ months gestational age. At the time of delivery, both mother and newborn tested positive for cocaine. Ms. McKnight, an African American, was 22 years old. She was a homeless, unemployed addict, the mother of three, and possibly suffering from a mental handicap—with an IQ of 72 (Herbert, 2001). She had started to use drugs after her mother, whom she had lived with, was killed in an automobile accident in 1998. In South Carolina, women are given toxicology tests if they have had no prenatal care or if the fetus dies with no explanation. When McKnight's test results were positive, a report was made to the Horry County Police Department. The case went to jury trial in May of 2001 (Bhargava, 2004).

The doctors who testified at the trial disagreed about the cause of fetal death. While existing medical research showed a link between cocaine use and fetal death in cases where there is placenta abruption or ruptured membranes, neither of these were present in McKnight's case. The defense further argued that the State failed to rule out more common causes of fetal death that were present in the case (syphilis, hypothyroidism, poverty, and the use of alcohol and tobacco). The jury in McKnight's case deliberated for just 15 minutes before rendering a verdict of guilty. McKnight was sentenced to 12 years in jail (Bhargava, 2004).

In 2002, the South Carolina State Supreme Court upheld McKnight's conviction. They maintained that it was appropriate to use the state's homicide laws to prosecute women who experience stillbirths if the women had engaged in behaviors that heightened the risk to their fetuses. The U.S. Supreme Court declined to review this decision (Paltrow & Newman, 2008).

In 2008, the case was again appealed to the South Carolina State Supreme Court on different grounds. This time McKnight's lawyers argued that she had not received a fair trial due to ineffective counsel. Specifically, it was argued that McKnight's attorney did not solicit appropriate medical experts to challenge the findings of the prosecution's experts. On May 11, 2008, the court ruled unanimously that McKnight had not received a fair trial. The court ruled that a factual error was made when the trial court accepted that there was a causal link between McKnight's use of cocaine and the stillbirth of her son. Further, the court noted that the medical evidence presented at trial that linked cocaine use and fetal harm was both outdated and inaccurate (Paltrow & Newman, 2008).

Discussion Questions

1. Was the jury right to convict McKnight of homicide?
2. What criteria were used to establish maltreatment in this case? Do you think they were influenced by political or cultural forces?
3. Was McKnight's sentence fair? If not, what punishment or intervention would you suggest?
4. The South Carolina State Supreme Court ruled twice on this case. Do you agree with these decisions?
5. If the U.S. Supreme Court heard this case, do you think it would agree or disagree with the lower courts? Why?

Although states continue to move forward with criminal prosecution of alleged fetal abuse, there are still many unanswered questions, legally and morally. The debate about whether this is an appropriate response to drug use during pregnancy is a heated one (see Debate 8.1: Should Cases of Alleged Fetal Abuse Be Prosecuted Criminally?).

DEBATE 8.1: SHOULD CASES OF ALLEGED FETAL ABUSE BE PROSECUTED CRIMINALLY?

YES

There are many who argue strongly that fetal abuse should be prosecuted in court because it is a crime. First, the use of illegal substances is already a criminal act. Second, many states now include viable fetuses in their child abuse statutes, which makes using any drugs that may harm the fetus during the end of a pregnancy a crime. Our court systems are set up to deal with crimes. From a justice perspective, this makes prosecution the right thing to do (Ondersma et al., 2000). In states that do not have laws protecting fetuses, prosecution is still appropriate because the fetuses become children when they are born alive. If they have injuries because of what they were exposed to prenatally, then a child has been harmed. Logli (1998) also points out that it is already well established, in both criminal and civil courts, that fetuses can be protected from people other than their mothers. Given that fetuses have legal rights in some contexts, they are valuable entities that deserve to be protected in all cases.

Logli (1998) further argues that using drugs, even legal ones, is not a right that women have. Additionally, if women chose to carry a pregnancy to term, then society can and should require them to do a good job.

Some opponents of prosecuting fetal abuse argue that such laws or prosecutions may prevent women from seeking prenatal care, but Logli (1998) says this is a weak argument. Arguably, the same logic could be applied to all current child maltreatment laws. One could say that because it is illegal to physically abuse your child, parents are less likely to bring them for medical care where the abuse could be discovered. Therefore, child maltreatment should not be illegal. If this argument is not valid, neither is the one regarding fetuses.

Prosecuting fetal abuse also opens the door to removing any children born alive if the mother is found guilty. This would serve to protect children from being raised in a home where substance abuse is occurring. It has been reported that households where substance abuse occurs are likely to have other problems including domestic violence, criminal activity, poverty, and stress, none of which are good for children. While not all women who use substances are going to maltreat their born children, substance abuse is certainly a risk factor for child maltreatment, especially considering the significant taboo and risk of getting caught during delivery when a woman uses drugs near the end of her pregnancy (Ondersma et al., 2000).

For all of these reasons, fetal abuse should be prosecuted in court.

NO

On the other side of the debate, there are many who argue equally vehemently that women who use drugs while pregnant should not be prosecuted criminally. One obvious place to start is that the laws of most states do not include fetuses in their child abuse statutes. The statutes governing child maltreatment refer specifically to children, which means they are in effect only after a child has been born (Paltrow, 1991).

While a simple solution to this point is to pass laws that include fetuses, as some states have done, there are still significant concerns. One argument is that substance abuse is considered a mental disease. The U.S. Supreme Court ruled in 1925 that addiction was a disease (Paltrow, 1991). The use of the drug is, therefore, not under the complete control of the addict. Not only is it true that a person should not be punished for something she cannot control, it is also true that laws will not change behavior that is not under a person's control. If an addict is not in control of her substance-using behavior, it is unlikely that she could choose to stop using a drug even if she knew she might be punished for engaging in that behavior. Perhaps it would be more effective, and more humane, to treat the addict than to punish her for her disease.

A practical argument is one of cost. While the estimated incidence of children who are parentally exposed to drugs ranges dramatically, even the lowest estimate of 380,000 incidents per year is daunting (Merrick, 1993). If all of these women were to be charged, tried, and punished, the cost would be astronomical. In addition to court and prison costs, the foster care system would need a substantial increase in funding to care for the children whose mothers were incarcerated. There are also intangible costs associated with separating the child from the mother. Unfortunately, our foster care system is not perfect, and there have been cases where family relationships have been disrupted because of drug use, but a healthy, alternative home was not established for the newborn (Paltrow, 1991).

With regard to constitutional issues, it has been argued that these laws violate the Fourteenth Amendment, which guarantees equal protection under the law. Because any laws that deal with issues related to pregnancy can only be used against women during their childbearing years, they cannot apply to everyone (Merrick, 1993). A second constitutional argument against the prosecution of fetal abuse is that it violates the mother's fundamental right to privacy. In addition, the U.S. Supreme Court ruled in *Ferguson v. The City of Charleston* (2000) that if mothers are tested randomly for drugs when they deliver babies, their Fourth Amendment rights have been violated (the right to be free of unreasonable search). Finally, the Eighth Amendment guarantees that only conduct may be punished, not status. However, the prosecution of fetal abuse is not about punishing women for using drugs, because other laws govern the use of illegal substances. These women are being prosecuted for using drugs while they are pregnant (Paltrow, 1991).

There is also significant concern that laws like these would not be applied fairly even within the group of pregnant women. Research already exists that provides convincing evidence that women who are poor and/or members of minority groups are more likely to be reported for using drugs while pregnant (Chasnoff, Landress, & Barrett, 1990).

Even those who focus on the well-being of the child, as opposed to the rights of the mother, have expressed concerns about the criminal prosecution of fetal abuse. The concern is that if women know that they will be arrested if they admit to using drugs while pregnant, they may keep this information from their doctors, or refuse to seek medical care at all. For example, following the very well publicized prosecution of Melanie Green for allegedly inducing the death of her newborn via prenatal drug use, the Prenatal Center for Chemical Dependence at Northwestern University began to receive calls from women who were afraid that they would be arrested if they came in for help. Women who in the past would have received care from this facility stopped seeking services to avoid arrest. In the extreme case, a drug-using mother may opt to terminate a pregnancy rather than attempt to carry and deliver a baby while she is struggling with drug addiction. Another concern regarding fetal health is that if women are jailed prior to giving birth, the fetus may be damaged by being carried and delivered within the prison system (Norton-Hawk, 1998). These concerns have led the major national health groups, including the "American Medical Association, the American Academy of Pediatrics, the American Public Health Association, the American College of Obstetricians and

Gynecologists, and the American Society of Law and Medicine" (Paltrow, 1991, p. 88), to oppose such criminal prosecution.

A final concern is that this approach punishes women addicts who may have desperately wanted to get help but were turned away from treatment centers (Norton-Hawk, 1998). The U.S. does not currently have a sufficient number of drug treatment facilities available for those who seek care. In addition, the majority of the existing programs will not accept patients who are currently pregnant. Other programs do not accept Medicaid, so poor women have no way to pay for treatment (Merrick, 1993). An additional problem is that the programs that do accept pregnant women may not allow these mothers to bring other children with them. This forces the women to choose between caring for their children or their fetuses. Finally, even programs that will accept pregnant women may be flawed because they were originally designed to treat male addicts. As such, programs frequently fail to address issues, such as prior victimization, that are nearly universal among female addicts (Paltrow, 1991).

For all of these reasons, criminal prosecution is not the best response to drug use during pregnancy.

Public Support for Prosecution. There does seem to be a good deal of public support for the criminal prosecution of fetal abuse. In one survey, 98% of the participants said that women who use drugs while pregnant should be prosecuted. Seventy-five percent of the participants indicated that they would be in favor of prosecution in any case—illegal or legal drugs. However, when participants were asked to indicate what sort of punishment, if any, they thought should be the result of a guilty finding, they were much gentler than the courts have been. Only 17.1% of participants recommended jail time, and most of those (10.4%) recommended sentences of less than a year. This does not mean that the participants did not think any sanctions were necessary. Only 3.7% of participants endorsed no sanctions at all for guilty women. Interventions that were more therapeutic than criminal were recommended most often (participants could select more than one option): 54% endorsed court-ordered counseling, 57% were in favor of court-ordered inpatient treatment, 42% recommended court-ordered outpatient treatment, and 65% wanted to see court-ordered parenting education (McCoy, 2003).

Civil Commitment

Yet another legal response to drug use during pregnancy is **civil commitment**. More than half of the states in the U.S. have laws that allow for the involuntary commitment of substance abusers to treatment programs. Some states specifically note that pregnant women who use drugs qualify. For instance, Michigan law states that pregnant women who use certain drugs (cocaine, heroin, phencyclidine, methamphetamine, or amphetamine) habitually or excessively can be committed to treatment without their consent. Another example is seen in Florida, where Hillsborough County has an Involuntary Drug Court that can sentence a pregnant woman to jail for as long as 5 months and 29 days if she uses drugs or refuses treatment (Chasnoff & Lowder, 1999). Although putting pregnant women who use drugs in prison may seem like an easy solution, this approach is contraindicated on two fronts. First, it means committing women to involuntary commitment who would not be likely to be committed if they were not pregnant. Second, the conditions in involuntary treatment centers and jails may pose a new set of threats to fetal health.

Motivation for Responding to Alleged Fetal Abuse

While some argue that professionals must intervene in cases of fetal abuse to protect children and society, others feel that the motivation for punitive intervention may be more complex than that. Philosophy professors Sonya Charles and Tricha Shivas (2002) raise an interesting point regarding the reasons for punishing women who use drugs while pregnant. They point out that mothers who attempt to carry high-order multiple fetuses also put their fetuses at risk, and they are not punished. In fact, high-order multiple births, almost always the result of fertility treatments, may put fetuses at greater risk than would exposure to cocaine. Charles and Shivas compared the media's response to the case of the McCaughey septuplets with its response to cases of women who used illegal drugs (generally cocaine) while pregnant. They speculated that if the main societal concern was for fetal health, the cases should have been handled in a similar manner. This, of course, was not what they found. McCaughey was praised for her decision, she was called brave, and she was even referred to as an "expert parent." Forty-two percent of the articles about the McCaughey family mentioned the many gifts of products, time, and property that were showered on the family. None of them mentioned bringing criminal charges against Bobbi McCaughey for fetal abuse. In contrast, 40% of the articles about the mothers who used illegal drugs while pregnant made a direct analogy to abuse, 73% discussed punitive approaches, 31% made negative comments about the character of the mother, and none mentioned gifts. With regard to life after birth, only 10% of the articles about the McCaughey's septuplets mentioned concern with the children's welfare (despite the fact that the children were born with serious medical problems), while 31% of the articles about mothers who used drugs addressed concerns about the subsequent development of the involved children.

If prosecution is not exclusively about protecting the fetus, what is the motivation behind this type of legal action? One possibility is that the character of the mother is being attacked. While Bobbi McCaughey put her fetuses at risk because her religious convictions prevented selective reduction, drug-using mothers are seen as merely seeking self-gratification. The fact that this is an oversimplified and inaccurate view of addiction does not mean it is not a prevalent view. It may also be that some mothers are seen as deserving of support. In this comparison, a mother who has higher-order multiples deserves help to raise her at-risk children, but a drug-using mother does not. In both cases, the fetuses are harmed or at risk for harm, but only one set of mothers gets help to raise her child(ren) and prevent further harm (Charles & Shivas, 2002). So instead of treatment, drug-using mothers face criminal charges. Certainly, it does not escape notice that the mothers prosecuted for using drugs while pregnant are largely poor, minority women, while those using fertility treatments that can lead to higher-order multiples are mostly Caucasian and middle or upper class.

Prenatal Exposure and Risk for Harm After Birth.   It is possible that the concern for children who are exposed to drugs prenatally is that they will continue to be at risk for harm after they are born. Some states go so far as to state that a positive drug test at birth is de facto child abuse or neglect. In these states the positive toxicology report is considered a substantiated charge of abuse or neglect. In other states, even without such laws, children have been removed from their mother's care, temporarily or even permanently, based on positive drug screenings (Chasnoff & Lowder, 1999).

Some research exists that examines the relationship between prenatal drug exposure and later child maltreatment. In a study done in 1992, Kelly found that mothers who used cocaine while pregnant had a subsequent maltreatment rate of 23%. This was significantly higher than the rate of 3% among matched controls. Another study, conducted in Illinois, followed 513 infants who had been exposed to cocaine prenatally. The researchers found that 19.9% of the children had later been found to be maltreated. This was three times higher than the rate of matched peers. A link has also been established between mothers who use drugs while pregnant and previous charges of child maltreatment. After reviewing 3,436 cases in which children had been born with positive toxicology reports, it was found that 40% of the families had previous substantiated charges of child maltreatment against them. Even if one takes prenatal exposure out of the picture, parental substance abuse is a risk factor for child maltreatment. Living with a substance abuser increases a child's risk of being abused 2.9 times and the risk of being neglected 3.24 times (Chasnoff & Lowder, 1999).

While the statistics presented above do document increased risk, they do not prove that all children prenatally exposed to drugs will suffer from later maltreatment. In fact, if 23% of the mothers are found guilty, that means that 77% were not. Assuming that many of these mothers are doing an adequate job of raising their children (and not simply that they have not been "caught" yet), would removing all children be a disservice? Perhaps offering services to all families who share this risk would be the best approach. For now, it seems clear that decisions should be made on a case-by-case basis as opposed to following a blanket approach.

CONCLUSION

Because the recognition of this type of maltreatment has a very short history, there are many unanswered questions. The law is still developing with regard to fetal abuse. As more cases are prosecuted, the role of the justice system in addressing cases of alleged fetal abuse will be clarified. Issues of what punishment, if any, is appropriate need to be figured out, as do questions of custody for children who are prenatally exposed to drugs. In the meantime, child advocates are called upon to find ways to protect children by preventing fetuses from being exposed to toxins.

DISCUSSION QUESTIONS

1. Should the child maltreatment laws cover fetuses? Why or why not?
2. Which should be more important in assessing fetal abuse: the use of an illegal drug, or how harmful the drug is known to be to fetal development?
3. If a mother ingests a substance that she does not know may harm her fetus, is she guilty of maltreatment? What if she does not know she is pregnant?
4. If you were given a $5 million grant to prevent fetal abuse in your community, how would you spend the money?
5. Does the criminal prosecution of alleged fetal abuse ultimately protect children?
6. Given that we do not know what level of drug exposure might be safe for fetal development, should there be a zero-tolerance policy for drug use during pregnancy (e.g., even one glass of wine or one cigarette is abusive)?
7. Compared to the other types of maltreatment covered so far, would you be more or less comfortable reporting suspicions of fetal abuse?

DEFINITIONS

Fetal Abuse: maternal behaviors that put the fetus at risk for harm.

National Institute on Drug Abuse (NIDA): an organization dedicated to bringing the power of science to bear on issues of drug abuse and addiction by supporting research and disseminating research findings related to drug prevention, treatment, and policy.

Postpartum Depression: prolonged sadness, crying spells, impatience, or mood swings following the birth of a child; may include mixed feelings about motherhood and/or an inability to care for the newborn.

Polydrug: multiple, different drugs.

Alcohol: an intoxicating beverage containing a chemical produced by yeast fermentation or hydration of ethylene.

Fetal Alcohol Syndrome (FAS): a series of birth defects resulting from a mother's consumption of alcohol during pregnancy. Symptoms include mental retardation, low birth weight, head and face abnormalities, and growth deficiencies.

Dysmorphic: an abnormality of the structure of part of the body that results from a developmental defect.

Down Syndrome: a chromosomal abnormality (an extra copy of the 21st chromosome) that results in mental retardation, abnormal facial features (flattened nasal bridge, widely spaced and slanted eyes), slowed growth, and other physical problems.

Spina Bifida: a congenital abnormality in which the fetus's spinal cord does not form properly, leaving part of the spinal cord unprotected.

Fetal Alcohol Effects: symptoms present in a child that are associated with maternal alcohol consumption during pregnancy but which do not meet the diagnostic criteria for fetal alcohol syndrome.

Perinatal: occurring shortly before or shortly after birth.

Cocaine: a crystalline alkaloid that comes from coca leaves. It is used illicitly as a stimulant and to induce euphoria.

Congenital: a condition that is present at birth.

Sudden Infant Death Syndrome: the unexplained and unexpected death of an infant (less than a year old) who was apparently healthy; generally occurs during sleep.

Neurobehavioral: the study of the way the brain affects emotion, behavior, and learning; the assessment of a person's neurological status by observing his or her behavior.

Methamphetamine (MA): a potent, highly addictive central nervous system stimulant that causes an increase in energy and a decrease in appetite.

Cleft Palate: a congenital condition that results in a crack in the roof of the mouth.

Marijuana: the dried leaves and female flowers of the hemp plant that are used as an intoxicant. It can be smoked or eaten and it produces mild euphoria and possibly distorted perceptions.

Nicotine: a toxic, addictive substance derived from tobacco that acts as a stimulant.

Heroin: a highly addictive narcotic derived from morphine; it decreases the ability to perceive pain.

Methadone: a synthetic narcotic that is used to relive pain and as a heroin substitute during treatment for heroin addiction.

Buprenorphine: a medication used during the treatment of heroin addiction that prevents the experience of withdrawal symptoms.

Cannabinoids: the chemical compounds that are the active components of marijuana.

Racial Bias: a negative opinion, attitude, or response toward a group of people who share a common physical attribute such as skin color.

Civil Commitment: the confinement of a person who is ill, incompetent or drug-addicted.

CHAPTER 9

Munchausen by Proxy Syndrome

DEFINITION

Munchausen by proxy syndrome (MPS) is a rare form of child maltreatment in which the caretaker, usually the mother, fabricates, simulates, or induces symptoms of physical or psychological illness in a child. The *Diagnostic and Statistical Manual of Mental Disorders* (Fourth Edition), which lists all psychological disorders and their symptoms, refers to this set of behaviors as **factitious disorder by proxy**. While the name in the *Diagnostic and Statistical Manual* is more self-explanatory, the more popular name of **Munchausen syndrome** has an interesting history. Baron Munchausen was an 18th century German nobleman who joined the Russian military, and later entertained his guests with tales of his adventures in the Russo-Turkish War. The Baron's stories were essentially true; however, a man by the name of Rudolph Erich Raspe published *Baron Munchausen's Narratives of His Marvelous Travels and Campaigns in Russia* in 1785. This book contained outlandish tales attributed to the Baron, including riding cannon balls, escaping from a swamp by pulling himself up by his own hair, and even of travelling to the moon! The Baron sued Raspe, but his suit was unsuccessful. That the Baron actually told these tales seems unlikely, but it became common to use the name Munchausen to mean someone who lies and/or exaggerates the truth (Lasher & Sheridan, 2004).

It was based on this historical background that the label Munchausen syndrome was given to persons who sought medical attention for induced, faked, or greatly exaggerated symptoms. There are many in the field who find this name to be unfortunate, because the disorder has little to nothing to do with the Baron's circumstances. However, despite the use of factitious disorder in the *Diagnostic and Statistical Manual*, the label of Munchausen syndrome persists in common usage. Dr. Richard Asher first described Munchausen syndrome in 1951, but it was not until 1977 that Sir Roy Meadow, a pediatrician, coined the term Munchausen syndrome by proxy. Dr. Meadow used this new term in a short article to describe parents who exaggerate or induce illness in their children (a proxy) instead of themselves. In this first MPS publication, Meadow (1977) described two cases of MPS in detail. He described the children's alleged medical problems, the procedures performed by the doctors, and the mothers' behavior and attitudes. This article marked the beginning of the public discussion of MPS.

Exaggeration, Fabrication, and Induction

There are three categories of behavior that are seen in MPS. Some caregivers may show all three, but others do not. First, a parent may **exaggerate** the child's symptoms. In these cases the parent is deliberately embellishing a genuine problem. This exaggeration must be beyond the normal use of hyperbole. Many mothers who are not perpetrators of MPS will say, "He *always*..." or "it has happened a *million* times." The difference between a parent with MPS and a nonmaltreating parent is the motivation behind the exaggeration and the response to clarifying questions. While the maltreating mothers are deliberately misleading in order to get more attention, the normal mothers are just using exaggerated speech without malicious intent. If a doctor questions a mother who is not guilty of MPS, she will focus on giving a more precise, accurate, and truthful answer; however, a mother with MPS will insist her exaggeration is accurate (Lasher & Sheridan, 2004). Second, a caregiver may **fabricate** symptoms by saying a child has a symptom he or she does not have. For instance, a mother may report that her child had a seizure when no such event had occurred. Third, a parent may actually **induce** an illness in a child. The myriad ways that parents have either made their children appear or actually become ill are almost impossible to believe. The "mixing of foreign blood with body fluids and excretions, the addition of, salt to urine or blood specimens, friction or chemicals to produce a rash, heating a thermometer with a match, laxatives for diarrhea, using drugs, suffocation or **carotid** sinus pressure to cause seizures, and injections of milk or other infectious materials are only some examples of what may be encountered" (O'Shea, 2003, p. 37). While exaggerating or fabricating may not seem bad at first glance, these behaviors can lead to unpleasant and dangerous consequences for the child. If a parent insists that a child is ill, the child will be subjected to medical examinations and tests, some of which are invasive and painful (see Case Example 9.1).

CASE EXAMPLE 9.1

In the journal *Pediatrics*, Epstein, Markowitz, Gallo, Holmes, and Gryboski (1987) reported a case example of MPS that includes many of the classic traits of the disorder. Their report describes a male infant who was first hospitalized at 3 months of age for diarrhea. The boy spent 2 months in the hospital undergoing a large number of costly and sometimes painful tests, all of which showed normal results. During this time, a central line was implanted surgically so that he could receive adequate nutrition. When the diarrhea stopped abruptly, he was discharged and remained healthy until he was 18 months old. At that time, he was readmitted to the hospital for intractable diarrhea that began after he had received multiple treatments of antibiotics to treat an unresponsive ear infection. Once again, a central line catheter was surgically implanted and extensive tests were done. Just as before, all of the test results were normal.

At this point, several things began to arouse the doctors' suspicions. First, despite extensive diarrhea, the boy was gaining weight and he stayed well hydrated. Second, the diarrhea generally occurred only when the boy was awake, and it ceased when he was away from his room for tests or procedures. The mother also displayed many of the traits seen in persons who perpetrate MPS: she was excessively complimentary to the medical staff, she developed extremely close relationships with the nurses, her relationship with her husband was estranged, she appeared to be overprotective of her child, and she had previous experience as a nurse's aide.

When the mother was persuaded to spend some time away from the hospital, she remarked that her son was likely to improve in her absence. The boy's diarrhea did cease when she was away and returned within days of her being back by his side. When the child was moved to a multibed room that was under constant observation by nurses, the diarrhea stopped again.

After discussion among the physicians, a social worker, the hospital administrators, and the hospital attorney, the decision to use covert video surveillance was made. The child was again placed in a private room, and within a day the mother was observed injecting liquid into her son's mouth with a syringe. A search of the room revealed "oily syringes, castor oil, milk of magnesia, phenobarbital, amitriptyline, oral hypoglycemics and other unidentified pills" (Epstein et al., 1987, p. 221).

When the mother was confronted, she became extremely agitated and was admitted to a psychiatric hospital. Once separated from his mother, the boy's diarrhea stopped and he was returned to his father's care.

CASE POINTS

This case illustrates many of the common features seen in MPS: a young victim, odd and/or conflicting laboratory findings, maternal behavior that can be indicative of MPS, and improvement when the mother is absent.

This case also highlights the use of covert video surveillance in order to prove allegations of MPS.

DISCUSSION QUESTIONS

1. If you were the pediatrician in this case, how long do you think it would have taken you to suspect MPS? What characteristics of the case might have delayed your recognition of the problem?
2. Without the information gathered from the covert video surveillance, would you have been confident in making a diagnosis of MPS?

If you are interested in reading more extensive case summaries of MPS written by the victims, consider the following sources:

For an article about being the victim of MPS, read Bryk, M., & Siegel, P. T. (1997). My mother caused my illness: The story of a survivor of Munchausen by proxy syndrome, *Pediatrics,* 100(1), 1–7.

For a well-reviewed book about being the victim of MPS, read: Gregory, J. (2003). *Sickened: The memoir of a Munchausen by proxy childhood.* New York: Bantam Dell.

Although most cases of MPS involve medical symptoms, a parent may also fabricate, exaggerate, or induce psychological or even educational problems (see Focus on Research 9.1). In any type of MPS case, the parent's behavior is not simply the result of ignorance or misunderstanding of how to care for a child. The perpetrator shows clear evidence of planning, and the acts are calculated to avoid detection. Furthermore, these acts tend to be repeated over a long period of time. Children who are the victims of MPS end up with medical records that fill many files. When it can be determined, the average length of time between the onset of symptoms and the diagnosis of MPS is reported to be 21.8 months, nearly 2 years (Lasher & Sheridan, 2004).

VICTIMS

The victims of MPS are, most often, infants and toddlers. In a study of MPS in New Zealand, the median age at the time of diagnosis was 2.7 years, and 66% of the victims were under the

FOCUS ON RESEARCH 9.1   MUNCHAUSEN BY PROXY IN SPECIAL EDUCATION

Most presentations of MPS involve medical symptoms, but it is also possible that a mother will fabricate, exaggerate, or create educational symptoms. Ayoub, Schreier, and Keller (2002) use the term *educational condition or disability falsification* (ECF) to describe this sort of case. They conducted a case review of five families (nine children) where this was strongly suspected or confirmed. In all cases, the mothers insisted that their child (or children) had significant educational problems, even though testing and teacher reports did not confirm these maternal concerns.

    After reviewing these cases the authors presented the following results:

1. The victims: The average victim age at the time of diagnosis was 9.1 years, with a range of 7 to 13 years. The average time from the onset of symptoms until diagnosis was 5.3 years, with a range of 2 to 8 years. In three of the five families, more than one of the children was presented as disabled. The children showed a host of symptoms while their mothers were engaging in educational condition or disability falsification, including aggressive behavior and depression as well as hypervigilance.
2. The perpetrators: All perpetrators were Caucasian mothers who were divorced. Two of the mothers had factitious disorder, two had previously attempted suicide, four either currently held positions in the educational system or were studying the field, and three had been banned from their child's school.
3. The outcome: Three of the families (representing six children) were referred to child protective services (CPS). In all of these cases, the mothers were found to be guilty and the children were placed in out-of-home care with only supervised visits with their mothers. All of the children showed marked improvement in their symptoms once they were removed from their mother. All six children stopped receiving Ritalin and were removed from special education classrooms. The mothers in these cases still deny the allegations of educational condition or disability falsification and have resisted treatment. The two cases that were not referred to CPS involved three children. These children remained with their mothers and showed no improvement. In fact, all three were moved to more specialized and more restrictive educational settings.

The authors conclude that educational condition or disability falsification is harmful not only to the children but also to the schools. The mothers' actions cost the schools financially and the staff emotionally. For all of these reasons, it is important to identify educational condition or disability falsification. Finally, the authors caution that their results are limited due to their small sample size.

age of 5 years (Denny, Grant, & Pinnock, 2001). Sheridan (2003) concluded, based on a review of the MPS literature, that most victims are 4 years of age or younger. Young children are particularly vulnerable to this type of maltreatment because they are not capable of speaking up for themselves and telling medical professionals what is actually occurring. It is not uncommon for a perpetrator to switch to a younger victim once their original victim begins to speak. One study revealed that 39% of children who were the victims of MPS had at least one sibling who had also suffered from a fabricated illness (O'Shea, 2003). This does not mean, however, that older children are never victims. MPS has been diagnosed with victims ranging from 1 month to 21 years of age (Moldavsky & Stein, 2003), and approximately 25% of all victims of MPS are over the age of 6 years.

What might make an older child go along with his or her mother's claims? One 14-year-old boy who had undergone 40 surgeries between the ages of 8 and 14 years reported that his mother promised him expensive rewards if he cooperated during a hospital stay. This same boy later revealed that his mother would frequently beat him with a belt. In this case, the mother used both reward and punishment to get her son to go along with her fabricated stories. In addition, many children are strongly motivated to maintain a relationship with their parents, even if the parents hurt them (Awadallah et al., 2005).

Male and female children are equally likely to be victimized in this way, and female perpetrators are as likely to have female victims as they are to have male victims. Male perpetrators are more likely to have male victims, but it is rare to find a male perpetrator (Parnell, 2002).

PERPETRATORS

The majority (at least 76.5%) of perpetrators of MPS are mothers, while fathers make up less than 3% of perpetrators. The other perpetrators are female caregivers such as grandmothers, foster mothers, and babysitters (Feldman, 2004). One possible explanation for this sex discrepancy is that women are largely in charge of children's healthcare, so they have more opportunities to fake illnesses (Parnell, 2002). Because most perpetrators of MPS are mothers, I will use "mother" throughout this chapter to refer to the alleged perpetrator. Racial information on perpetrators of MPS has not been consistently recorded, so the data is incomplete in this area. In an analysis of 33 cases that documented race, 26 of the perpetrators (78.79%) were Caucasian (Sheridan, 2003). When compared to the perpetrators of other types of child maltreatment, parents engaging in MPS tend to be older and better off financially (i.e., you do not see the preponderance of young, low-class perpetrators like you do with neglect or physical abuse; Meadow, 1982).

Perpetrators of MPS generally appear to be normal and good mothers who are concerned with their child's welfare (Meadow, 1977). Very few mothers charged with MPS have any previous involvement with child protective services (CPS). However, upon careful study, they may be found to be good liars and manipulators who are simply doing a good job of portraying themselves as doting mothers. One striking finding is that many of these women have a good deal of knowledge about healthcare and are more likely to have worked in a health-related field than are other mothers. Between 14.16% and 30% of MPS perpetrators have been either employed or trained in a field related to health, most commonly nursing (Rosenberg, 1996; Sheridan, 2003). This gives them the necessary background to induce or make up credible symptoms. Perpetrators of MPS tend to have a dramatic flair, and they may seek attention from a wide variety of sources including professionals and nonprofessionals. Many of these mothers have a history of being abused themselves, and they are more likely than others to have dealt with a somatizing disorder, borderline personality disorder, or depression (Bools, Neale, & Meadow, 1994; Moldavsky & Stein, 2003). However, it is not true that all perpetrators of MPS have a mental illness. In a good number of cases, the mothers have not received any diagnostic labels beyond MPS (Meadow, 1982). If the mother is challenged by the medical staff that is caring for her child, she is likely to deny the allegations but not to stop the behavior. Instead, she will take her child to other doctors who have not questioned her motivations. This "doctor shopping" can result in the child being subjected to even more medical procedures.

INCIDENCE

It is not clear how common MPS is at this time, and data for the U.S. is particularly lacking. Some incidence studies indicate that it is quite rare in other countries. For instance, Adshead and Bluglass (2001) report that the incidence of MPS in the UK is between 0.1 and 0.8 cases per

100,000. The incidence is a bit higher in New Zealand, 2 cases per 100,000, but still uncommon (Denny, Grant, & Pinnock, 2001). Although a systematic study of incidence is lacking, there are over 550 published case reports of MPS from over 30 countries (Lasher & Sheridan, 2004), which means that professionals across the globe are starting to pay attention to this form of child maltreatment. One estimate is that there are approximately 1,200 new cases of MPS reported each year in the U.S. (Feldman, 2004). Some medical doctors are beginning to express their belief that MPS may be more common than was generally thought but that it often goes unrecognized. Sir Roy Meadow cites Goethe, who wrote, "We see only what we know," to indicate that as doctors learn to look for MPS, there may well be an increase in documented cases (Meadow, 1982). As recently as 1988, a survey of pediatric nursing staff revealed that 55% had never even heard of MPS and 70% did not feel prepared to handle such a case (Feldman, 2004).

RISK FACTORS

An obvious question is, "What would motivate a parent to fake or create illness in her own child?" The motivation for MPS is complex, but it appears that the mothers are drawn to the attention they receive because their child is ill. Playing the role of "mother to a seriously ill child" becomes their claim to fame. Mothers crave the gratification that comes from being seen as a good, attentive mother. They like being seen as a woman willing to be a martyr for her child by giving up her own life to remain at her child's side. It may be that an MPS mother first had a child with a true illness or had a child who had died, which resulted in attention and support. Denny, Grant, and Pinnock (2001) reported that more than half of the victims of MPS in their study (55%) had an underlying chronic illness. They speculated that early exposure to intense medical attention when caring for a newborn may make a mother who is otherwise isolated crave this sort of attention. Once the true crises passed, they needed to create new situations that would elicit the same type of response. Some mothers seem particularly motivated to maintain a relationship with the medical community. They are comfortable in medical settings such as hospitals, and they want to feel a part of the unit. For some mothers, an additional benefit is that being in the hospital with a child relieves them of all other parenting responsibilities. A mother with a very ill child cannot, after all, be expected to cook, clean, or do laundry. Neglecting these tasks to care for a sick child is not frowned upon. In fact, others are eager to cover the more mundane aspects of childcare while the mother attends to her ill child.

In some cases, this need for attention predates their maternal role. For about 10% of MPS perpetrators, their first victim was themselves; before making their child ill, they suffered from Munchausen syndrome. The theory that MPS perpetrators are motivated by a need for attention is supported by the finding that many MPS mothers report that they have a poor relationship with the child's father (Moldavsky & Stein, 2003). It may be that when their partner is not meeting their need for attention, they use the child to force others to pay attention, or they use the sick child to force their spouse to engage with the family. Furthermore, spouses with very conflicted relationships may find that their arguing ceases when they face a common adversity such as a child's illness. However, the relationship between MPS and poor spousal relationship is only a correlational finding, so we cannot assume cause and effect. It is possible that some third factor causes women to have poor spousal relationships and to commit MPS.

It is also possible that a woman who had a good relationship with her spouse would not harm her child out of love for her spouse (i.e., she would not hurt him by hurting his child). If this is the case, a poor spousal relationship would fail to prevent MPS but would not cause it.

Some experts stress that the diagnosis of MPS should only apply to mothers who are motivated by the desire for medical attention, but others have noted that you may see the same behaviors for other reasons. A possible motivation for MPS behaviors may be that the mother

LEGAL EXAMPLE 9.1

Lorena Victorina Hernandez was charged with child abuse after she injected her 9-month-old, nondiabetic son, Isaiah, with insulin. The case was discovered when Isaiah was brought to the hospital, where he fell into a coma. The boy's blood sugar levels were dangerously low, and manufactured insulin was detected in his blood. The injection could have been fatal, but Isaiah did survive. Investigation revealed that Hernandez had used her mother's diabetes supplies to inject her son on at least two occasions.

At trial, Hernandez's attorney claimed that Hernandez was not guilty because she suffered from MPS. Terry Bowman, the district attorney, argued that while MPS may explain what Hernandez did, it did not excuse the behavior. Hernandez's defense was not successful, and she was convicted of two counts of child abuse (Romano, 2001).

is desperate to keep the child at home with her. She does not want the child to start school or even to go to a friend's house. The mother is so attached to the child that she cannot tolerate the idea of separation. It is socially unacceptable to keep a healthy child socially isolated; however, a mother who forgoes all outings to be with her ill child will receive only praise. Many researchers have noted that MPS mothers seem to be overly attached to their children. In one case report, a mother actually attended school with her daughter so that she could monitor her at all times. The mother did this despite the fact that there was already in-class nursing supervision (von-Hahn et al., 2001).

Finally, a less selfish motivation for MPS behaviors may be that the mother is seeking help with parenting. In this scenario, the mother would be so overwhelmed by parenting and so worried that she will fail on her own that she would do whatever was necessary to ensure that others will help her.

Regardless of the mother's motivation, MPS is considered a form of child abuse and not only a psychological disorder. Most perpetrators of MPS do not have any symptoms of psychological problems beyond what they are doing to their children. To this end, mothers who attempt to use MPS as a legal defense when they are charged with making their children ill have not been successful (see Legal Example 9.1).

CONSEQUENCES OF MPS

A review of the literature shows that all victims of MPS suffer at least in the short-term. In cases where symptoms are induced, the child will be subjected to the pain, suffering, and injury that are inflicted. Serious cases may result in permanent physical damage to the child. In approximately 7% of cases, long-term or permanent disability is documented (Sheridan, 2003). One common effect of MPS is the development of feeding disorders because so many cases involve negative interactions around feedings (e.g., when food is contaminated, when vomiting is induced, or when food is withheld). Other doctors have reported that victims of MPS suffer psychological as well as physical effects. These victims are immature, they are overly dependent on their mothers, and they suffer from **separation anxiety**. The children may also be more irritable and more aggressive than their peers (McGuire & Feldman, 1989). Finally, some studies have noted attention deficits, poor school performance, and symptoms of post-traumatic stress disorder in these children (Moldavsky & Stein, 2003).

In situations with fabricated, exaggerated, or induced symptoms, children will face painful medical tests and procedures and may suffer from taking unnecessary medication or even hospitalization. In a review of 19 children, Meadow (1982) noted that the greatest physical harm to the children was inflicted by the doctors, not directly by the mothers. The time spent seeking medical treatment is also time taken from normal social and educational experiences, so the child suffers from missed opportunities as well. This is an indirect effect, but it can be a substantial one. If a mother is trying to convince the world that her child is gravely ill, she cannot let the child out to play or even to attend school. For example, one 6-year-old male victim spent a full 13 months out of school, and he was hospitalized for 5 of those months (Meadow, 1982). Another indirect effect of MPS is that the child's siblings may be injured. Research on MPS victims shows that 25% of their siblings are deceased and 61.32% of their siblings have symptoms of illness with no known cause (Lasher & Sheridan, 2004; Sheridan, 2003). A third, indirect effect is tied to cases where mental illness is faked. In these cases, the child is likely to suffer from embarrassment and shame because of the stigma that can be attached to hospitalization in a psychiatric ward (Lasher & Sheridan, 2004). In addition, children who are found to be the victims of MPS may be removed from their homes. While this stops the abuse, it also means that the children may lose contact with many or all members of their family. Of course, the worst possible cases are those that are fatal. It is estimated that MPS has a mortality rate that is between 6% and 10% (Schreier & Libow, 1993; Sheridan, 2003). The victims who die seem to represent the lower age range of all MPS victims. In an examination of 21 MPS deaths, the average age at the time of death was 18.83 months (Sheridan, 2003).

As the child ages, if the abuse does not stop, the child may begin to aid the parent in the deception, and the child may develop Munchausen syndrome as an adult (Epstein, Markowitz, Gallo, Holmes, & Gryboski, 1987). It is not clear why the child would continue this painful cycle, but Libow (2002) suggested that if the child becomes the initiator, he may achieve a sense of control missing when the parent was creating the symptoms. An alternative theory, also proposed by Libow, is that the child may be angry with the doctors for failing to protect him or her and seeks revenge by tricking or deceiving the doctors.

Adult Survivors

Almost no research exists that examines which effects of MPS may persist into adulthood. One exception is the work of Libow (1995) that involved interviewing 10 self-identified, adult survivors of MPS and having them complete a questionnaire and a post-traumatic stress disorder checklist. Although this was a small, nonrandom sample and a retrospective design, it provides a first look at what MPS victims might be like as adults.

All of these adults reported that they were aware that something was wrong or unusual about their experiences as children, and all felt unloved and unsafe. Four of the 10 tried to tell an adult about the abuse, but none were believed. While this may seem shocking, imagine that a child you believe to have serious medical problems tells you that his mother made him drink something that tasted funny and made him sick. Would you think MPS, or would you assume this child did not like to take medicine?

As adults, all victims placed the blame on the perpetrator (nine mothers and one father), and simply saw the other parent, who failed to protect them, as weak. At the time of the study, eight of the abusing parents were still alive, and four of the adult children had some contact with them, but none had a close relationship with the offending parent. No parent had admitted to abusing his or her child (Libow, 1995).

Furthermore, only two of the participants felt that their experience with MPS had not had a significant impact on their adult life. The other eight reported lasting negative effects from the MPS. The commonly stated problems resulting from being the victim of MPS included, "a struggle to avoid playing the victim role, difficulty maintaining relationships, insecurity and 'constantly doubting myself,' a fruitless search for mother's love, and difficulty separating fantasy from reality—especially in relation to illness and the need for medical treatment" (Libow,

1995, p. 1137). Not only did the participants admit difficulties to researchers, but seven of them had previously sought psychiatric/psychological services. On the checklist administered by the author, the participants' responses indicated a significant degree of post-traumatic stress disorder. On a positive note, it did not appear than any of the participants were repeating the MPS on their own children. Despite these preliminary findings, much more research is needed on survivors of MPS across their life span.

INVESTIGATION OF MPS

If medical professionals suspect MPS, they should begin a careful review of the alleged victim's chart. One indicator of MPS is a child who presents with multiple problems that do not respond to traditional treatment. In other words, the treatment that is prescribed based on the history given by the parent does not result in the expected alleviation of symptoms. A second indicator is odd or conflicting laboratory findings that do not support the symptoms reported by the parents. Medical staff should also check the signs of illness carefully. For instance, blood in the child's stool or vomit may not even be the child's blood. Some mothers add their own blood to their child's feces or vomit to simulate illness. While a hospital may not be able to differentiate a mother's blood from her child's blood, a police **forensic** laboratory could assist (Meadow, 1982). To this end, specimens from children should be kept for detailed examination in cases where there is suspicion. Doctors should also look for a discrepancy between the medical history of the child provided by the mother and the clinical findings and/or the general health of the child. Medical staff might also become suspicious if there is a previous, unexplained child death in the family. Another suspicious finding is when the child's symptoms decrease when the alleged perpetrator is away, and return or increase when contact is resumed (Moldavsky & Stein, 2003).

With regard to the attitude of the caregiver, doctors look for parents who do not seem to be relieved by good news (or who go so far as to be angry about negative test results), who appear to enjoy the hospital environment, and/or who are unusually calm when confronted with medical problems. These mothers may appear excited about invasive procedures that most parents would be reluctant to allow before they were convinced that the tests were absolutely necessary (Meadow, 1982). Perpetrators of MPS also have a tendency to take over the child's medical care to a degree that is far greater than normal. They are also described as overly attentive to their children when staff is present (Moldavsky & Stein, 2003). Finally, doctors assess how the caregiver interacts with them. Parents who are guilty of MPS tend to have extreme responses to doctors. On the one hand they may be particularly encouraging of the doctors, and on the other hand they will express intense anger at the doctors and constantly switch doctors in search for one who will give them the attention they crave. Some parents also prohibit the dismissed doctors from sharing medical information with other physicians who become involved with the case.

Individually, none of these indicators proves that the case involves MPS, but a cluster of them should raise suspicion. Unfortunately, it is feared that many cases of MPS go undetected because medical personnel fail to consider the possibility that the parent is making the child ill. Given the rarity of MPS and the very real concern of most parents, this is understandable. However, if doctors are suspicious, they are advised to put together a multi-disciplinary team to investigate the case. Parnell (2002) suggests that the team should include the following personnel: "child protective services worker, law enforcement officer, psychologist or psychiatrist, prosecutor, hospital social worker, nurse, pediatrician, and other members of the child's medical team" (p. 134). She further recommends that the team should include a physician who specializes in MPS and that the team should meet quickly. While this certainly seems to be a sound plan, it may be a challenge to get so many professionals together to discuss an event that is statistically unlikely. Once gathered, the team should review all of the child's medical records with MPS in mind. They should also conduct an "educated toxicology work-up." Instead of testing for conditions suggested by the history provided by the parents, the doctors should look specifically for signs of MPS.

Separation of Parent and Child

If this review is inconclusive, further investigation is necessary. Two courses of action, both controversial, may be pursued. One involves limiting the access that the suspected parent has to the child, and not allowing that parent to participate in the child's care. This approach will generally require a court order. If professionals are able to separate the parent and the child, they can determine whether the child improves in the absence of the caregiver. However, because it seems counterintuitive to separate an ill child from his or her parent, judges may be reluctant to grant such a request.

Covert Video Surveillance

A second way to pursue suspicions of MPS is via **covert video surveillance**, generally in a hospital setting. This involves making audio and/or video recordings of events in a child's room without the knowledge or consent of the involved family. This approach raises issues concerning cost, legalities, and ethics (see Focus on Research 9.2).

The Fourth Amendment to the U.S. Constitution protects citizens from unreasonable search and seizure. This has been interpreted to mean that information cannot be collected from any place where you can reasonably expect privacy unless there is probable cause that has been demonstrated to the court and a warrant has been obtained. If evidence is collected in violation of the Fourth Amendment, it is not admissible in court. However, the court has allowed exceptions to this rule in cases where there is imminent threat to human life. What this means for covert video surveillance is that it would be clearly permissible in cases where the hospital has obtained a warrant prior to recording. It is less certain that hospitals can record without a warrant based on the exception of imminent threat, because it generally does not take long to get a warrant and most MPS cases go on for months or even years before being diagnosed. If a doctor has had suspicions for months, it could be difficult to argue that waiting one day for a warrant would result in a threat to life. Another approach that has been argued by hospitals is that patients cannot reasonably expect privacy in the hospital. A patient is in the hospital specifically to be monitored by medical staff. Certainly, if you have ever been in a hospital, you know that you are not granted much privacy! Even Ron Madick, the director of the **American Civil Liberties Union** (ACLU), has stated that the use of covert video surveillance in hospitals is permissible because the expectation of privacy in such a setting is so low. Given that the goal of the American Civil Liberties Union is to protect our constitutional liberties, this is a strong statement in favor of covert video surveillance (Morrision, 1999).

A more practical concern about the use of covert video surveillance is the expense involved. Not only do hospitals have to pay for the equipment, but they must also pay staff to monitor the surveillance in real time. If a mother is taped while smothering her child and intervention is not begun immediately, the hospital may be considered negligent. The cost of constant monitoring can quickly deplete a budget.

Hospitals also face concerns of being considered negligent if they do not use covert video surveillance in cases where there is suspicion of MPS, or if they use covert video surveillance and the child is harmed. Some argue that it may be better to seek a court order to separate the child from the alleged perpetrator instead of performing surveillance that still allows the child to be harmed (Foreman & Farsides, 1993). However, because courts are reluctant to separate ill children from their parents, this may not always be feasible. One final concern about covert

Hall, Eubanks, Meyyazhagan, Kenney, and Johnson (2000) wanted to determine the value of covert video surveillance in diagnosing MPS. From 1993 until 1997, 41 patients were monitored via covert video surveillance at Children's Healthcare of Atlanta at Scottish Rite when their doctors suspected MPS. The rooms were wired with multiple cameras that recorded audio and video information. All parts of the patients' rooms, except the bathroom, were monitored. Before any patient was taped, a multi-disciplinary team convened to discuss the case and whether covert video surveillance was appropriate. The team only elected to use covert video surveillance when they had agreed that a diagnosis of MPS was more than likely.

The hospital secured permission for covert recording in two ways. First, they posted a sign at the entrance to the hospital that said the facility was monitored and recorded via hidden cameras. Second, the hospital admission forms for consent to treatment contained the statement, "Closed circuit monitoring of patient care may be used for educational or clinical purposes" (p. 2 of 20). No patients or parents were directly informed that they were being recorded.

Once covert video surveillance began, trained security guards monitored a live feed 24 hours a day. In order to keep the monitors alert, they watched for only an hour at a time. Logs were kept that detailed what happened in the room, and a floor nurse was paged immediately if the guard saw any suspicious behavior. When necessary, the nurse would intervene to protect the child. Finally, all instances of possible MPS were reviewed by hospital supervisors. The average length of observation was 3.57 days.

Evidence of MPS was found in 23 (56%) of the cases, but was not detected in 18 (44%) of the cases. Of these 18 cases, four of the mothers seemed to know that they were being observed. These mothers looked for cameras and made comments about being watched. In the 23 cases where inappropriate parental behavior was seen, the recording was necessary for the diagnosis of MPS in 13 (56.5%) cases, supportive of the diagnosis in 5 (21.7%) cases and not needed in 5 (21.7%) cases. In the 5 cases where the video was not needed, 2 were confirmed by laboratory tests of drug levels, 2 by staff observation of abuse, and 1 by a maternal confession following confrontation.

The videos revealed the following behaviors:

4 suffocations
1 injection of a bodily fluid (urine)
5 instances of oral medication administration
1 gastrostomy tube medication administration
1 burn
10 instances of fabrication

In addition to these behaviors, mothers were heard coaching their children to fabricate symptoms. Mothers were also recorded telling lies to family and friends on the phone. One mother reported that her child was having constant seizures, when in fact no seizures were observed. Some of the mothers were also seen to be extremely attentive to their children while others were present, only to virtually ignore the children when they were alone. After confrontation with the video, 9 of 20 cases (45%) resulted in a maternal confession. The maternal response in 3 of the confirmed cases was not known.

With regard to demographic variables, the authors reported that all perpetrators were mothers who were an average of 24.8 years old. Fifty-five percent of these mothers had a history of healthcare work or study, and another 25% had worked in a daycare. Thirty-five percent of the guilty mothers reported a history of having been abuse victims themselves. Ninety-three percent of the mothers were Caucasian, which is greater than the percentage of Caucasians in the general hospital population (68%). While some of the mothers fit the stereotype of MPS perpetrators (great interest in and enthusiasm for medical tests, poor relationship with spouse, extremely close to medical staff), none of these factors was sufficient to prove MPS.

The victims of MPS were as likely to be male (13) as female (10). The average age of the victims at the time of diagnosis was 26 months. Only one victim had a sibling who had died. When this mother was confronted with the current case of MPS, she also admitted to having smothered the sibling.

In four cases, the covert video surveillance resulted in the realization that the mothers were innocent despite strong suspicion of MPS. No instances of inducing or fabrication were seen on the videos, and in one case the child's true symptoms were recorded, which confirmed the mother's reports.

The authors conclude that covert video surveillance is a valuable tool for the diagnosis of MPS. In many cases, MPS would go unproven if the videos were not available, and the child would be exposed to further pain and danger. In addition to catching guilty parents, covert video surveillance can also show when parents are innocent. The authors believe that the efficacy of covert video surveillance overrides the ethical concerns inherent in the procedure. They also argue that covert video surveillance is not likely to be overused because it is only begun when a team of professionals believes it is necessary. In addition, covert video surveillance is an expensive process that is not covered by insurance, so hospitals would be motivated to use it judiciously. Covert video surveillance is an important tool in protecting children.

video surveillance is that it may interfere with the trust relationship between a family and their doctor. For now, each patient's situation is assessed on a case-by-case basis by the medical staff along with legal consultation.

CONTROVERSIES RELATED TO MPS

Despite an increase in the interest in and attention to MPS, there are still many unanswered questions. Although there has been a significant increase in the number of articles and books published about MPS in the last decade, these publications are mostly the presentations of case studies or theoretical papers. There is still a definite lack of empirical research on this disorder (Mart, 2002). This lack of definitive data underlies the many controversial issues surrounding MPS.

Who Should Be Diagnosed with MPS?

One of the first questions is who is diagnosed with MPS. Is this a diagnosis given to the parent or to the child? If it is a diagnosis given to the parent, it is complicated because it is largely based on the parent's motivation. If a parent is to meet the criteria for MPS he or she must be making the child ill in order to receive attention from others. What if the parent is making the child ill in order for some other type of gain? For instance, a parent may make the child ill in order to get money or earn an advantage in a custody battle. In these situations, the child would still be ill, but MPS does not fit. The American Professional Society on the Abuse of Children suggests that children who are made ill or simply described as ill when they are not be diagnosed with **pediatric condition falsification** (PCF). This diagnosis would say nothing about the parent's motivation, but it would simply describe what is happening to the child. In addition, the case could involve MPS if the parent's motivation was attention, but this would not always be the motivation. If the medical professionals could not determine the parental motivation or if they thought the motive was to gain something other than attention, they would not diagnose MPS. So, you could have pediatric condition falsification without MPS, but you could not have MPS without pediatric condition falsification (Mart, 2004).

Focus on Motivation or Harm?

Some professionals argue that we should not try to determine something as subjective as motivation at all. Instead, we should simply focus on and describe the behaviors that are harming the child. However, parental motivation does become important if the case goes to court. A possible compromise is to have a two-tiered approach to diagnosis. First, the specific acts committed could be described without any prejudicial labels. Then, the second tier would involve an analysis of the perpetrator's behavior. What is the parent gaining by this behavior? Does the perpetrator suffer from some sort of psychopathology? How serious is the behavior? The answers to these questions would be important not only in determining guilt in a court case, but also in devising treatment programs for the family if the child is to remain in their care (Mart, 2004).

The Placement of the Disorder in the *Diagnostic and Statistical Manual*

This lack of definitional clarity is highlighted by the position of the factitious disorder by proxy in the *Diagnostic and Statistical Manual*. Factitious disorder by proxy is not listed among the official diagnoses, but it is found in an appendix entitled "Criteria Sets and Axes Provided for Further Study." The manual's authors warn that the diagnoses in this section can only be considered tentative because the research supporting them is insufficient (Mart, 2002).

Malingering by Proxy

What if the parent coaches the child to fake symptoms in order to obtain something external, such as money? In these cases, the term **malingering by proxy** may be used. Consider the following case. A 13-year-old boy was injured in an accident at school. A concession stand window fell, cutting his hand, and he was pushed against a building. He was taken to the emergency room where he received sutures. The doctor who treated him noted that there was no injury to his tendons. Over the next year, the boy was taken repeatedly to the emergency room and to doctors' offices, where he received many tests. The complaints were that the boy would frequently drop things, his hand would shake, he suffered from numbness and he had a limited range of motion. Two things were suspicious about the case. First, the mother did most of the talking for the boy even though he did not disagree with her, and he did hold his arm stiffly. Second, none of the tests revealed any signs of damage. It should also be noted that the family was involved in litigations with the school where the accident had occurred. In this case, video surveillance revealed that the boy did have full range of motion, and the litigation was stopped. In other cases, mothers have falsely reported behavioral problems in their children in order to obtain disability benefits after the children received a psychiatric diagnosis (Stutts, Hickey, & Kasdan, 2003). Using the criteria recommended by the American Professional Society on the Abuse of Children, these children could all receive the diagnosis of pediatric condition falsification with the additional note of parental malingering by proxy.

Incorrect Diagnoses

A second concern is the possibility of a false diagnosis of MPS. Imagine how terrible it would be if you were separated from your seriously ill child because the medical professionals were suspicious of your behavior. As awareness of MPS increases, it is likely that the rate of false positive diagnoses will also increase. (A false positive is a case where a diagnosis of MPS is made when, in fact, the child is not being maltreated.) There is some evidence of an increased rate of false positives in the U.S. and the UK, based on the fact that we have seen an increase in the number of cases where parents have been convicted of MPS and later exonerated after further examination of the case (Mart, 2004). The concern about false positives is tied to the fact that MPS is rare and, therefore, has a low base rate. For instance, one common manifestation of MPS is sleep apnea (the child stops breathing while asleep). In cases of MPS this is either fabricated or induced by the parent. However, a doctor would not want to assume that a child with sleep apnea was the victim of MPS. In one study of 20,090 cases of sleep apnea, only 54 (0.27%) involved the suspicion of MPS. In another study of 340 infants with serious, episodic health problems, only 5 cases (1.5%) involved likely MPS (Mart, 1999). What these studies show is that because MPS is rare, the explanation for most child illnesses is not MPS, but a true medical condition.

Certainly, the stories of false positive diagnoses of MPS can be heartbreaking. One mother was charged with MPS after her infant died. After she had served 5 years in prison, her conviction was overturned when it was discovered that her child had died of a rare medical condition (spontaneous methylmalonic acidemia) that had been unrecognized (Rand & Feldman, 1999). Here you have a case where an innocent mother was sent to prison while she was grieving the loss of her infant. Other mothers have been kept away from their very ill children because medical doctors suspected MPS. Unfortunately, in some of these cases, the child died of an unrecognized, true illness while the mother was not present. Some of these mothers are fighting back by suing the doctors for this horrible mistake. A group of women who say they were falsely accused of MPS have gone so far as to form an organization they call MAMA (Mothers Against Munchausen by Proxy Allegations).

Suggestions to Prevent Misdiagnoses.　After reviewing 11 cases of misdiagnosed MPS, Rand and Feldman (1999) offered the following suggestions. First, they encouraged professionals not to rely on subjective criteria. Although many parents who are guilty of MPS are unusually attached to their children, this is also true of many parents who are not maltreating their children. Using unhealthy attachment to diagnose MPS would result in a very high false positive rate. The same can be true of other subjective criteria, such as having an unhealthy interest in the child's medical situation or being resentful toward doctors who say the child is not ill. Many professionals note that MPS mothers are extremely demanding. While this may be true, other mothers may be demanding because they sincerely believe their children are ill and/or because they have done a great deal of research on the condition, and they feel informed enough to be assertive. Doctors must be careful not to assume any aggressive mother is making her child ill. Even if these are warning signs of MPS, none of them is a confirming sign.

Second, doctors are encouraged to do a complete review of all medical records and discuss those records with the parent. A mother who is engaging in MPS may take her child to many doctors and have many tests done, and the same could be true of a parent who is not abusive. If a mother believes her child is ill and her current doctor cannot find a problem, it would seem appropriate to seek a second and even a third opinion. Also, many doctors want to run their own tests instead of relying on forwarded tests from other offices. A thorough discussion with the mother could shed more light on the situation.

Rand and Feldman (1999) also caution that just because a child improves in his or her mother's absence does not prove that the mother is making the child ill. It may simply mean that the most recent treatment is working for the child, and the separation is a coincidence. In fact, many childhood illnesses do improve with time, so the illness may have simply run its course. Related to this point, an illness that has an unusual course does not necessarily mean MPS. It is also possible that the child has been misdiagnosed, especially if there is an underlying medical problem that is rare (Mart, 1999).

Certainly, exaggeration does not necessarily mean MPS. A parent may be using exaggeration to get the child's case prioritized. If the mother feels that her child is not receiving adequate, needed attention, she may be motivated to exaggerate in order to get the child the care that she truly believes is needed. Doing what you deem necessary to ensure that the doctors pay attention to your sick child does not seem like child maltreatment. It is also possible that the mother sees every symptom in her child as a sign of a major problem. While she may well be wrong, she is not trying to make the child appear ill to gain attention; she is genuinely concerned about her child's health (Mart, 1999).

Another common pitfall in the diagnosis of MPS is the belief that parents who are guilty of MPS will deny the abuse when they are confronted. While this is true in most cases, what about the parent who is *not* guilty of MPS? If a doctor asks an innocent person about making his or her child ill, this person will also say no. Because there are many more innocent parents than guilty parents, one cannot assume that a denial of abuse is proof of maltreatment. In some cases, parents have been told that they cannot see their child until they admit to making the child sick. Obviously, a "confession" based on this type of coercion is problematic. If your child is ill, it is possible that you would say or do anything in order to get to his or her side.

Expert Testimony Regarding MPS

Added to the inherent difficulty in diagnosing cases of MPS is the controversy concerning expert testimony provided by Dr. Meadow, who first identified the disorder. Dr. Meadow became a frequent expert witness in cases of MPS in Britain, especially in cases where a family had experienced the loss of more than one child to cot death (known as sudden infant death syndrome in the U.S.). His now infamous dictum that one infant death was a tragedy, two were suspicious, and three were murder became known as Meadow's law. Dr. Meadow testified, as an expert, that the chance of two babies dying this way in one family was 1 in 73 million. He arrived at this number by starting with the chance that one child in a middle-class, nonsmoking home would die of cot death (1 in 8,500) and squaring it. The problem with this approach is that it works only if the event in question is totally random (like the roll of a dice). However, it is quite likely that cot death is a nonrandom event that has some unknown cause, possibly genetic (The probability of injustice, 2004).

After several controversial cases were appealed in Great Britain, the appeals court ruled that a mother could not be convicted in a case of cot death based solely on the testimony of an expert witness. The court also ordered the review of 258 cases in which parents had been accused of murder, and 5,000 cases of children taken into care based on Meadow's testimony (Cohen, 2004). While this ruling found that Meadow's statistical testimony was inaccurate, it did not find that MPS is not possible. The courts merely urged prosecutors to rely more on the medical facts of the case and less on analysis of maternal behavior beyond the direct acts against the child.

CONCLUSION

The history of documented MPS is a short one, so as may be expected, there are still many difficulties to iron out. As more professionals become educated about MPS, it is likely that more research will be conducted on this disorder. Having more information will hopefully mean that precise recommendations can be made in the future. It is also possible that medical advances will help to clarify many of the issues that relate to diagnosing MPS. Just as the invention of the x-ray machine dramatically improved the diagnosis of child physical abuse, the development of more sensitive blood tests may eventually make it easier to detect MPS. The goal in dealing with

MPS, as in all areas of child maltreatment, is to protect children who are being harmed without interfering with families who are not abusive.

DISCUSSION QUESTIONS

1. Which term do you think is the best description of the behaviors described in this chapter: Munchausen by proxy syndrome, factitious disorder by proxy, or pediatric condition falsification? Why?
2. Some people argue that only medical doctors need to know about MPS. What arguments could you suggest to counter that claim?
3. Compared to the other types of maltreatment covered in this text book, would you be more or less comfortable reporting suspicions of MPS to CPS?
4. Many people confuse hypochondria and Munchausen syndrome. How would you differentiate between these conditions?
5. Is there any way to prevent cases of MPS? If so, what type of prevention program do you think might be effective?
6. Is it ethical to use covert video surveillance in cases of suspected MPS?

DEFINITIONS

Munchausen by Proxy Syndrome (MPS): a rare form of child maltreatment in which the caretaker, usually the mother, fabricates, exaggerates, or induces symptoms of physical or psychological illness in a child.

Factitious Disorder by Proxy: the term used by the *Diagnostic and Statistical Manual of Mental Disorders* to describe the behaviors also referred to as Munchausen by proxy syndrome.

Munchausen Syndrome: a psychiatric disorder that involves exaggerating or creating symptoms of illness in oneself, or acting as if ill, in order to receive attention and sympathy.

Exaggerate: to overstate; to increase to an abnormal degree.

Fabricate: to falsify; to report something that is not true.

Induce: to cause or bring about.

Carotid: an artery in the neck that supplies the brain with oxygenated blood.

Separation Anxiety: distress and/or anxiety a child experiences when separated from a primary caregiver.

Forensic: related to, or appropriate for, use in legal settings.

Covert Video Surveillance: making a video recording without making it clear to the participants that they are being taped.

American Civil Liberties Union (ACLU): a national organization that advocates for individual rights by preserving the protections and guarantees listed in the Bill of Rights.

Pediatric Condition Falsification (PCF): a description suggested by the American Professional Society on the Abuse of Children to refer to any children who are described as ill when they are not, regardless of parental motivation.

Malingering by Proxy: a parent's coaching a child to fake symptoms in order to gain something external such as money from a lawsuit or an insurance claim.

PART III

Legal Issues

CHAPTER 10

Forensic Interviewing of Children

CHILDREN PROVIDING TESTIMONY

Forensic interviewing is the term used to describe attempts to elicit information from witnesses for use in a legal setting. Following the increase in attention given to the sexual abuse of children in the 1980s, states began to make changes in their laws that made it easier for children to provide **testimony** in court. Because children are frequently the only witnesses in cases of alleged abuse, it was imperative to have their testimony if prosecutors hoped for a conviction. In order to allow children to provide this type of evidence, two significant changes were made. First, children were allowed to provide **uncorroborated** testimony in cases of alleged sexual abuse. This meant that children could testify to an event even if what they said was not supported or confirmed by any other evidence or authority. Second, states eliminated the competency requirement for child witnesses. Prior to the changes made in the 1980s, many states had age requirements related to competency, such as 10 or 14 years of age. However, the trend has been to move away from age requirements and to presume competence. In federal courts, the competency rules were abolished by **Federal Rule of Evidence 601**, which states that all witnesses are presumed competent, and it is up to the jury to assess the accuracy of testimony. This trend has been followed on the state level to varying degrees (Sagatun & Edwards, 1995). The result is that there has been a significant increase in the number of children who are providing testimony in court.

THE ACCURACY OF CHILDREN'S TESTIMONY

The concern about these changes revolves around the question of how good children are at providing testimony. In the early 1980s when concern about sexual abuse was at a peak, little was known about how accurate children would be in a legal setting. The attention given to some very high profile cases, like the McMartin case in California, focused the media spotlight on children as witnesses and raised a plethora of questions (see Case Example 10.1). The research that has taken place in the last two decades has demonstrated some strengths and some serious weaknesses in children's ability to provide accurate testimony. The concerns are related specifically to information that is gathered from children for forensic purposes. In other words, the

The case that captured the nation's attention with regard to child sexual abuse was the McMartin day care case in California. Virginia McMartin, 79 years old, had started a preschool and hired family members to help her run the facility. Her daughter, Peggy Buckey, served as an administrator, and her grandchildren, Ray and Peggy Ann Buckey, were teachers. All was going well until 1983, when a mother, Judy Johnson, called the day care and was told that the center was at capacity and her son could not attend at that time. Ms. Johnson ignored this information and proceeded to drop off her 2-year-old son, Matthew, at the day care, where she left him in the yard. In a decision they would come to regret, the adults at the preschool began to provide day care for Matthew (Ramsland, 2007).

Ms. Johnson was a psychologically unstable woman who was separated from her husband. She also seemed overly concerned with her son's anus. Apparently, at some point Matthew had complained that it hurt when he had bowel movements. Ms. Johnson then specifically asked if Ray, the only male teacher the day care, had hurt Matthew's bottom. Matthew denied that Ray had hurt him, but Ms. Johnson persisted in her questioning. Finally, Matthew said that Ray had taken his temperature. Ms Johnson then took Matthew to the hospital for a rectal exam. At that time she told the doctors that Matthew had been tied up and photographed naked at the school. She also added that other children had been similarly abused. Matthew was then taken to the Children's Institute International (CII) at UCLA, where he was seen by an intern. This intern accepted Ms. Johnson's story and diagnosed Matthew with penile penetration of the anus. Matthew was then sent to the Richstone Center for counseling for sexual abuse victims. Because Ms. Johnson said that Matthew had told her that other children were involved, police told parents who had children at the day care to question their children. All of the children denied having been abused. Ms. Johnson continued to tell stories of sexual abuse, and the media began to cover her allegations (Ramsland, 2007).

On September 7, 1983, Ray Buckey was arrested. However, because there was no physical evidence and no confession, he was soon released. The police then sent a letter to parents who had, at any time, had a child at the day care. They told the parents what to look for in their children, and told them to question their children. The parents were told not to take no for an answer. Priests instructed parents on the techniques used by satanic cults and joined the police in telling the parents to question their children. At first the children continued to deny abuse, but as they were questioned repeatedly and counseled at CII, they began to make allegations. This intensified the police's search for evidence, especially pictures. Their search for physical evidence was not successful (Ramsland, 2007).

The interviews of the children continued. The interviewers used anatomically detailed dolls and puppets in attempts to help the children tell about what had happened. The children were pressured, even coerced, to tell. One young girl finally said that she was abused, but not by Ray. She pointed the finger at Peggy Buckey. Allegations later spread to the entire staff at the day care. Children who made allegations were promptly reinforced for their bravery. Children who continued to deny abuse were thought to be repressing memories, and the therapists set to work uncovering those memories. The children began to tell stories, not just of sexual abuse but of bizarre happenings. Children talked of underground tunnels, being taken to cemeteries to dig up and cut corpses, and torturing and killing animals. Matthew's mother said her son reported being taken by plane to visit a goat-man, and once there, Matthew was forced to stick his finger in the goat's anus. As the media hysteria grew, people began to attack the McMartins and the Buckeys. Their property was vandalized, and they were physically accosted (Ramsland, 2007).

The grand jury indicted all seven members of the staff at the day care on more than 150 counts. The district attorney added counts to bring the total to 208. In April of 1987, the defendants were imprisoned, and all but Virginia were denied bail. This denial of bail was based on an unsubstantiated claim by the prosecution that the defendants would intimidate witnesses if they were released. Following these events, paranoia seemed to run rampant. The children continued to make allegations against the seven who had already been arrested and against neighbors, babysitters, and coaches. Interestingly, these allegations were never pursued by the police. In the meantime, the behavior of Ms. Johnson continued to deteriorate. She claimed someone had raped her dog, she wrote a letter to the prosecuting attorney saying that she could not tell fantasy from reality, she accused her husband of sexually abusing their son, and she was drinking heavily. Ms. Johnson was eventually diagnosed with paranoid schizophrenia, and her son, Matthew, went to live with relatives (Ramsland, 2007).

At the preliminary hearing, much of the children's testimony was bizarre. The result was that the charges against five of the defendants were dropped. Only Ray and Peggy were to be tried. At this point Peggy was released on bail, but Ray remained in jail. Shortly after this, the original accuser, Ms. Johnson, died due to problems associated with alcohol use. Later, the defense learned of Ms. Johnson's letter, which the prosecution had failed to share with them (Ramsland, 2007).

Despite these events, at the time of the trial, members of the community were convinced that the McMartin day care staff was guilty. In one survey, 97.5% of respondents said that they thought the employees of the McMartin day care should be convicted. Even with this information, the judge denied a change of venue, and the trial began in April of 1987. The best 11 children from the preliminary hearing were called to testify. The medical evidence presented by the prosecution was controversial in that the expert they used, Dr. William Gordon, was not a medical doctor, and he had no formal education in diagnosis. Furthermore, he had been banned from testifying as an expert in other countries. The jurors also saw some videotaped interviews that contained very poor interviewing techniques. A defense expert, Dr. Michael Maloney, testified about the problematic nature of the interviews. The trial lasted 28 months and cost the state more than 15 million dollars. In January of 1990, the jury was hung on 13 charges (all related to Ray, not Peggy) and acquitted on all others. Five months later, Ray was tried again on those 13 charges. When the jury deadlocked, the charges were dismissed. By then, Ray had spent five years in jail (Ramsland, 2007).

As a postscript to this story, in November of 2005, the Associated Press reported that Kyle Zirpolo, one of the children who had made accusations, admitted that he had lied. Zirpolo stated, "I'm not saying nothing happened to anyone else at the McMartin Preschool. I can't say that—I can only speak for myself. But I never forgot I was lying" (Associated Press, 2005, p. 1). Zirpolo was one of the older children in the case. He was eight years old at the time he made allegations. Although he testified before the grand jury, he did not testify at the trial. Zirpolo said he was coming forward now to provide an example for his children about doing the right thing (Associated Press, 2005).

The media attention given to this case greatly increased public awareness of childhood sexual abuse. It also prompted researchers to explore how children respond to interviewing techniques.

research presented here is focused on whether the statements given by children are appropriate for use in a court of law.

Conditions Related to Accurate Testimony

The good news is that under certain conditions, even young children can provide accurate testimony about events they have experienced. First, children who give spontaneous accounts of abuse are generally believed to be truthful and accurate. So, if a child comes up to you and tells you, without prompting, that he or she is being abused, you should make the assumption that the account is likely accurate and make the appropriate report to child protective services (CPS). Because this untainted testimony is believed to be more accurate than what a child might say after repeated questioning, you should do your best to record exactly what the child said to you. Professionals are even more confident about the accuracy of a child's memory if there is a minimal delay between the alleged incident occurring and the telling of it. Because memory decays with time, the more immediate the telling, the more confidence we have in the details (see Case Example 10.2).

The problem is probably one that you have already recognized. Many children do not spontaneously tell others that they are being abused. Some children are afraid, others are ashamed, and still others do not realize that what is happening is wrong or unusual. Therefore, it is frequently necessary for concerned adults to ask children questions about what is going on in their

CASE EXAMPLE 10.2

When Samantha Runnion was abducted, she was taken in the presence of her 5-year-old playmate, Sarah. When the police arrived, just 4 minutes after the abduction, Sarah explained that the man had asked the girls to help him find his dog. She also described his appearance, his car, and his accent. The details Sarah provided were excellent and accurate. For instance, she reported that the car was green and that it had an "H" on the trunk. Sarah even worked with a sketch artist and created a picture that was a close match to the perpetrator, Alejandro Avila, who was subsequently arrested and charged with Samantha's abduction and murder (Lewin, 2002).

CASE POINT

Despite Sarah's young age, she was able to provide good information when questioned immediately after the event by an interviewer who had no preconceived notions about what had happened.

DISCUSSION QUESTIONS

1. Would you expect all 5-year-old witnesses to be as competent as Sarah?
2. What did the investigators do correctly in this case?

lives. Research has shown that children tend to be accurate when responding to open-ended, **unbiased questions. Open-ended questions** are those that cannot be answered with a single word. An interviewer should not ask a child, "Did Mr. Bob hurt you at day care?" A better question would be, "What do you do at day care?" The first question is not only closed, it is also biased. By associating Mr. Bob's name with "hurt," the child is being led to give the expected answer. Interviewers should avoid providing the child with names or specific events in the context of their questions. If this sounds easy, try to come up with a series of questions that you could ask a three-year-old that are open-ended and unbiased. Given that many young children do not provide much detail when they respond to open-ended questions, getting information can be a real struggle. If an interviewer believes the child is being abused, there is an incentive to push the child with more pointed questions. The question for researchers was whether a child could be convinced that something bad had happened when it did not, simply by the way the child is questioned.

Suggestibility

Children seem to be especially prone to **suggestibility.** Early studies demonstrated that it was relatively easy to change a child's memory for story details. For instance, Ceci, Ross, and Toglia (1987) had researchers read a story to 182 children between 3 and 12 years of age. Part of the story included the information that the main character, Loren, had eaten eggs for breakfast and later got a stomach ache. The story was accompanied by eight pictures. One day after hearing the story, half of the children received misleading information. In the biased condition, children were asked, "Do you remember the story about Loren, who had a headache because she ate her cereal too fast? Then she felt better when she got to play with her friend Tricia's Pac Man game?" (Ceci et al., 1987, p. 40). In the unbiased condition, the children were simply asked, "Do you remember the story of Loren, who was sick? Then she felt better when she got to play with her friend Tricia's Pac Man game?" (Ceci et al., 1987, p. 40). Two days later, all children were asked to pick which two out of four pictures had been in the story. The pictures were of Loren eating eggs, Loren eating cereal, Loren with a stomach ache, and Loren with a headache. Children in the biased condition made significantly more errors than did children in the unbiased condition. Instead of choosing photos that represented the original story, they selected photos that depicted what the biased interviewer had suggested. There were no age differences in the unbiased condition, but in the biased condition, young children made significantly more errors than did older children. This research showed that children, especially young children, were very sensitive to suggestion by adults.

Although a number of other studies replicated the finding by Ceci et al. (1987), some researchers argued that the errors made in those studies were about peripheral details that were not relevant to the child. The argument was that while a child may confuse eggs and cereal, it did not follow that a child would falsely recall or report being abused. To this end, researchers tried to create events that were ethical but more relevant to questions about child abuse. Empirical studies began to appear in the literature that provided evidence that even children as young as 3 or 4 years of age were able to provide good information about action-related, salient events (London, 2006). For instance, in 1991, Rudy and Goodman had pairs of children (both 4 years old or both 7 years old) enter a trailer and join an unfamiliar male there. One child was selected to be a participant while the other watched. When the children entered the trailer, the man used puppets to interact with the girls, and he spoke with them about general topics such as siblings, pets, and school. During this time, the man also put on a mask for a brief period. After drawing marbles, he assigned one child to watch and one to participate. The participating child played a series of games with the man, including Simon Says, putting on a clown costume (over the child's clothes), posing the child for photographs, having the child tickle the man and touch his nose (acting like a clown who is trying to make someone laugh), and thumb wrestling. Finally, the man helped the child remove the costume. Both children were praised for doing a good job, and both were given a small toy. Between 10 and 12 days later, the children returned individually to be interviewed. The interview began with open-ended, unbiased questions concerning what happened in the trailer, what the man looked like, and what games were played. The experimenter than asked specific (e.g., Did he kiss you?) and misleading (e.g., What color was the hat he was wearing on his head?) questions.

Rudy and Goodman (1991) found that the older children gave more correct information in response to free-recall questions and specific questions. However, participants and observers did not differ. They did find that participants were more resistant to suggestion than were observers, and that older children were less suggestible regarding actions that had taken place. Most important, Rudy and Goodman found that regardless of age or role, children made very few errors that would be relevant in the assessment of abuse allegations. The conclusion from studies like this was that children were not suggestible about events that were relevant to themselves.

This research did not allay all concerns about children's testimony. First, Ceci and Bruck (1993) pointed out that while most of the children in Rudy and Goodman's study did not make false reports in response to abuse-relevant questions, some did. In response to misleading abuse questions, 12% of the 4-year olds falsely assented, as did 6% of the 7-year olds. The rate of false reports was even higher in response to direct abuse questions (18% for 4-year olds and 10% for 7-year olds). If we are considering basing a prosecution for alleged child abuse on the basis of testimony, a false positive rate of 1 in 10 children is a bit scary. The second concern about Rudy and Goodman's (1991) results was that they had only asked the leading questions once. In real abuse cases, children are questioned repeatedly by their parents, the police, therapists, and CPS workers. Would children be able to resist an erroneous suggestion about central experiences if they were questioned repeatedly?

Repeated Questions

On average, a child involved in an abuse investigation will be interviewed 11 times (London, 2006). It is imperative to know whether asking questions more than once has an impact on children's reports. To explore this question, a series of experiments was conducted to assess the impact of repeated questioning on preschool children's memories. Ceci, Crotteau-Huffman, Smith, and Loftus (1994) asked children to pick a card from a set held by an adult. Written on the cards were certain events, some of which the children had actually experienced and others that they had not. The adult then read the card to the child and asked the child to think hard about it and then tell the adult whether it had ever happened to them. False events included getting a finger caught in a mousetrap and having to go to the hospital, and seeing alligators eating apples on an airplane. The children were given prompts to help them think about each event (e.g., who was with you? What were you wearing? How did you feel?). This procedure was followed once a week for 10 weeks. Then, the children were interviewed by a new adult and simply asked if the various things had happened to them. If the child said yes, he or she was asked to provide more details (e.g., what happened next?). The results were surprising. Fifty-eight percent of the children assented to at least one of the false events, and 25% assented to the majority of the false events. Not only did they say that the false events happened to them, they gave elaborate, rich details, and provided coherent, convincing stories. It seemed that the children were not lying or making up the stories; they seemed to believe them.

After the study was completed, John Stossel of *20/20* aired a story about the experiment. The parents of one boy, Bill, gave Stossel permission to interview their 4-year-old son, but they told

Stossel that they had briefed Bill 2 days before. They had told Bill all about the experiment, and they told him that the mousetrap story was all in his imagination. The parents said that it took some time to convince Bill of the truth, but that he finally admitted that the mousetrap story never happened. However, when Stossel interviewed Bill, he was still able to tell the mousetrap story. Bill's story was rich with detail, including which finger was injured, and who had gone to the hospital with him. When Stossel challenged the accuracy of Bill's story, the 4-year-old insisted, "But it really happened! It wasn't just in my imagination." This study showed that children could be made to believe that something had happened that was relevant to them simply by repeating a question. Keep in mind that this happened after weeks of simple questioning. In real abuse cases, not only are children questioned repeatedly, they are also questioned in ways that are leading and even coercive (see Case Examples 10.1 and 10.3).

You may wonder why it is so problematic to ask a child a question more than once. One possible explanation is that adults know the answer to most of the questions they pose to young children. Think about the things we generally ask children: What color is my shirt? What is her name? What is this called? In all cases, the adult knows the correct answer. If the child provides the correct answer, the exchange ends, or the answer is rewarded. So, if I am wearing a red shirt and I ask a child what color my shirt is, and the answer is red, I either let it go or respond with something like, "You are so smart!" But what happens if they say it's blue? A typical response from adults is to simply repeat the question, "What color is my shirt?" You will often hear an emphasis on the word "what," which compounded with the second asking communicates to the child that the first response was wrong. Most of the time children sense this and try another answer. Now, to put this in the context of an interview assessing allegations of abuse, consider the following question: "Did Mr. Bob hurt you at day care?" The child says, "No." The adult says, "It's OK; you can tell me. Did Mr. Bob hurt you at day care?" Well, there are only two answers to that question. "No" seems not to have worked, so the child tries "yes." A concerned adult may then say, "You are so brave to tell me. You are a strong little boy. I am so proud of you!" This, of course, reinforces the answer of "yes." While the adult knows that questions about shirt color and questions about abuse are very different, a young child would not necessarily know this.

Of course, it can be argued that thinking you had your finger caught in a mousetrap is still a long way from thinking that someone molested you. In order to explore the question of children's accuracy in an even more realistic scenario, researchers decided to question children following medical exams. After all, during a medical exam, a child is undressed and touched by an adult who is in a position of authority. Would a child say that a doctor touched their private parts when the doctor had not gone anywhere near their private parts during an exam? Would the children continue to be accurate in reports of touching if asked leading questions or presented with anatomically detailed dolls? Anatomically detailed dolls have vaginal, anal, and oral openings, and the adult dolls also have pubic and underarm hair. The theory behind using dolls is that a child may be able to show what he does not have the words to tell or is too embarrassed to talk about.

Anatomically Detailed Dolls

Researchers have found that dolls are frequently used by professionals during the assessment of child sexual abuse allegations. Conte, Sorenson, Fogarty, and Dalla Rosa (1991) surveyed 212 professionals (84 child protection workers, 98 mental health professionals, and 30 "others" including police officers and attorneys) who worked with sexually abused children. They found that 92% of professionals reported using **anatomically detailed dolls** in their interviews. Kendall-Tackett and Watson (1992) conducted a similar study in Boston. They also found that police (62%) and mental health workers (80%) were likely to use anatomically detailed dolls. Kendall-Tackett and Watson also reported that, contrary to what others had reported, almost all

Figure 10.1 Anatomically detailed dolls are generally presented to the children dressed as are the child dolls in this photograph. Photo credit: Monica L. McCoy.

the professionals who used dolls (96.6%) were trained in using them, and many (77.8%) used a standard protocol. Furthermore, almost all of the professionals (98.6%) were careful to avoid the leading practices of presenting the dolls naked or undressing the dolls.

Given the high rate of doll use, researchers have attempted to evaluate the dolls' strengths and weaknesses as interview tools. As mentioned earlier, researchers have examined the impact

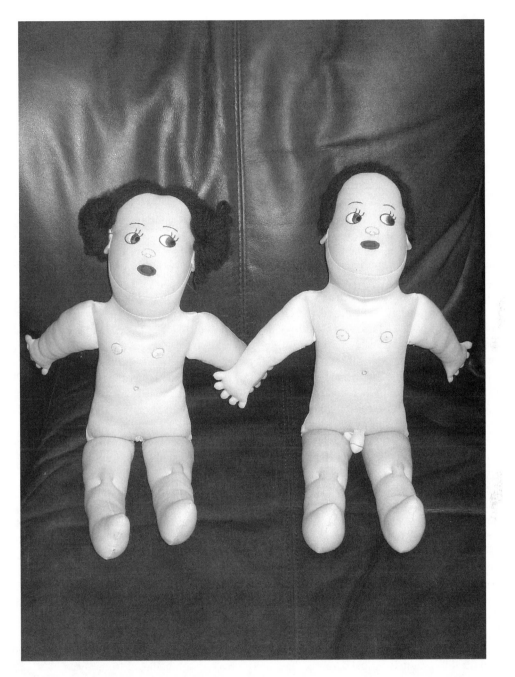

Figure 10.2 Anatomically detailed dolls have anal and vaginal openings and genitalia as seen on these child dolls. Photo credit: Monica L. McCoy.

of using anatomically detailed dolls on young children's reports about a medical exam (Bruck, Ceci, & Francoeur, 2000; Bruck, Ceci, Francoeur, & Renick, 1995). Bruck et al. (1995, 2000) interviewed children following a pediatric exam. Forty children age 3 (24 girls and 16 boys) and 44 children age 4 (24 girls and 20 boys) were randomly assigned to an exam with no genital touching or an exam with genital touching. After giving consent, the child's parent accompanied the child to the examination room. The parent undressed the child, leaving underwear on, and dressed the child in a Mickey Mouse T-shirt and white socks that had been presented by the experimenter. The pediatrician, Dr. Francoeur, conducted a normal exam, with or without a genital exam, and added three odd steps. He measured the child's wrist with a ribbon, he put a sticker on the child's stomach, and he tickled the child's foot with a stick.

Immediately after the exam, while still dressed in the T-shirt, socks, and underwear, children were interviewed in the presence of their parents. The children were shown two anatomically detailed dolls. One was dressed like the doctor, and the other was dressed like the child (Mickey Mouse T-shirt, underwear, and socks). The "child doll" was the same sex as the child being interviewed. The children were first asked to name 11 body parts on the child doll. The experimenter then undressed the child doll and showed the child that it was a special doll. The children were then asked to provide their name for the buttocks and the genitals and to describe the function of those parts. Next, the children were asked direct, doll-assisted questions. For instance, the experimenter would say, "Did Dr. F. touch you here?" (Bruck et al., 2000, p. 76). This was asked while pointing to the genitals, and again while pointing to the buttocks. After these questions, the experimenter redressed the doll and asked the child to demonstrate, using the doll, what the doctor had done with a stethoscope, a ribbon, a sticker, and a stick. Finally, children were asked to show the experimenter how things happened by using the dolls. These demonstration questions required the children to "Show me on the doll how Dr. F. touched your _____." The blank was filled in with the child's term for buttocks, and then their term for genitals. In the next phase of questioning, the children were given a spoon and asked what Dr. F. did with the spoon. If they reported, correctly, that there was no spoon involved, they were asked what he could have done with the spoon, and to demonstrate that with the dolls. While this may seem to be a bizarre series of questions, it was based on questions used in the Kelly Michaels case (see Case Example 10.3). Finally, children were asked to demonstrate what had occurred using their own bodies instead of the dolls.

Bruck et al. (2000) found that children were not more accurate in the doll condition than they were in the no-doll (using their own body) condition. The dolls did not seem to improve recall. There was, as expected, an age effect, with the 4-year olds being more accurate than were the 3-year olds. On the doll-assisted questions and the doll-demonstration questions, the children were more accurate if they had not had genital exams (64% correct for 3-year olds and 86% correct for 4-year olds) than if they had received a genital exam (38% correct for 3-year olds and 45% correct for 4-year olds). This means that children were making more **omission errors** (failing to admit to genital touch) than **commission errors** (saying that genital touching occurred when it did not). However, as you can see from the percentage of correct answers, errors of both types were prevalent. Bruck et al. also noted that, on average, boys were more accurate than were girls. Looking at the spoon questions, 38 of the children (45%) said Dr. F. had used a spoon in some way. Another 35 (42%) were willing to demonstrate what Dr. F. might have done with a spoon. While most of the 73 demonstrations involved nonsexual touching or feeding, 15% of the children either touched the genitals with the spoon or inserted the spoon into the doll's vaginal or anal opening. This was more common behavior from 3-year olds (18%) than from 4-year olds (9%). In addition to these sexualized acts, 12 of the children (14%) used the props (stickers, stick, stethoscope) in a sexual way, and 11 (13%) showed aggressive behavior toward the doll (e.g., hit the doll with their hands or with objects). The authors concluded that 58% of 3-year olds and 43% of 4-year olds showed some sort of suspicious behavior during the interviews, with girls being more likely to do so than were boys. Bruck et al. caution that in light of minimal evidence to suggest that anatomically detailed dolls help children's memories, and a growing literature of evidence that they can mislead children, dolls should not be used when questioning children under 5 years of age.

CASE EXAMPLE 10.3

Kelly Michaels, a preschool teacher at Wee Care, was charged with the sexual molestation of the children under her care. The case started after Michaels had left Wee Care and went to work at another day care. She had been at Wee Care for 7 months, and during that time there were no complaints about her, and nobody reported seeing or hearing anything odd. Then, a boy who Michaels used to look after during naptime was having his temperature taken rectally by a nurse, when he commented that his teacher at day care did this to him. He did not seem upset or scared when he made the comment, and when queried, he said, "Her takes my temperature" (Ceci & Bruck, 1995, p. 12). Upon further questioning the boy said the teacher's name was Kelly, and that she also took the temperature of two other boys. At this point, his concerned mother called the police, and the investigation began (Manning, 2007). The two other boys denied that Michaels had taken their temperature, but when questioned by the assistant prosecutor one said that Michaels had touched his penis. Two days later, this boy inserted his finger into the anal opening of an anatomically detailed doll (Ceci & Bruck, 1995).

After months of interviews, Michaels, 25 years old, was charged with 235 counts of sexual misconduct. The allegations were based solely on the testimony of young children, and they ranged from odd (e.g., playing the piano while naked, licking peanut butter off the children) to impossible (e.g., changing a child into a mouse). There was no physical evidence, even though many of the claims would have left such evidence (e.g., amputating children's penises). Despite every effort to find physical evidence, the prosecution was not successful. For instance, after children claimed they had been forced to urinate on a piano bench, the bench was sent to the FBI for testing. The tests came back negative for urine. In addition, there were no adult witnesses to the alleged abuse (Manning, 2007).

Following a 9-month trial, the jury deliberated for 13 days before finding Michaels guilty. Michaels was convicted on 115 counts and sentenced to 47 years in prison. For the first 18 months of her sentence, Michaels was in solitary confinement for her own protection. As Michaels sat in jail, her case was discovered by several journalists, including Debbie Nathan and Dorothy Rabinowitz, who raised public awareness about how her case was handled. Eventually, Morton J. Stavis, a well-respected attorney, decided to take Michaels's case. An assistant to the defense team, Robert Rosenthal, asked researchers Bruck and Ceci (1995) to examine the interviews from the Wee Care case (Manning, 2007). After psychologists reviewed transcripts of the interviews conducted with the children, they had serious concerns about the children's testimony. Maggie Bruck and Steve Ceci filed an amicus brief on Michaels's behalf that highlighted problems with the interviews.

First, the children were asked the same question repeatedly. Consider the following exchange (Bruck & Ceci, 1995, p. 276) between an interviewer (Q) and a child (A):

Q: When Kelly kissed you, did she ever put her tongue in your mouth?
A: No.
Q: Did she ever make you put your tongue in her mouth?
A: No.
Q: Did you ever have to kiss her vagina?
A: No.
Q: Which of the kids had to kiss her vagina?
A: What's this?
Q: No, that's my toy, my radio box. Which kids had to kiss her vagina?
A: No.

The children were also coerced. Specifically, the children were told repeatedly that their friends had already told the interviewers about bad things that Kelly Michaels had done to them (Bruck & Ceci, 1995, pp. 283–284).

Q: All the other friends I talked to told me everything that happened. 29C told me. 32C told me…And now it's your turn to tell. You don't want to be left out, do you?

Q: Boy, I'd hate having to tell your friends that you didn't want to help them.

The interviewers also suggested to the children that Kelly Michaels was bad (Bruck & Ceci, 1995, p. 276).

Q: Do you think that Kelly was not good when she was hurting you all?
A: Wasn't hurting me. I like her.
Q: I can't hear you. You got to look at me when you talk to me. Now when Kelly was bothering kids in the music room—
A: I got socks off.
Q: Did she make anybody else take their clothes off in the music room?
A: No.
Q: Yes.
A: No.

Other authors have highlighted different sections of questioning that also conveyed the idea that Michaels was bad (Manning, 2007, p. 5):

Q: You Wee Care kids seem so scared of her.
A: I wasn't. I'm not even.
Q: But while you were there, were you real scared?
A: I don't know.
Q: What was so frightening about her, what was so scary about her?
A: I don't know. Why don't you ask her?

Finally, there were aspects of the interviewer's questions that provided the children with explicit sexual information (Bruck & Ceci, 1995, pp. 276–278).

Q: Did you ever see Kelly have blood in her vagina?
A: This is blood.
Q: Kelly had blood in her vagina.
A: Yeah.
Q: She did? Did you ever get any of that blood on your penis?
A: No. Green blood.
Q: Did you ever see any of your friends get blood on their penis from her vagina?
A: Not green blood but red blood.
Q: What did you put there?
A: I put jelly right there.
Q: Jelly.
A: And I put jelly on her mouth and on the eyes.
Q: You put jelly on her eyes and her vagina and her mouth.
A: On her back, on her socks.

Q: And did you have to put anything else down there?

A: Right there, right here, and right here and there.

Q: You put peanut butter all over? And where else did you put the peanut butter?

A: And jelly.

Q: And jelly?

A: And we squeezed orange on her.

Q: And you had to squeeze orange on her?

A: Put orange juice on her.

Q: And did anybody—how did everybody take it off? How did she make you take it off?

A: No. Lick her all up, eat her all up and lick her all up.

Q: You had to lick her all up?

A: And eat her all up.

Q: Yeah? What did it taste like?

A: Yucky.

Q: So she made you eat the peanut butter and jelly and the orange juice off the vagina too?

A: Yeah.

Q: Was that scary or funny?

A: Funny, funny and scary.

In addition, the interviewers would not take "no" for an answer. If children admitted abuse, they were telling the truth. If they denied abuse they were too scared to tell. There was no response a child could give to convince the interviewers that he or she had not been abused (Manning, 2007).

After reviewing all of the evidence, Ceci told a reporter, "The interviews with the children in the Michaels case are some of the worst I have ever heard. The children were undoubtedly abused, but probably not until they met the investigators" (Manning, 2007, p. 11).

Attorney Morton J. Stavis died before he could present his arguments to the appeals court, but his friend William Kunstler stepped in to take his place. The defense used research like what is covered in this chapter to raise concerns about the accuracy of the children's testimony. Based on this evidence, the state appellate court overturned Michaels's conviction. The judges were very critical of the way the children had been interviewed. This did not, of course, mean that Michaels was innocent, but only that her trial was flawed. Prosecutors originally planned to retry her. However, in June of 1994, the Supreme Court of New Jersey ruled that there could not be a new trial without a taint hearing. This meant that it had to be determined whether the children's testimony had been so tainted by the interviewers that it held no value, or that truth could be discovered despite the poor techniques used. Knowing that there was no way to determine the truth after all that happened during the investigation, the charges were dropped in December of 1994. At the age of 32, Kelly Michaels was free (Manning, 2007).

While this case may seem extreme, it is sadly not unique. If you are interested in reading about other cases, go to http://members.shaw.ca/imaginarycrimes/othercases.htm.

DISCUSSION QUESTIONS

1. What mistakes were made in the investigation of Michaels' case?
2. Given the way that information was collected in this case, is it possible to know, for certain, whether or not abuse occurred at the day care?

There are a number of reasons why play with dolls should be interpreted carefully. First, young children may not fully understand what they are being asked to do. Use of a doll in this manner requires children to be capable of **dual representation,** the understanding that one thing can be two things at once. The child needs to understand that the child doll is not only a doll, but it is also a symbol, or representation, of the child. Likewise, the adult doll is both a doll and the representation of the alleged perpetrator. DeLoache and Marzolf (1995) explored whether young children were able to comprehend this sort of task. They had 72 children who were 2 ½, 3, or 4 years old play games with a male experimenter. Before the games started, the children were asked to pick a pillow to sit on and a necklace to wear. They were also given the opportunity to wear a cape if they wanted to. After these selections were made, the children played three games in random order: a sticker activity, Simon Says, and a puppet activity. Immediately after playing, the children were interviewed by a female interviewer. She used a doll in the interview, with the prompt, "Let's pretend this doll is you. This can be the [child's name] doll" (DeLoache & Marzolf, p. 161). If the child had worn a cape, the interviewer put a cape on the doll and pointed out the similarity. If the child had refused the cape, the interviewer noted that the doll would also not wear a cape. Then, the child was instructed to pick a necklace for the doll that was like the one the child had worn. If the child made an error, the interviewer corrected him or her. This same routine was followed for the pillow selection. All of this was done to stress that the doll was representing the child. Following this, children were provided with miniature (doll-sized) props and asked to show what they had done with the male experimenter. None of the children spontaneously used the dolls to answer this question. Next, the interviewer asked the children to re-enact the play session using the doll to represent themselves. The researchers wanted to see if the children could map on the doll what had happened to them.

DeLoache and Marzolf (1995) concluded that you cannot assume that young children can use dolls as representations of themselves. First, some children flat-out refused to even pretend the doll was them. One child said, "No, that is not the Evan Doll. You think I'm a doll or what... Doll not me" (DeLoache & Marzolf, p. 168). The children who attempted the representation were not accurate with even a simple task prior to the age of 4 years. For example, the children were not able to show, using the doll, how the male experimenter had put stickers on them. Regarding the touch-related questions with the Simon Says game, no child spontaneously used the dolls to demonstrate touch, and most failed to show on the doll what they had reported verbally, even when prompted to do so. Finally, when asked to demonstrate touch with the doll, children tended to touch a different place on the doll than what they had reported verbally. The dolls did not help the children add any new, correct information.

A second reason to be cautious when interpreting doll play is that there is evidence that an expert cannot determine abuse status based solely on interviews using dolls. Realmuto, Jensen, and Wescoe (1990) had a child psychiatrist interview 15 children (6 abused, 5 nonclinical controls, and 4 clinical/psychiatric but nonabused controls). The psychiatrist did not know the children's status prior to the interview. He followed a standardized protocol for the interview that included 10 minutes of free play, followed by presentation of the dolls for 10 additional minutes. Based on the interviews, the psychiatrist attempted to assess each child's abuse status. He was correct 53% of the time (8 of the 15 cases). Because this success rate is not significantly different from chance, the authors concluded that interviews with dolls are not sufficient for diagnosis of abuse. However, they did note that their study was limited by a small sample size. Part of the difficulty inherent in using dolls to diagnosis sexual abuse is that even nonabused children will sometimes play with doll in ways that appear to be quite sexual. Children may not realize that what they are doing is even sexual; they may simply be playing.

Despite these concerns, some researchers do advocate the use of anatomically correct dolls. Their argument is that although the dolls should not be used as a diagnostic test for sexual abuse, they can be used in other ways that are productive. For instance, anatomically correct dolls can be used as an anatomical model. Using this detailed model, the children can demonstrate for the interviewer what they call various body parts. Because many parents do not teach their children the standard names for private parts, it is important that the interviewer is able to learn what words a child uses to refer to a bottom or a penis. The doll can also be used to question the child about the function of various body parts (Everson & Boat, 1994). The current state of knowledge seems to be that dolls can be used if the interviewer is well trained and aware of the necessity to avoid leading or aggressive questioning.

Interviewer Bias

You may be asking yourself why investigators would question children so aggressively. The answer is that the interviewers assume the abuse has taken place, and it is their job to get the conviction. They are motivated to get a dangerous perpetrator off the streets. While this passion can be a good motivator, it can also be dangerous when it comes to uncovering the truth. There is a long list of research studies, dating as far back as 1929, that show how powerful **interviewer bias** can be in shaping reports. It seems that humans are very good at eliciting the responses they expect to hear. Social psychologists use the term **self-fulfilling prophecy** to refer to the process by which one person's expectations about another person will actually lead that other person to behave in the expected way. One of the classic studies in this field was conducted by Robert Rosenthal and Lenore Jacobson in 1968. Rosenthal and Jacobson told elementary school teachers that certain students in their class were on the verge of an intellectual growth spurt. The teachers were told that this prediction was based on an IQ test, but in fact the children were selected at random. Eight months later, the children who had been selected actually showed greater increases in IQ scores than did a control group from the same class, and their teachers rated them more positively. This finding has since been replicated and is accepted as a true description of what can occur. The researchers chose, for ethical reasons, to increase teacher expectations, but this could also theoretically work in the opposite direction. For instance, a teacher may have preconceived negative ideas about a child who is poor or who has a difficult older sibling. What is unfortunate about this research is that the teachers were not even aware they were treating the children differently.

Research has also demonstrated that an interviewer's bias can change what a child reports about an event. A 1990 study by Pettit, Fegan, and Howie (as cited in Ceci & Bruck, 1995) tested the impact of interviewer bias on children's subsequent reports. The researchers had two actors, pretending to be park rangers, visit a preschool classroom. The rangers' task was to have the children help a bird find a nest so that it could lay eggs. During the presentation, one of the rangers knocked a cake off the piano, and it was smashed all over the floor. The response to this event was shocked silence on the part of the rangers. Two weeks later the children were interviewed about the event by one of three interviewers. The first interviewer was given no information about the event ahead of time, the second interviewer was given an accurate description of the event, and the third interviewer was given inaccurate information about what had occurred. All of the interviewers were warned not to ask leading questions. Despite this advice, 30% of the interviewers did ask leading questions, and half of the leading questions were actually misleading. Children agreed with 41% of the misleading questions. What was most telling, though, was that the interviewer who had been given inaccurate information was almost five times more likely to ask leading questions than were the other interviewers. Translated to abuse investigations, this could mean that an investigator who had a mistaken idea going into an interview would be more likely to ask misleading questions than would an investigator who had an open mind or one who was armed with accurate information.

Negative Stereotypes

Another thing that can alter children's memories of events is the creation of negative stereo-types. If adults convince a child that someone is bad, or clumsy, or mean, it is easier to lead that child to recall the maligned adult behaving inappropriately. Leichtman and Ceci (1995) tested this empirically with their Sam Stone study. Children from 3 to 6 years of age were told that Sam Stone was going to visit their classroom. Prior to the visit, some of the children were told that Sam Stone was very clumsy (stereotype group). They were told stories about Sam accidentally breaking things and creating messes. Then, Sam Stone visited the room. While there, he did not do anything clumsy; he did not break anything, nor did he have any accidents. Following the visit, children were interviewed four times over a 10-week period. Some children were inter-viewed in a suggestive manner (suggestion group). These interviews included misleading ques-tions about events that had not occurred (tearing a book and getting a teddy bear dirty). After these interviews, the children were interviewed by another adult who asked general questions about the book and the teddy bear. Children in the control group (no stereotype induction, nonsuggestive interviews) were the most accurate. None of these children made false claims in response to being asked to tell what happened the day Sam Stone came to visit. When asked specific questions about a book or a bear, only 10% of the children 3 or 4 years old erroneously said that Stone had caused the damage, and only 5% said they had seen Stone do the misdeed. When these children were gently challenged with the question, "You didn't really see him do anything to the book/teddy bear?" only 2.5% maintained their false report. Among the children ages 5 and 6 in the control condition, only 3.7% made any false claims, and this disappeared when they were asked if they had seen the misdeeds themselves.

The children who had the preconceived negative stereotype of Sam Stone did not respond as accurately. Twenty-one percent of the younger children and 14% of the older children made false statements in their free narrative. When asked specifically about the bear and the book, 53% of the young children falsely blamed Sam Stone, as did 38% of the older children. When asked if they actually saw Sam hurt the book or the toy, 35% of the young children said yes, and 12% maintained this response when challenged. For older children, these percentages were 11% and 5% respectively. Finally, the third group was exposed to both the negative stereotype and the misleading questions. They were, not surprisingly, the most likely to give incorrect responses. Among the 3- and 4-year-old children, 72% said that Sam Stone was responsible for at least one misdeed. If the children were asked if they actually saw Sam Stone do the bad thing, the rate of allegations dropped to 44%, and when they were challenged, 21% main-tained that they had seen the events. Furthermore, the children provided many details about the events that never occurred. Their stories, illustrated with hand movements and appropriate facial expressions, were very convincing. Although older children (5 and 6 years old) were more resistant to suggestion, they still made false reports (39% said Stone was responsible, 14% said they actually saw Stone damage the toys, and 5% maintained their story when challenged). Not only does this study show the danger of creating negative stereotypes, but it also shows how this problem can be increased by the use of misleading questions, especially when dealing with very young children.

A Word of Caution

Thomas D. Lyon (2001), a law professor at the University of Southern California School of Law, wrote an article entitled "Let's Not Exaggerate the Suggestibility of Children." While he applauds the research that has been conducted about the possible suggestibility of young children, he cautions against overusing the "suggestibility defense" (p. 12). Lyon points out that although the highly leading techniques reviewed in this chapter have occurred in some high-profile cases, they are not the norm. He asserts that most real-life interviewers do not use techniques that are as problematic as those seen in Kelly Michaels's case and many cases do not involve testimony from very young children who seem especially suggestible in research settings. Lyon notes that particularly dangerous techniques such as stereotype induction and coercive questioning are rare. Lyon further notes that in research studies children are generally being led to make false statements about events that involved relative strangers, not loved ones. His argument is that children may be more resistant to the suggestion that a person they are close to hurt them. Since the majority of child sexual abuse cases involve familiar adults, this is forensically relevant. Because of these concerns, Lyon suggests that it is not appropriate in all child abuse cases for experts to testify about the literature on suggestibility. Instead, this sort of testimony should be limited to cases in which the investigators did, in fact, use improper techniques. This decision, according to Lyon, should be left to the judge in the case. In addition, when experts do testify, they should be very specific about what the research shows and avoid over-generalized statements that indicate that all testimony from children is suspect. Lyon is not, however, naïve. Even though Lyon maintains that investigators are not regularly making the most egregious errors, he acknowledges that real-world interviewers are not perfect. His own review of interviews found that the questioners ask very few open-ended questions and too many yes/no or forced-choice questions.

Reviews of Forensic Interviews

A more negative review of real interviews was reported by Warren, Woodall, Hunt, and Perry (1996). Warren et al. examined the transcripts of 42 sexual abuse interviews that were conducted by CPS personnel. The goal of their research was to compare what was being done in "regular" as opposed to high-profile cases, and how the interviewers' techniques compared to the best practices suggested by research. In the interviews they reviewed, the children being interviewed ranged in age from 2 to 13 years, with a mean age of 6 years.

The first thing assessed by Warren et al. (1996) was whether the interviewer attempted to build **rapport** with the children. All of the interviewing guidelines the authors had reviewed stressed that it was important to establish a relationship with a child before asking questions about the alleged abuse. This is necessary to help the child relax and be willing to share important information. The good news is that 71% of the interviews reviewed began with at least a minimal attempt to build rapport. The bad news is that in some cases the rapport-building section of the interview was very brief, and in 29% of the interviews this important step was skipped entirely. Furthermore, Warren et al. noted that during the rapport-building stage, the interviewers did the majority of the talking. In fact, the interviewers spoke three times more than the children and asked specific rather than open-ended questions. Even though this is not problematic in and of itself, it does set the stage for the rest of the interview. The expectation that is being created is that the interviewer will do most of the talking.

The next thing Warren et al. (1996) looked at was whether the interviewers established ground rules for the interview. Because a forensic interview is very different from discussions a child normally engages in, it is recommended that the children be told that there are "rules" for this talk. Children should know, before questioning begins, that (1) they do not have to answer a question if they do not know the answer; "I don't know" is an acceptable answer; (2) the interviewer does not know what happened and does not know the right answer; (3) the child may ask the interviewer to clarify a question that is unclear; and (4) the child may correct the interviewer if the interviewer is wrong. Not only is it important to tell the child about these rules, it is necessary to practice them. If an investigator was interviewing a child, Chris, who was 4 years old, she might say to him, "You turned 3 on your last birthday. Isn't that true?" If Chris agrees with her or is silent, the interviewer should remind him that he may correct her when she is wrong. She should also try a question like, "Is my blouse chartreuse?" If he answers, she would ask if he understood the question. Assuming he did not, she would remind him that it is all right to ask for clarification or to say "I don't know." By practicing the rules with neutral material, she is preparing Chris to give a better interview when they get to the abuse-specific questions. Of the interviews reviewed by Warren et al., only 29% (12 cases) made any reference to ground rules. All 12 of these included a reminder to tell the truth. In 6 cases, the children were informed that "I don't know" was an acceptable answer, and in 3 cases the child was told to tell the interviewer if he or she did not understand a question. Only one child was told that it was appropriate to say he or she did not remember, and none of the children were told that they could correct the interviewer. The fact that children do not spontaneously correct adults was illustrated by the following exchange (Warren et al., 1996, p. 235):

Interviewer: Is it good or bad to tell a lie?
Child: G.A. touched me.
Interviewer: Jesus loves me? Is that what you said?
Child: Yeah.

Researchers also recommend that interviewers do a **practice interview** with the children prior to asking about the abuse. These interviews should deal with neutral topics. In addition to allowing more time for rapport building, this allows the interviewer the opportunity to assess the child's language ability and narrative style. It is also the chance to establish roles. The interviewer will ask question and then listen to the child, who will do the majority of the talking. Research has shown that when children are given practice interviews, they give more information in the abuse-related part of the interview. Only 2 of the 42 interviews reviewed made use of this technique.

With regard to the types of questions asked, Warren et al. (1996) found that interviewers asked very few open-ended questions. The most frequent style of question used (62.8%) involved specific questions with yes/no answers. Furthermore, when asking about the abuse, only 10.5% of the questions were open-ended. Interviewers were also guilty of asking multiple questions. This is when the interviewer asks more than one question without allowing the child the chance to respond. For instance, consider the following exchange (Warren et al., 1996, p. 240):

Interviewer: He never kissed you? Did he ask you to kiss him? Have you touched him?
Child: No.

Clearly, it is difficult to interpret what the child's response means. Looking at only a subset of 20 of the 42 interviews, Warren et al. noted 520 series of multiple questions. This common practice is one that interviewers need to learn to avoid.

Warren et al. (1996) were able to detect a number of interviewer oversights and errors, but it was impossible to determine whether the interviewers introduced any false information because there was no way to know what had actually occurred. However, Warren et al. did note that 93.9% of the interviewers introduced new information. In addition, the interviewers were introducing more than one piece of new information (the average across interviews was seven). It is probably not realistic to assume that all of this information was accurate.

Warren et al. (1996) concluded that because the interviews they reviewed were conducted during the late 1980s and the early 1990s, interviewers may not have been aware of the recent research on interviewing. It is possible that interviews have gradually become better since the

Figure 10.3 The Children's Advocacy Center of Spartanburg, South Carolina. Photo credit: Monica L. McCoy.

study was conducted. As CPS workers have found out about the research on interviewing techniques, they may have improved their techniques. Warren et al.'s work does, however, make it clear that mistakes are not found only in high-profile cases.

Others have suggested that we should not think simply in terms of "good" or "bad" interviews. Wood and Garven (2000) suggest that it would be helpful to assess whether a poor interview was likely to elicit false information (improper) or to have other negative consequences that did not include false allegations (clumsy). **Improper interviews** would be those that contained elements known to increase the risk for false allegations. **Clumsy interviews** were defined as those in which the interviewer failed to do at least one of the following things: make the child comfortable; convey interest in and warmth toward the child; use vocabulary that the child could easily comprehend; ask open-ended questions; introduce the topic of abuse in a nonsuggestive manner; encourage the child to tell the story in his own words from the beginning to the end; avoid interrupting the child; or finish by telling the child what would happen next. There can be overlap between improper and clumsy interviewing, but Wood and Garven assert that it is helpful to consider them as separate categories. Improper interviews can lead to false allegations. Clumsy interviews are more likely to lead to a disclosure that is less coherent, less detailed, and less convincing than what would result from a good interview. As a result, these cases are less likely to be prosecuted; and if prosecuted, they are less likely to lead to a guilty verdict. The authors propose that clumsy interviewing is much more common and more difficult to improve than improper interviewing. Training sessions that tell interviewers what not to do can greatly reduce the number of improper interviews. However, quick remedies do not seem to be available for improving clumsy interviewing. For example, after training, the interviews conducted by CPS workers in one agency were rarely improper (5%), but many were still clumsy (50%–70%). The authors suggest possible solutions that range from internships for interviewers, to using interviewing specialists, to relying on structured interviews. All of these methods may be promising, but they still lack empirical evidence to demonstrate that they are effective.

While there is no way to determine how many false reports of abuse exist, estimates generally range between 5% and 8% of sexual abuse cases. Assuming there are approximately 200,000 cases of alleged sexual abuse each year, this would mean approximately 13,000 false allegations. There is also some evidence to suggest that the number of false allegations may be significantly higher among children in families that are currently going through a divorce (London, 2006).

Figure 10.4   The interview room at the Children's Advocacy Center of Spartanburg, South Carolina. Photo credit: Monica L. McCoy.

CONCLUSION

The research reviewed in this chapter has hopefully convinced you that children must be interviewed carefully in order to prevent the creation of false memories. Perhaps the most important lesson is that forensic interviewing is outside of the mandated reporter's area of expertise and that it is *not* something you should attempt. While it is appropriate to listen to a spontaneous report from a child, you should leave the interviewing to the experts. This area of investigation has become so specialized that most police officers and social workers do not do this sort of work. Instead, cities have established special centers, generally called **child advocacy centers** (CACs), where carefully trained forensic interviewers conduct all interviews, especially in cases of alleged sexual abuse. Not only are these interviewers specially trained, but the facilities are set up for this type of information gathering. For instance, the interview rooms are generally set up to allow for audio and video recording as well as observation through a one-way mirror. All of these techniques are designed to reduce the number of interviews required and to provide an accurate record of not only what the child said but what the interviewer said. Child advocacy centers also allow for services for children to be centralized. In many cases, interviews, medical examinations, and therapy are all offered under one roof.

The interviewers at child advocacy centers are well trained in forensic interviewing, and they follow established guidelines for interviewing. There are general and specific rules that have been recommended for interviewing that go beyond avoiding the pitfalls described in this chapter. In the book *Investigative Interviews of Children*, Poole and Lamb (1998) provide the following five general guidelines:

Figure 10.5 Electronic recording devices are in a room adjacent to the interview room at the Children's Advocacy Center of Spartanburg, South Carolina. This room also allows real-time observation of the interview via a one-way mirror. Photo credit: Monica L. McCoy.

Figure 10.6 The child-friendly medical exam room at the Children's Advocacy Center of Spartanburg, South Carolina. Photo credit: Monica L. McCoy.

Figure 10.7   One of the therapy rooms at the Children's Advocacy Center of Spartanburg, South Carolina. Photo credit: Monica L. McCoy.

1. Interview the children as soon as possible. It is important to minimize the time delay between the alleged event and the interview.
2. Give the child the opportunity to get used to the interview setting before you ask about the alleged abuse. Take time to build rapport with the child, and take the time to do a practice interview about a neutral event before moving on to the abuse. Let the child know that it is OK to say that he or she does not understand a question or does not know an answer. It is even permissible to disagree with the interviewer.
3. Whenever possible, interviewers should ask open-ended questions.
4. The person conducting the interview should remain neutral and open. He or she should not convey that the child is correct or incorrect. The interviewer should be willing to consider multiple explanations for a child's statements.
5. If the child is old enough, he or she should be given the opportunity to review and clarify the information that has been gathered.

London (2006) adds the following recommendations:

1. Use language that the child can fully comprehend. Interviewers must be aware that even some basic words like "touch" and "remember" can be confusing for children. For instance, a child who says, "He put his finger inside me" (p. 39) may say no in response to the question, "Did he touch you?" (p. 39). In other words, the child did not think that putting something inside and touching were the same thing. A child may also think that he can only remember something that he had previously forgotten. Therefore, if he always recalled an event, he may indicate that he cannot remember it. Children also struggle with emotional words, time, passive voice, and negatively phrased questions. These deficits persist until children are between 8 and 13 years of age.
2. The environment for the interviews should be carefully selected. Ideally, the child will be interviewed in a room with few distractions. A cheerful room that is not cluttered or threatening is ideal. Along with this, the interviewer should not be in a police uniform or wearing a gun. Finally, the setup of the room should allow for video- and audiotaping, as well as discreet observation via one-way mirrors.

Poole and Lamb (1998) use the next two sections of their book to cover interview protocols and how interviews can be customized. Their information moves beyond the scope of this book, but it is excellent reading for those interested in forensic interviewing and who may be considering a career in the field. Well-conducted interviews are good for everyone. They lead to fewer false allegations and to better prosecution of true allegations. In cases where so much rests on a child's testimony, professionals must be committed to doing whatever they can to ensure that the information obtained from witnesses is as accurate as it can possibly be.

DISCUSSION QUESTIONS

1. After reading this chapter, would you be interested in pursuing a career in forensic interviewing? What would be the benefits and the drawbacks of this type of career?
2. Should expert witnesses be called to provide testimony on interviewing in all cases of alleged child maltreatment? Why or why not?
3. Listen to the way adults talk to children, especially when they are trying to elicit information from them. Note whether their questions are appropriate. If you do not have any access to children, television shows like *Jon & Kate Plus 8* (TLC) show a good deal

of dialogue between adults and young children. Share your observations with your classmates.

4. For ethical reasons, we cannot deliberately try to make a child believe he or she was abused when he or she was not. Did the researchers go too far in the studies you read in this chapter? (e.g., Is it right to make a child believe he had his hand caught in a mouse trap when this did not happen? Do the benefits of this research outweigh the potential costs to the children who participated?)

DEFINITIONS

Forensic Interviewing: an interviewing technique used to elicit verbal information from witnesses for use in a legal setting.

Testimony: evidence given by a witness who is under oath at trial or in an affidavit or deposition.

Uncorroborated: a fact or statement that is not supported or confirmed by additional evidence or authority.

Federal Rule of Evidence 601: a rule governing the admissibility of evidence at trials in federal courts that states that every person is presumed competent unless otherwise noted in the Federal Rules. Because the rules do not list age as a requirement, children are presumed competent.

Unbiased Question: a question that is worded in such a way that it does not influence the respondent's answer.

Open-Ended Question: a question with no set of anticipated responses; the respondent is free to give any answer.

Suggestibility: accepting or acting on something that is implied by another person.

Anatomically Detailed Doll: a doll with anatomical details such as a penis or a vaginal opening, an anal opening, pubic hair, chest hair, and underarm hair.

Omission Errors: mistakes that involve failure to report something that did occur.

Commission Errors: mistakes that involve saying something occurred when it did not.

Dual Representation: the ability to think of one object as being or representing two things at once.

Interviewer Bias: the attitudes or actions of the interviewer influencing the respondent's answers.

Self-Fulfilling Prophecy: the process by which one's expectations about a person leads that person to behave in ways that confirm those expectations.

Rapport: a feeling of connection and trust that is established between two people.

Practice Interview: a question-and-answer session about a neutral topic that allows the person being interviewed to become comfortable with the process before addressing the issue of interest.

Improper Interview: an interview that contains elements known to increase the risk for eliciting false allegations.

Clumsy Interview: an interview that is not likely to lead to false allegations but is conducted poorly. Clumsy interviews lead to statements that are less coherent, less detailed, and less convincing than those garnered from good interviews.

Child Advocacy Center (CAC): a center designed to assess allegations of maltreatment and to treat victims by enlisting a multidisciplinary team of law enforcement, medical, social service, legal, and clinical professionals.

CHAPTER 11

The Legal System and Child Maltreatment

CHILDREN AND THE COURTROOM

For the most part, the U.S. court system is not set up to meet the needs of child witnesses. The court system in the U.S. is an **adversarial system**, or accusatorial. This means that each side presents its case to the court, and it is the job of the judge or the jury to decide which argument is more persuasive. The heart of the adversarial system is the use of **cross-examination** to challenge and discredit opposing witnesses. This can be contrasted with an inquisitorial system, in which the court's role is to figure out the truth by gathering information and asking questions of lay witnesses and experts. Generally, an inquisitorial system is more child friendly (Myers, 1996).

The rules that govern testifying in an adversarial court system were designed with adult witnesses in mind. Being aggressively challenged by opposing counsel is frightening enough for adult witnesses, who have some understanding of the process. It can be overwhelming for children. It is obvious that children may struggle to communicate clearly in this adult context. One major drawback of being asked to perform in a developmentally inappropriate arena can be that children appear incompetent. Saywitz, Jaenicke, and Camparo (1990) suggest that some children may appear incompetent in a court setting, not because they are incapable of giving good testimony, but because the adults who question them are not asking the questions appropriately. Specifically, adults may be using legal terms and/or advanced vocabulary that young children cannot comprehend. For instance, the authors provide the anecdote of a young child who surprised the adults in court when failing to perform when she was asked to "identify her assailant"—a task she had completed easily in the past. However, in previous questioning, the child had been asked to "point to" the person who had harmed her. The jury would have no way of knowing the child was suffering from a vocabulary problem. Instead, it looked like the child could not recognize the defendant. Stories like this prompted Saywitz et al. (1990) to study children's understanding of legal terms from the ages of 5 to 11 years (see Focus on Research 11.1).

Saywitz, Jaenicke, and Camparo published a paper entitled "Children's Knowledge of Legal Terminology" in *Law and Human Behavior* in 1990. They were interested in assessing children's ability to define legal terms and how their skills change with age. They used a sample of 60 participants: 20 kindergartners (average age of 5 years and 10 months), 20 third graders (average age of 8 years and 8 months), and 20 sixth graders (average age of 11 years and 11months). The sample came from primarily middle-class households in the Los Angeles area, and the majority were Caucasian (63%). All of the participants were of normal intelligence.

The researchers compiled a list of 35 terms that were used frequently in cases that involved child witnesses. College students then rated each word or phrase in terms of difficulty on a 3-point scale. The children were asked to define the terms to someone who knew nothing about them (they were asked to think about explaining the words to a spaceman who was from another planet). Participants were prompted to give complete definitions by interviewers who asked "can you tell me more?" Responses were scored on a 5-point scale from 0 to 4. Zero represented *I don't know*, while 4 was reserved for definitions that included the defining features of the term. Scores were then collapsed with 0, 1, and 2 considered incorrect, and 3 and 4 rated as correct. Collapsed scores had an interrater reliability of 99% (this means that two raters agreed on the score 99% of the time).

The researchers found significant differences among all three of the grade levels. Third graders were significantly more accurate than were kindergartners, and sixth graders were significantly more accurate than third graders. However, this difference was not evident for all terms, only terms of moderate difficulty such as "duty," "identify," "case," and "oath." Terms that were easy or hard did not reveal a grade-related trend. Nearly all of the children could accurately define easy terms such as "lie," "police," and "remember," while almost none of the children could identify the difficult terms such as "defendant," "allegation," and "minor."

The authors noted three types of errors. First, many children simply said they did not know what a term meant. This decreased significantly with age (42%, 17%, and 5%). Second, children made auditory discrimination errors. In these cases they defined a legal term as a similarly sounding, familiar term. For instance, children would define "jury" as if it were "jewelry" or "journey." Thirdly, children made homonym errors in which they gave only the nonlegal definition for a term and not the legal definition. In fact, they said that the term could not mean anything else in court. For example, a "charge" was something you did with a credit card, a "motion" was something like moving your arms, and "parties" were places you went to get presents. Errors of auditory discrimination and homonyms were both less common with the older children (sixth grade) than they were with the younger children.

The authors concluded that some terms should be avoided when dealing with child witnesses, and others should be used only with older children. They also noted that older children were less likely to say "I don't know" and more likely to attempt to give a response even if they did not fully comprehend the question. Therefore, they proposed that children may move from a lack of understanding, to a mistaken understanding, and then to accurate knowledge of legal terms.

Based on their research, they concluded that children need to be prepared to testify, attorneys must be trained in age-appropriate questioning, and judges should be encouraged to monitor the vocabulary used in cases involving children.

The Court Prep Group

As professionals recognize that court can be confusing and even traumatic for children, they are beginning to devise and implement programs to make the experience less stressful. The benefits of these programs are twofold. First, children are less likely to experience additional trauma if they are adequately prepared, and second, children will be able to provide better testimony if they are not anxious. One such program is the **court prep group** devised by the National Children's Advocacy Center. This program evolved in response to feedback that simply taking children on a single tour of the courtroom prior to their giving testimony was not sufficient (Keeney, Amacher, & Kastanakis, 1992).

The court prep group involves a series of 6 group sessions with children who are going to testify in court. Ideally, the children in the groups will be similar in age (ranges of 6–12 and 13–17 are recommended, with individual work for those who are younger or older). When possible, the sessions are held at a time that is close to the trial date. The groups are led by various types of professionals including social workers, victim advocates, prosecutors, and therapists. During the first session, which takes place in a natural setting, the leader explains the goals of the group and engages the children in ice-breaking activities, frequently engaging them in artwork. The children also assemble puzzles of court personnel and are given the opportunity to discuss their feelings. In the second session, also in a natural setting, the children engage in artwork and writing on what they have learned about court and what they need to know, as well as their feelings about court. The leader also gives a good deal of concrete information about the court and the people who work there. Finally, the children engage in role-play with court props such as a judge's robe and gavel. For example, children may be asked to role-play a court case where the crime is an alleged robbery and the defendant is a friend of theirs. Sessions 3, 4, and 5 take place in the courthouse. During session 3, the children get a tour of the entire courthouse. This part of the program was added once professionals learned that many children are intimidated by the courthouse itself, not just the courtroom. It gives the children the opportunity to see the courtroom, the jury room, the victim advocate's office, and the bathrooms. Then the children play a game where they have to find numbers that are placed around the courtroom and match them to the person who would be there during a trial. This gives the leader another chance to review the roles that various people play in the court system. Sessions 4 and 5 involve engaging the children in a mock court in the actual courtroom. The children get to take turns playing the different roles—judge, witness, attorney, and so forth. The leader stresses appropriate witness behavior and helps the children focus on their feelings during the exercise. For very young children, the mock court would be replaced with watching a video of court proceedings. In the final session, the group returns to a natural setting to draw about what they have learned and what they feel. They also review key concepts and discuss individual case plans. At the conclusion of this session, the children receive graduation certificates. In addition to learning about the court process, the children receive support from the other members of the group along with a sense that they are not alone (Keeney, Amacher, & Kastanakis, 1992).

The Child Victim/Witness Program

A similar program, the **Child Victim/Witness Program** (CVWP), is offered in Canada. However, there is no group work. The advocates work individually with each family. There are also some unique aspects to the program. For instance, the victim advocate identifies someone in the child's life as the support person for the child (often this will be the nonoffending parent).

This person is then given the education necessary to allow him or her to fully support the child. The advantage of this tactic is that the person will have much more contact with the child than would an advocate with a large caseload. Another technique used by the Child Victim/Witness Program is to allow the child to visit court while it is in session, although not for a sexual abuse case. This gives the child the opportunity to see a trial in action, which can be quite different from seeing an empty courtroom (Doueck, Weston, Filbert, Beekhuis, & Redlich, 1997). As more programs like this emerge, it will be the job of research psychologists to assess their effectiveness so that the techniques used can be refined. The ultimate goal is to elicit accurate testimony while minimizing trauma to the child.

TYPES OF COURTS

Not only can court be intimidating, but the entire court process can also be confusing for both adults and children. In addition to the fact that there are many different types of maltreatment, the cases are handled in different court systems, depending upon the specific problem addressed (questions of who should raise the child versus questions of whether someone should be punished for maltreating behavior, for example). Not surprisingly, the legal handling of child maltreatment is almost as complex as the problem itself. There are many places within the vast legal system that issues of child abuse and neglect are dealt with. In the following section, I will address, in detail, four legal contexts where allegations of child maltreatment may be addressed: juvenile court, domestic relations court, criminal court, and civil court.

Juvenile Court

Juvenile court was designed to serve the interests of children and their families. These courts were first established in Illinois in 1899. With the foundation of this court system, the government was saying that even though we generally rely on the family to provide for children, if that family fails, it is the responsibility of the court system to intervene for the sake of the child and society. The juvenile court was founded to meet two major goals. The first was to rehabilitate youthful offenders, and the second was to protect children (Sagatun & Edwards, 1995). This second role of "State as parent" is referred to with the Latin phrase *parens patriae*. A literal translation of the phrase is "parent of the country" (Garner, 1996, p. 465).

Juvenile Delinquency Cases.   Juvenile court deals with three types of cases. First, judges in juvenile court hear cases of **juvenile delinquency**. These cases involve acts committed by children that would have been criminally prosecuted if the defendants were legal adults at the time of the crime. The reason these cases were moved to juvenile court from criminal court is that the founders believed that children who commit crimes should be dealt with differently from adults who commit crimes. In short, the focus of juvenile court was to be on treating and rehabilitating children more than on punishing them. To this end, the juvenile court was based on a clinical or medical model of intervention. Because the focus was on treatment, rather than punishment, it was determined that child defendants would not need the same constitutional protections that were granted to adult defendants (e.g., the right to legal counsel, the right to avoid self-incrimination, the right to a jury trial). While this policy sounded good, it did not work out exactly as planned. Over time it seemed evident that child defendants were punished, not treated. Punishing child defendants, who were not protected by the constitutional guarantees enjoyed by adult defendants, was challenged in 1967 (Feller, Davidson, Hardin, & Horowitz, 1992).

The Supreme Court ruled *In re Gault* (1967) that the juvenile court system was not meeting the needs of child defendants. In this case, a 15-year-old boy, Gerald Francis Gault, was committed to a state industrial school in Arizona for 6 years for making lewd remarks over the phone. The trial court described the remarks as being offensive and sexual. If Gault had been tried as an adult in criminal court, the maximum sentence he could have received was 2 months in jail and a fine of $50. Further, Gault had not been advised of his right to a lawyer or his right to remain silent. The Supreme Court ruled that, in order to ensure that child defendants were not punished unfairly, they must have due process rights such as the right to a lawyer, the right to be notified of the charges against them, the right to examine and cross-examine witnesses, and the right to avoid self-incrimination. Following this decision, the only significant right still denied to defendants in juvenile court is the right to a jury trial (Bartol & Bartol, 2004).

Status Offenses.   In addition to cases of juvenile delinquency, juvenile courts also hear cases that involve **status offenses**. An act that is against the law only because the person who commits the act is a child is considered a status offense (Bartol & Bartol, 2004). For instance, truancy is a status offense. A child who skips school can be punished legally. If you, as an adult, skip class, you only have to deal with your professor (and maybe your parents when they see your grade!), not the legal system. Underage drinking, underage smoking, and curfew violations are additional examples of status offenses. In most jurisdictions, attempts are made to keep children who are guilty of status offenses separated from children who are juvenile delinquents.

Dependency Cases.   The third type of course heard by juvenile court judges is the most relevant to child maltreatment. This is this court that hears **dependency cases**. The purpose of these cases is to determine whether the child's needs are met by the current guardians, generally the parents, or if the State needs to take temporary or permanent custody of the child. This court is charged with the mandates to protect children and to preserve families (Sagatun & Edwards, 1995). As you can imagine, in cases of child maltreatment it can be difficult, if not impossible, to meet both of these goals.

This court system follows a strict timetable. Once a child has been removed from his or her home based on allegations of maltreatment, a petition to declare the minor a dependent child must be filed with the court within 48 hours. During this time the child has the right to make two phone calls, one to parents and one to a lawyer. Within an additional 24 hours, the case must be before a judge for a detention hearing. This hearing is often referred to as the **72-hour hearing** (simply adding the original 48 hours and the next 24). The purpose of this court appearance is for the judge to decide whether there is sufficient evidence to hold the child pending further investigation. Generally, the attorney for child protective services (CPS) argues the case against the parents or guardians (Sagatun & Edwards, 1995).

If the judge finds sufficient reason to keep the child in care, a second hearing, the **jurisdictional hearing**, is scheduled (between 15 and 30 days later). This gives CPS time to perform additional investigation. The parents may also use this time to prepare their own defense. At the jurisdictional hearing, the judge decides whether the child meets the description of a dependent child. The format of these hearings is more relaxed than what you would see in a criminal court. Many of the traditional evidentiary protections are not enforced at this hearing. For instance, **hearsay** evidence is generally allowed, and children are often allowed to testify outside of their parents' presence. Finally, neither a husband nor a wife can claim spousal protection in this court. Because of these relaxed evidentiary standards, evidence gathered in these hearings cannot necessarily be used in other courts, such as criminal court (Feller et al., 1992; Sagatun & Edwards, 1995).

The judge then enters a decision at the **dispositional hearing**. This can take place immediately after the testimony is presented at the jurisdictional hearing, or up to 10 days later. At this time, the court decides what is to be done in the case. The major decision revolves around the physical placement of the child: returned to parents, placed with a relative, placed in a foster home, and so forth. The standard for judgment in this court is **clear and convincing evidence**. If the judge determines that there is clear and convincing evidence that the child is in danger, the ruling will favor CPS. If the judge does not see danger, the ruling will favor the parents. In cases where the judges rule for CPS, in addition to deciding placement, they lay out mandatory treatment plans. For example, the court may order the parent(s) to attend parenting classes and/ or drug and alcohol treatment. Other aspects of the treatment plan might involve contributing financially to the child's care, securing employment, and/or finding an appropriate place to raise the child. If appropriate, when a child is not returned home, a visitation schedule is devised and the details regarding how the visitation will occur are specified. For instance, the court will determine where visitation will take place and whether it will be supervised (Feller et al., 1992; Sagatun & Edwards, 1995).

Six months later, a **review hearing** takes place. The purpose of this court appearance is to assess the progress that has been made on the treatment plan. The judge's job is to decide if the parent(s) have made enough progress to ensure the safe return of the child to the home and the termination of court involvement with the family. If adequate progress has not been made, the treatment plan is reviewed and perhaps revised, and another review hearing is scheduled. By the time the child has been in out-of-home care for 12 to 18 months, the courts must hold a **permanency planning hearing**. Instead of allowing a child to languish in foster care, professionals are required to prepare a long-term plan for each child. If the parents are not meeting the goals of the treatment plan, the permanency plan may involve steps to terminate the parents' rights and make the child eligible for adoption (Feller, Davidson, Hardin & Horowitz, 1992; Sagatun & Edwards, 1995).

Domestic Relations Court

The function of the **domestic relations court** is the resolution of legal issues surrounding marriage and the rearing of children. In practical terms, this means the court deals mostly with issues of divorce, child custody, and child support. The presumption of this court is that parents are fit and proper adults and that they know what is best for their own children. The court is, therefore, set up to make the parents' decision legally binding. It is only if parents cannot agree that a court hearing may occur. However, before scheduling a hearing, many jurisdictions require that the adults first meet with a mediator in an attempt to resolve these issues in a less adversarial way. If **mediation** fails, the court will move forward with a hearing. Studies have shown that the vast majority of custody decisions are made by parents, not by the courts. Only a small percentage of cases, between 6% and 20%, are ultimately decided by the courts (Bartol & Bartol, 2004).

In domestic relations court, proceedings are initiated by parents. This differs from the juvenile courts, where proceedings are begun by CPS or the police. This means that any allegations of child maltreatment also come from parents. Because this court makes the presumption that the parents are "fit and proper," it is not set up to deal with child maltreatment. In fact, many recommend that any allegations of abuse that arise during divorce or custody proceedings should be referred to the juvenile court or CPS. Since the domestic relations court does not have the mechanisms in place to investigate charges of child maltreatment, it is up to the parent making the allegations to provide the evidence to support his or her claims. This can cause problems, because it means that the quality of the investigation and evidence is tied to the abilities and resources of the parent who is alleging abuse.

The domestic relations court judge can have a psychologist brought in to evaluate any children involved in custody disputes. The professional is then asked to report his or her findings to the court with a focus on the best interest of the child (Bartol & Bartol, 2004). In addition to having children go through a court-ordered evaluation, parents may hire additional professionals to further assess the children involved. The court sets no limits on the number of times a child can be assessed. In hotly contested cases, a child may be subjected to many psychological evaluations, and this is only one of the common problems faced by children in domestic relations court. These children are rarely assigned a lawyer of their own. So, while both parents have representation, the most vulnerable parties, the children, are on their own. In addition, children may be asked to testify in the presence of both of their parents. During custody disputes it is not uncommon for a judge to ask a child about how his parents take care of him or even whom he would prefer to live with after the divorce. To make matters even more challenging, children are often asked to respond to these questions in the presence of their parents. A child who may have strong ties to both parents is put in an extremely difficult situation. The ability of judges to elicit information from children, in private chambers or in court, varies widely. Judges are not required to have any specialized training in child development, and they can also be extremely intimidating.

After hearing the testimony, the judge makes a decision that is thought to be in the **best interest of child**. Until about 30 years ago, in accordance with the tender years presumption, modern courts frequently ruled in the mother's favor as a matter of routine. It was the overwhelming belief that young children needed their mothers more than their fathers. Today, other factors are considered by the court. For instance, a judge may consider who has been serving as the primary caregiver for the child, which parent is the better parent, and which adult is more likely to encourage a healthy relationship between the child and the noncustodial parent, as well as parental problems such as mental illness, substance abuse, and even extramarital affairs if the affair can be shown to have hurt the child. Courts will also consider violence within the home, including domestic violence and child abuse. Finally, especially with older children, the judge will weigh the stated preference of the child. Based on this evaluation, the judge not only determines custody but also sets up a visitation plan. Court-ordered visitation ranges from no visitation at all to supervised visits to unsupervised visits (Sagutan & Edwards, 1995).

After decisions have been made, the court has little enforcement power. The domestic relations court does not have the powers to investigate, prosecute, or supervise the cases it rules on. If one party fails to fulfill the court order, it is up to the injured party to bring a new complaint. If a parent does not pay court-ordered child support, it is up the parent who did not receive the money to bring a new complaint before the court. The custodial parent can also violate the court order by, for example, failing to produce the child for visitation. In this case, the noncustodial parent would have to bring the custodial parent back to court. With regard to child maltreatment allegations, the parent making the claims must report, prove, and then monitor the situation. If a parent is in clear violation of an order of the domestic relations court, he or she would be found to be in civil contempt. As such, they can be fined or jailed while they are violating the order. However, once they end the violation (e.g., they make the payment or produce the child), they are no longer in contempt of court (Sagatun & Edwards, 1995). Clearly, this court is not the best response to allegations of child maltreatment.

Criminal Courts

The most powerful response to child abuse and neglect is criminal prosecution. The **criminal courts** are the venues that can result in imprisonment for behavior. The vast majority of child maltreatment cases never make it to criminal court. This court is generally used only for the most severe cases of physical abuse (those causing severe, permanent harm or death) and, more recently, cases of sexual abuse. Only cases of extreme physical neglect (that result in severe harm or death) are likely to be heard in criminal court. Criminal charges are rarely used to deal with maltreatment; however, they are the most intense charges. Additionally, the number of these cases that are brought to criminal court does appear to be increasing (see Focus on Research 11.2).

FOCUS ON RESEARCH 11.2

In 2003, Cross, Walsh, Simone, and Jones published a meta-analysis of rates of crimi-nal justice decisions in cases alleging child abuse. Although child abuse cases have not, historically, been heard in great numbers in criminal court, some surveys of prosecutors indicated that this was changing during the 1980s and 1990s. To determine rates of refer-ral for prosecution, charges, and guilty pleas, the authors reviewed 21 studies that had examined criminal prosecution in cases of child abuse. In order to be included in the meta-analysis, the study had to present quantitative data on at least one of the following aspects of case flow: referral to district attorneys, charging rate, the percentage of cases that were carried forward (they resulted in either a guilty plea or a trial), the rate of guilty pleas or verdicts, or the incarceration rate. With one exception (a study done in 1969), all studies were fairly recent (5 were conducted in the 1980s, 11 in the 1990s and 4 in the 2000s).

The authors found that rates varied dramatically across studies. For instance, the referral rate of child abuse claims to the district attorney ranged from a low of 40% to a high of 85%. Although the mean rate of referral was greater than 50%, the authors noted that the extreme variability makes the mean difficult to interpret. Once cases were referred to the district attorney, the rate of charging also varied significantly (from a low of 28% to a high of 94%). However, once charges were filed, a consistently high percent-age (79%) of cases were carried forward and not dismissed or transferred. The majority of studies also showed high plea rates (82%) and low trial rates (18%). Although 14 of 19 studies reported trial rates that were equal to or less than 16%, the range across all studies was from 3% to 61%. The incarceration rate also varied greatly across studies, from a low of 24% to a high of 96%, with a mean rate of 54%.

The authors summarized the data by projecting the likely results of 100 hypotheti-cal cases referred for prosecution of child abuse claims (Cross, Walsh, Simone, & Jones, 2003, p. 324):

66 would be charged
43 would plead guilty
12 would be dismissed or transferred
2 would be diverted to treatment
6 would be convicted at trial
3 would be acquitted at trial
26 would be incarcerated

The decision to press criminal charges is usually decided by law enforcement and prosecut-ing attorneys. However, in some areas, there is increased contact between CPS and law enforce-ment. Their interaction is complex because, although they both strive to protect victims, they often have different goals. CPS and the dependency courts are designed as therapeutic models with hopes of reuniting families; the criminal courts are focused on gathering evidence for the purpose of criminal prosecution, punishment, and the protection of potential future victims. It is not always clear which approach is the best in cases of maltreatment. Since the early 1970s there have been calls for "interdisciplinary collaboration" between CPS and the police. When these interdisciplinary teams are created, they appear to be most successful when there are equal numbers of participants from each area, the participants from each area are perceived to be equal in power, there is mutual respect between team members, and there is regular and direct communication at meetings in neutral locations (Sedlack et al., 2006). As you can imagine, it is difficult to meet these ideal standards among teams who come to the table with some fundamental differences in goals.

Charges and Pleas. Unlike the other court systems covered so far, when a case is heard in criminal court, someone must be charged with an offense. Charges regarding child maltreatment can be **felony** or misdemeanor charges. Furthermore, once a person has been charged with a crime, the person has all of the rights for due process that are guaranteed by the Constitution: the right to an attorney, the right to be notified of the charges, the right to confront and cross-examine witnesses, the right to remain silent, the right to a reasonable bail, the right to a jury trial, and the right to appeal the verdict of the court. The defendant is granted these rights in criminal court because the potential outcomes (prison, death penalty) are so severe. In addition to these rights, a further protection for defendants is the standard of proof used in criminal court. In order to find a defendant guilty, the prosecution must prove guilt **beyond a reasonable doubt**. While there is much debate about exactly what this phrase means, all agree that it is the highest standard of proof used in the American courts (Brooks, 1996).

In criminal court, the case is called *Name of State v. Name of Accused*. If I were charged by South Carolina, the case would be called *South Carolina v. McCoy*. This helps to remind you that the party pressing charges is the State, not the victim. In fact, the State can press charges even if a victim would prefer that the defendant was not prosecuted (Brooks, 1996). The process begins when the charges are filed and bail is set. In most jurisdictions, this is followed by a grand jury hearing. The purpose of these hearings is to make sure that the State has probable cause to try the case. Only the prosecution presents evidence at this time, and the jury decides by a majority vote. The purpose of this system is to prevent the State from harassing citizens whom they do not have sufficient evidence against and to control court costs by preventing trials that are highly unlikely to result in a guilty verdict (Shaw & Brenner, 2006).

If the State proceeds with its case, the next step is the **arraignment**. At this time the defendant officially enters a plea. There are four possible pleas: guilty, not guilty, not guilty by reason of insanity, and no contest. A plea of no contest is not an admission of guilt; it simply means that the accused will not fight the charge(s). In this situation, the defendant then accepts whatever sentence is given. These sentences are frequently less than sentences imposed when a defendant is tried and found guilty. A defendant may choose this option if the case is likely to result in a subsequent civil action, because a plea of no contest may not be used against a defendant in later civil cases (Garner, 1996). In order to plead no contest, both parties and the judge need to agree that the verdict is acceptable.

After a plea of not guilty has been entered, plea bargaining begins. Most cases will end with this process. Generally, the defendant agrees to plead guilty to a lesser charge or to plead guilty to only some of the charges that have been filed. In other cases, the defendant pleads guilty in return for a predetermined sentence. This type of plea bargaining, when permitted, is limited in many jurisdictions and generally requires the approval of a trial judge (Larson, 2000). This has some advantages and disadvantages for the child victims in maltreatment cases. On the positive side, the defendant is found guilty of some offense and the child is not forced to testify at trial. On the other hand, the defendant often pleads guilty to a much less severe crime than that allegedly committed against the child. It is possible that this leaves the child feeling further victimized. To make matters worse, the victim has no official say in what type of plea is offered.

Accommodations for Children Who Testify. If the case does go to trial, the defendant has significant rights, including the right to confront any witnesses who testify against them. As mentioned previously, this can be problematic for children who may be unable to testify in the presence of their alleged abusers. Attempts have been made to reduce the potential trauma of being a child witness. Instead of testifying in court, some children have been allowed to testify from a nearby location via closed-circuit television, and exceptions to hearsay laws have been granted to let adults testify about what a child said to them. While these techniques may protect a child victim from further trauma, they can be problematic legally because they limit the defendant's constitutional guarantee to confront and cross-examine witnesses against them (see Legal Example 11.1). Furthermore, Goodman et al. (2006) reported that jurors found children who testified in person to be more credible and that the jurors felt more empathy for these alleged victims. In addition, jurors were more confident about the defendant's guilt when the child's testimony was presented in person and not via closed-circuit television.

Other minor changes can be made in the criminal court proceedings to make testifying easier on child victims while still having them testify in person. For example, a child's testimony can be given in shorter segments with frequent recesses. In addition, if a child is going to testify, cases can be given priority so as to lessen the delay between the alleged crime and the child's testimony. Simple changes may also be made to the physical setting of the courtroom. For example, a trial judge in Massachusetts allowed a child witness to testify while sitting at a child-sized table in front of the jury instead of from the witness stand. This decision was upheld by the Massachusetts Supreme Judicial Court. A **guardian ad litem**, or support person, may also be appointed to the child so that there is always someone who is looking out for the child's rights. Not only does this relieve some of the child's fears, but research has suggested that it also increases a child's ability to provide answers during direct examination (Goodman et. al, 1992). Other judges have required attorneys to remain seated while questioning children, allowed the witness chair to be turned slightly away from the defendant, or forbidden people to enter or leave the courtroom during a child's testimony. Finally, the judge can restrict public access to the courtroom while a child is testifying. Any of these things may make the experience easier for a young victim (Myers, 1996).

While courts seem to be moving in the direction of accommodating child witnesses, these changes are not always upheld on appeal. In a number of cases, state supreme courts have ruled that some changes are not appropriate, especially in criminal courts. For instance, a trial judge was ruled to have gone too far by allowing a child witness to sit on his lap (*State v. Michaels,* 1993), and another judge was faulted for promising to give a child ice cream if she told what was "real" (*State v. R. W.,* 1986). In this case, the child refused to proceed with cross-examination before getting the promised treat. When the judge provided the reward in the courtroom, it appeared that the judge was agreeing that the child had, indeed, told what was real. While the reasoning behind these decisions may seem clear, other cases are less obvious. For instance, the Hawaii Court of Appeals ruled in *State v. Palabay* (1992) that a 12 year-old witness should not have been allowed to hold a teddy bear while testifying unless the State was able to provide a compelling reason for allowing this (Myers, 1996).

Another accommodation to child witnesses has been to allow hearsay evidence under some conditions. *Hearsay* is defined by *Black's Law Dictionary* as, "testimony that is given by a witness who related not what he or she knows personally, but what others have said, and that is therefore dependent on the credibility of someone other than the witness; such testimony is generally inadmissible under the rules of evidence" (Garner, 1996, p. 287). Because child abuse victims may disclose to adults (parents, teachers, professionals, etc.) and still be ineffective as witnesses themselves, hearsay exceptions exist to get their statements admitted at trial. For instance, all U.S. courts recognize the **excited utterance exception**. This exception allows witnesses to testify about things a child said immediately after a startling event (Myers, 1996). The reasoning is that statements made by an upset or emotional child right after a traumatic event are likely to be true because such children are not in a state to make up plausible lies. A second hearsay exception is the medical diagnosis or treatment exception. This allows medical

A major issue that professionals deal with when considering child witnesses is the confrontation clause. According to the Sixth Amendment of the U.S. Constitution, a defendant is guaranteed the right "to be confronted with the witnesses against him." This has been interpreted to mean that a witness must provide testimony in the presence of the accused, and the defendant has the right to cross-examine that witness. The basis of this guarantee is the belief that direct and cross-examinations are the best way to ensure truthful testimony. In opposition to this guarantee is research that finds that being forced to testify in the presence of the accused is a highly negative scenario for child witnesses (Bussey, Lee, & Grimbeek, 2003). Various attempts have been made to protect children without depriving defendants of their constitutional rights. It has proven to be a tough ethical and legal dilemma. This issue has been heard twice by the U.S. Supreme Court in *Coy v. Iowa* (1988) and in *Maryland v. Craig* (1990).

COY V. IOWA (1988)

In *Coy v. Iowa* the defendant was charged with the sexual molestation of two girls, both 13 years old. It was alleged that he entered the tent where they were camping in their backyard and sexually assaulted them. At the time of his jury trial, the judge allowed a screen to be placed in the courtroom between the witnesses and the defendant. The screen was used based on a state statute that existed to protect child victims of sexual abuse. With the screen in place, and the lighting in the room adjusted, the defendant was able to see the witnesses dimly, and he could hear their testimony. The witnesses were not able to see the defendant. Coy was found guilty on two counts of lascivious acts with a child by the trial court. Coy appealed to the Iowa Supreme Court on the grounds that he had been denied the right to face his accusers. Coy's team also argued that the use of the screen made him appear guilty, and therefore interfered with the presumption of innocence. Coy's conviction was upheld by the Iowa Supreme Court. The court ruled that because his attorney was able to cross-examine the witnesses, his right to confrontation had not been violated. The court further stated that the screen was not inherently prejudicial.

Coy's case was then appealed to the Supreme Court of the U.S. on the grounds that his Sixth Amendment rights had been violated by use of the screen. The U.S. Supreme Court ruled in favor of Coy, stating, "That core guarantee serves the general perception that confrontation is essential to fairness, and helps to ensure the integrity of the fact-finding process by making it more difficult for witnesses to lie" (p. 2). While the court acknowledged that this could be traumatic for witnesses by writing, "It is a truism that constitutional protections have costs" (p. 6) the court argued further that the use of the screen by the trial court violated this right. The Supreme Court justices wrote that there may be some exceptions to this guarantee, but they did not apply to this case. Even though Iowa had a statute designed to protect child witnesses, it was not established that this protection was needed in this case. The justices noted that there was no evidence that these particular witnesses were in need of special protection. Therefore, the use of the screen was not acceptable.

This decision was a 6 to 2 ruling by the court (Justice Kennedy did not take part in either the consideration or the decision of the case; hence, only eight justices were involved). The dissenting justices (Blackmun and Rehnquist) felt that the screen had not violated Coy's Sixth Amendment rights. They noted that the following conditions were met: the witnesses were under oath; they were subject to cross-examination; the jury, judge, and defendant could see and hear the witnesses; the jury and judge could see the defendant while the witnesses testified; and the witnesses were aware that the defendant could see and hear them. Because all of these things were true, Coy's Sixth Amendment rights were not violated. The dissenting justices went on to say that focusing narrowly on witnesses "seeing" the defendant while they testified could obscure the more fundamental aspects of the confrontation clause—the right to cross-examine witnesses and the opportunity for the jury to observe the witnesses while they testify. The justices raised the following thought-provoking question: If seeing the defendant is an absolute requirement of the confrontation clause, how would the court handle a blind witness? The dissenting justices also argued that the use of the screen was not inherently prejudicial. Although wearing prison garb or being shackled does make a defendant look guilty, the same cannot be said of the screen because screens are not associated with convicts. Further, the trial court judge had instructed the jury not to draw any inference of guilt from the use of the screen.

Finally, the dissenting justices point out that face-to-face confrontation is preferred, but it is not an absolute. Because testifying may be traumatic for children, they should be protected. If face-to-face testimony is overwhelming for children, procedures can be used to protect the children and possibly increase the accuracy of their testimony as a result of lowered anxiety. The justices wrote that it could be assumed that child witnesses would benefit from the use of the screen without an individualized finding of trauma for each case.

Discussion Questions

1. Which court decision do you agree with in the Coy case? Why?
2. If you were a juror in this case, do you think that the use of the screen would have made the defendant appear guilty?
3. Can you think of ways that children could testify that would protect them without violating the rights of the defendant?

As you can see, this is not an easy issue to resolve. People have very strong feelings on both sides of this debate. Therefore, it is not overly surprising that the same issue was back before the U.S. Supreme Court only 2 years later in the case of *Maryland v. Craig*.

MARYLAND V. CRAIG (1990)

In 1986, Sandra Craig was charged with sexually abusing a 6-year-old who had attended the pre-kindergarten/kindergarten center that she operated. The child had attended the center for 2 years prior to the allegations of abuse. During her trial, the judge permitted the child witness to testify via one-way closed-circuit television. This was allowed after an expert had testified that the child would suffer serious emotional distress if forced to testify in front of the defendant, and that this distress would likely interfere with her ability to provide accurate testimony. During the trial, the child witness testified in a separate room with only the prosecutor and defense counsel present. Her testimony was broadcast live to the courtroom, where the defendant, jury, and judge were able to see and hear the child. The defendant was also able to communicate with her counsel. Craig was found guilty by the trial court, but she appealed on the grounds that her Sixth Amendment rights had been violated. The Maryland Court of Special Appeals affirmed the decision of the trial court, but the Maryland Court of Appeals reversed the decision of the trial court. The court of appeals did not agree with Craig that her right to face her accusers was absolute, but they said the current case did not meet the necessary standards to allow an exception. Specifically, the court wrote that it was not enough to have an expert say the child would be emotionally distressed if forced to testify in front of the accused. They suggested that this determination could only be made by attempting to question the child in front of the defendant and seeing if the child was too distressed to communicate. Further, they said the court should have explored an intermediate option like two-way television. The case was appealed to the U.S. Supreme Court.

In a 5 to 4 decision, the Supreme Court ruled to affirm the trial court. The justices wrote that the confrontation clause does not guarantee a defendant the right to be face-to-face with their accuser. Maryland's desire to protect a child witness was a sufficient reason to waive the right to face-to-face confrontation as long as the trial court established individual trauma. The ruling of an expert is sufficient for this purpose. It is not necessary, as advocated by the Maryland Court of Appeals, to establish this by exposing the child to the defendant. The justices did add that the expert must find that the child would be traumatized specifically by facing the defendant and not by other aspects of testifying such as the courtroom itself.

The opinion of the four dissenting justices was written by Justice Scalia and begins with this very strong statement, "Seldom has this Court failed so conspicuously to sustain a categorical guarantee of the Constitution against the tide of prevailing current opinion" (p. 14); and the introduction ends, "Because the text of the Sixth Amendment is clear, and because the Constitution is meant to protect against, rather than conform to, current 'widespread belief,' I respectfully dissent" (p. 15). Scalia goes on to argue that face-to-face confrontation is a constitutional guarantee and not a mere preference. While it may be nice to shield children, it is necessary to protect defendants by ensuring that they receive what they are guaranteed. Because research shows that children are, in fact, more vulnerable to suggestion and to confusing fantasy with reality, it is even more imperative to have them present their testimony live, in court, so it can be most fully assessed by the jurors. Scalia concludes by saying, "I have no need to defend the value of confrontation because the Court has no authority to question it" (p. 18).

Given the intense debate on this issue, most prosecutors prefer to have children testify so that cases cannot be appealed on grounds like these. This means, of course, that children are exposed to the emotional distress that this entails. For this reason, professionals continue to strive to find ways to make this experience easier without violating the rights of the accused.

Discussion Questions

1. Which court decision do you agree with in the Craig case? Why?
2. If you were a juror in this case, do you think that the use of closed-circuit television would have made the defendant appear guilty?
3. What do you think is necessary to establish that a witness would be traumatized by facing a defendant in court? (e.g., is expert testimony sufficient?)
4. Which technique do you think is better for the child: closed-circuit television or the use of a screen? Which is better for the defendant?

professionals to testify to statements made to them by children they were treating (Myers, 1996). The assumption is that a person would not lie to a person who was using the information to treat him or her. Some states have gone so far as to add more general exceptions for cases of child sexual abuse or for child witnesses in general (Myers, 1996).

Are Criminal Courts an Appropriate Venue for Allegations of Child Abuse?.   Given all of these controversial issues, there is still much debate about whether the criminal courts are the appropriate arena for addressing charges of child maltreatment. Certainly, the criminal court is not helping as would a therapeutic approach. If the perpetrator is jailed, the likelihood of family reunification is low. Even when the child may not ever be safe with the perpetrator, criminal cases can tear apart the extended family as each person chooses a side. Second, criminal prosecution ignores the root of the problem. It does not attempt to address what caused the parent to behave inappropriately. If the root cause is not identified, it will not be fixed. Third, as mentioned earlier, children often experience significant stress if they have to testify in criminal court. In addition, a victim may feel guilty if his or her testimony sends a family member to jail. For all of these reasons, some argue that cases of child maltreatment are best handled in the dependency courts.

On the other hand, there are some strong arguments in favor of prosecuting child maltreatment cases in criminal court. Perhaps the most striking reason is that criminal prosecution makes child maltreatment a real crime—one that has real penalties. Some argue that for too long, what goes on inside a family's home has been too protected from legal intervention. A child who is victimized deserves to have the perpetrator prosecuted, even if that perpetrator is a family member. Also, because criminal courts can imprison guilty defendants, this court system is best set up to protect potential future victims from the perpetrator. Finally, because the standard of proof is so high in criminal court, it is less likely that a false allegation of abuse would be found to be true in this court. In this way, criminal prosecution offers extra protection to the wrongly accused. Given this controversy, it is not surprising that only a small number of child maltreatment cases are tried in criminal court.

Civil Court

Child maltreatment cases have not traditionally been heard in **civil court**. However, in recent years, there has been an increase in civil cases related to child abuse. The use of the civil court was often the only avenue available for people who allegedly recovered memories of child abuse after they were adults. Because they were no longer dependents, the cases could not be heard in juvenile courts or domestic relations courts. Criminal courts were not an option in any states that had a **statute of limitations** for criminal charges. If too much time (usually seven years) had passed between the alleged event and the claim, the defendant could not be prosecuted criminally.

Tort Laws.   Child maltreatment cases heard in civil court have usually been related to **tort laws**. The tort laws allow people to sue others based on the claim that some conduct, product, or service has caused harm because it does not meet minimal, acceptable standards (Garner, 1996). You are probably familiar with cases using the term *personal injury*, and you have likely had the greatest exposure to cases dealing with product liability. If a person was injured by a product that was not well made, he or she could sue the manufacturer. In cases of child maltreatment, the **plaintiff** (person making the charges) is saying that the defendant did not meet society's standard for child rearing. These cases can involve intentionally inflicted harm (what I have been referring to as abuse) or negligence and carelessness (which would be appropriate for cases of neglect). The goal of taking someone to civil court is to recover damages. If you are found guilty in civil court, you do not go to jail, but you must pay reparations to the alleged victim. Because this court can only impose monetary punishment, as opposed to imprisonment, it does not offer as many protections to defendants. For instance, defendants still have the right to a trial by jury, but they do not have the right to have an attorney provided for them (Brooks, 1996).

It is easier to get a guilty verdict in civil court than in criminal court because the standard of proof is lower. In order to find the defendant guilty in civil court, the jury or judge needs to find that the **preponderance of evidence** favors the plaintiff (Loar, 1998). In other words, there is more evidence to support the plaintiff than there is to support the defendant. When jury members believe that more than 50% of the evidence supports one party, he or she must rule for that party.

The plaintiff in a civil court case must be an adult. However, this does not mean that a child is forced to wait until age 18 in order to pursue a civil case. An adult can bring civil charges on a child's behalf. Civil cases are labeled with the names of the parties involved (Carp, Stidham, & Manning, 2004). So, if I sued my neighbor, John Jones, the case would be *McCoy v. Jones*. Like criminal court cases, most civil court cases are settled prior to trial, but most courts require a review before an action brought on behalf of a child can be settled. If the case goes to trial, the procedure is similar to that used in criminal court and, once again, the child may be forced to testify.

Class Action Suits.   **Class action suits** are filed in civil court. In these cases, an action is brought by a few people on behalf of a group. The goal is to seek relief for all members of the group. Often the purpose is to force a systemwide change so that an entire group is treated more fairly by an agency. With regard to child maltreatment, a group may sue the State under the general premise that children are not properly served because the agencies designed to protect them are understaffed. They may also allege that maltreated children are at greater risk once in the care of the Department of Social Services than they were in their homes, or that the agency is not following the federal regulations that address child maltreatment. In some cases, individual claims are made against the State. In general, the civil courts have found for the State if a child is injured at home. In other words, failure to protect the child is not something that the State is liable for. Furthermore, if a parent voluntarily places his or her child in the care of the State, the State is not liable if the child is harmed while in the State's care. The only cases where suits against the State on behalf of an individual child tend to be successful are when the child is harmed while in involuntary placement. In these cases, a child is removed from home against the wishes of parents and is maltreated or harmed while in the State's care (Sagatun & Edwards, 1995).

Possible Defendants in Civil Suits.   Some civil cases against the State have been successful, as have cases against abusive parents. In addition, suits against nonabusive parents have been successful when it was shown that they allowed the abuse to occur. While it is obvious that the most common defendants would be parents, there is a problem with this choice of defendant. Because civil courts can only issue financial penalties, it is not very productive to sue parents who are poor. In response to this, some plaintiffs have attempted to sue insurance companies, usually under homeowner policies. In this scenario, the claim is that the child was harmed in the home and, therefore, the insurance company is liable. This approach has not proven to be successful because the policies insure against accidental injury, not injury that results from intentional or willful acts (Loar, 1998).

In other cases, civil charges have been filed against professionals who came in contact with the child and failed to report suspected abuse. In fact, the courts have gone beyond failure to report suspected abuse and found professionals responsible if they failed to notice signs of abuse that a trained professional should have noticed. (For an example, see the case of *Landeros v. Flood* in chapter 3.)

CONCLUSION

In conclusion, the law regarding child maltreatment is complex, as is the American court system. While nearly everyone agrees that the government needs to have a role in protecting the child, there is much less agreement about what that role should be. In addition, it is clear that even if protecting children is a goal of the courts, the courts were not set up with children in mind. Finally, some argue that little of this legal finagling actually helps to prevent child maltreatment. Still, given that this is the current state of the legal system, it is important for all of those who work with children to be aware of the basics of our court systems.

DISCUSSION QUESTIONS

1. What are the benefits and weaknesses of each court system when handling cases of alleged child maltreatment? Should maltreatment cases be heard in all four court systems?
2. Is it possible to protect child witnesses while preserving the rights of defendants in criminal court? If not, who should be protected first?
3. If you were given a $1 million grant to protect child witnesses in your community, how would you spend the money?

DEFINITIONS

Adversarial System: a court system that involves active and unhindered parties contesting with each other in the presence of an independent decision maker (judge or jury).

Cross-Examination: the questioning of a witness by the opposing party, especially for the purpose of clarifying or discrediting the witness's testimony.

Court Prep Group: a program devised by the National Children's Advocacy Center to prepare groups of children for court through education, understanding of emotional issues, role-play, and touring of a courthouse.

Child Victim/Witness Program (CVWP): an individualized Canadian program that prepares children for court by educating them, by appointing and educating a support person to assist them, and by visiting a court in session.

Juvenile Delinquency: antisocial behavior by a minor, especially if the behavior is in violation of the law and would be punished criminally if committed by an adult.

Status Offense: an act that is against the law only because the person engaging in it is a minor.

Dependency Case: a case to determine whether a child's needs are being met by his or her guardians or if the State needs to take temporary or permanent custody of the child.

Detention Hearing: a hearing for the purpose of determining whether there is sufficient evidence for the State to hold the child pending further investigation; also referred to as the 72-hour hearing.

Jurisdictional Hearing: a hearing where evidence is presented by child protective services and parents and a guardian ad litem so the judge can determine whether the child meets the description of a dependent child.

Hearsay: testimony based not on what one knows personally but on what someone else has said.

Dispositional Hearing: a hearing when the judge enters their decision as to what is in the best interest of the child.

Clear and Convincing Evidence: a degree of evidence that indicates that the issue being proven is highly probable. It is a higher standard of proof than the preponderance of evidence, but a lower standard than beyond a reasonable doubt.

Review Hearing: a hearing that takes place approximately 6 months after a care plan has been enacted, for the purpose of reviewing the progress that has been made on the treatment plan.

Permanency Planning Hearing: a review of the child's current placement and progress with the goal of establishing long-range goals if the child requires continued care. Permanent plans include the termination of parental rights and adoption.

Domestic Relations Court: a court that is dedicated to hearing cases related to divorce, child custody and support, paternity and other family-law issues; it is also called family court.

Mediation: a neutral person's helping two disputing parties arrive at a solution that is mutually acceptable; however, the mediator's decision is not legally binding.

Best Interest of the Child: the principle that drives the judge's decisions in domestic relations courts when deciding issues of custody and support.

Criminal Court: the court charged with the administration of justice via penalty or punishment.

Felony: a serious crime that is punishable with imprisonment of greater than 1 year or even death.

Beyond a Reasonable Doubt: the burden of proof in criminal court; the doubt that prevents one from being firmly convinced of a defendant's guilt; the highest burden of proof.

Arraignment: an initial step in criminal prosecution where defendants hear the charges against them and enter a plea.

Guardian ad Litem: an adult who is appointed by the court to represent the best interests of the child during court proceedings.

Excited Utterance Exception: an exception regarding a statement that is made while under stress about an event, which is admissible as hearsay testimony.

Civil Court: a court that hears noncriminal cases where parties seek to settle disputes and be awarded damages.

Statute of Limitations: a law that sets a time frame for the prosecution of a crime or for suing to ensure that cases are resolved while the evidence is still reasonably available.

Tort Laws: laws that allow people to sue others based on the claim that some conduct, product, or service that does not meet minimal, acceptable standards has caused harm.

Plaintiff: the party that brings the suit in civil court.

Preponderance of Evidence: the burden of proof in a civil trial; the greater weight of evidence, however slight.

Class Action Suit: a lawsuit in which one person or a small group of people sue as representatives of a larger group of affected people because the group is so large that individual suits would not be practical.

PART IV

What Happens Next

CHAPTER 12

The Maltreated Child and Child Protective Services' Response

What Happens After a Report Is Made?

STEFANIE M. KEEN

Raising a family in the manner and style deemed personally appropriate and desirable is a fundamental parental right. With this right, however, comes obligation. Society presumes that parents will raise their children with the children's best interests at heart. When this does not occur and parents do not protect their children from harm or do not meet their children's basic needs, then society has the responsibility to intervene on behalf of the children (Goldman, Salus, Wolcott, & Kennedy, 2003).

In the U.S., the governmental agency that receives and responds to reports of child maltreatment is broadly known as child protective services (CPS). Each state is responsible for maintaining and operating its own child protective agency, which may vary in name from one state to another (Department of Children and Families, Department of Social Services, etc.). While law enforcement may also be involved in the child protection process, the majority of child protection efforts fall on the shoulders of CPS agencies.

Although the primary responsibility for CPS **jurisdiction** lies at state and local levels, there are several federal laws that mandate and subsequently govern CPS agencies. The **Child Abuse Prevention and Treatment Act** (CAPTA) was passed in 1974 and authorizes the expenditure of federal dollars to individual states for their child protection efforts. To receive these funds, states must conform their child abuse reporting laws to federal standards and adhere to the minimum federal definitions of child abuse and neglect (Myers, 2002). The Child Abuse Prevention and Treatment Act was most recently amended and reauthorized in 2003 by the **Keeping Children and Families Safe Act**.

Additional federal legislation includes the **Adoption Assistance and Child Welfare Act** (1980), which requires states to make **reasonable efforts** to prevent the removal of children from their parents (i.e., family preservation). If removal is unavoidable, this act further requires states to make reasonable efforts to reunify children with their parents (i.e., family reunification). Lastly, the **Adoption and Safe Families Act** (1997) was passed in an attempt to clarify the "reasonable efforts" requirement previously established by the Adoption Assistance and Child Welfare Act with respect to **family preservation and reunification** ("In making reasonable efforts, the child's health and safety shall be the paramount concern." Public Law 105-89) and to correct problems inherent in the foster care system that deterred the adoption of children with special needs (Myers, 2002).

    The **Office on Child Abuse and Neglect** (OCAN), a division within the Children's Bureau of the **Administration for Children and Families** (ACF) has developed a *User Manual Series* to provide state agencies with up-to-date knowledge and practice guidelines regarding child protection. As part of this series, *Child Protective Services: A Guide for Caseworkers* (2003) provides guidance to state agencies regarding their specific child protection policies and regulations. According to this manual, the basic philosophical tenets of CPS are as follows:

- A safe and permanent home and family is the best place for children to grow up.
- Most parents want to be good parents, and when adequately supported, they have the strength and capacity to care for their children and keep them safe.
- Families who need assistance from CPS agencies are diverse in terms of structure, culture, race, religion, economic status, beliefs, values, and lifestyles.
- CPS agencies are held accountable for achieving outcomes of child safety, permanence, and family well-being.
- CPS efforts are most likely to succeed when clients are involved and actively participate in the process.
- When parents cannot or will not fulfill their responsibilities to protect their children, CPS has the right and obligation to intervene directly on the children's behalf.
- When children are placed in out-of-home care because their safety cannot be assured, CPS should develop a permanency plan as soon as possible.
- To best protect a child's overall well-being, agencies want to assure that children move to **permanency** as quickly as possible (DePanfilis & Salus, 2003).

As should be clear from these tenets, the main role of any CPS agency is to help families function to the best of their ability by providing services necessary to preserve the family structure. The ultimate goal of CPS is to help parents protect their children and to keep children with their families whenever possible. If the child's home environment is not safe, then it is CPS's obligation to intervene on the child's behalf and establish a safe environment in which the child can live. Whenever possible, this entails allowing the child to remain at home and working with the family to improve the child's living conditions and remedy any safety concerns. Only if this is not possible or cannot be readily accomplished should CPS remove children from their homes and place them in out-of-home care. Even under these circumstances, it is the agency's responsibility to make every reasonable attempt to reunify a family before developing an alternate plan for residency. Regardless of the eventual outcome, it is understood that both **continuity** and permanency with respect to a child's living environment and overall developmental trajectory are paramount concerns and should be achieved as quickly and as smoothly as possible.

    In accordance with these tenets, the **National Association of Public Child Welfare Administrators** (NAPCWA) has outlined the mission of CPS agencies to include assessing the safety of children, intervening to protect children from harm, strengthening the ability of families to protect their children, and providing either family reunification or an alternative, safe family for the child. To fulfill its mission, CPS agencies should provide **culturally responsive**

services to children and their families to achieve safety, well-being, and permanency for children. In doing so, CPS agencies often facilitate collaborations with community agencies and enlist the help of these agencies to provide the necessary services and resources to support families and protect children from maltreatment (NAPCWA, 1999).

A large portion of CPS efforts are spent in activities centered on receiving and responding to **allegations** of child maltreatment. These allegations may reach CPS through a number of sources including law enforcement, legally mandated reporters (e.g., physicians, mental health professionals, educators), concerned relatives or neighbors, or anonymous telephone calls to a 24-hour hotline. As part of this process, CPS agencies generally perform a variety of functions, including:

- *Intake.* This process includes the receipt and evaluation of reports of suspected child maltreatment. During this process, it will be determined whether the reported information meets the statutory and agency guidelines for child maltreatment. Furthermore, based on the information reported, the urgency with which the agency must respond to the report will be determined.
- *Investigation and Initial Assessment.* After receiving a report of child maltreatment, the agency will conduct an investigation to determine whether child maltreatment actually occurred. In addition, the immediate safety of the child is assessed and appropriate action taken if that safety is in jeopardy. Furthermore, the assessment will likely include a determination of any future risk to the child, the level of that risk, and whether additional agency services are necessary to address any effects of child maltreatment and/or to reduce the risk of future maltreatment.
- *Family Assessment.* Following the investigation and initial assessment, the CPS **caseworker** collaborates with family members toward identifying and understanding their strengths and any areas of need. Specifically, the caseworker may encourage the family's use of available resources, identify potential risk factors for future maltreatment, and help children cope with the effects of maltreatment.
- *Case Planning.* In order to achieve CPS goals, three types of plans are developed: (1) a **safety plan**, which is developed whenever a risk of immediate harm is determined; (2) a case plan, which includes the goals and desired outcomes determined by the family assessment; and (3) a concurrent permanency plan, which includes the steps by which family reunification may be achieved, while also outlining a plan to establish legal permanency with an alternate family in the event that reunification efforts are not achieved.
- *Service Provision.* During this stage the case plan is implemented. To some extent it may be the responsibility of CPS to arrange, provide, and coordinate service delivery for children and their families. Ideally, these services are individually tailored to a particular child's and/or family's needs.
- *Family Progress.* Ongoing assessment continues throughout the duration of an open CPS case. The caseworker will routinely evaluate safety issues, assess the presence of any risk factors for maltreatment, address any effects of maltreatment, and ensure that the family is achieving the goals established in the case plan.
- *Case Closure.* Ideally, a case is closed when the family has achieved their goals and the risk of maltreatment has been significantly reduced or eliminated. In reality, a case may be closed for any one of several reasons, including situations in which at least some measure of risk reduction has been obtained, the family prematurely discontinues CPS services, or legal permanency with an alternate family is achieved (DePanfilis & Salus, 2003).

It is important to note that not all families will experience all of the previously mentioned CPS activities. For example, a report may be *screened out* during the intake process and no further CPS involvement may be required, or a report may be **unsubstantiated** following an investigation or initial assessment and the case will be closed at this point in the process (although referrals to community agencies may be made). See Figure 12.1 for a flow chart outlining the various child protective procedures and decision-making options. Factors such as the nature of a report, the available evidence for substantiation of a maltreatment allegation, the severity of the maltreatment, and individual family-based issues may determine which of these specific activities a particular family will receive. Many mandated reporters feel frustrated when they make calls to CPS and it looks like nothing was done. However, if the behavior in question does not meet legal definitions of maltreatment, or if CPS cannot find evidence to support the allegations, there is nothing more it can legally do at that time. Reporters should continue to observe the child in question and call CPS again if they see further cause for concern. In addition, making the initial report (and any subsequent reports) is important because CPS agencies keep a computerized record of all the calls received. So, even if an initial allegation is not supported by evidence, a pattern of allegations may be enough to warrant further investigation.

INTAKE

Intake is generally the first stage of the CPS process. It is a crucial decision-making point in the child protection system, as it is the point at which reports of suspected child maltreatment are received. During the intake process, certified caseworkers gather information to determine safety concerns (i.e., whether the child is at risk of imminent harm), maltreatment risk (i.e., the likelihood that some form maltreatment will occur in the near future), and the type of CPS response that is required (whether the situation is an emergency that needs an immediate response, whether a call to law enforcement is necessary, whether further investigation by CPS is warranted, etc.). At intake, caseworkers should also perform a public relations function by responding to all reports in a professional and sensitive manner, and a public awareness function by clarifying the role of the agency to referral sources (Pecora, Whittaker, Maluccio, Barth, & Plotnick, 2000). Unfortunately, this goal is not always achieved due to time constraints that result from understaffing. This is just one more reason why it is helpful for mandated reporters to be knowledgeable about the system and what they can reasonably expect from CPS.

Although the specific nature of the intake process may vary somewhat from one jurisdiction to another, the basic process will be similar across jurisdictions. The primary tasks caseworkers should accomplish during the intake process include:

- Gathering sufficient information from the reporter to be able to identify and locate the child and parents/**primary caregiver**, to assess whether the child is safe, to determine if the report meets the statutory and agency guidelines for child maltreatment, and to determine the credibility of the report/reporter.
- Handling emergency situations including calming the reporter and determining how to best meet the immediate safety needs of the child and family (e.g., involving law enforcement).
- Checking agency records and the state's **central registry** (a centralized database containing information on all substantiated reports of child maltreatment) to determine whether the family and/or child are known to the agency (DePanfilis & Salus, 2003).

The intake may be the only opportunity the agency has to obtain information from the reporter. The more comprehensive the information provided by the reporter, the better able the intake caseworker will be to determine the safety of the child, the urgency of the situation, and the

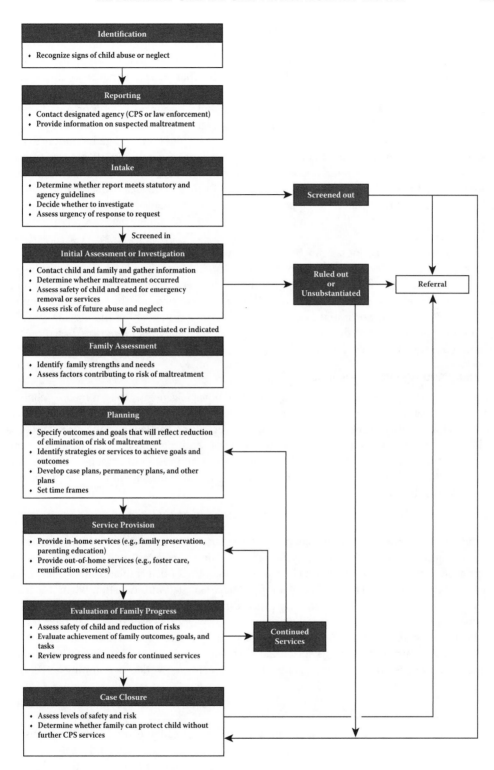

Figure 12.1 Flow chart outlining child protective procedures and decision-making options. Courtesy of U.S. Department of Health and Human Services.

appropriateness and type of CPS intervention. Reports that are lacking in important or significant amounts of information may prevent the caseworker from being able to adequately address the reporter's concerns and/or accept the case for further investigation. Additionally, the information obtained from the reporter may help to identify other potential sources of information about the family and the possibility of past, previously undocumented maltreatment. Finally, this information may assist the caseworker responsible for the investigation or initial assessment in locating all relevant parties (child, primary caregiver, and perpetrator) and in planning an effective investigation (DePanfilis & Salus, 2003). It is helpful for mandated reporters to have a detailed list of information and concerns in hand before they call CPS. If you are worried about a child, make specific notes about your concerns. For instance, instead of saying, "She is bruised all the time," a better report would note, "Four times in the last 6 weeks, I noticed significant bruising on the back of her upper thighs." The more detailed and specific information you can give, the easier it will be for a CPS caseworker to determine whether a report requires further investigation.

In addition to collecting as much information as possible from the reporter, the intake caseworker must also analyze that information and make decisions based on that analysis. This analysis will likely involve ensuring that the report meets criteria established by statutory and agency guidelines, evaluating the credibility of the reporter and the report, determining whether an investigation or initial assessment is warranted, establishing the urgency of CPS's response to the report, and determining the appropriate agency response time based on that urgency (DePanfilis & Salus, 2003).

Statutory and Agency Guidelines

Whether the report meets statutory and agency guidelines is generally determined by comparing the information obtained from the report to state law regarding the definition of various forms of child maltreatment and agency policies interpreting the law and practice standards. Additionally, the caseworker will likely determine the requirements for state or local county response, including the involvement of law enforcement and required response times. Lastly, practical issues such as jurisdictional authority and caseload management may need to be considered (Wells, 1997).

Credibility of Reports

During the intake process, a crucial component is determining the consistency and accuracy of the information reported. Determining the full credibility of a report may not occur until the investigation or initial assessment phase, but some measure of determination will likely occur during the intake phase. The validity of a report may be called into question when it is influenced by a contentious divorce or custody proceedings, general family dysfunction or conflict, or poor neighborly relations. Ultimately, despite any suspicions a caseworker may have regarding the motives of the reporter, the case must be accepted for investigation if the allegations meet statutory and agency requirements for child maltreatment. However, documentation of these suspicions may assist the investigation or initial assessment caseworker in planning an effective investigation (DePanfilis & Salus, 2003).

Accepting a Report for Further Investigation

The decision whether or not to accept a report for CPS investigation is the primary responsibility of the intake caseworker. This decision is based on law, agency policy (and implementation of that policy), and specific information about the case that indicates harm or likely harm to the child (Wells, 2000a). This decision may also depend on a number of other factors including whether the child is at risk of harm due to noncaregiver maltreatment (e.g., physical abuse committed by a babysitter) or whether the risk is of a more indirect rather than direct nature (e.g., intimate partner violence, parental substance abuse, parental physical or mental health issues). In either of these cases, the situation may be more appropriately addressed by an alternate agency, for example, law enforcement or a domestic violence shelter. Ultimately, if the caseworker determines that the child's safety is more directly compromised or that caregiver responsibility needs further investigation in any of the above-mentioned situations, then CPS involvement may also be warranted (DePanfilis & Salus, 2003). In making these determinations, it is critical that the caseworker have all necessary information available and easily accessible, including any agency policy guidelines and screening tools, while responding to a report (Wells, 2000a)

Urgency and Response Time

Part of the intake process will include a **safety assessment** in which, pending face-to-face contact by the agency, establishing the child's immediate risk of harm is the primary concern (Child Welfare League of America, 1999). Reports that likely require immediate CPS response (e.g., 2–3 hours) include situations in which the child's injuries are severe enough to have caused serious physical harm; the child is particularly vulnerable due to age, illness, or disability; the behavior of the caregiver is known to have previously caused harm to the child; there is no one able and/or willing to assure the child's safety; the family is likely to flee the area with (or abandon) the child; the report involves sexual abuse and the child continues to have contact with the alleged perpetrator; or the child has physical injuries that require immediate documentation (Wells, 2000b). Mandated reporters should keep in mind that only the most severe cases of maltreatment are addressed immediately. There will likely be a 1–3 day delay before most cases are investigated.

If the report does not require immediate response either by CPS and/or law enforcement, the intake caseworker must determine the level of response (and the time frame for response) that is required. Many states have specific criteria for determining the response time to a report, based on the nature of that report and the urgency of the situation. These criteria generally include the severity of the incident or harm to the child, the person responsible for the alleged maltreatment, and specific information regarding the family's situation (e.g., maternal mental health issues, parental employment status, family access to resources). For example, a case in which a day care provider reports bruising on a child's legs and buttocks may not require immediate action, especially if the day care provider also notes that she has been caring for this child for over a year, has never noticed bruises before, and there have been no previous reports of maltreatment filed for this family. A case such as this would likely require a more standard CPS intervention time frame of 24 hours. Other reports may require CPS response but do not involve immediate or continuous danger of harm to the child. For example, a case in which a schoolteacher reports that a 10-year-old girl in his class routinely comes to school in dirty, smelly clothes and often falls asleep in class. Cases such as these may allow for a slight delay (48–72 hours or longer) in the standard CPS response time. Varying state and local agencies will establish their own criteria for determining standard response times based on the nature and particular details of each case (DePanfilis & Salus, 2003).

INVESTIGATION OR INITIAL ASSESSMENT

The purpose of the investigation or initial assessment process is to gather information in response to reports filed with CPS, to interpret the agency's obligation to the children and their families, and to determine whether a family needs and will benefit from further agency intervention. After gathering all of the relevant information, the caseworker must determine whether the report is *substantiated* or *founded* (i.e., credible evidence indicates that maltreatment has occurred) or whether the report is *unsubstantiated* or *unfounded* (i.e., there is a lack of credible evidence to indicate that maltreatment has occurred—this does not necessarily mean that the child was not maltreated, only that there is a lack of evidence to support the allegation). See Case Examples 12.1 and 12.2 for substantiated and unsubstantiated reports of child maltreatment. Depending on the particular state law, agencies may have 30, 60, or 90 days after receiving the report to complete the investigation or initial assessment and make a final determination (DePanfilis & Salus, 2003). Again, this calls for patience on the part of the mandated reporter. Although a reporter is rightly concerned about the child, conducting a thorough and accurate investigation is important and, therefore, is a process that takes time.

An effective investigation or initial assessment is cooperative in nature. The CPS worker should form an alliance with the child and family in order to gather relevant information and provide support to the family. This requires involving the child and family in exploring the nature of the allegations and obtaining their perceptions of the situation, focusing on the family's strengths and resources, listening to the family's concerns and expressing sensitivity and empathy regarding any anxiety or fears they may have, and involving the child and family in any decisions that affect them by providing choices and opportunities for input whenever possible (Goldman, Salus, Wolcott, & Kennedy, 2003).

Effective decision making during this process requires competent interviewing skills; an ability to gather, organize, and analyze information; and the capacity to arrive at accurate conclusions. Methods typically employed in this process include the use of **structured interview** protocols with, and observations of, all relevant parties (identified victims, siblings and any other children living in the home, all nonoffending adults living in the home, and the alleged maltreating caregiver), information gathered from **collateral sources** (e.g., relatives, babysitters, day care providers, schoolteachers, physicians, clergy), and a careful analysis of all of the information obtained. One important note with regard to interviewing collateral sources is that special attention needs to be given to the family's **confidentiality** and any state regulations regarding contact with collateral sources. Ideally, interviews should be conducted both individually and with the family as a whole. Following the completion of data gathering, the caseworker should reconvene with the family to describe the findings of the investigation or initial assessment, address any family concerns, and (if warranted) discuss options for further CPS, law enforcement, and/or court involvement (DePanfilis, & Salus, 2003). If you feel that you would be good at conducting this type of investigation and that you would find such work rewarding, you might want to consider a career in social work.

Decisions that must be achieved by the conclusion of the investigation and initial assessment process include determining whether the initial allegation of maltreatment is substantiated, assessing child/familial risk factors, evaluating child safety, determining emergency needs for the family, and determining whether to offer additional services to the family (DePanfilis & Salus, 2003).

Substantiation of Maltreatment

The decision to substantiate maltreatment depends on whether the harm (or threat of harm) to the child is severe enough to constitute maltreatment and whether there is sufficient evidence to support the incident as a case of child maltreatment (Drake, 2000). Regardless of the final decision, if possible, all information collected should be documented and retained, as unsubstantiated reports may eventually yield a pattern of incidents that warrant substantiation. An agency's ability to maintain these records may vary based on statutory guidelines regarding the **expungement** of records. Following the completion of the initial assessment, the disposition of the report must be determined based on state laws, agency policies, and implementation of

The following fictitious case is an example of a report that was substantiated following an investigation by CPS.

Mr. Jones is a third-grade teacher at Bennett Elementary School. Approximately a week into the new school year he noticed that one of his students, Daniel, had a large bruise on his forearm. At the end of the day he asked Daniel to talk with him for a few minutes. Mr. Jones learned that Daniel lives with his mother and her boyfriend of 5 years, and that they recently moved to the area from out-of-state. Daniel told him that he got the bruise when he fell down some stairs the day before. Mr. Jones was suspicious of his story because the bruise looked very much like a handprint, and he decided to call CPS to file a report. During the investigation, the CPS caseworker learned from Daniel's mother that money was tight because her boyfriend had been out of work for awhile and they had moved to town at the beginning of the summer because he got a job at the local factory. She also mentioned that her boyfriend has a drinking problem and a temper, but denied that he would ever hurt her son. Her boyfriend corroborated most of this information, and also denied ever hurting Daniel. The caseworker spoke with a few of Daniel's neighbors, who mentioned that they often heard yelling coming from Daniel's apartment and have considered calling CPS themselves because Daniel seems very "accident prone" and has had noticeable bruises on his arms and legs on several occasions since he moved in. The caseworker also spoke with Daniel's maternal grandmother, who reported that Daniel's mother begged her not to tell anyone when she confessed that her boyfriend had hit Daniel on at least one occasion. She feared his temper, Daniel's maternal grandmother said. The caseworker obtained Daniel's medical records, which revealed a history of "accidental" bruising and broken bones over the past 5 years. No reports of child abuse had ever been filed, most likely because Daniel's mother took him to a different clinic or hospital on almost every occasion. Finally, the caseworker had a physician examine the current bruise on Daniel's arm, and she confirmed that it was likely made by a hand grabbing his forearm. Through x-ray, the doctor also discovered several old rib fractures that had healed improperly because they did not appear to have ever been set. Based on all of the above information, the CPS caseworker determined that Mr. Jones' report of physical abuse was substantiated and temporarily placed Daniel with his maternal aunt, who lived in the next town.

DISCUSSION QUESTIONS

1. Based on what you have learned so far, was the teacher obligated to file a report in this case?
2. Should the teacher have conducted any further investigation prior to filing his report?
3. What procedures and/or methods did the CPS caseworker employ during this investigation?
4. Is there anything additional the caseworker could have done to make this investigation more complete?
5. What element(s) of this case and/or the investigation clearly indicate that Daniel was physically abused?

CASE EXAMPLE 12.2

The following fictitious case is an example of a report that was unsubstantiated following an investigation by Child Protective Services (CPS).

During a "tickle fest" with her mother, 6-year-old Susie mentioned that that it was just like the "special time" she had with her uncle Steve. After talking with Susie about this further, she also learned about other concerning incidents including a lot of play time in Uncle Steve's bedroom and one particular game called "hide the snake." Her mother became alarmed and questioned Steve about Susie's comments, but he denied that they were true. Susie's mother was still concerned, however, and contacted CPS. During the investigation, the CPS caseworker learned that Steve is Susie's paternal uncle who has been living with the family for the past year. He takes care of Susie quite a bit because her mother works full-time outside the home, her father is often out of town on business, and Steve has been unable to work while he has been recovering from a serious car accident that occurred shortly before he moved in with Susie's family. The caseworker interviewed Susie, her parents, and Uncle Steve. She also spoke with Susie's teacher and a few neighbors. Susie's report of her interactions with Uncle Steve remained fairly consistent, but the caseworker was unable to find additional evidence of sexual abuse. Furthermore, the results of a physical examination were inconclusive. Based on the results of the investigation, the caseworker determined that the report of sexual abuse was unsubstantiated.

DISCUSSION QUESTIONS

1. What procedures and/or methods did the CPS caseworker employ during this investigation?
2. Is there anything additional the caseworker could have done to make this investigation more complete?
3. Based on what you've learned so far, how credible is the testimony of a 6-year-old?
4. While the report was determined to be unsubstantiated, does this mean that Susie definitely was not sexually abused?

those policies. Each state has developed its own laws and policies that outline the guidelines for determining whether child abuse or neglect has occurred. Most states have a two-tiered system of substantiated-unsubstantiated (or founded-unfounded), although a third tier (**indicated**) may be included. This third tier generally allows the caseworker to determine that some evidence of maltreatment exists, but not enough to substantiate the case (DePanfilis & Salus, 2003).

When evaluating a report of neglect, it is important to consider whether the conditions or circumstances indicate that a child's basic needs are unmet and what harm or threat of harm has resulted (or may result) from these conditions or circumstances (DePanfilis, 2000). In deciding if a report of physical abuse should be substantiated, the caseworker will need to determine the plausibility of the caregiver's and child's accounts of the injury. This is generally accomplished by evaluating whether the injury could have occurred in a nonabusive manner and comparing the explanation given for the injury to available physical evidence (Dubowitz, 2000). Substantiation of a sexual abuse report may be more challenging, as there is often little or no physical evidence to review. Important considerations include the nature of the allegation, any statements made by the child, and any behaviors exhibited by the child (Adams, 2000). Lastly, substantiating a report of psychological maltreatment may prove even more challenging and requires information on caregiver behavior over time and indicators from the child (behavioral, cognitive, social, emotional and/or physical) with respect to any effects of this behavior (Brassard & Hart, 2000).

Risk Factors

Assessing risk factors entails identifying the factors in the family's environment that increase the likelihood that a child will be maltreated, evaluating the family's strengths and resources, and determining available agency and community services (Pecora et al., 2000). In evaluating the risk factors for maltreatment that may be present, caseworkers should organize the risk-relevant information by category (e.g., child factors, parental factors, family-functioning issues), establish whether there are any interactions between risk factors and strengths, and determine the significance of each of the risk factors and strengths (Holder & Morton, 1999). Special cases of **risk assessment** include situations that involve parental substance abuse, situations that involve intimate partner violence, and any specific cultural factors (e.g., language barriers, parenting strategies, discipline techniques, cultural or religious practices) that may need to be considered as part of the investigation and initial assessment process (DePanfilis & Salus, 2003).

Child Safety

The Adoption and Safe Families Act requires that states assess and assure a safe living environment for children. This safety may, in part, be related to the risk factors and strengths present in the family, but risk assessment and safety assessment are separate decisions. Caseworkers must assess child safety during at least two points of the investigation and initial assessment process, the beginning and the end. During the first contact, the caseworker must decide whether the child will be safe for the duration of the investigative process. Upon completing the assessment, the caseworker must determine whether the child will remain safe without ongoing CPS involvement and services. Additionally, safety should be assessed at any other point the caseworker deems necessary. Developing a safety plan is a key component in safety assessment. The interventions in the safety plan are designed to control the risk factors that pose a safety threat to the child. These interventions should generally progress from least to most intrusive and include in-home services, partial out-of-home services (i.e., day care/respite services), removal of the abusive caregiver from the home, kinship care, or **out-of-home placement**. Ultimately, the safety plan should include interventions that strive to preserve or reunify families (DePanfilis & Salus, 2003).

Emergency Needs

In addition to services aimed directly at child protection, CPS is often in a unique position to help families address other problems they may be facing. As child maltreatment is rarely an isolated issue, adopting an **ecologically based approach** may be more helpful to the family on a long-term basis. Examples of emergency services may include health care (physical and/or mental), food, clothing, shelter, crisis counseling, and job placement services. Assisting a family with these additional emergency needs and arranging for emergency services for the child and family may be a crucial step in alleviating family dysfunction and reducing the risk for child maltreatment (DePanfilis & Salus, 2003).

Additional Services

Upon completion of the investigation or initial assessment, the caseworker must decide if the family should receive ongoing child protective or additional agency services. This decision may be based on a variety of factors including whether a report is substantiated, the perceived level of risk for future maltreatment, the state or local guidelines, and the availability of services (DePanfilis & Salus, 2003). Traditionally, the role of CPS has been a primarily investigative one in which caseworkers are narrowly focused on obtaining evidence of maltreatment and then referring substantiated cases to law enforcement. More recently, states are incorporating greater flexibility in their response to allegations of child maltreatment by utilizing a "dual track" approach that provides a differential response system based on the child's needs for safety, degree of maltreatment risk, and the family's need for support or services. Typically, in cases where severe maltreatment has occurred, the more traditional investigative route will be pursued. However, in less serious cases a more thorough assessment that focuses on the family's strengths and needs will be conducted. This type of assessment is designed to form a collaborative partnership with the family to determine the most beneficial resources and services for the family. However, at any point during the course of the assessment, a family may be transferred to the investigative track if deemed necessary (Goldman et al., 2003).

Adult/Child Removal

One important consideration within the decision-making process during the investigation or initial assessment phase is the potential need to remove either the alleged perpetrator or child from the home. Removing the alleged perpetrator is generally the less intrusive (and therefore preferred) intervention. However, this intervention requires an agreement by the family (and a certainty on the part of the caseworker) that there will be no unsupervised contact between the alleged victim and perpetrator. Removing a child from the home is a more involved process requiring out-of-home placement needs that may have a more negative effect on the child. In addition to separating the child from the offending caregiver, removal also separates the child from the nonoffending caregiver and other potentially supportive relatives and friends. The effects of out-of-home placement are likely much greater than simply the loss associated with physical separation from the family. Unfortunately, in some situations, removing the child from the home may be the only viable option and the only way to assure separation between alleged victim and perpetrator (DePanfilis & Salus, 2003).

FAMILY ASSESSMENT

The initial assessment focuses on identifying the risk factors and concerns present in a family, but the family assessment emphasizes the relationship between a family's strengths and risks to a much greater extent. The family assessment is more thorough and in-depth. It focuses on the change that is necessary in a family to keep the child safe, reduce the risk of future maltreatment, and enhance overall family well-being. The family assessment promotes an understanding of the problems present in a family and becomes the basis for subsequent intervention (Goldman, Salus, Wolcott, & Kennedy, 2003).

In order to be effective, family assessments should be culturally sensitive, strengths-based, and developed in collaboration with the family. Ideally, the goal is to allow children to reside safely in their homes by helping caregivers identify and resolve areas of concern (NAPCWA, 1999).

Culturally Sensitive and Strengths-Based Assessment

A culturally sensitive assessment acknowledges and respects the fact that diversity exists among families. It considers parenting practices within the context of ethnic, racial, and religious differences and recognizes that a wide range of practices exist within the parameters of the law (Dunst, Trivette, & Deal, 1994; as cited in DePanifils & Salus, 2003). A strengths-based assessment recognizes that all people are capable of change, especially when the focus of change is on building their strengths. While a standard protocol may assist the family assessment process, an individualized approach based on the particular strengths and needs of each family is likely to be most effective (Child Welfare League of America, 1999).

Interviews and Referrals

After reviewing all pertinent information regarding a particular family, the family assessment caseworker will conduct interviews with the child and family to determine the family's treatment needs. During these interviews, the caseworker should meet with the family as a whole and also with family members individually. While meeting with the child, the caseworker will generally try to determine any and all effects of the maltreatment. While meeting with the caregivers, determining the causes of the maltreatment and the conditions under which it is likely to recur will be the caseworker's primary objective. During this phase of CPS intervention, the caseworker may also identify family issues that are in need of additional services (substance abuse, mental health concerns, or undiagnosed physical health conditions) and make the appropriate referrals to qualified professionals (DePanfilis & Salus, 2003).

Ultimately, the family assessment should be a comprehensive reporting of the family's strengths, risk factors, and needs. It should include information such as the reason the family was referred for continuing CPS intervention, a description of the family system and all of its members, family background and history, the presenting problems as conceptualized by the family, the present status of the family, and a tentative disposition based on an analysis of all relevant information. The comprehensiveness of this assessment is crucial as it will likely form the basis for case planning and service provision (DePanfilis & Salus, 2003).

CASE PLANNING

In addition to outlining the risks and problems present in a family, the case plan identifies the strategies and interventions that will be employed to facilitate the changes necessary to assure child safety and for the family's overall well-being. It also outlines the specific tasks, goals, and expected outcomes associated with these changes. Two crucial components of a case plan are flexibility and creativity: flexibility because families and their needs and resources are constantly changing, and creativity because this helps to generate new approaches to challenging, and often deeply entrenched, problems (DePanfilis & Salus, 2003).

The purpose of case planning is to identify strategies that address the effects of maltreatment and change the behaviors and/or conditions that contribute to its risk, provide clear and specific guidelines to implement these strategies, establish criteria to measure the family's progress in achieving specified outcomes, and develop a framework with the family for case decision-making. Throughout case planning, it is important to involve the family in the decision-making process as much as possible. Families who feel as though their input was regarded during case planning are much more likely to be engaged in carrying out and adhering to the case plan (DePanfilis & Salus, 2003).

Family Meetings

Since the early 1990s, CPS agencies have utilized a **family group decision-making model** to optimize family strengths in the case-planning process. This model includes the family and members of the family's social support network in the decision-making process for ensuring the family's safety and well-being. These family meetings have been effective in increasing the willingness of family members to accept the services outlined in the case plan, have improved relationships between the family and professionals, and have increased the support available to families through network connections (Merkel-Holguin, 2001; as cited in DePanfilis & Salus, 2003).

Outcomes

With the passage of the Adoption and Safe Families Act, child protection agencies have been federally mandated to design intervention programs around the achievement of outcomes

(DePanfilis & Salus, 2003). The primary outcomes targeted through case planning comprise four broad domains and include child safety, child permanence, child well-being, and family well-being (Courtney, 2000). In order to achieve these broad-based outcomes, more specific outcomes must be outlined in each of four areas: child-level outcomes (e.g., peer relationships, behavioral control), caregiver outcomes (e.g., mental health functioning, parenting skills), family outcomes (e.g., communication patterns, social support), and environmental outcomes (e.g., housing issues, neighborhood safety; DePanfilis & Salus, 2003).

Goals and Tasks

The successful achievement of outcomes depends on the goals and tasks outlined in the case plan. If the goals are unrealistic or the tasks are overwhelming, the outcomes will never be realized. Goals should indicate the specific changes necessary to accomplish the outcomes. The objective is not to create a perfect family but one in which children will be safe and have their developmental needs met. Goals should be **SMART**, that is, Specific, Measurable, Achievable, Realistic, and Time-limited. In order to promote change, goals should also be framed within the context of positive behaviors or conditions that will result, and not highlight negative behaviors or conditions. Furthermore, goals should be broken down into smaller tasks with specified time frames for completion. These tasks incorporate the services and intervention necessary to achieve the goals and outcomes (DePanfilis & Salus, 20030). For example, if a broad-based outcome for a particular family includes the development of effective parenting skills, then a goal for that family will likely include the consistent use of nonphysical discipline techniques for the violation of family rules, and a task for that family may include instruction in an effective time-out procedure that can be used for infractions surrounding chores and bedtime routines. As evidenced by this example, each step in the case-planning process becomes more specific and clearly defined so that the family is aware of the exact procedures necessary to achieve the overall target outcomes.

Concurrent Planning

As part of the case plan, concurrent planning works toward family preservation and/or reunification while also establishing alternate permanency plans that can be implemented if preservation or reunification becomes impossible. In accordance with this model, caseworkers need to develop two or more distinct case plans so that children can be transferred as quickly and smoothly as possible from one living environment to another if necessary. Since some families may be unwilling or unable to change, and the risks associated with maltreatment are high, caseworkers need to make early decisions and plans regarding a permanent living environment for the child (Lutz, 2000; as cited in Goldman et al., 2003).

SERVICE PROVISION

The provision of services for families involved with CPS agencies will largely depend on the family's level of maltreatment risk. Accordingly, a conceptual framework developed by the National Association of Public Child Welfare Administrators (1999) outlines the level of service appropriate to the level of risk present in a family. See Figure 12.2 for a diagrammatic representation of the service strategies and agencies appropriate for families at various levels of risk for child maltreatment.

High-Risk Families

Families that pose the highest risk of child abuse and neglect (serious physical injury, sexual abuse, and severe neglect) require service strategies related to court-ordered services, intensive family preservation, child removal, foster care, adoption, and criminal prosecution. The

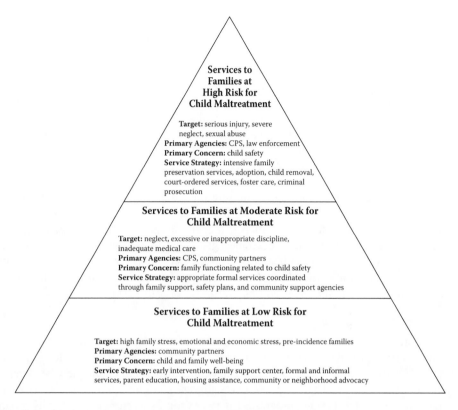

Figure 12.2   Service strategies and service agencies appropriate for families at various levels of risk for child maltreatment. Courtesy of U.S. Department of Health and Human Services.

agencies involved with these families are CPS and law enforcement, and the primary concern is child safety.

Moderate-Risk Families

Families that pose moderate risk for child abuse and neglect (excessive or inappropriate discipline, inadequate medical care, some supervisory neglect) require service strategies related to safety plans, family support, and community support agencies. The agencies involved with these families are CPS and community service agencies, and the primary concern is family functioning relative to child safety.

Low-Risk Families

Families that pose the lowest risk for child abuse and neglect but may require CPS involvement (high level of family stress, emotional and economic stress, and pre-incidence risk factors) require service strategies related to early intervention, family support, parent education, housing assistance, and community and/or neighborhood advocacy. CPS may be involved with these families, although community service agencies are more likely to provide service delivery. The primary concern among these families is child and family well-being.

Intervention

CPS is responsible for identifying and providing access to all treatment and intervention services deemed necessary for ensuring child safety and reducing maltreatment risk. These services may be available directly through the CPS agency or may be offered through collaborations with community agencies. Services may range from supportive in nature to long-term psychological treatment. Some may be offered specifically to children, others to caregivers, and others to the family as a whole. Specific services and programs may include art and/or play therapy for younger child victims; trauma-focused therapies for older children and adolescents; parent training/skills courses; parent-child interaction therapy; family preservation services; respite programs and support groups for caregivers or children; and anger management, batterer's treatment, and sex offender treatment programs for perpetrators (DePanfilis & Salus, 2003).

FAMILY PROGRESS

A key feature of CPS intervention is determining the extent and nature of family progress. Monitoring this type of change generally begins with the onset of program implementation and continues until case closure. Evaluation is a continual process that focuses on the family's progress toward the attainment of outcomes, goals, and tasks established in the case plan. Additionally, the evaluation is an opportunity to reassess child safety. While informal evaluations are more continual in nature, formal case evaluations generally occur at regular and predetermined intervals (e.g., every 3–6 months; DePanfilis & Salus, 2003).

Evaluating Family Progress

The evaluation of family progress includes a review of the case plan, the collection of information from all service providers, the measurement of change, and the documentation of progress attained. During this process, CPS caseworkers may consult with other professionals (therapists, guardians ad litem, etc.) who have been involved with case planning and/or service provision to assist them in evaluating a family's progress. The issues addressed through the family progress evaluation include determining whether changes to the safety plan are required, determining whether any changes in risk factors have occurred, evaluating the progress toward achieving case goals and outcomes, evaluating the services provided with respect to their ability to effect change, evaluating social support availability, and determining the potential for continued family preservation or for initiating family reunification. Routine monitoring of family progress allows both the caseworker and family to track family change and be aware of the status of case plan completion. Any decisions based on the family progress evaluation should be discussed with the family and documented for future case determination (DePanfilis & Salus, 2003).

CASE CLOSURE

Case closure is the point at which CPS no longer maintains an active relationship with the family. The closing of a case may occur for several reasons. The best case scenario is when case closure occurs as the result of the completion of the case plan in which all outcomes have been achieved. During this situation, both the caseworker and family may mutually agree that it is time to end the relationship between family and agency and that the family is ready to continue without agency involvement (DePanfilis & Salus, 2003).

More realistically, case closure occurs when most of the goals and outcomes have been achieved and there is sufficient reason to believe that the child is safe (although some risk may still be present). Cases may also be "closed" with respect to CPS intervention, but may still continue with services through community agencies. In some situations, cases may be closed due to premature discontinuation by the family. Under these circumstances, a family receiving voluntary services makes a unilateral decision to end its relationship with the agency. This decision may be communicated to the caseworker verbally or behaviorally (the family does not attend scheduled appointments and does not respond to the caseworker's attempts at contact). A family that is receiving involuntary (i.e., court-mandated) services, however, cannot legally discontinue services in this manner. Lastly, a case may be closed following the termination of parental rights and child adoption (DePanfilis & Salus, 2003).

Clearly, the investigation of child maltreatment and the necessary follow-up for substantiated cases is an extremely time-consuming process. While the steps outlined above describe an ideal response, caseworkers are limited with regard to both time and resources.

DECISION MAKING

While it may appear that the general CPS process is fairly straightforward, this is generally not the case. One major factor that significantly affects the nature of this process for any particular family is decision making. Throughout the course of CPS involvement with a family, decisions are made. Whether the intake caseworker screens in or out a report, whether the investigation or initial assessment caseworker finds a report substantiated or unsubstantiated, the outcomes and goals outlined in a family's case plan, and whether a case is to be closed are all decisions that must be made by individual and supervisory agency employees. This process can leave room for wide variations in consistency, both within and among CPS cases.

Unfortunately, expert consensus regarding decision-making criteria has been difficult to achieve. In a study of CPS decision-making (Rossi, Schuerman, & Budde, 1996; as cited in Wilson & Morton, 1997), the authors reported an overall level of agreement among experts that was below levels expected to provide clear standards for expert consensus. In this same study, the authors found that even when experts used the same factors in making decisions and combined these factors in a similar manner, they still arrived at differing decisions.

The very nature of the difficult decisions faced by CPS workers (for example, whether a child should be removed from his or her home) contributes to the difficulty in establishing consistent criteria for decision making. To some extent, decision makers' values and beliefs regarding the goals of child protection may influence this inconsistency, such that statutory and agency guidelines are applied differentially from one situation to another (Wilson & Morton, 1997). A caseworker's beliefs concerning the importance of family, for example, may affect decisions regarding out-of-home placements. This may be more or less of an issue depending on who exactly is making the decisions (i.e., caseworker vs. supervisor vs. multidisciplinary team).

The **National Study of Child Protective Services Systems and Reform Efforts**, conducted by the **U.S. Department of Health and Human Services** (2003), reported that while most state policies included a decision protocol for forwarding cases from intake to investigation, there were considerable differences with regard to who made those decisions. Of the 29 states indicating one approach to decision making across cases, 13 primarily relied on the caseworker's decision with supervisory approval, 7 relied on supervisory decisions, 5 relied on joint decisions between caseworker and supervisor, 2 relied on the caseworker's decision alone, and 2 reported other decision-making protocols. Of the remaining 21 states, different protocols were reported depending on case circumstances. Whether one, two, or more people are involved in the decision-making process (and their different levels/types of training) can have dramatic effects on decision-based outcomes.

This inconsistency may also be influenced by the ambiguity inherent in statutory guidelines and agency policies. Legal definitions of maltreatment are often vaguely worded; phrases such as "reasonable efforts" and "**reason to believe**" are common among legal statutes. Consequently, agency policies may lack clear operational guidelines for decision makers to follow. In a study of the basis for ongoing CPS intervention (i.e., family assessment, case planning, service provision, and family progress evaluations), Holder (2000) noted that approximately 34% of survey respondents (CPS workers from 31 states) reported that their agency did not employ a specific assessment process to develop case/treatment plans. Unfortunately, nonspecific guidelines are likely to result in inconsistent decision making.

It is relatively clear that a lack of consistency in decision making exists, and that this inconsistency likely affects the CPS process in significant ways; however, the underlying causes of this inconsistency remain largely undetermined. More comprehensive training of agency employees and clearer guidelines with respect to statutory and agency policies are likely necessary to improve consistency in the decision-making process.

CONCLUSION

While variations in the investigative and intervention processes may exist from one CPS agency to another, largely as a result of varying state laws and agency policies, the child protection process generally follows the guidelines as described in this chapter, and this general process is fairly consistent nationwide. When differences do exist, they are most likely related to factors such as CPS response time frames, issues regarding the determination of jurisdiction, individually based decision-making issues, and variations with respect to statutory and agency definitional guidelines for maltreatment. In some cases these differences may be substantial. Jurisdictional differences may result in cases that "fall through the cracks," for example, if the agency policy for the state in which the maltreatment occurred dictates that the case be referred to the child's home state, while the agency policy for the child's home state dictates that the case remain in the jurisdiction of the agency where the maltreatment occurred (A. Robinson, personal communication, November 8, 2007). Situations such as these create a veritable "no man's land" and have the potential for dire consequences on an individual child's safety and well-being. However, despite such individual cases, the overall impact of agency differences may remain largely unknown.

Child maltreatment is a problem with severe, and potentially fatal, consequences. Therefore, CPS intervention must function, first and foremost, to protect children. However, the goal of CPS intervention is not, as many believe, to break families apart. Rather, CPS's role in family intervention is to protect the safety of children by improving family functioning. In fact, a large factor in the mission of child protective agencies is family preservation and reunification, that is, to keep families together. The hope is that this can be accomplished through the variety of services and resources provided by CPS and community agencies. Unfortunately, this hope is not always fulfilled and, in these situations, child safety must take precedence.

DISCUSSION QUESTIONS

1. Should child protective agencies conform to a set of uniform regulations imposed at the federal level, or should they remain in operation on a state-by-state basis?
2. Does the child welfare principle of family preservation and reunification mean that CPS caseworkers should make every effort to keep biological families together?
3. Does a caseworker's ability to substantiate a report of child maltreatment vary depending on the type of maltreatment that is reported?
4. Should CPS caseworkers be allowed to interview collateral sources during a CPS investigation? Does doing so violate a family's privacy and/or confidentiality?
5. If an alleged case of child maltreatment is determined to be unsubstantiated by CPS, does this mean that no child maltreatment occurred in this case?
6. What are the advantages and disadvantages to including the family in case planning decisions?

7. Does the idea of concurrent planning run counter to that of family preservation and reunification?

8. Do you think that individual values and beliefs often affect the decisions made by CPS professionals? Should they?

DEFINITIONS

Jurisdiction: the authority to deal with legal matters and the limits within which that authority may be exercised.

Child Abuse Prevention and Treatment Act (CAPTA): legislation passed in 1974 that sets forth a minimum definition of child abuse and neglect, establishes the Office on Child Abuse and Neglect (OCAN), authorizes the expenditure of federal dollars to support state child protection efforts, and provides grants to public agencies to support child maltreatment research.

Keeping Children and Families Safe Act: legislation passed in 2003 to make improvements to and reauthorize programs under the Child Abuse Prevention and Treatment Act (CAPTA).

Adoption Assistance and Child Welfare Act: legislation passed in 1980 to encourage case-workers to work toward reunifying families and to avoid long-term and/or multiple foster care placements for children if possible.

Reasonable Efforts: according to the Adoption Assistance and Child Welfare Act, the responsibility of state child welfare agencies to avoid foster care placement and/or to reunify a family whenever possible. This definition was amended in the Adoption and Safe Families Act, providing exceptions to the family preservation and reunification requirements (especially in consideration of child safety issues).

Adoption and Safe Families Act: legislation passed in 1997 to promote the adoption of children in foster care (in the event that reunification with biological parents is not possible), especially children with special needs. It describes safety, permanency, and well-being as key principles in the implementation of child welfare legislation.

Family Preservation and Reunification: an underlying principle of federal legislation (particularly the Adoption Assistance and Child Welfare Act) that encourages child protective agencies to maintain biological families whenever possible. Adherence to this principle has lessened since the passing of the Adoption and Safe Families Act, which focuses more on the child's safety and well-being than maintaining a biological family.

Office on Child Abuse and Neglect (OCAN): established by the Child Abuse Prevention and Treatment Act (CAPTA) in 1974, this agency is part of the Children's Bureau in the Department of Health and Human Services. It funds resources for improving state responses to child abuse and neglect.

Administration for Children and Families (ACF): a division of the Department of Health and Human Services. It is responsible for federal programs that promote the economic and social well-being of children and families, and assists local agencies (both public and private) with relevant funding, policy direction, and educational services.

Permanency: the principle that a child's ideal living environment is one that will be long-lasting and stable.

Continuity: the principle that a child's ideal living environment should be disrupted as little as possible.

National Association of Public Child Welfare Administrators (NAPCWA): founded in 1983, this organization represents public child welfare agencies by contributing to child welfare policy and ensuring that children in the public child welfare system have safe, permanent homes.

Culturally Responsive Services: child welfare services that include the acknowledgement and acceptance of other people's cultures and cultural values.

Allegation: an unproven assertion that child maltreatment has occurred.

Intake: process by which reports of suspected child maltreatment are received and initially evaluated by a CPS agency.

Investigation and Initial Assessment: the process by which a child protective agency verifies reports of child maltreatment and determines the immediate safety of the alleged child victim.

Family Assessment: following a child protective services investigation and initial assessment, the process by which a caseworker collaborates with family members to identify needed services.

Caseworker: a professional employed by child protective services to investigate child maltreatment, ensure the safety of children in their homes, and provide necessary services to families.

Case Planning: the developing of three types of plans by the caseworker during a family's involvement with child protective services: a safety plan for the child, a case plan aimed at allowing the family to remain together, and a concurrent permanency plan that establishes an alternate living arrangement for the child in the event that the case plan is not successful.

Safety Plan: a plan that is developed following a safety assessment whenever a risk of immediate harm is discovered in order to minimize and/or eliminate that immediate risk.

Service Provision: the process by which a child protective services case plan is implemented.

Family Progress: the ongoing assessment of an open child protective services case by a caseworker.

Case Closure: the process by which an open child protective services (CPS) case is resolved and the family no longer receives CPS services.

Unsubstantiated (Unfounded): a report of child maltreatment that has been investigated, but not confirmed, by CPS.

Primary Caregiver: a person primarily responsible for the health and well-being of a child (e.g., mother, father, legal guardian).

Central Registry: a database maintained by a state's child protective agency that contains information on all substantiated reports of child maltreatment for that state.

Safety Assessment: the process by which a caseworker evaluates a child's living environment and determines whether there is any immediate risk of harm to that child's safety.

Structured Interview: a face-to-face method of collecting information that follows a series of pre-established questions.

Collateral Sources: individuals who are interviewed by caseworkers as part of a CPS investigation (e.g., neighbors, teachers, babysitters).

Confidentiality: an ethical principle associated with people in many human service professions whereby these professionals may not divulge information about their clients to third parties.

Expungement: the act of destroying or sealing records following a specified period of time.

Indicated: a designation utilized by some child protective agencies during the course of an investigation that allows the caseworker to determine that some evidence of child maltreatment exists, but not enough to substantiate the case.

Risk Assessment: the process by which a caseworker evaluates a child's living environment and determines whether any factors are present that increase the likelihood for child maltreatment.

Out-of-Home Placement: often referred to as foster care, the condition by which children are temporarily removed from their home and placed in an alternative living environment (e.g., with a relative, in an emergency shelter, in a group home).

Ecologically Based Approach: a strategy in the delivery of human services that focuses on family and community as a whole, rather than focusing solely on the individual.

Family Group Decision-Making Model: a strategy used by child protective agencies to optimize family strengths in the case-planning process. As part of this strategy, the family and members of the family's social support network are included in the decision-making process during case planning.

SMART: strategy used during the case-planning process whereby established goals are Specific, Measurable, Achievable, Realistic, and Time-limited.

National Study of Child Protective Services Systems and Reform Efforts: a 2-year study (2000–2001) conducted to assess and evaluate the status of the child protective services system in the U.S.

U.S. Department of Health and Human Services: established in 1979 with the goal of protecting the health of all Americans and providing essential human services.

Reason to Believe: a term often used in child welfare legislation with regard to mandatory reporting guidelines. Includes the notion of a reasonable professional standard for mandated reporters, such that their professional training and experience informs their ability to recognize the presence of child maltreatment.

CHAPTER 13

Preventing Child Maltreatment

STEFANIE M. KEEN

Given the high prevalence of child maltreatment and the seriousness of its consequences, efforts to **prevent** child abuse and neglect are critical. In addition to the harmful short-term effects of child maltreatment, negative outcomes often persist throughout the remainder of a victim's life and may even be perpetuated in future generations. Additionally, once child maltreatment has begun, it tends to be a chronic condition that is fairly resistant to intervention efforts. This is often true in regard to both the perpetrator's behavior and the consequences to the victim. Finally, it is expensive. Costs associated with social welfare services, medical care, and intervention are astronomical and must generally be subsidized through state and federal funding sources.

Most people, especially in the U.S., are not accustomed to thinking preventively. Medical care is sought most often when we are sick; mental health professionals are contacted after psychological or adjustment problems have already begun; even cars are usually brought into maintenance garages only in response to repair needs—and not for routine "checkups." As such, in the area of child maltreatment, we have had a tendency to devote more time, money, and resources to intervening once abuse or neglect has already occurred, and not on identifying and addressing the **precursors** of maltreatment risk. In part, this tendency is influenced by current laws and priorities such that child protection agencies have few resources for families who have not yet violated any statutory guidelines or agency policies. Unfortunately, the present system is primarily designed for protection, which does not often permit offering assistance to parents who could benefit from an early intervention/prevention model (Wolfe, Reppucci, & Hart, 1995). Sadly, this means that children generally have to suffer before assistance is available.

Working in the prevention arena poses unique challenges to mental health clinicians and researchers. First, because target families have not (yet) demonstrated acts of maltreatment, they may not be aware or believe that they have a problem. Therefore, they are less likely to seek out services and may be more difficult for professionals to identify. Second, families need to be motivated to participate in preventive services when they are offered. Since their participation is largely voluntary, they may refuse or be unwilling to participate fully. Third, given constraints related to funding and available resources, it is important to identify potential participants who are at greatest risk and, therefore, most likely to benefit from services (Leventhal, 1997).

OVERVIEW OF PREVENTION PROGRAMS

In general, prevention programs for physical abuse and neglect (unfortunately, psychological maltreatment is rarely targeted for prevention) attempt to reduce the likelihood of maltreatment by focusing on service delivery to parents. The underlying model of this approach is that maltreatment often stems from issues related to poor parenting and dysfunctional parental practices (e.g., excessive physical discipline, failure to provide children with basic needs, substance abuse, and intimate partner violence), which are best resolved by improving parenting skills, increasing parental knowledge regarding child development and behavioral expectations, and offering supportive services to parents. The fundamental assumption of this approach is that physical abuse and neglect are less likely to occur if parents are armed with knowledge about appropriate child care, child development, and healthy family relationships. To this end, parent education and support programs (e.g., home visitation programs, family or community support centers, programs for new and/or teenage mothers, and programs offering individual counseling and support groups) have been developed and implemented in an attempt to achieve these goals (Olsen & Widom, 1993).

Alternatively, child sexual abuse prevention programs typically target preschool through school-age children. While these programs may include a parent education component, such as providing parents with information regarding the prevalence and nature of child sexual abuse and encouraging parent-child discussions of child sexual abuse-related issues, the focus is on educating children. These programs tend to be school- or community-based, and their emphasis is on empowering children and improving their ability to resist assault. They may be included as part of a larger child safety program that provides classroom-based instruction on how children can protect themselves from sexual assault and ways to cope with actual or potential sexual abuse. The fundamental assumption of these programs is that by arming children with information and skills associated with the prevention of child sexual abuse, they will be capable of protecting themselves from victimization (Olsen & Widom, 1993).

The majority of prevention programs target and serve families who recognize their limitations with respect to caregiving and seek out services to address these limitations. However, fewer resources are available (and their effectiveness is limited) for families who do not even recognize they need assistance or are unable or unwilling to access resources. This is reflected in the 30%–50% **attrition** rate observed throughout child abuse prevention programs (McCurdy, Hurvis, & Clark, 1996; as cited in Daro & Donnelly, n.d.). Furthermore, many child abuse prevention programs fail to achieve their desired outcomes. Despite our good intentions and best efforts, we continue to see high child abuse report rates, child abuse-related injuries, and child abuse fatalities among families receiving prevention services. It is estimated that as many as one third of parents will abuse their children either during, or within one year of, their participation in a therapeutic program (Karski, Gilbert, & Frame, 1997; as cited in Daro & Donnelly, n.d.). Given these facts, efforts at prevention are clearly falling short of their goals. However, by continuing to develop prevention programs and evaluate their effectiveness we will hopefully be able to improve our success rate and offer safety to children as a guarantee of childhood development.

A PUBLIC HEALTH ISSUE

Over the course of the past 20–30 years child maltreatment has come to be recognized as a serious public health issue—injury, accidental or intentional, is a leading cause of death for children in the U.S. The **Centers for Disease Control and Prevention**, a public health agency, has been involved in child maltreatment prevention efforts since the 1980s, with an initial focus on child deaths that has since expanded to include the prevention of all cases of premature death and disability caused by injuries to children. More specifically, the **Division of Violence Prevention** has as part of its mission the prevention of injuries and deaths to children caused by violence. The range of health outcomes related to child maltreatment also poses a significant public health burden, further ensuring its basis as a public health issue. For example, exposure to child maltreatment often increases risk factors for many of the leading causes of death among adults, including heart disease, cancer, alcoholism, and suicide (Hammond, 2003).

Given the interpretation of child maltreatment as a public health issue, it seems appropriate that the remainder of this chapter should address child maltreatment prevention efforts within a public health context. That is, specific prevention efforts will be outlined and evaluated according to **epidemiological** terminology, which describes prevention efforts as primary (i.e., targeting the general population), secondary (i.e., targeting **at-risk** individuals), or tertiary (i.e., targeting affected individuals).

Unfortunately, it is sometimes difficult to translate this categorization system into a psychological arena and categorization can lead to some confusion regarding the definitions of and distinctions between different types of prevention approaches. This confusion is especially true for primary versus secondary prevention approaches, as one person may consider a program to be primary in nature while another may consider it to be more of a secondary approach. For example, a home visitation program that targets at-risk families based on income level, educational level, single-parent status, maternal age, and so forth (but without any previous or current history of child maltreatment), may be considered a **primary prevention** program by some because there is no evidence of child maltreatment among the recipients of services. However, others may categorize this same approach as a **secondary prevention** program because it targets a specific, as opposed to the general, population. For the purposes of this review (and in an attempt to simplify this distinction), any program that targets a high-risk group or specific subgroup will be considered a secondary prevention program, while the term *primary prevention* will be reserved for programs that are more universally available.

Furthermore, discussions of tertiary (or indicated) prevention, which targets affected individuals in an attempt to prevent further incidences and reduce the progression of an already existing problem, can create confusion because these programs are often considered to be synonymous with treatment/intervention (Harder, 2005). The goals of **tertiary prevention** programs are to minimize the negative effects of an existing problem, decrease the intensity and/or severity of a problem, reduce complications associated with the problem, and decrease **recidivism**. Examples of tertiary prevention programs related to child maltreatment include parent training classes and intensive family preservation services for families currently receiving child protective services, mental health services for children and families affected by maltreatment, and parent mentor programs with nonmaltreating families. Therefore, as the intent of this chapter is to evaluate prevention programs, and not intervention programs, tertiary prevention will not be a focus of subsequent discussion.

It is important to note that, when evaluating prevention programs, drawing comparisons among them can be difficult due to program diversity (even within a specific type of prevention program, e.g., home visitation). Variability includes (but is not limited to) the selection of participants, the duration of the program, the length of follow-up, the qualifications of program personnel, and outcome measurement (MacMillan, MacMillan, Offord, Griffith, & MacMillan, 1994a). Additionally, many programs claim to target the primary and/or secondary prevention of child maltreatment, but then do not include outcome variables that can be directly connected to the measurement of child maltreatment such as reports to child protective agencies, medical records, or prospective information regarding sexual abuse victimization (Peterson, Tremblay, Ewigman, & Saldana, 2003). These are just a few of the issues associated with evaluating child maltreatment prevention programs, and these should be kept in mind during the remainder of this review.

PRIMARY PREVENTION

Primary prevention programs universally target the general population (e.g., public service announcements) or individuals defined by geographical and/or chronological parameters (e.g., home visiting services for all women giving birth at a particular hospital during a specified period of time) in order to reduce the incidence of all new cases of a problem (Harder, 2005). Sanders, Cann, and Markie-Dadds (2003) argue for a universal population-based approach to the prevention of child maltreatment, noting that an exclusive focus on intervention programs creates a developmental disadvantage for children since they are usually only applied after maltreatment has already occurred. Further, they note that these interventions may only address part of a larger problem with family interactions, ignoring important factors such as parents' negative attributions toward child behavior and parents' anger control issues. They propose that the enhancement of parental competence, prevention of dysfunctional parenting practices, changing parental attributions (for both their behavior and children's behavior), and promotion of teamwork between parents are necessary in order to universally reduce family risk factors associated with child maltreatment. Critical aspects of such an endeavor include easy access to services, culturally appropriate family interventions, the use of effective parenting and family interventions, evidence demonstrating that decreases in dysfunctional parenting and increases in parental competence are directly linked to child functioning, and knowledge of the prevalence/incidence of family risk factors and targeted child outcomes (Sanders, Cann, & Markie-Dadds, 2003).

Public Awareness Campaigns

Primary prevention programs that are geared toward public education and awareness campaigns have as their goal informing citizens about child maltreatment and how to report it if suspected. They include the ability to create awareness of a problem, improve knowledge of a problem, change attitudes regarding a problem, and either directly or indirectly change behavior (Daro & Donnelly, n.d.). They may include such media outlets as public service announcements on television and radio programming, billboards, advertisements in newspapers and magazines, Internet sources, and distributed pamphlets or brochures. For examples of awareness campaign advertisements, see Figure 13.1. These types of media campaigns allow prevention programmers to target a large audience frequently and consistently. Unfortunately, they tend to be considered the least important approach to prevention.

Despite this mentality toward public awareness campaigns, they can be quite influential. In the mid 1970s, more than 90% of Americans were unaware of the extent of the child maltreatment problem in the U.S. Following a media campaign in the 1970s and 1980s, studies showed that more than 90% of the public were aware of the problem and knew what to do in order to help resolve it (Daro & Gelles, 1992). During this same period, child protection reports increased from 100,000 in 1976 to over 1 million in the early 1980s, many of which were made by the general public (McCurdy & Daro, 1994).

The use of public awareness campaigns in an attempt to alter specific parental attitudes and behaviors has been viewed as more challenging and often considered a less appropriate prevention strategy when compared to more targeted prevention efforts (e.g., home visitation). However, a campaign during the 1980s that targeted the use of physically and emotionally

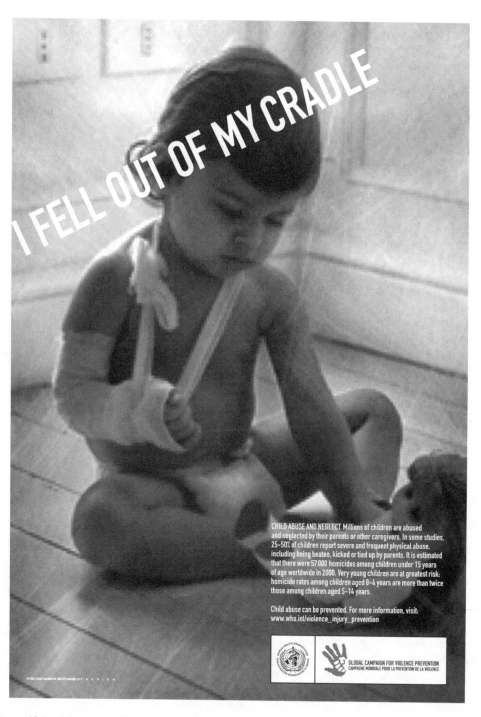

Figure 13.1 Advertisement for a public awareness campaign sponsored by the Global Campaign for Violence Prevention. Photo credit: World Health Organization.

abusive discipline techniques demonstrated a reduction in the use of both corporal punishment and verbal aggression when disciplining children. These results, however, come strictly from parental report, so it is unclear whether they reflect a true change in behavior or reluctance by parents to admit using discipline strategies they have been admonished against utilizing (Daro & Gelles, 1992).

Parent Education Campaigns

This type of primary prevention program is specifically targeted toward parents and is generally offered through certain venues (e.g., school system, medical facilities) but is available to all parents who choose to utilize these services. These programs have the advantage of being available to a large number and potentially wide range of parents. In addition, they provide a more universal level of support to parents, without the stigma associated with more targeted programs (Daro & Donnelly, n.d.). They do, however, require that parents recognize that they need help raising their children and that they be both willing and able to attend and learn from them. Unfortunately, many of the risk factors for child maltreatment (e.g., substance abuse, high stress, low education levels, lack of support) may also prevent parents from taking advantage of programs like these.

Several of these programs have been developed for use in medical settings including the **Detroit Family Project** and **Don't Shake the Baby**. In the Detroit Family Project, parent facilitators visit waiting rooms of health clinics with a mobile cart containing snacks, brochures, and toys for children. The facilitators initiate informal discussions with the parents about a variety of parenting-related topics and also give parents brochures and suggestions for obtaining additional information. This program reaches approximately 25,000 parents annually, and many report having learned information of which they were not previously aware (Whitelaw Downs & Walker, 1996; as cited in Daro & Donnelly, n.d.). Don't Shake the Baby was developed to increase parental knowledge regarding the dangers of shaking infants and reduce the occurrence of shaken baby syndrome. Over a 1-year period, information was distributed to parents on maternity wards. Parents reported that the information was helpful (Showers, 1992), but no attempts were made to determine whether this program affected the prevalence of shaken baby syndrome. By taking the program to where the parents already are instead of waiting for parents to come to the program, more parents, including those who are less capable or motivated, may also be reached.

Child Sexual Abuse Programs

As previously mentioned, prevention efforts to reduce the rates of sexual abuse have taken a different approach from programs targeted at physical abuse and neglect in that child sexual abuse prevention programs target potential victims rather than perpetrators. The approach of these programs is primarily educational in nature. Children are provided with general information regarding sexual abuse and more specific information regarding how to protect themselves from and respond to sexual abuse. Programs also provide opportunities for children to discuss issues surrounding child sexual abuse with their parents and disclose past or current abuse to an adult. Child sexual abuse prevention programs may be provided directly through the school system and through community and nationally based organizations (Daro & Donnelly, n.d).

Many people are concerned about the suitability of these programs, particularly with respect to potential negative effects on children, but research generally shows few negative side effects as a result of program participation (MacMillian, MacMillan, Offord, Griffith, & MacMillan, 1994b; Wurtele & Miller-Perrin, 1987). Additionally, studies report that these programs yield a slight increase in children's knowledge of sexual abuse and how to respond (Carroll & Miltenberger, 1992; Rispens, Aleman, & Goudena, 1997). As with any program, there appear to be some differences with respect to how this information is received. Children have more difficulty accepting that this type of abuse can occur by someone they know than by strangers (Finkelhor & Strapko, 1992), and among younger children, the more complex concepts such as secrets and ambiguous feelings are often misunderstood (Berrick, 1989). Furthermore, programs that incorporate more active components (i.e., modeling, rehearsal, vignettes) tend to yield more positive results (Davis & Gidycz, 2000).

In an attempt to determine children's exposure and response to child sexual abuse prevention programs, a national survey of children age 10–16 years found that 67% had attended at least one program in their lifetime (Finkelhor & Dziuba-Leatherman, 1995). Topics covered in these programs included information regarding **intrafamilial** and **extrafamilial** sexual abuse, appropriate versus inappropriate touch, strategies for stopping abuse attempts, the importance of disclosure, and reassurance that abuse is not the child's fault. Few of these programs included parents, although more than half of the children reported that they discussed the program with their parents. Most evaluations of the programs were positive; 95% of participants said they would recommend it to other children. With regard to potential negative effects of program participation, younger children, minority children, and children from lower socioeconomic families reported more fear and anxiety. However, these same children reported the most positive reactions to the program and the most use of program information and skills.

In a related study of the same group of participants, Finkelhor, Asdigian, and Dziuba-Leatherman (1995) reported results regarding the effectiveness of child sexual abuse prevention programs. Children who attended programs scored higher on a knowledge test related to child sexual abuse information and reported more disclosures of current and past sexual abuse. Many of the children also reported that they had used the skills learned in the program during a variety of later real-life situations (e.g., saying no to an adult, disclosure, helping a friend). Furthermore, they reported feeling better able to handle threats of victimization, although they were not any more effective in thwarting actual assaults. That is, they did not have a lower level of completed victimizations. Unfortunately, these children were also more likely to be injured during sexual victimizations, probably resulting from a greater tendency to fight back. Accordingly, it is recommended that care be taken with respect to the strategies that children are taught to prevent abuse attempts, especially because these strategies may not reduce a child's likelihood to actually prevent these attempts.

While most child sexual abuse prevention programs are developed and marketed as efforts to prevent the occurrence of child sexual abuse, most evaluations of these programs focus on child knowledge (which is generally improved by intervention), but not actual ability to avoid sexual abuse in real life. In an attempt to discern whether these programs affect the incidence of child sexual abuse, Gibson and Leitenberg (2000) conducted a retrospective survey of female college students. They found that students who had not participated in a school-based child sexual abuse prevention program were twice as likely to experience subsequent child sexual abuse compared with the students who had participated in one of these programs. They did not find any differences in rates of sexual abuse disclosure, although the students who had participated in a program tended to make earlier disclosures than students who had not attended a program. Furthermore, any sexual abuse they had experienced was of shorter duration. In order to address public concerns regarding the potential negative impact of child sexual abuse programs on later sexual functioning, Gibson and Leitenberg evaluated sexual satisfaction and behavior among women who had not experienced child sexual abuse. The results of these analyses indicated that there were no differences in sexual satisfaction or behavior between students who had and had not previously participated in a prevention program. Overall, the results from this study suggest that attendance at prevention programs can have long-term positive effects on the incidence of child sexual abuse without negatively impacting sexual functioning.

FOCUS ON RESEARCH 13.1

Several of the studies investigating the effectiveness of child sexual abuse prevention programs mentioned in this chapter (Finkelhor & Dziuba-Leatherman, 1995; Finkelhor, Asdigian, & Dziuba-Leatherman, 1995; Gibson & Leitenberg, 2000) required research participants to remember a program they had attended at some point in their lifetime (that is, the studies are retrospective in nature). A primary concern with retrospective studies is that they rely on the ability of people to remember the details of events that occurred sometime in the past. In the case of these child sexual abuse prevention studies, the participants were required to recall the details of an event that occurred many years in the past. In evaluating the results of these retrospective studies, we must consider whether people are able to remember adequately the details of a program they attended as many as 15 years ago. Additionally, we must consider the value of a prospective research design in evaluating the effectiveness of prevention programs—a design that is often underutilized because it tends to be more costly and time consuming than a retrospective design.

See Focus on Research 13.1 for further discussion on the validity of results obtained through retrospective studies.

Many feel that parents may be in a better position to protect their children from sexual abuse than are children to protect themselves and have suggested that child sexual abuse prevention programs should more regularly incorporate parental involvement (Reppucci, Jones, & Cook, 1994). While some programs do include parental components, these are likely to be voluntary, and attendance may be poor. In fact, one study of parental involvement in a child sexual abuse prevention program for preschoolers reported that only 34% of parents attended the parent-focused meeting (Berrick, 1988). Furthermore, the results of this study indicated that the parents who did attend did not learn very much, as there were no differences in parental knowledge between those who attended and those who did not. Even those who did attend had difficulty identifying the indicators of child sexual abuse, primarily noting an intuitive ability to recognize sexual abuse among their children ("I'd just know"). Despite these findings, others have suggested strategies for encouraging parental attendance, including program involvement with parent-teacher associations (Brassard, Tyler, & Kehle, 1983), scheduling workshops on a Saturday with alternate activities (i.e., movies, games) for children, and forming smaller discussion groups rather than the typical larger lecture format (Reppucci, Jones, & Cook, 1994).

SECONDARY PREVENTION

Due to monetary and resource costs associated with primary prevention efforts, many programs targeting child maltreatment adopt a more selective approach. In order to effectively reach those most in need of service, and to be able to offer them more comprehensive services from a limited pool of resources, prevention programs tend to target individuals at risk for maltreatment rather than offering services to the general population.

This more selective approach to prevention efforts is called secondary prevention, which targets at-risk individuals in order to reduce the incidence of new cases of a problem among those determined to be at some identified risk. These individuals may include single parents, young parents, parents with a psychiatric history, parents with a history of having been abused themselves, and low-income families among others (Harder, 2005). Helfer (1976) proposed that a "**disease model**" be applied to our understanding of secondary prevention efforts for child maltreatment, in which the goal is to inoculate susceptible parents against abusing/neglecting their children (as cited in McMurtry, 1985). The general approach is governed by the principle that, while everyone can presumably benefit from services aimed at the prevention of child maltreatment, not everyone needs it. Therefore, secondary prevention approaches may offer advantages in service efficiency. Unlike the more conventional disease model, however, the prevention of child maltreatment is faced with some formidable difficulties. First, there is no clear definition of child maltreatment, and therefore, its existence (to some extent) is a matter of subjective interpretation. Furthermore, it is not a discrete phenomenon that a parent clearly demonstrates or does not, but may actually lie on a continuum that also includes good parenting characteristics. Third, a clear and useful **etiology** of the problem is unknown (McMurtry, 1985). The problem, therefore, is deciding who exactly should be targeted for prevention programs.

Findings From Specific Prevention Programs

Most secondary prevention programs for child maltreatment focus their efforts primarily on reducing the likelihood for physical abuse, although they may indirectly address factors related to neglect as well. Few attempt to investigate any effects on psychological maltreatment, either directly or indirectly. Additionally, recognizing the many challenges associated with the prevention of physical abuse and neglect, especially once risk factors are present and have been identified, most secondary prevention programs tend to be fairly comprehensive in nature. They incorporate components from models of parenting education, family support, crisis intervention, therapeutic interventions, and home visitation.

Several secondary prevention programs, in particular, have had a large impact on the overall child maltreatment prevention field. One such program is **Hawaii's Healthy Start Program**, which began in the mid-1980s and focused on home visitation for families identified as being at risk for maltreating their newborn children. Families participating in this program were enrolled during the mother's pregnancy, and they began receiving home visits shortly after childbirth. Families received services for the fist three years of the child's life. Home visits were conducted by trained **paraprofessionals** and initially occurred on a weekly basis. Over the course of the program, visits gradually decreased to quarterly appointments. Although this initial program did not include a control group comparison, results indicated that there were no child protection reports of physical abuse and only four reports of neglect (out of 234 participating families) among program enrollees (Duggan et al., 1999).

The success of Hawaii's Healthy Start Program spearheaded home visitation efforts across the U.S., particularly **Healthy Families America** (HFA), is a program that was initiated by **Prevent Child Abuse America** in 1992 and, by 1997, had been implemented in approximately 38 states and the District of Columbia. Healthy Families America programs include weekly home visits that begin shortly after childbirth, with visit frequency tapering over time. Home visits are conducted by paraprofessionals, and services are available to families for the first five years of a child's life. Daro and Harding (1999) reviewed Healthy Families America data related to CPS reports of child physical abuse and neglect and found a 6% child maltreatment rate among program participants. This percentage is higher than the national average at the time (4.7% in the late 1990s), but two to three times lower than the estimated rate for families with at-risk characteristics (e.g., low income, single mothers) similar to those of the program participants. However, studies conducted with control group comparisons have not demonstrated different child maltreatment rates between treatment and control group families.

Hawaii's Healthy Start Program and Healthy Families America have more recently come under fire, especially given their apparent inability to produce results similar to those obtained by the initial project in Hawaii. Duggan et al. (2004) reviewed the results from 12 of Hawaii's Healthy Start Programs. In general, the authors found no program impact on preventing child physical abuse or promoting nonviolent discipline techniques, and only modest effects related to child neglect. Given these negative findings, researchers have generally concluded that the use of paraprofessionals to deliver prevention services may not be appropriate for high-risk families who often have complex and multiple psychosocial risk factors (e.g., parental substance abuse, poor maternal mental health, domestic violence). Interestingly, in a survey of Healthy Families America home visitors, LeCroy and Whitaker (2005) noted that the biggest challenges faced by home visitors in conducting visitations included limited resources, family mental illness (e.g., threatening suicide), substance abuse in the home, domestic violence, families in constant crisis, safety issues, and unmotivated families.

Another secondary prevention program that has had a significant impact on child maltreatment prevention efforts is the **Nurse Home Visitation Program**. Participants in this program included pregnant women whose fetuses are at risk for later health and developmental problems due to factors such as maternal age, single parenthood, and low socioeconomic status. The program consisted of weekly home visits conducted by nurses. Home visits generally began during the second trimester of pregnancy and gradually decreased in frequency until program termination at the child's second birthday. Results of this program revealed a significant reduction in substantiated CPS reports among home-visited families (compared to control group participants) by the child's second birthday. This effect was especially dramatic among a subsample of poor, unmarried teenage mothers. During a 15-year follow-up, results indicated half as many substantiated CPS reports among home-visited families compared to control group participants. Again, this effect was strongest among poor and unmarried women (Olds et al., 1999). The Nurse Home Visitation Program results are certainly more positive than those from the more recent Hawaii's Healthy Start Program and Healthy Families America evaluations. Many have credited the difference in program effectiveness to the utilization of more qualified and highly trained home visitors in the Nurse Home Visitation Program (i.e., nurses vs. paraprofessionals). Whether it is this difference in professional qualifications that explains the resulting difference in findings remains unknown. However, it is encouraging to know that positive reports from a well-executed home visitation program are attainable.

A meta-analysis of reports on secondary prevention programs revealed an overall positive effect. Positive outcomes were specifically connected to decreases in abusive and neglectful acts; a reduction in risk factors related to child, parent, and family functioning; and improvements in parent-child interaction. Although this meta-analysis did not reveal any beneficial program effects based on actual indicators of maltreatment (i.e., CPS reports), the fact that positive effects were found on several other measures of child maltreatment is noteworthy. This suggests that the use of proxy measures (i.e., risk factors) may be preferable to direct outcome measures that may not accurately reflect the true prevalence of abuse and neglect and that are difficult to detect given their rarity (Geeraert, Van den Noortgate, Grietens, & Onghena, 2004).

Given the potential difficulties and methodological issues in using CPS reports as an indicator of child maltreatment, an alternative outcome measure in the study of child abuse is parental discipline styles. Prevention programs may examine factors associated with an increased risk for child abuse, such as harsh physical discipline. One such program assessed seven components related to successful parenting: parenting skills, awareness of developmentally appropriate behaviors, parental beliefs, parental affect, parental role, maternal role, and parental efficacy. Participants included low-income mothers with children from 18 months to 4 years of age. Intervention included weekly group therapy sessions and weekly home visits for 16 weeks. Compared to control groups, measures of harsh discipline revealed a significant treatment effect—such that harsh discipline among the treatment group decreased, while it remained the same among control groups. This study did not directly measure child maltreatment, as there was no inclusion of reports to CPS, emergency room visits, injuries, hospitalizations, and the like. It did, however, examine "harsh discipline" (e.g., shouting, threatening, shoving, slapping) within the context of parenting skills, which is a potential risk factor for child maltreatment. As such, this study is of interest because it demonstrates the range of variability with regard to methodological considerations that is apparent among prevention efforts (Peterson, Tremblay, Ewigman, & Saldana, 2003).

Lastly, Barth (1991) reported results for the **Child Parent Enrichment Project**. This program included 6 months of home visitation that began during pregnancy. Participants were primarily high-risk mothers (e.g., low IQ, mental illness, history of maternal abuse). The program received high consumer satisfaction scores but did not show any evidence of child abuse and neglect prevention. These results highlight the need to include objective (rather than relying solely on subjective) outcome measures. While it is helpful to know that the mothers liked the program, it is not the same as knowing that the program was effective at reducing child maltreatment.

Prevention Targeting Child Neglect

Although neglect is the most often reported form of child maltreatment, little is known regarding effective methods for prevention. Given the complex, and likely chronic, nature of neglect, a simple prevention program is unlikely to have much impact. Consequently, prevention programs do not often target neglect directly or explicitly. In a study conducted by DePanfilis and Dubowitz (2005), residents of an impoverished urban neighborhood with several additional risk factors for neglect (e.g., nonreportable neglectful characteristics, parental mental health issues, child behavior problems) and a child between the ages of 5 and 11 years old were recruited as participants. Participants were assigned to either a 3- or 9-month **Family Connections Program**. Components of the program included home-based interventions (e.g., social support, behavior management), referrals to community services (e.g., substance abuse treatment), supportive recreational activities (e.g., trips to museums, baseball games, holiday celebrations), and emergency (e.g., eviction notice, lack of food, intimate partner violence) assistance. Although some improvements in risk and protective factors were seen (and maintained at 6-month follow-up), issues related to child safety and maltreatment reports were still present following program termination. Furthermore, there were no observed differences between the treatment groups based on duration of program participation.

One explanation for the lack of positive findings relevant to child maltreatment in this study is the possibility that the program was not long enough to evidence any subsequent effects. That is, 3 or 9 months is likely not enough time to resolve issues related to a problem as pervasive as child neglect. Furthermore, a methodological issue present in this study is that without a control group comparison it is impossible to determine whether the effects observed resulted from program implementation, the passage of time, or issues associated with participant and researcher expectations. Despite the limited positive findings from this study, the fact that it directly addressed the prevention of child neglect makes it a unique contribution to the prevention field. This is an issue that is worthy of continued consideration. Hopefully, more researchers will begin focusing on child neglect as an area worthy of more targeted prevention efforts.

CONCLUSION

Unfortunately, we are faced with the reality that that we do not yet know how to effectively prevent child maltreatment. With continued development and evaluation of prevention programs, we stand a better chance of achieving success. Additional research that is **empirically** tested is necessary to attain this goal. In conducting these evaluations, several methodological issues should be taken into consideration. First, the lack of clear statutory definitions and guidelines for identifying maltreatment complicate our ability to conduct effective outcome research. Second, incorporating follow-up protocols is necessary to determine any long-term programmatic gains and/or **"sleeper" effects** (i.e., those that emerge some time after program completion). Third, the role of potential **mediators** of maltreatment risk, such as parental attitudes, should be considered in research designs. Finally, researchers need to develop ways to make program participation more appealing so that families are willing to take part in these programs before it becomes too late to help them reverse dysfunctional patterns of behavior (Wolfe, Reppucci, & Hart, 1995). This is by no means intended as an exhaustive list of methodological issues associated with prevention research, but certainly some of the important factors to consider.

Finally, some have argued for an overhaul in our thinking about child maltreatment and its prevention. Rather than viewing poor parental practices and lack of support as indicators of dysfunction and therefore adopting a stigmatizing intervention approach, a truly prevention-focused model encourages us to recognize the need for varying levels of services among all families (Wolfe, Reppucci, & Hart, 1995). In other words, who wouldn't benefit from a little extra support, a few more resources, or a bit of education? These services are important for the healthy functioning of all families, and this model encourages us to view family functioning from a developmental perspective in which the goal is to promote positive behaviors from the beginning, rather than eliminate negatives ones after they have occurred.

DISCUSSION QUESTIONS

1. Provide an additional example of how U.S. society is more intervention, than prevention, focused. Why do you think this is the case?
2. How can primary and secondary prevention efforts be distinguished from each other?
3. Should agencies devote the bulk of their resources to primary or secondary prevention methods?
4. Do you consider tertiary prevention to be a form of prevention or intervention?
5. What are the advantages and disadvantages of public awareness campaigns?
6. In the prevention of child sexual abuse, do you think it makes sense to target potential child victims (the focus of most current prevention programs) rather than parents and/or potential perpetrators?
7. Does the "disease model" for secondary prevention efforts seem appropriate?
8. What are the primary methodological issues in researching the prevention of child maltreatment? How might we overcome these methodological issues?

DEFINITIONS

Prevent: to reduce the likelihood of an occurrence.

Precursor: any factor that precedes the onset of child maltreatment and may function as a risk factor.

Attrition: the loss of participants during a research study, which may occur for a variety of reasons (e.g., loss of interest in the study, relocation, death).

Centers for Disease Control and Prevention: a division of the Department of Health and Human Services whose mission is to promote health and quality of life by preventing and controlling disease, injury, and disability.

Division of Violence Prevention: a division of the Centers for Disease Control and Prevention that is dedicated to the prevention of all forms of violence including child maltreatment, intimate partner violence, school violence, and youth violence.

Epidemiological: that which pertains to factors affecting the health and illness of populations (i.e., public health).

At-Risk: an individual (or group of individuals) who are predisposed to developing a maladaptive behavior pattern (such as child maltreatment).

Primary Prevention: targets the general population to reduce the incidence of all new cases of a problem.

Secondary Prevention: targets a specific group of individuals to reduce the incidence of new cases of a problem among those determined to be at some identified risk.

Tertiary Prevention: intended to minimize the negative effects of an already existing problem.

Recidivism: the tendency for something (such as a disease or maladaptive behavior pattern) to recur.

Detroit Family Project: a primary prevention program in which facilitators engaged in informal discussions on parenting-related topics with parents in the waiting rooms of health clinics.

Don't Shake the Baby: a primary prevention program developed to increase parental knowledge regarding the dangers of shaking infants and reduce the occurrence of shaken baby syndrome.

Intrafamilial: occurring within a family.

Extrafamilial: occurring outside of a family.

Disease Model: a term borrowed from medical science to refer to maladaptive behavior patterns (e.g., addiction, child maltreatment) as lifelong illnesses that involve both biological and environmental sources of origin.

Etiology: the study of causation; why things occur and/or the reasons for behavior.

Hawaii's Healthy Start Program: a secondary prevention program that provides home visitation for families identified as being at risk for maltreating their newborn children.

Paraprofessional: a job title given to people in occupations for which they have received some specialized training but are not professionally licensed.

Healthy Families America: a home visitation program that was modeled after Hawaii's Healthy Start Program.

Prevent Child Abuse America: an organization that began in 1972 with the mission of preventing all forms of child abuse and neglect in the U.S.

Nurse Home Visitation Program: a secondary prevention program that targets pregnant women whose fetuses are at risk for later health and developmental problems.

Child Parent Enrichment Project: a secondary prevention program involving home visitation for high-risk mothers.

Family Connections Program: a secondary prevention program specifically targeting the prevention of child neglect.

Empirically: obtained through experimental and/or experimental observation methods; derived from science and the scientific method of gathering evidence.

"Sleeper" Effect: an outcome that emerges some time after a program has been completed.

Mediator: a factor that may explain the relationship between two other variables. For example, the relationship between race and parenting style may be explained by socioeconomic status (SES). That is, SES may mediate the relationship between race and parenting style so that when you remove the effect of SES, the relationship between race and parenting style is no longer apparent.

Appendix of Abbreviations

ACF	Administration for Children and Families
ACLU	American Civil Liberties Union
ADHD	Attention Deficit Hyperactivity Disorder
APSAC	American Professional Society on the Abuse of Children
ASPCA	American Society for the Prevention of Cruelty to Animals
BDI	Beck Depression Inventory
CAC	Child Advocacy Center
CAPTA	Child Abuse Prevention and Treatment Act
CBCL	Child Behavior Checklist
CHILD	Children's Healthcare is a Legal Duty
CPA	Child Physical Abuse
CPS	Child Protective Services
CSA	Child Sexual Abuse
CTS	Conflict Tactics Scale
CVS	Covert Video Surveillance
CVWP	Child Victim Witness Protection Program
DCS	Department of Children's Services
DID	Dissociative Identity Disorder
DSM	*Diagnostic and Statistical Manual of Mental Disorders*
DSS	Department of Social Services
DUI	Driving Under the Influence
ECF	Educational Condition or Disability Falsification
FAE	Fetal Alcohol Effects
FAS	Fetal Alcohol Syndrome
FDBP	Factitious Disorder by Proxy
FE	Family Environments
HFA	Healthy Families America
IRB	Institutional Review Board
MA	Methamphetamine
MAMA	Mothers Against Munchausen by Proxy Allegations
MHP	Mental Health Professionals
MMPI	Minnesota Multiphasic Personality Inventory
MPD	Multiple Personality Disorder
MPS	Munchausen by Proxy Syndrome
NAPCWA	National Association of Public Child Welfare Administrators
NAMBLA	North American Man/Boy Love Association
NCAND	National Child Abuse and Neglect Data System
NCCAN	National Clearinghouse on Child Abuse and Neglect

NFTT	Nonorganic Failure to Thrive
NIDA	National Institute on Drug Abuse
NIS	National Incidence Studies
NIS-3	Third National Incidence Study
OCAN	Office on Child Abuse and Neglect
OI	Osteogenesis Imperfecta
PA	Physical Abuse
PCF	Pediatric Condition Falsification
PLS	Preschool Language Scale
PTSD	Post-Traumatic Stress Disorder
RBPC	Revised Behavior Problem Checklist
SBS	Shaken Baby Syndrome
SD	Standard Deviation
SES	Socioeconomic Status
SIS	Shaken Impact Syndrome
SMART	Specific, Measurable, Achievable, Realistic, and Time-limited
SPCA	Society for the Prevention of Cruelty to Animals
SPCC	Society for the Prevention of Cruelty to Children
STD	Sexually Transmitted Disease
STI	Sexually Transmitted Infection
VD	Venereal Disease
WISC	Wechsler Intelligence Scale for Children

Glossary

Abandonment: desertion; severing ties with and failing to support one's own child.

Abrogated: cancelled or annulled by official means or authority.

Administration for Children and Families (ACF): a division of the Department of Health and Human Services. It is responsible for federal programs that promote the economic and social well-being of children and families, and assists local agencies (both public and private) with relevant funding, policy direction, and educational services.

Adoption and Safe Families Act: legislation passed in 1997 to promote the adoption of children in foster care (in the event that reunification with biological parents is not possible), especially children with special needs. It describes safety, permanency, and well-being as key principles in the implementation of child welfare legislation.

Adoption Assistance and Child Welfare Act: legislation passed in 1980 to encourage caseworkers to work toward reunifying families and to avoid long-term and/or multiple foster care placements for children if possible.

Adversarial System: a court system that involves active and unhindered parties contesting with each other in the presence of an independent decision maker (judge or jury).

Aggression: behavior that is intended to cause harm or pain; a disposition to behave in a violent way even when not provoked.

Alcohol: an intoxicating beverage containing a chemical produced by yeast fermentation or hydration of ethylene.

Allegation: an unproven assertion that child maltreatment has occurred.

American Academy of Pediatrics: an organization of approximately 60,000 pediatricians dedicated to the health of all children.

American Civil Liberties Union (ACLU): a national organization that advocates for individual rights by preserving the protections and guarantees listed in the Bill of Rights.

American Professional Society on the Abuse of Children (APSAC): a national nonprofit organization that is committed to preventing child maltreatment, promoting research, informing American public policy, and educating the public about maltreatment.

Anatomically Detailed Doll: a doll with anatomical details such as a penis or a vaginal opening, an anal opening, pubic hair, chest hair, and underarm hair.

Anorexia: an eating disorder characterized by the relentless pursuit of thinness through starvation.

Arraignment: an initial step in criminal prosecution where defendants hear the charges brought against them and enter a plea.

At-Risk: an individual (or group of individuals) who are predisposed to developing a maladaptive behavior pattern (such as child maltreatment).

Attachment: a strong, affectionate bond between two people. Infants typically form an attachment to their primary caregiver between 6 and 12 months.

Attention Deficit Hyperactivity Disorder (ADHD): a mental disorder characterized by a limited attention span, overactivity, restlessness, and impulsiveness.

Attributions: determinations about what caused an event or condition; explanations for one's own behavior or the behavior of others.

Attrition: the loss of participants during a research study, which may occur for a variety of reasons (e.g., loss of interest in the study, relocation, death).

Avoidant Attachment: an insecure attachment style in which infants tend to avoid or ignore their caregivers.

Beck Anxiety Inventory: a 21-item scale designed to measure anxiety and to discriminate between anxiety and depression.

Best Interest of the Child: the principle that drives the judge's decisions in domestic relations courts when deciding issues of custody and support.

Beyond a Reasonable Doubt: the burden of proof in criminal court; the doubt that prevents one from being firmly convinced of a defendant's guilt; the highest burden of proof.

Borderline Personality Disorder: a mental disorder marked by significant impairment in interpersonal relationships, problems with self-esteem and self-image, and impulsivity.

Bruising: injury in which capillaries are damaged, allowing blood to seep into the surrounding tissue; generally caused by striking or pressing that does not break the skin.

Bulimia: an eating disorder characterized by cycles of bingeing and purging.

Buprenorphine: a medication used during the treatment of heroin addiction that prevents the experience of withdrawal symptoms.

Burns: injuries caused by fire, heat, or acid; first-degree burns cause red skin, second-degree burns result in blisters, and third-degree burns cause deep skin destruction.

***Caida de Mollera*:** a sunken anterior fontanelle (space between the bones in an infant's skull) that can be the result of severe illness, significant weight loss, or dehydration.

Cannabinoids: the chemical compounds that are the active ingredients of marijuana.

***Cao Gio*:** a Southeast Asian practice in which a practitioner massages a heated ointment or oil on an ill child's neck, spine, and ribs, and then runs a coin or spoon along the child's skin with firm, downward strokes.

Carotid: an artery in the neck that supplies the brain with oxygenated blood.

Case Closure: the process by which an open child protective services (CPS) case is resolved and the family no longer receives CPS services.

Case Planning: the developing of three types of plans by the caseworker during a family's involvement with child protective services: a safety plan for the child, a case plan aimed at allowing the family to remain together, and a concurrent permanency plan that establishes an alternate living arrangement for the child in the event that the case plan is not successful.

Case Study: an in-depth analysis of one person or event. This research method provides significant detail about one case, but the findings cannot be generalized to other persons or events.

Caseworker: a professional employed by child protective services to investigate child maltreatment, ensure the safety of children in their homes, and provide necessary services to families.

Centers for Disease Control and Prevention: a division of the Department of Health and Human Services whose mission is to promote health and quality of life by preventing and controlling disease, injury, and disability.

Central Registry: a database maintained by a state's child protective agency that contains information on all substantiated reports of child maltreatment for that state.

Child Abuse: an act, generally deliberate, by a parent or caregiver that results in harm or death to a child.

Child Abuse Prevention and Treatment Act (CAPTA): legislation passed in 1974 that sets forth a minimum definition of child abuse and neglect, establishes the Office on Child Abuse and Neglect (OCAN), authorizes the expenditure of federal dollars to support state child protection efforts, and provides grants to public agencies to support child maltreatment research.

Child Advocacy Center (CAC): a center designed to assess allegations of maltreatment and to treat victims by enlisting a multidisciplinary team of law enforcement, medical, social service, legal, and clinical professionals.

Child Behavior Checklist (CBCL): a 118-item scale designed to measure a child's behavioral problems and social competencies based on parental report.

Child Endangerment: placing a child in a situation that is potentially harmful.

Child Maltreatment: the abuse and/or neglect of children. Specific definitions vary by state and purpose (legal, research, etc.).

Child Neglect: the failure of a parent or caregiver to meet the minimal physical and psychological needs of a child.

Child/Parent Enrichment Project: a secondary prevention program involving home visitation for high-risk mothers.

Child Physical Abuse: an act by a caregiver that results in a nonaccidental injury to a child.

Child Protective Services (CPS): a government agency charged with protecting children and preserving families. This is the agency that responds to charges of child maltreatment. Not all states use the title CPS; variations include department of family services (DFS) and department of social services (DSS).

Child Sexual Abuse (CSA): the involvement of a child in any sexual activity where consent is not or cannot be given.

Child Victim Witness Program (CVWP): an individualized Canadian program that prepares children for court by educating them, by appointing and educating a support person to assist the child, and by visiting a court in session.

Children's Bureau: the oldest federal agency for children. This agency is charged with providing for the safety, permanence, and well-being of children.

Civil Commitment: the confinement of a person who is ill, incompetent, or drug-addicted.

Civil Court: a court that hears noncriminal cases where parties seek to settle disputes and be awarded damages.

Class Action Suit: a lawsuit in which one person or a small group of people sue as representatives of a larger group of affected people because the group is so large that individual suits would not be practical.

Clear and Convincing Evidence: a degree of evidence that indicates that the issue being proven is highly probable. It is a higher standard of proof than the preponderance of evidence, but a lower standard than beyond a reasonable doubt.

Cleft Palate: a congenital condition that results in a crack in the roof of the mouth.

Clinical Population: a group of people defined by their association as patients with a treatment facility.

Clumsy Interview: an interview that is not likely to lead to false allegations but is conducted poorly. Clumsy interviews lead to statements that are less coherent, less detailed, and less convincing than those garnered from good interviews.

Cocaine: a crystalline alkaloid that comes from coca leaves. It is used illicitly as a stimulant and to induce euphoria.

Collateral Sources: individuals who are interviewed by caseworkers as part of a child protective services investigation (e.g., neighbors, teachers, babysitters).

Commission Errors: mistakes that involve saying something occurred when it did not.

Conduct Disorder: a personality disorder of childhood marked by persistent disruptive behavior and repeated violation of the rights of others and societal norms.

Confidentiality: an ethical principle associated with people in many human service professions whereby these professionals may not divulge information about their clients to third parties.

Conflict Tactics Scale (CTS): a scale that measures psychological and physical maltreatment as well as nonviolent discipline. The parent/child version was designed to gather information about how parents have disciplined their child over the past year. The child fills out one form, and a parent fills out another.

Congenital: a condition that is present at birth.

Continuity: the principle that a child's ideal living environment should be disrupted as little as possible.

Control Group: participants in a study who are not exposed to the variable being explored.

Corporal Punishment: physical punishment such as spanking or slapping.

Correlational Research: a study in which two or more variables are measured so that the degree of relationship between them can be measured.

Court Prep Group: a program devised by the National Children's Advocacy Center to prepare groups of children for court through education, understanding of emotional issues, role-play, and touring of a courthouse.

Covert Video Surveillance: making a video recording without making it clear to the participants that they are being taped.

Criminal Court: the court charged with the administration of justice via penalty or punishment.

Cross-Examination: the questioning of a witness by the opposing party, especially for the purpose of clarifying or discrediting the witness's testimony.

Culturally Responsive Services: child welfare services that include the acknowledgement and acceptance of other people's cultures and cultural values.

Culture: the socially transmitted behaviors, arts, beliefs, and institutions that characterize a group of people.

Denying Emotional Responsiveness: a caregiver's ignoring their child or showing no emotional reactions while interacting with their child.

Dependency Case: a case to determine whether a child's needs are being met by guardians or if the State needs to take temporary or permanent custody of the child.

Detention Hearing: a hearing for the purpose of determining whether there is sufficient evidence for the State to hold the child pending further investigation; also referred to as the 72-hour hearing.

Detroit Family Project: a primary prevention program in which facilitators engaged in informal discussions on parenting-related topics with parents in the waiting rooms of health clinics.

Diagnostic and Statistical Manual of Mental Disorders (DSM): a manual published by the American Psychiatric Association that lists the criteria for diagnosing mental disorders as well as providing information on causes, age of onset, gender differences, and prognosis.

Disclosure: the act of revealing; telling someone else or making known what has previously been hidden.

Disease Model: a term borrowed from medical science to refer to maladaptive behavior patterns (e.g., addiction, child maltreatment) as lifelong illnesses that involve both biological and environmental sources of origin.

Disinhibition: a loss of the ability to restrain from or suppress behaviors or impulses.

Dispositional Hearing: a hearing when the judge enters their decision as to what is in the best interest of the child.

Dissociation: the separation of some mental processes from conscious awareness.

Dissociative Experience Survey: a 28-item self-report measure designed to be a screening test for dissociative identity disorder (DID), formerly called multiple personality disorder (MPD).

Division of Violence Prevention: a division of the Centers for Disease Control and Prevention that is dedicated to the prevention of all forms of violence including child maltreatment, intimate partner violence, school violence, and youth violence.

Domestic Relations Court: a court that is dedicated to hearing cases related to divorce, child custody and support, paternity and other family law issues; it is also called family court.

Domestic Violence: violence, abuse, or intimidation that takes place in the context of an intimate relationship.

Don't Shake the Baby: a primary prevention program developed to increase parental knowledge regarding the dangers of shaking infants and reduce the occurrence of shaken baby syndrome.

Down Syndrome: a chromosomal abnormality (an extra copy of the 21st chromosome) that results in mental retardation, abnormal facial features (flattened nasal bridge, widely spaced and slanted eyes), slowed growth, and other physical problems.

Dual Representation: the ability to think of one thing as being or representing two things at once.

Dysmorphic: an abnormality of the structure of part of the body that results from a developmental defect.

Dysthymia: a chronic, mild depression that persists for more than 2 years.

Ecologically Based Approach: a strategy in the delivery of human services that focuses on family and community as a whole, rather than focusing solely on the individual.

Educational Neglect: the failure to meet legal requirements for school enrollment or attendance, or the lack of attention to special educational needs.

Emotional Neglect: the failure to meet a child's emotional needs.

Empirically: obtained through experimental and/or experimental observation methods; derived from science and the scientific method of gathering evidence.

Epidemiological: pertaining to factors affecting the health and illness of populations (i.e., public health).

Erikson: a psychologist who proposed a theory of psychosocial development in which people develop across their entire life span by confronting various social issues.

Etiology: the study of causation; why things occur and/or the reasons for behavior.

Exaggerate: to overstate; to increase to an abnormal degree.

Excited Utterance Exception: an exception regarding a statement that is made while under stress about an event, which is admissible as hearsay testimony.

Experiment: a form of scientific research in which a researcher manipulates one or more variables in order to see the effects on another variable or variables.

Exploiting/Corrupting: encouraging children to develop and engage in inappropriate behaviors.

Expungement: the act of destroying or sealing records following a specified period of time.

Extrafamilial: occurring outside of a family.

Fabricate: to falsify; to report something that is not true.

Factitious Disorder by Proxy: the term used by the *Diagnostic and Statistical Manual of Mental Disorders* to describe the behaviors also referred to as Munchausen by proxy syndrome.

Family Assessment: following a child protective services investigation and initial assessment, the process by which a caseworker collaborates with family members to identify needed services.

Family Connections Program: a secondary prevention program specifically targeting the prevention of child neglect.

Family Group Decision-Making Model: a strategy used by child protective agencies to optimize family strengths in the case-planning process. As part of this strategy, the family and members of the family's social support network are included in the decision-making process during case planning.

Family Preservation and Reunification: an underlying principle of federal legislation (particularly the Adoption Assistance and Child Welfare Act) that encourages child protective agencies to maintain biological families whenever possible. Adherence to this principle has lessened since the passing of the Adoption and Safe Families Act, which focuses more on the child's safety and well-being than maintaining a biological family.

Family Progress: the ongoing assessment of an open child protective services case by a caseworker.

Federal Rule of Evidence 601: a rule governing the admissibility of evidence at trials in federal courts that states that every person is presumed competent unless otherwise noted in the Federal Rules. Because the rules do not list age as a requirement, children are presumed competent.

Felony: a serious crime that is punishable with imprisonment of greater than 1 year or even death.

Fetal Abuse: maternal behaviors that put the fetus at risk for harm.

Fetal Alcohol Effects: symptoms present in a child that are associated with maternal alcohol consumption during pregnancy but which do not meet the diagnostic criteria for fetal alcohol syndrome.

Fetal Alcohol Syndrome (FAS): a series of birth defects resulting from a mother's consumption of alcohol during pregnancy. Symptoms include mental retardation, low birth weight, head and face abnormalities, and growth deficiencies.

Folk Medicine: health practices that come from cultural traditions; native remedies.

Forensic: related to, or appropriate for, use in legal settings.

Forensic Interviewing: an interviewing technique used to elicit verbal information from witnesses for use in a legal setting.

Fracture: the partial or complete breaking of bone or cartilage.

Freud: a Viennese physician who developed the psychoanalytic theory that stresses the importance of the unconscious mind and the constant conflict within each person's personality.

Guardian ad Litem: an adult who is appointed by the court to represent the best interests of the child during court proceedings.

Hawaii's Healthy Start Program: a secondary prevention program that provides home visitation for families identified as being at risk for maltreating their newborn children.

Healthy Families America: a home-visitation program that was modeled after Hawaii's Healthy Start Program.

Hearsay: testimony based not on what one knows personally but on what someone else has said.

Heroin: a highly addictive narcotic derived from morphine; it decreases the ability to perceive pain.

Hypersexual: excessively or unusually interested in sexual matters.

Hypervigilance: excessive watchfulness or wariness; constant scanning of the environment for signs of danger.

Immunity (legal): exception from civil or criminal liability or prosecution.

Impetigo: a contagious skin infection that is marked by blisters that erupt and form crusts.

Improper Interview: an interview that contains elements known to increase the risk for eliciting false allegations.

Incidence: the number of new cases occurring or diagnosed in a year.

Indicated: a designation utilized by some child protective agencies during the course of an investigation that allows the caseworker to determine that some evidence of child maltreatment exists, but not enough to substantiate the case.

Induce: to cause or bring about.

Infanticide: the killing of an infant, particularly a newborn.

Infantile Amnesia: the inability of adults to remember much, if anything, about the first 3 years of their lives.

Informed Consent: the ethical requirement that participants voluntarily agree to take part in an experiment only after they have been told what their participation will entail.

Institutional Review Board (IRB): a group of professionals charged with determining whether the benefits of a proposed research project outweigh the potential costs to participants.

Intake: process by which reports of suspected child maltreatment are received and initially evaluated by a CPS agency.

Intergenerational Transmission: the passing down of a trait or behavior from one generation to the next.

Interpersonal Relationships: social association, connection, and involvement between two people.

Interviewer Bias: the attitudes or actions of the interviewer influencing the respondent's answers.

Intrafamilial: occurring within a family.

Investigation and Initial Assessment: the process by which a child protective agency verifies reports of child maltreatment and determines the immediate safety of the alleged child victim.

Isolating: confining a child or not allowing a child to have the opportunity to socialize with others.

Jurisdiction: the authority to deal with legal matters and the limits within which that authority may be exercised.

Jurisdictional Hearing: a hearing where evidence is presented by child protective services and parents and a guardian ad litem so the judge can determine whether the child meets the description of a dependent child.

Juvenile Court: a court established in 1899 to hear cases of dependency and juvenile delinquency.

Juvenile Delinquency: antisocial behavior by a minor, especially if the behavior is in violation of the law and would be punished criminally if committed by an adult.

Keeping Children and Families Safe Act: legislation passed in 2003 to make improvements to and reauthorize programs under the Child Abuse Prevention and Treatment Act (CAPTA).

Language Delays: the failure to develop language skills according to the usual timetable resulting in development that is significantly below the norm for a child of a given age.

Longitudinal Research: a research design that involves repeated observations of a group of participants at regular intervals over a relatively long period of time.

Malingering by Proxy: a parent's coaching a child to fake symptoms in order to gain something external such as money from a lawsuit or an insurance claim.

Malnourished: having a medical condition caused by an improper or insufficient diet.

Malpractice: professional negligence; failure to exercise the minimum degree of care expected by professional standards.

Mandated Reporters: people required by law because of their occupation to report suspected cases of child maltreatment to the proper authorities.

Marijuana: the dried leaves and female flowers of the hemp plant that are used as an intoxicant. It can be smoked or eaten and it produces mild euphoria and possibly distorted perceptions.

Maslow: considered to be the father of humanistic psychology, Maslow studied healthy people and classified human needs into a hierarchy.

Meconium: dark greenish-brown material that builds up in the digestive tract before birth; excreted as fecal matter shortly after birth.

Mediation: a neutral person's helping two disputing parties arrive at a solution that is mutually acceptable; however, the mediator's decision is not legally binding.

Mediator: a factor that may explain the relationship between two other variables. For example, the relationship between race and parenting style may be explained by socioeconomic status (SES). That is, SES may mediate the relationship between race and parenting style so that when you remove the effect of SES, the relationship between race and parenting style is no longer apparent.

Medical Neglect: the failure to seek medical treatment or to provide treatment that has been prescribed.

Mental Health, Medical, and Educational Neglect: caregivers' failing to meet a child's psychological, medical, or educational needs.

Mental Health Neglect: the failure to seek help for a child's severe psychological problems or to comply with recommended therapeutic procedures.

Meta-Analysis: a statistical technique that allows researchers to combine the results of several different studies.

Metabolite: a product of metabolism.

Methadone: a synthetic narcotic that is used to relive pain and as a heroin substitute during treatment for heroin addiction.

Methamphetamine (MA): a potent, highly addictive central nervous system stimulant that causes an increase in energy and a decrease in appetite.

Minnesota Mother-Child Interaction Project: a longitudinal study of 267 children who were born to high-risk mothers.

Minnesota Multiphasic Personality Inventory (MMPI): a 576-item, true/false questionnaire that provides scores on 10 clinical scales and 1 scale designed to assess whether the participant was truthful.

Misdemeanor: a crime that is less serious than a felony and is usually punished with a lesser penalty (a fine, forfeiture, or less than one year in prison).

Molestation: the act of subjecting someone to unwanted or improper sexual activity.

Mongolian Spot: a birthmark that is a smooth, flat, bluish gray spot that looks like a bruise.

Munchausen by Proxy Syndrome: a rare form of child maltreatment in which the caretaker, usually the mother, fabricates, simulates, or induces symptoms of physical or psychological illness in a child.

Munchausen Syndrome: a psychiatric disorder that involves exaggerating or creating symptoms of illness in oneself, or acting as if ill, in order to receive attention and sympathy.

National Association of Public Child Welfare Administrators (NAPCWA): founded in 1983, this organization represents public child welfare agencies by contributing to child welfare policy and ensuring that children in the public child welfare system have safe, permanent homes.

National Clearinghouse on Child Abuse and Neglect (NCCAN): a national resource for professionals that provides information regarding child maltreatment including prevalence, incidence, treatment, statistics, and statutes.

National Child Abuse and Neglect Data System (NCAND): a voluntary, national data collection and analysis system that gathers and maintains data relevant to child maltreatment.

National Child Abuse Hotline: 1-800-4-A-CHILD; a phone line that is staffed 24 hours a day, 7 days a week, by professional counselors who can answer questions about child maltreatment. The counselors have access to a very large database of resources including emergency, social services, and support services.

National Institute on Drug Abuse (NIDA): an organization dedicated to bringing the power of science to bear on issues of drug abuse and addiction by supporting research and disseminating research findings related to drug prevention, treatment, and policy.

National Study of Child Protective Services Systems and Reform Efforts: a 2-year study (2000–2001) conducted to assess and evaluate the status of the child protective services system in the U.S.

Neurobehavioral: the study of the way the brain affects emotion, behavior, and learning; the assessment of a person's neurological status by observing their behavior.

Nicotine: a toxic, addictive substance derived from tobacco that acts as a stimulant.

Nonorganic Failure to Thrive: a child's failing to reach normal milestones for physical growth (falling below the third percentile) when the child has no known organic disease.

Nurse Home Visitation Program: a secondary prevention program that targets pregnant women whose fetuses are at risk for later health and developmental problems.

Obsessive Compulsions: the persistent intrusion of unwanted thoughts accompanied by ritualistic actions.

Office on Child Abuse and Neglect (OCAN): established by the Child Abuse Prevention and Treatment Act (CAPTA) in 1974, this agency is part of the Children's Bureau in the Department of Health and Human Services. It funds resources for improving state responses to child abuse and neglect.

Omission Errors: mistakes that involve failure to report something that did occur.

Open-Ended Question: a question with no set of anticipated responses; the respondent is free to give any answer.

Operational Definition: a precise definition of a variable in terms of observable procedures or measurements.

Oppositional Defiant Disorder: a disruptive pattern of behavior in childhood that is characterized by defiance and disobedience as well as hostile behavior. These behaviors persist for at least 6 months and interfere with everyday functioning.

Osteogenesis Imperfecta: a genetic disorder in which bones fracture easily.

Out-of-Home-Placement: often referred to as foster care, the condition by which children are temporarily removed from their home and placed in an alternative living environment (e.g., with a relative, in an emergency shelter, in a group home).

Paranoid Ideation: abnormal suspicion that is not based on fact.

Paraprofessional: a job title given to people in occupations for which they have received some specialized training but are not professionally licensed.

Parens Patriae: a Latin term meaning that the State acts on behalf of a child or mentally ill person. The State is the guardian of those who cannot protect themselves.

Parent-Child Relational Problem: a mental disorder marked by clinically significant impairment in the interaction between parent and child that impacts family functioning or leads to the development of negative psychological symptoms in the parent or child.

Pediatric Condition Falsification (PCF): a description suggested by the American Professional Society on the Abuse of Children to refer to any children who are described as ill when they are not, regardless of parental motivation.

Perinatal: occurring shortly before or shortly after birth.

Permanency: the principle that a child's ideal living environment is one that will be long-lasting and stable.

Permanency Planning Hearing: a review of the child's current placement and progress with the goal of establishing long-range goals if the child requires continued care. Permanent plans include the termination of parental rights and adoption.

Permissive Reporter: a person who is allowed, but not required, to report suspected child maltreatment.

Perpetrator: a person who commits an offense or crime.

Phobic Anxiety: worry about irrational fears.

Physical Neglect: the failure to meet the minimal physical needs of the child.

Plaintiff: the party who brings a suit in civil court.

Platelet Aggregation Disorder: a medical condition that occurs when platelets do not form plugs at injury sites.

Polydrug: multiple, different drugs.

Postnatal: occurring after birth.

Postpartum Depression: prolonged sadness, crying spells, impatience, or mood swings following the birth of a child; may include mixed feelings about motherhood and/or an inability to care for the newborn.

Post-Traumatic Stress Disorder (PTSD): an anxiety disorder that occurs in response to experiencing extreme stress (generally involving actual or threatened death or serious injury). The person experiences symptoms including re-experiencing the event, avoiding stimuli reminiscent of the event, and increased arousal for at least one month.

Poverty: a situation in which income and resources are inadequate to obtain and maintain an acceptable standard of living. Official poverty levels are set by the Social Security Administration.

Practice Interview: a question-and-answer session about a neutral topic that allows the person being interviewed to become comfortable with the process before addressing the issue of interest.

Precursor: any factor that precedes the onset of child maltreatment and may function as a risk factor.

Preponderance of Evidence: the burden of proof in a civil trial; the greater weight of evidence, however slight.

Prevalence: the number of cases that exist in a specified population at a given point in time.

Prevent: to reduce the likelihood of an occurrence.

Prevent Child Abuse America: an organization that began in 1972 with the mission of preventing all forms of child abuse and neglect in the U.S.

Primary Caregiver: a person primarily responsible for the health and well-being of a child. (e.g., mother, father, legal guardian).

Primary Prevention: targets the general population to reduce the incidence of all new cases of a problem.

Psychological Abuse: a parent's engaging in behaviors that actively harm their child's mental health.

Psychological Neglect: a parent's failing to meet the emotional needs of his or her child.

Psychomotor: pertaining to the function of voluntary muscles.

Psychotic: mental disorders marked by the loss of contact with reality; generally marked by delusions, hallucinations, or serious thought disturbance.

Psychoticism: impaired contact with reality.

PsycINFO: an electronic database produced by the American Psychological Association that indexes the psychology literature.

Racial Bias: a negative opinion, attitude, or response toward a group of people who share a common physical attribute such as skin color.

Rapport: a feeling of connection and trust that is established between two people.

Reason to Believe: a term often used in child welfare legislation with regard to mandatory reporting guidelines. Includes the notion of a reasonable professional standard for mandated reporters, such that their professional training and experience informs their ability to recognize the presence of child maltreatment.

Reasonable Efforts: according to the Adoption Assistance and Child Welfare Act, the responsibility of state child welfare agencies to avoid foster care placement and/or to reunify a family whenever possible. This definition was amended in the Adoption and Safe Families Act, providing exceptions to the family preservation and reunification requirements (especially in consideration of child safety issues).

Recidivism: the tendency for something (such as a disease or maladaptive behavior pattern) to recur.

Repression: a defense mechanism in which painful or unacceptable memories or fears are rejected by the conscious mind and buried in the unconscious.

Resilient: having the ability to recover from adversity.

Resistant Attachment: an insecure attachment style in which infants cling to their caregivers at times and resist closeness at other times.

Retrospective Design: a research design that uses data that are recollections of past events. This type of design is limited because of concerns about memory degradation over time.

Review Hearing: a hearing that takes place approximately 6 months after a care plan has been enacted, for the purpose of reviewing the progress that has been made on the treatment plan.

Risk Assessment: the process by which a caseworker evaluates a child's living environment and determines whether any factors are present that increase the likelihood for child maltreatment.

Safety Assessment: the process by which a caseworker evaluates a child's living environment and determines whether there is any immediate risk of harm to that child's safety.

Safety Plan: a plan that is developed following a safety assessment whenever a risk of immediate harm is discovered in order to minimize and/or eliminate that immediate risk.

Secondary Prevention: targets a specific group of individuals to reduce the incidence of new cases of a problem among those determined to be at some identified risk.

Secure Attachment: an infant's using a caregiver as a secure base from which to explore his or her surroundings.

Self-Actualization: according to Maslow, the highest level of psychological development; a person's reaching full potential.

Self-Efficacy: a person's belief that he or she is capable of doing what is necessary to produce the desired result in a given situation.

Self-Fulfilling Prophecy: the process by which one's expectations about a person leads that person to behave in ways that confirm those expectations.

Separation Anxiety: distress and/or anxiety experienced when a child is separated from his or her primary caregiver.

Service Provision: the process by which a child protective services case plan is implemented.

Sexual Dysfunction: any problem during the sexual response cycle from desire to arousal to orgasm that prevents the achievement of sexual satisfaction.

Sexual Exploitation: use of a child (under the age of 18 years) for the purpose of prostitution or pornography.

Sexually Transmitted Diseases (STDs): diseases that are most commonly spread via sexual contact; also called venereal disease (VD) or sexually transmitted infections (STIs).

Shaken Baby Syndrome (SBS): a condition of severe internal bleeding, particularly around the brain or eyes, that is caused by violently shaking an infant or young child.

"Sleeper" Effect: an outcome that emerges some time after a program has been completed.

SMART: strategy used during the case planning process whereby established goals are Specific, Measurable, Achievable, Realistic, and Time-limited.

Social Referencing: reading another person's facial expressions in order to decide on an appropriate response.

Socially Isolated: lacking sufficient social ties or support.

Society for the Prevention of Cruelty to Children (SPCC): a nonprofit organization that was founded in1875 to protect children and strengthen families. The SPCC offers mental health, legal, and educational services.

Socioeconomic Status (SES): a measure of a person's standing within a social group based on factors such as income and education.

Somatization: the expression of psychological distress as physical symptoms.

Spina Bifida: a congenital abnormality in which the fetus's spinal cord does not form properly, leaving part of the spinal cord unprotected.

Spurning: caregiver behaviors that are hostile and rejecting toward a child.

Status Offense: an act that is against the law only because the person engaging in it is a minor.

Statute: a law passed by a legislative body.

Statute of Limitations: a law that sets a time frame for the prosecution of a crime or for suing to ensure that cases are resolved while the evidence is still reasonably available.

Strange Situation Task: a laboratory task designed to measure an infant's attachment to his or her caregiver.

Structured Interview: a face-to-face method of collecting information that follows a series of pre-established questions.

Substantiated: a report of child maltreatment that has been confirmed by child protective services.

Sudden Infant Death Syndrome: the unexplained and unexpected death of an infant (less than a year old) who was apparently healthy; generally occurs during sleep.

Suggestibility: accepting or acting on something that is implied by another person.

Tabula Rasa: a blank slate; a mind that has not yet been affected by experiences or impressions.

Terrorizing: a caregiver's threatening a child or a child's loved ones or possessions with violence or abandonment, or placing a child in a dangerous situation.

Tertiary Prevention: intended to minimize the negative effects of an already existing problem.

Testimony: evidence given by a witness who is under oath at trial or in an affidavit or deposition.

Therapeutic Relationship: the working alliance between a counselor and patient.

Tort Laws: laws that allow people to sue others based on the claim that some conduct, product, or service that does not meet minimal, acceptable standards has caused harm.

Toxicology: the study of poisons and drugs and their effects.

Unbiased Question: a question that is worded in such a way that it does not influence the respondent's answer.

Uncorroborated: something that is not supported or confirmed by additional evidence or authority.

Unsubstantiated (Unfounded): a report of child maltreatment that has been investigated, but not confirmed, by child protective services.

U.S. Department of Health and Human Services: established in 1979 with the goal of protecting the health of all Americans and providing essential human services.

References

2 wandering toddlers lead to 3 child-neglect arrests. (2005, September 9). *St. Petersburg Times*. Retrieved September 28, 2005, from http://web.lexis-nexis.com

Adams, J. (2000). How do I determine if a child has been sexually abused? In H. Dubowitz & D. DePanfilis (Eds.), *Handbook for child protection practice* (pp. 175–179). Thousand Oaks, CA: Sage Publications, Inc.

Adams, J., McClellan, J., Douglass, D., McCurry, C., & Storck, M. (1995). Sexually inappropriate behaviors in seriously mentally ill children and adolescents. *Child Abuse and Neglect, 19*(5), 555–568.

Adshead, G., & Bluglass, K. (2001). Attachment representation and factitious illness by proxy: Relevance for assessment of parenting capacity in child maltreatment. *Child Abuse Review, 10*, 398–410.

Alapo, L. (2005, November 11). Probation for sitter in abuse case. *Knoxville News-Sentinel*. Retrieved September 6, 2006, from http://web.lexis-nexis

Allen, R. E., & Oliver, J. M. (1982). The effects of child maltreatment on language development. *Child Abuse and Neglect, 6*, 299–305.

Allen, D. M., & Tarnowski, K. J. (1989). Depressive characteristics of physically abused children. *Journal of Abnormal Child Psychology, 17*(1), 1–11.

American Academy of Pediatrics, Committee on Bioethics (1988). Religious exemptions from child abuse statutes. *Pediatrics, 81*(1), 169–171.

American Professional Society on the Abuse of Children (APSAC). (1995). *Guidelines for the psychosocial evaluation of suspected psychological maltreatment in children and adolescents.* Chicago: Author.

American Psychiatric Association. (1994). *Diagnostic and statistical manual of mental disorders* (4th ed.). Washington, DC: Author.

Ammerman, R. T., Kolko, D. J., Kirisci, L., Blackson, T. C., & Dawes, M. A. (1999). Child abuse potential in parents with histories of substance use disorder. *Child Abuse and Neglect, 23*(12), 1225–1238.

Arria, A. M., Derauf, C., LaGasse, L. L., Grant, P., Shah, R., Smith, L., et al. (2006). Methamphetamine and other substance use during pregnancy: Preliminary estimates from the infant development, environment, and lifestyle (IDEAL) study. *Maternal and Child Health Journal, 10*(3), 293–303.

Ashton, V. (1999). Worker judgments of seriousness about reporting of suspected child maltreatment. *Child Abuse and Neglect, 23*(6), 539–548.

Asser, S. M., & Swan, R. (1998). Child fatalities from religion-motivated medical neglect. *Pediatrics, 101*(4), 625–629.

Associated Press (2005, September 29). Mother indicted in case where child became ill after navel piercing. *The Boston Globe*. Retrieved October 5, 2005, from http://www.boston.com/news/local/massachusetts/articles/2005/09/29/mother_indicted_in_case_where_child_became_ill_after_navel_piercing/

Associated Press Worldstream (2005, November 1). Accuser in notorious McMartin Preschool abuse case admits lying. *Associated Press*. Retrieved September 6, 2007, from http://www.lexisnexis.com

Awadallah, N., Vaughan, A., Franco, K., Munir, F., Sharby, N., & Goldfarb, J. (2005). Munchausen by proxy: A case, chart series, and literature review of older victims. *Child Abuse and Neglect, 29*, 931–941.

Ayoub, C. C., Schreier, H. A., & Keller, C. (2002). Munchausen by proxy: Presentations in special education. *Child Maltreatment, 7*(2), 149–159.

Balisy, S. S. (1987). Maternal substance abuse: The need to provide legal protection for the fetus. *Southern California Law Review, 60*, 1209–1238.

Balloch, J. (2005, June 12). Motions could delay Baby Haley trial: Potential jurors report Monday for Campbell court. *Knoxville News-Sentinel*. Retrieved November 1, 2005, from http://web.lexis-nexis

Balloch, J. (2005, June 29). Testimony begins in Haley case: Campbell lawman says he held injured child until ambulance arrived. *Knoxville News-Sentinel*. Retrieved November 1, 2005, from http://web.lexis-nexis

Balloch, J. (2005, June 30). Baby Haley's half-sister says she's behind some injuries: Father says he never hurt daughter: Jury expected to get abuse case today. *Knoxville News-Sentinel*. Retrieved November 1, 2005, from http://web.lexis-nexis

Balloch, J. (2005, October 12). Baby Haley's father gets 95 years: Ex-wife advises him to just 'sit and rot' for abuse. *Knoxville News-Sentinel*. Retrieved September 5, 2006, from http://web.lexis-nexis

Barlow, B., Niemirska, M., Gandhi, R. D., & Leblanc, W. (1983). Ten years of experience with falls from a height in children. *Journal of Pediatric Surgery, 18*(4), 509–511.

Barth, R. P. (1991). An experimental evaluation of in-home child abuse prevention services. *Child Abuse and Neglect, 15,* 363–375.

Bartol, C. R., & Bartol, A. M. (2004). *Psychology and the law: Theory, research, and application.* Belmont, CA: Wadworth/Thomson Learning.

Bath, H. I., & Haapala, D. A. (1992). Intensive family preservation services with abused and neglected children: An examination of group differences. *Child Abuse and Neglect, 17,* 213–225.

Belsky, J. (1993). Etiology of child maltreatment. *Psychological Bulletin, 114*(3), 413–434.

Berk, L. E. (1997). *Child development* (4th ed.). Needham Heights, MA: Allyn and Bacon.

Berliner, L., & Elliott, D. M. (2002). Sexual abuse of children. In J. E. B. Myers, L. Berliner, J. Briere, C.T. Hendrix, C. Jenny, & T.A. Reid (Eds.), *The APSAC handbook on child maltreatment* (2nd ed., pp. 55–78). Thousand Oaks, CA: Sage.

Berrick, J. D. (1988). Parental involvement in child abuse prevention training: What do they learn? *Child Abuse and Neglect, 12,* 543–553.

Berrick, J. D. (1989). Sexual abuse prevention education: Is it appropriate for the preschool child? *Children and Youth Services Review, 11,* 145–158.

Bhargava, S. (2004). Challenging punishment and privatization: A response to the conviction of Regina McKnight. *Harvard Civil Rights-Civil Liberties Law Review 39*(2), 513–542. Retrieved July 10, 2006, from www.lexis-nexis.com

Bishop, S. J., & Leadbeater, B. J. (1999). Maternal social support patterns and child maltreatment: Comparison of maltreating and non-maltreating mothers. *American Journal of Orthopsychiatry, 69*(2), 172–181.

Black, I. B. (1998). Genes, brain and mind: The evolution of cognition. *Neuron, 20,* 1073–1080.

Bolton, R. G., Laner, R. H., & Kane, S. P. (1980). Child maltreatment risk among adolescent mothers: A study of reported cases. *American Journal of Orthopsychiatry, 50,* 489–503.

Bools, C., Neale, B. A., & Meadow, R. (1994). Munchausen syndrome by proxy. *British Journal of Psychiatry, 169,* 268–275.

Bousha, D. M., & Twentyman, C. T. (1984). Mother-child interactional style in abuse, neglect, and control groups: Naturalistic observations in the home. *Journal of Abnormal Psychology, 93* (1), 106–114.

Bowlby, J. (1982). *Attachment* (2nd ed.). New York: Basic Books.

Cantwell, H. B. (1997). The neglect of child neglect. In M. E. Helfer, R. S. Kempe, & R. D. Krugman (Eds.), *The battered child,* (pp. 347–373). Chicago: The University of Chicago Press.

Brassard, M., & Hart, S. (2000). How do I determine whether a child has been psychologically maltreated? In H. Dubowitz & D. DePanfilis (Eds.), *Handbook for child protection practice* (pp. 215–219). Thousand Oaks, CA: Sage Publications, Inc.

Brassard, M. R., Tyler, A. H., & Kehle, T. J. (1983). School programs to prevent intrafamilial child sexual abuse. *Child Abuse and Neglect, 7,* 241–245.

Brick, J. (2005). Fetal drug effects. *Intoxikon International,* 1–2.

Briere, J., & Runtz, M. (1988). Post sexual abuse trauma. In G. E. Wyatt & G. J. Powell (Eds.). *Lasting effects of child sexual abuse.* Newbury Park, CA: Sage.

Briere, J., & Runtz, M. (1990). Differential adult symptomology associated with three types of child abuse histories. *Child Abuse and Neglect, 14,* 357–364.

Briere, J., & Runtz, M. (1993). Childhood sexual abuse: Long-term sequelae and implications for psychological assessment. *Journal of Interpersonal Violence, 8*(3), 312–330.

Briere, J., & Zaidi, L. Y. (1989). Sexual abuse histories and sequelae in female psychiatric emergency room patients. *American Journal of Psychiatry, 146*(12), 1602–1606.

Brodeur, A. E., & Monteleone, J. A. (1994). *Child maltreatment: A clinical guide and reference.* St. Louis, MO: G.W. Medical Publishing, Inc.

Bronfenbrenner, U. (2000). Ecological theory. In A. Kazdin (Ed.), *Encyclopedia of psychology*. Washington, DC: American Psychological Association and Oxford University Press.

Brooks, C. M. (1996). The law's response to child abuse and neglect. In B. D. Sales & D. W. Shuman (Eds.), *Law, mental health, and mental disorder* (pp. 464–486). Pacific Grove, CA: Brooks/Cole Publishing Company.

Brown, J., Cohen, P., Johnson, J. G., & Salzinger, S. (1998). A longitudinal analysis of risk factors for child maltreatment: Findings of a 17-year prospective study of officially recorded and self-reported child abuse and neglect. *Child Abuse and Neglect, 22*(11), 1065–1078.

Brown, R., & Strozier, M. (2004). Resisting abuse at what cost? The impact of mandated reporting laws on the process and content of therapy. *Contemporary Family Therapy, 26*(1), 45–60.

Bruck, M., & Ceci, S. J. (1995). Amicus brief for the case of *State of New Jersey v. Michaels*, presented by committee of concerned social scientists. *Psychology, Public Policy, and Law, 1*(2), 272–322.

Bruck, M., Ceci, S. J., & Francoeur, E. (2000). Children's use of anatomically detailed dolls to report genital touching in a medical examination: Developmental and gender comparisons. *Journal of Experimental Psychology: Applied, 6*(1), 74–83.

Bruck, M., Ceci, S. J., Francouer, E., & Renick, A. (1995). Anatomically detailed dolls do not facilitate preschoolers' reports of a pediatric examination involving genital touching. *Journal of Experimental Psychology: Applied, 1*(2), 95–109.

Burke, J., Chandy, J., Dannerbeck, A., & Watt, J. W. (1998). The parental environment cluster model of child neglect: An integrative conceptual model. *Child Welfare, 77*(4), 389–406.

Burnett, B. B. (1993). The psychological abuse of latency age children: A survey. *Child Abuse and Neglect, 17,* 441–454.

Bussey, K., Lee, K., & Grimbeek, E. J. (1993). Lies and secrets: Implications for children's reporting of sexual abuse. In G. S. Goodman & B. L. Bottoms (Eds.), *Child victims, child witnesses: Understanding and improving testimony* (pp. 147–168). New York: Guilford Press.

Canadian Hemophilia Society. (2006). Types of platelet function disorder. Retrieved September 19, 2006, from http://www.hemophilia.ca/en/2.4.4.php

Carroll, L. A., & Miltenberger, R. G. (1992). A review and critique of research evaluating child sexual abuse prevention programs. *Education and Treatment of Children, 15,* 335–355.

Ceci, S. J., & Bruck, M. (1993). Suggestibility of the child witness: A historical review and synthesis. *Psychological Bulletin, 113*(3), 403–439.

Ceci, S. J., & Bruck, M. (1995). *Jeopardy in the courtroom*. Washington, D.C.: American Psychological Association.

Ceci, S. J., Crotteau-Huffman, M., Smith, E., & Loftus, E. W. (1994). Repeatedly thinking about non-events: Source misattributions among preschoolers. *Consciousness and Cognition, 3,* 388–407.

Ceci, S. J., Ross, D. F., & Toglia, M. P. (1987). Suggestibility of children's memory: Psycholegal implications. *Journal of Experimental Psychology: General, 116*(1), 38–49.

Carp, R. A., Stidham, R., & Manning, K. L. (Eds.). (2004). *The civil court process* (pp. 256–275). Washington, DC: CQ Press.

Chadwick, D. L., Chin, S., Salerno, C., Landsverk, J., & Kitchen, L. (1991). Deaths from falls in children: How far is fatal? *Journal of Trauma, 31,* 1353–1355.

Chandra, P. S., Bhargavaraman, R. P., Raghunandan, V. N. G. P., & Shaligram, D. (2006). Delusions related to infant and their associations with mother-infant interactions in postpartum psychotic disorders. *Archives of Women's Mental Health, 9*(5), 285–288.

Charles, S., & Shivas, T. (2002). Mothers in the media: Blamed and celebrated—an examination of drug abuse and multiple births. *Pediatric Nursing, 28*(2), 142–145.

Chasnoff, I. J. (1989). Drug use and women: Establishing a standard of care. In D. E. Hutchings (Ed.), *Prenatal abuse of licit and illicit drugs* (pp. 208–210). New York: New York Academy of Sciences.

Chasnoff, I. J., Landress, H. J., & Barrett, M. E. (1990). The prevalence of illicit-drug or alcohol use during pregnancy and discrepancies in mandatory reporting in Pinellas County, Florida. *The New England Journal of Medicine, 322*(17), 1202–1206.

Chasnoff, I. J., & Lowder, L. A. (1999). Prenatal alcohol and drug use and risk for child maltreatment. In H. Dubowitz (Ed.), *Neglected children: Research, practice and policy* (pp. 132–155). Thousand Oaks, CA: Sage Publications.

Chavkin, W., Breitbart, V., Elman, D., & Wise, P. H. (1988). National survey of the states: Policies and practices regarding drug-using pregnant women. *American Journal of Public Health, 88*(1), 117–119.

Child Welfare League of America. (1999). *CWLA standards of excellence for services for abused and neglected children and their families* (Rev. ed.). Washington, DC: Author.

Children's Bureau, Administration for Children and Families, U.S. Department of Health and Human Services. (2005). *Safe Children and Healthy Families are a Shared Responsibility: 2005 Community Resource Packet.* Retrieved August 9, 2005, from http://nccanch.acf.hhs.gov/topics/prevention/childabuse_neglect/reporting.cfm

Cicchetti, D. (1991). Defining psychological maltreatment: Reflections and future directions. *Development and Psychopathology, 3,* 1–2.

Claussen, A., & Crittenden, P. (1991). Physical and psychological maltreatment: Relations among types of maltreatment. *Child Abuse and Neglect,15,* 5–18.

Cohen, J. (1988). *Statistical power analysis for the behavioral sciences, 2nd ed.* Hillsdale, NJ: Lawrence Erlbaum Associates.

Cohen, D. (2004, January 23). He doesn't like women, says ex-wife. *The Evening Standard (London).* Retrieved June 21, 2004, from http://www.msbp.com/Munchausendiscredited3.htm

Condon, J. T. (1986). The spectrum of fetal abuse in pregnant women. *The Journal of Nervous and Mental Disease, 174*(9), 509–516.

Condon, J. T. (1987). "The battered fetus syndrome": Preliminary data on the incidence of the urge to physically abuse the unborn child. *The Journal of Nervous and Mental Disease, 175*(12), 722–725.

Conte, J. R., Sorenson, E., Fogarty, L., & Dalla Rosa, J. (1991). Evaluating children's reports of sexual abuse: Results from a survey of professionals. *American Journal of Orthopsychiatry, 61*(3), 428–437.

Couple accused of starving 7-year-old. (2002, September 22). *St. Petersburg Times.* Retrieved September 28, 2005, from http://web.lexis-nexis.com

Courtney, M. (2000). What outcomes are relevant for intervention? In H. Dubowitz & D. DePanfilis (Eds.), *Handbook for child protection practice* (p. 373). Thousand Oaks, CA: Sage Publications, Inc.

Coy v. Iowa, 487 U.S. 1012 (1988). Retrieved February 12, 2007, from http://laws.findlaws.com/us/487/1012.html

Crenshaw, W. B., & Bartell, P. A. (1994). Proposed revisions to mandatory reporting laws: An exploratory survey of child protective service agencies. *Child Welfare, 73*(1), 15–27.

Crenshaw, W. B., & Lichtenberg, J. W. (1993). Child abuse and the limits of confidentiality: Forewarning practices. *Behavioral Sciences and the Law, 11,* 181–192.

Cross, T. P., Walsh, W. A., Simone, M., & Jones, L. M. (2003). Prosecution of child abuse: A meta-analysis of rates of criminal justice decisions. *Trauma, Violence, and Abuse, 4*(4), 323–340.

Crosson-Tower, C. (2005). Understanding child abuse and neglect (6th ed.). Needham Heights, MA: Allyn and Bacon.

Crouch, J. L., & Milner, J. S. (1993). Effects of child neglect on children. *Criminal Justice and Behavior, 20*(1), 49–65.

Dallam, S. J., Gleaves, D. H., Cepeda-Benito, A., Silberg, J. L., Kraemer, H. C., & Spiegel, D. (2001). The effects of child sexual abuse: Comment on Rind, Tromovitch, and Bauserman. *Psychological Bulletin, 127*(6), 715–753.

Dammeyer, M. D., Nightingale, N. N., & McCoy, M. L. (1997). Repressed memory and other controversial origins of sexual abuse allegations: Beliefs among psychologists and clinical social workers. *Child Maltreatment, 2*(3), 252–263.

Daro, D., & Donnelly, A. C. (n.d.). *Child abuse prevention: Accomplishments and challenges.* Unpublished manuscript.

Daro, D., & Gelles, R. (1992). Public attitudes and behaviors with respect to child abuse prevention. *Journal of Interpersonal Violence, 7,* 517–531.

Daro, D., & Harding, K. A. (1999). Healthy families America: Using research to enhance practice. *The Future of Children, 9,* 152–176.

Davis, M. K., & Gidycz, C. (2000). Child sexual abuse prevention programs: A meta-analysis. *Journal of Clinical Child Psychology, 29,* 257–265.

Davis, R. E. (2000). International scene: Cultural health care or child abuse? The Southeast Asian practice of Cao Gio. *Journal of the American Academy of Nurse Practitioners, 12,* 89–95.

Delaronde, S., King, G., Bendel, R., & Reece, R. (2000). Opinions among mandated reporters toward child maltreatment reporting policies. *Child Abuse and Neglect, 24*(7), 901–910.

DeLoache, J. S., & Marzolf, D. P. (1995). The use of dolls to interview young children: Issues of symbolic representation. *Journal of Experimental Child Psychology, 60,* 155–173.

DeMause, L. (Ed.). (1974). *The history of childhood.* New York: The Psychohistory Press.

Denny, S. J., Grant, C. C., & Pinnock, R. (2001). Epidemiology of Munchausen syndrome by proxy in New Zealand. *Journal of Pediatric Child Health, 37,* 24–243.

DePanfilis, D. (2000). What is inadequate supervision? In H. Dubowitz & D. DePanfilis (Eds.), *Handbook for child protection practice* (pp. 134–136). Thousand Oaks, CA: Sage Publications, Inc.

DePanfilis, D., & Dubowitz, H. (2005). Family connections: A program for preventing child neglect. *Child Maltreatment, 10,* 108–123.

DePanfilis, D., & Salus, M. K. (2003). *Child protective services: A guide for caseworkers.* Washington, DC: U.S. Department of Health and Human Services.

Dorne, C. K. (2002). *An introduction to child maltreatment in the United States: History, public policy and research.* Monsey, NY: Criminal Justice Press.

DiLillo, D., Tremblay, G. C., & Peterson, L. (2000). Linking childhood sexual abuse and abusive parenting: The mediating role of maternal anger. *Child Abuse and Neglect, 21*(6), 767–779.

The Disaster Center. (2007). United States crime rates 1960–2006. Retrieved October 24, 2007, from http://www.disastercenter.com/crime/uscrime.htm

Dorne, C. K. (2002). *An introduction to child maltreatment in the United States: History, public policy and research* (3rd ed.). Monsey, NY: Criminal Justice Press.

Doueck, H. J., Weston, E. A., Filbert, L., Beekhuis, R., Redlich, H. F. (1997). A child witness advocacy program: Caretakers' and professionals' views. *Journal of Child Sexual Abuse, 6*(1), 113–122.

Doward, J. (2006, September 17). Curse of a rotten childhood. *The Observer (England),* Observer Home Pages, p. 21.

Doyle, C. (1997). Emotional abuse of children: Issues for intervention. *Child Abuse Review, 6,* 330–342.

Drake, B. (2000). How do I decide whether to substantiate a report? In H. Dubowitz & D. DePanfilis (Eds.), *Handbook for child protection practice* (pp. 113–117). Thousand Oaks, CA: Sage Publications, Inc.

Driver in crash facing DUI, child neglect charges. (2005, August 30). *St. Petersburg Times.* Retrieved September 28, 2005, from http://web.lexis-nexis.com

Dubowitz, H. (1999). The families of neglected children. In M. E. Lamb (Ed.), *Parenting and child development in "nontraditional" families* (pp. 327–345). Mahwah, NJ: Lawrence Erlbaum Associates Publishers.

Dubowitz, H. (2000). How do I determine whether a child has been physically abused? In H. Dubowitz & D. DePanfilis (Eds.), *Handbook for child protection practice* (pp. 134–136). Thousand Oaks, CA: Sage Publications, Inc.

Dubowitz, H., Black, M., Starr, R. H., & Zuravin, S. (1993). A conceptual definition of child neglect. *Criminal Justice and Behavior, 20*(1), 8–26.

Duggan, A., McFarlane, E., Fuddy, L., Burrell, L., Higman, S. M., Windham, A., et al. (2004). Randomized trial of a statewide home visiting program: Impact in preventing child abuse and neglect. *Child Abuse and Neglect, 28,* 597–622.

Duggan, A. K., McFarlane, E. C., Windham, A. M., Rohde, C. A., Salkever, D. S., Fuddy, L., et al. (1999). Evaluation of Hawaii's healthy start program. *The Future of Children, 9,* 66–90.

East Tennessee man convicted of abusing young daughter. (2005, June 30). *Knoxville News-Sentinel.* Retrieved November 1, 2005, from http://web.lexis-nexis

Eckenrode, J., Laird, M., & Doris, J. (1993). School performance and disciplinary problems among abused and neglected children. *Developmental Psychology, 29,* 53–62.

Egeland, B., Sroufe, A., & Erickson, M. A. (1983). The developmental consequence of different patterns of maltreatment. *Child Abuse and Neglect, 7,* 459–469.

Emery, R. E., & Laumann-Billings, L. (1998). An overview of the nature, causes, and consequences of abusive family relationships: Toward differentiating maltreatment and violence. *American Psychologist, 53*(2), 121–135.

Epstein, M. A., Markowitz, R. L., Gallo, D. M., Holmes, J. W., & Gryboski, J. D. (1987). Munchausen Syndrome by Proxy: Considerations in diagnosis and confirmation by video surveillance. *Pediatrics, 80*(2), 220–224.

Erickson, M. F., Egeland, B., & Pianta, R. (1989). The effects of maltreatment on the development of young children. In D. Cicchetti & V. Carlson (Eds.), *Child maltreatment: Theory and research on the causes and consequences of child abuse and neglect* (pp. 647–684). New York: Cambridge University Press.

Erickson, M. F., & Egeland, B. (2002). Child neglect. In J. E. B. Myers, L. Berliner, J. Briere, C. T. Hendrix, C. Jenny, & T. A. Reid (Eds.). *The APSAC handbook on child maltreatment* (2nd ed., pp. 21–54). London: Sage Publications.

Erikson, E. H. (1963). *Childhood and society* (2nd ed.). New York: Norton.

Everson, M. D., & Boat, B. W. (1994). Putting the anatomical doll controversy in perspective: An examination of the major uses and criticisms of the dolls in child sexual abuse evaluations. *Child Abuse and Neglect, 18*(2), 113–129.

Farberman, H. A., & Finch, S. J. (1997). Confidentiality vs. mandated reporting of child abuse: A social work research dilemma. *Applied Behavioral Science Review, 5*(1), 101 –111.

Feldman, K. W. (1997). Evaluation of physical abuse. In M. E. Helfer, R. S. Kempe, & R. D. Krugman (Eds.), *The battered child* (5th ed., pp. 175–220). Chicago: The University of Chicago Press.

Feldman, M. D. (2004). *Playing sick*. New York: Routledge.

Feller, J. N., Davidson, H. A., Hardin, M., & Horowitz, R. M. (1992). *Working with the courts in child protection*. McLean, VA: The Circle Inc.

Fergusson, D. M., & Mullen, P. E. (1999). *Childhood sexual abuse: An evidence based perspective*. Thousand Oaks, CA: Sage Publications.

Finkelhor, D. (1990). Early and long-term effects of child sexual abuse: An update. *Professional Psychology: Research and Practice, 21*(5), 325–330.

Finkelhor, D. (1994). Current information on the scope and nature of child sexual abuse. *The Future of Children, 4*(2), 31–53.

Finkelhor, D., Asdigian, N., & Dziuba-Leatherman, J. (1995). The effectiveness of victimization prevention instruction: An evaluation of children's responses to actual threats and assaults. *Child Abuse and Neglect, 19*, 141–153.

Finkelhor, D., & Dziuba-Leatherman, J. (1995). Victimization prevention programs: A national survey of children's exposure and reactions. *Child Abuse and Neglect, 19*, 129–139.

Finkelhor, D., & Strapko, N. (1992). Sexual abuse prevention education: A review of evaluation studies. In D. J. Willis, E. W. Holden, & M. Rosenberg (Eds.), *Prevention of Child Maltreatment: Developmental and Ecological Perspectives* (pp. 150–167). New York: John Wiley & Sons, Inc.

Foreman, D. M., & Farsides, C. (1993). Ethical use of covert videoing techniques in detecting Munchausen Syndrome by Proxy. *British Medical Journal, 307*, 611–613.

Fox, L., Long, S. H., & Langlois, A. (1988). Patterns of language comprehension deficit in abused and neglected children. *Journal of Speech and Hearing Disorders, 53*, 239–244.

Frank, D. A., Augustyn, M., Knight, W. G., Pell, T., & Zuckerman, B. (2001). Growth, development, and behavior in early childhood following prenatal cocaine exposure. *Journal of the American Medical Assocaition, 285*(12), 1613–1625.

Fromuth, M. E., & Burkhart, B. R. (1989). Long-term psychological correlates of childhood sexual abuse in tow samples of college men. *Child Abuse and Neglect, 13*, 533–542.

Galanti, G. (1997). *Caring for patients from different cultures: Case studies from American hospitals* (2nd ed.). Philadelphia, PA: University of Pennsylvania Press.

Gallup, G. H., Moore, D. W., & Schussel, R. (1995). *Disciplining children in America: A Gallup poll report*. Princeton, NJ: The Gallup Organization.

Garner, B. A. (Ed.). (1996). *Black's law dictionary*. St. Paul: West Publishing Company.

Geeraert, L., Van den Noortgate, W., Grietens, H., & Onghena, P. (2004). The effects of early prevention programs for families with young children at risk for physical child abuse and neglect: A meta-analysis. *Child Maltreatment, 9*, 277–291.

Gelles, R., & Straus, M. (1988). *Intimate violence*. New York: Simon and Schuster.

Giardino, A. P. & Giardino, E. R. (2002). Recognition of child abuse for the mandated reporter (3rd ed.). St. Louis, MO: G. W. Medical Publishing, Inc.

Gibson, L. E., & Leitenberg, H. (2000). Child sexual abuse prevention programs: Do they decrease the occurrence of child sexual abuse? *Child Abuse and Neglect, 24*, 1115–1125.

Glaser, D. (2002). Emotional abuse and neglect (psychological maltreatment): A conceptual framework. *Child Abuse and Neglect, 26*, 697–714.

Goldman, J., Salus, M. K., Wolcott, D., & Kennedy, K. Y. (2003). *A coordinated response to child abuse and neglect: The foundation for practice*. Washington, DC: U.S. Department of Health and Human Services.

Gomby, D. S., & Shiono, P. H. (1991). Estimating the number of substance exposed fetuses. *The Future of Children, 1,* 17–25.

Good, J. B. (2004, May 1). Man sentenced for starving girlfriend's daughter. *Tampa Tribune.* Retrieved September 28, 2005, from http://web.lexis-nexis.com

Goodman, G. S., Myers, J. B., Qin, J., Quas, J. A., Castelli, P., Redlich, A. D., et al. (2006). Hearsay versus children's testimony: Effects of truthful and deceptive statements on juror's decisions. *Law and Human Behavior, 30*(3), 363–401.

Goodman, G. S., Taub, E. P., Jones, D. P. H., England, P., Port, L. K., Rudy, L., et al. (1992). Testifying in criminal court. *Monographs of the Society for Research in Child Development, 57* (5, Serial No. 229).

Gowan, J. (1993). *Effects of neglect on the early development of children: Final report.* Washington, DC: National Clearinghouse on Child Abuse and Neglect, National Clearinghouse on Child Abuse and Neglect, Administration for Children and Families.

Graham-Bermann, S. A. (2002). Child abuse in the context of domestic violence. In J. E. B. Myers, L. Berliner, J. Briere, C. T. Hendrix, C. Jenny, & T. A. Reid (Eds.), *The APSAC handbook on child maltreatment* (2nd ed., pp. 119–129). Thousand Oaks, CA: Sage Publications.

Green, A. H. (1993). Child sexual abuse: Immediate and long-term effects and intervention. *Journal of the American Academy of Child and Adolescent Psychiatry, 32*(5), 890–902.

Hall, D. E., Eubanks, L., Meyyazhagan, S., Kenney, R. D., Johnson, S. C. (2000). Evaluation of covert video surveillance in the diagnosis of Munchausen syndrome by proxy: Lessons from 41 cases. *Pediatrics, 105*(6), 1305–1312.

Hall, R. C. W., Tice, L., Beresford, T. P., Wooley, B., & Hall, A. K. (1989). Sexual abuse in patients with anorexia nervosa and bulimia. *Psychosomatics, 30,* 73–79.

Hamarman, S., & Bernet, W. (2000). Evaluating and reporting emotional abuse in children: Parent-based, action-based focus aids in clinical decision-making. *Journal of the American Academy of Child and Adolescent Psychiatry, 39*(7), 928–934.

Hamarman, D., Pope, K. H., & Czaja, S. J. (2002). Emotional abuse in children: Variations in legal definitions and rates across the United States. *Child Maltreatment, 7*(4), 303–311.

Hammond, W. R. (2003). Public health and child maltreatment prevention: The role of the Centers for Disease Control and Prevention. *Child Maltreatment, 8,* 81–83.

Hansen, K. K. (1997). Folk remedies and child abuse: A review with emphasis on *Caida de Mollera* and its relationship to shaken baby syndrome. *Child Abuse and Neglect, 22*(2), 117–127.

Harder, J. (2005). *Prevention of child abuse and neglect: Best practices.* Unpublished manuscript, University of Nebraska at Omaha.

Hart, S. N., Binggeli, N. J., & Brassard, M. R. (1998). Evidence for the effects of psychological maltreatment. *Journal of Emotional Abuse, 1*(1), 27–58.

Hart, S. N., & Brassard, M. R. (1987). Psychological maltreatment: Integration and summary. In M. R. Brassard, R. Germain, & S. N. Hart (Eds.). *Psychological maltreatment of children and youth* (pp. 254–273). New York: Pergamon Press.

Hart, S. N., Germain, R., & Brassard, M. R. (1987). The challenge: To better understand and combat psychological maltreatment of children and youth. In M. R. Brassard, R. Germain, & S. N. Hart (Eds.), *Psychological maltreatment of children and youth* (pp. 3–24). New York: Pergamon.

Hart, S. N., Brassard, M. R., Binggeli, N. J., & Davidson, H. A. (2002). Psychological maltreatment. In J. E. B. Myers, L. Berliner, J. Briere, C. T. Hendrix, C. Jenny, & T. A. Reid (Eds.), *The APSAC handbook on child maltreatment* (2nd ed., pp. 79–99). Thousand Oaks, CA: Sage Publications.

Haugaard, J. J. (2000). The challenge of defining child sexual abuse. *American Psychologist, 55*(9), 1036–1039.

Hekmatpanah, J., Pannaraj, P., & Callans, L. (2002). Head injury in abused children (review of 190 cases over 30 years). *Journal of Neuroscience Nursing, 34,* 14–19.

Helfer, R. E., Slovis, T. L., & Black, M. (1977). Injuries resulting when small children fall out of bed. *Pediatrics, 60,* 533–535.

Herbert, B. (2001, May 24). In America. *New York Times.* Retrieved October 11, 2001, from http://www.mapinc.org/drugnews

Herman, J. L. (1992). *Trauma and recovery: The aftermath of violence from domestic abuse and political terror.* New York: Basic Books.

Hindman, H. D. (2002). Child labor in American history. New York: M. E. Sharpe.

Holder, T. (2000). Basis for ongoing CPS intervention: CPS staff-focused survey summary. In T. D. Morton & W. Holder (Eds.), *Issues and strategies for assessment approaches to child maltreatment.* (pp. 14–25). Atlanta, GA: Child Welfare Institute.

Holder, W., & Morton, T. D. (1999). *Designing a comprehensive approach to child safety.* Atlanta, GA: Child Welfare Institute.

Huizink, A. C., & Mulder, E. J. H. (2006). Maternal smoking, drinking or cannabis use during pregnancy and neurobehavioral and cognitive functioning in human offspring. *Neuroscience and Biobehavioral Reviews, 30,* 24–41.

Humphrey, J. (2002, September 22). Dad saves abused, emaciated daughter. *Tampa Tribune.* Retrieved September 28, 2005, from http://web.lexis-nexis.com.In re E. G. 549 N. E. 2d 322 (Ill., 1989).

In re Gault, 387 U.S. 1 (1967).

Jones, J. Y. (1978). Child abuse: History, legislation and issues. *Congressional Research Service, Library of Congress,* 78-12 ED, 1–30.

Jones, L. M., & Finkelhor, D. (2003). Putting together evidence on declining trends in sexual abuse: A complex puzzle. *Child Abuse and Neglect, 27,* 133–135.

Jones, H. E. (2006). Drug addiction during pregnancy: Advanced in maternal treatment and understanding child outcomes. *Current Directions in Psychological Science, 15*(3), 126–130.

Johnson, C. F. (2002). Physical abuse: Accidental versus intentional trauma in children. In J. E. B. Myers, L. Berliner, J. Briere, C. T. Hendrix, C. Jenny, & T. A. Reid (Eds.), *The APSAC handbook on child maltreatment* (2nd ed., pp. 249–268). Thousand Oaks, CA: Sage Publications.

Kahr, B. (1991). The sexual molestation of children: Historical perspectives. *Journal of Psychohistory, 19*(2), 191–214.

Kalichman, S. C. (1999). *Mandated reporting of suspected child abuse: Ethics, law & policy* (2nd ed.). Washington, DC: American Psychological Association.

Kalichman, S. C., Craig, M. E., & Follingstad, D. R. (1989). Factors influencing the reporting of father-child sexual abuse: Study of licensed practicing psychologists. *Professional Psychology: Research and Practice, 20*(2), 84–89.

Kazdin, A. E., Moser, J., Colbus, D., & Bell, R. (1985). Depressive symptoms among physically abused and psychiatrically disturbed inpatient children. *Journal of Abnormal Psychology, 94,* 298–307.

Kearney, M. H., Murphy, S., & Rosenbaum, M. (1994). Mothering on crack cocaine: A grounded theory analysis. *Social Science Medicine, 38*(2), 351–361.

Keeney, K. S., Amacher, E., & Kastanakis, J. A. (1992). The court prep group: A vital part of the court process. In H. Dent & R. Flin (Eds.), *Children as witnesses* (pp. 201–209). New York: John Wiley & Sons.

Kelly, S. J. (1992). Parenting stress and child maltreatment in drug-exposed children. *Child Abuse and Neglect, 16,* 317–328.

Kelley, S. J. (2002). Child maltreatment in the context of substance abuse. In J. E. B. Myers, L. Berliner, J. Briere, C. T. Hendrix, C. Jenny, & T. A. Reid (Eds.), *The APSAC handbook on child maltreatment* (2nd ed., pp. 105–118). Thousand Oaks, CA: Sage Publications.

Kempe, C. H., Silverman, F. N., Steele, B. F., Droegemueller, W., & Silver, H. K. (1962). The battered-child syndrome. *Journal of the American Medical Association, 181*(1), 17–24.

Kenny, M. C. (2001). Compliance with mandated child abuse reporting: Comparing physicians and teachers. *Journal of Offender Rehabilitation, 34*(1), 9–23.

Kendall-Tackett, K. A., & Watson, M. W. (1992). Use of anatomical dolls by Boston-area professionals. *Child Abuse and Neglect, 16,* 423–428.

Kent, L., Laidlaw, J. D. D., & Brockington, I. F. (1997). Fetal abuse. *Child Abuse and Neglect, 21*(2), 181–186.

Knight, B. (1986). The history of child abuse. *Forensic Science International, 30*(2-3), 135–141.

Kolko, D. J. (2002). Child physical abuse. In J. E. B. Myers, L. Berliner, J. Briere, C. T. Hendrix, C. Jenny, & T. A. Reid (Eds.), *The APSAC handbook on child maltreatment* (2nd ed., pp. 21–54). Thousand Oaks, CA: Sage Publications.

Krugman, R. D., & Krugman, M. K. (1984). Emotional abuse in the classroom. *American Journal of Diseases of Children, 138,* 284–286.

Kuczkowski, K. M. (2005). Drug addiction in pregnancy and pregnancy outcome: A call for global solutions. *Substance Use and Misuse, 40,* 1749–1750.

Kuehnle, K., & Sparta, S. N. (2006). Assessing child sexual abuse allegations in a legal context. In S. N. Sparta & G. P. Koocher (Eds.) *Forensic mental health assessment of children and adolescents* (pp. 129–148). Oxford: Oxford University Press.

Labbe, J. (2005). Ambroise Tardieu: The man and his work on child maltreatment a century before Kempe. *Child Abuse and Neglect, 29*(4), 311–324.

Larson, A. (2000, March). How does "plea bargaining" work? Retrieved February 12, 2007, from http://www.expertlaw.com

Larzelere, R. E., & Johnson, B. (1999). Evaluations of the effects of Sweden's spanking ban on physical child abuse rates: A literature review. *Psychological Reports, 85,* 381–392.

Lasher, L. J., & Sheridan, M. S. (2004). *Munchausen by proxy: Identification, intervention, and case management.* Binghamton, NY: The Haworth Press.

Lawson, L., & Chaffin, M. (1992). False negatives in sexual abuse disclosure interviews: Incidence and influence of caretaker's belief in abuse in cases of accidental abuse discovery by diagnosis of STD. *Journal of Interpersonal Violence, 7*(4), 532–542.

LeCroy, C. W., & Whitaker, K. (2005). Improving the quality of home visitation: An exploratory study of difficult situations. *Child Abuse & Neglect, 29,* 1003–1013.

Lee, B. J., & Goerge, R. M. (1999). Poverty, early childbearing, and child maltreatment: A multinomial analysis. *Children and Youth Services Review, 21*(9/10), 755–780.

Leichtman, M. D., & Ceci, S. J. (1995). The effects of stereotypes and suggestions on preschoolers' reports. *Developmental Psychology, 31*(4), 568–578.

Leshner, A. I. (1999). Research shows effects of prenatal cocaine exposure are subtle by significant. *NIDA Notes, 14*(3), 1–4.

Leventhal, J. (1997). The prevention of child abuse and neglect: Pipe dreams or possibilities? *Clinical Child Psychology and Psychiatry, 2,* 489–500.

Levenon, M., & Jadhav, A. (2005, August 7). Hyde Park mother in neglect case held: 13-year-old clinging to life with infection. *The Boston Globe.* Retrieved September 28, 2005, from http://web.lexis-nexis.com

Lewin, T. (2002, July 28). Above expectation: A child as witness. *The New York Times.* Retrieved August 1, 2002, from http://web.lexis-nexis.com

Libow, J. A. (1995). Munchausen by proxy victims in adulthood: A first look. *Child Abuse and Neglect, 19*(9), 1131–1142.

Libow, J. A. (2002). Beyond collusion: Active illness falsification. *Child Abuse and Neglect, 26,* 525–536.

Lindsey, D. (1994). Mandated reporting and child abuse fatalities: Requirements for a system to protect children. *Social Work Research, 18*(1), 41–45.

Little, R. & Streissguth, A. (1981). Effects of alcohol on the fetus: Impact and prevention. *Canadian Medical Association Journal, 125,* 159–164.

Loar, L. (1998). Child abuse and neglect: A guide to effective advocacy. In L.L. Palmatier (Ed.), *Crisis counseling for a quality school community: Applying Wm. Glasser's choice theory* (pp.151–174). Washington, DC: Accelerated Development.

Loeber, R., & Strouthamer-Loeber, M. (1986). Family factors as correlates and predictors of juvenile conduct problems and delinquency. In M. Tonry & N. Morris (Eds.). *Crime and justice: An annual review of the research* (Vol. 7, pp. 29–149). Chicago: University of Chicago Press.

Loftus, E., & Ketcham, K. (1994). *The myth of repressed memory: False memories and allegations of sexual abuse.* New York: St. Martin's Griffin.

Logli, P. A. (1998). Drugs in the womb: The newest battlefield in the war on drugs. In S. Nolen-Hoeksema (Ed.), *Clashing views on abnormal psychology: A taking sides custom reader* (pp. 178–183). Guilford, CT: Dushkin/McGraw-Hill.

London, K. (2006). Investigative interviews of children: A review of psychological research and implications for police practices. In C. R. Bartol and A. M. Bartol (Eds.), *Current perspectives in forensic psychology and criminal justice* (pp. 35–53). Thousand Oaks, CA: Sage Publications.

Lyon, T. D. (2001). Let's not exaggerate the suggestibility of children. *Court Review, 38,* 12–14.

MacMillan, H. L., MacMillan, J. H., Offord, D. R., Griffith, L., & MacMillan, A. (1994a). Primary prevention of child physical abuse and neglect: A critical review. Part I. *Journal of Child Psychology and Psychiatry, 35,* 835–856.

MacMillan, H. L., MacMillan, J. H., Offord, D. R., Griffith, L., & MacMillan, A. (1994b). Primary prevention of child physical abuse and neglect: A critical review. Part II. *Journal of Child Psychology and Psychiatry, 35,* 857–876.

Malinosky-Rummell, R., & Hansen, D. J. (1993). Long-term consequences of childhood physical abuse. *Psychological Bulletin, 114,* 68–79.

Man accused of letting 3-year-old brandish gun. (2005, April 2). *St. Petersburg Times.* Retrieved September 28, 2005, from http://web.lexis-nexis.com

Manning, L. (2007). Nightmare at the day care: The Wee Care case. *Crime Magazine: An Encyclopedia of Crime,* 1–16. Retrieved August 20, 2007, from http:/crimemagazine.com/daycare.htm

Mart, E. G. (1999). Problems with the diagnosis of factitious disorder by proxy in forensic settings. *American Journal of Forensic Psychology, 17*(1), 69–82.

Mart, E. G. (2002). Munchausen's syndrome (factitious disorder) by proxy: A brief review of its scientific and legal status. *The Scientific Review of Mental Health Practice, 1*(1), 55–61.

Mart, E. G. (2004). Factitious disorder by proxy: A call for the abandonment of an outmoded diagnosis. *The Journal of Psychiatry and Law, 32,* 297–314.

Maryland v. Craig, 497 U.S. 836 (1990). Retrieved February 12, 2007, from http://caselaw.lp.findlaw.com/scripts/printer.pl?page=us/497/836.html

Maslow, A. H. (1962). *Toward a psychology of being.* Princeton, NJ: Van Nostrand.

McCord, J. (1983). A forty year perspective on effects of child abuse and neglect. *Child Abuse and Neglect, 7,* 265–270.

McCoy, M. L. (1994). *Sexual abuse research: What is being done?* Poster session presented at the Rocky Mountain Psychological Association, Las Vegas, Nevada.

McCoy, M. L. (2003). Factors impacting the assessment of maternal culpability in cases of alleged fetal abuse. *Journal of Drug Education, 33*(3), 275–288.

McCurdy, K., & Daro, D. (1994). Current trends in child abuse fatalities and reporting. *Journal of Interpersonal Violence, 9,* 75–94.

McGee, R. A., & Wolfe, D. A. (1991). Psychological maltreatment: Toward an operational definition. *Development and Psychopathology, 3,* 3–18.

McGuire, T. L., & Feldman, K. W. (1989). Psychologic morbidity of children subjected to Munchausen syndrome by proxy. *Pediatrics, 83*(2), 289–292.

McMurtry, S. L. (1985). Secondary prevention of child maltreatment: A review. *Social Work, 30,* 42–48.

Meadow, R. (1977). Munchausen's syndrome by proxy: The hinterland of child abuse. *Lancet, 2,* 343–345.

Meadow, R. (1982). Munchausen syndrome by proxy. *Archives of Disease in Childhood, 57,* 92–98.

Medline Plus Medical Enclyclopedia. (2006). Impetigo. Retrieved September 19, 2006, from http://www.nlm.nih.gov/medlineplus/ency/article/000860.htm

Merrick, J. C. (1993). Maternal substance abuse during pregnancy: Policy implications in the United States. *The Journal of Legal Medicine, 14,* 57–71.

Miller-Perrin, C. L., & Perrin, R. D. (1999). *Child maltreatment: An introduction.* Thousand Oaks, CA: Sage Publications.

Moehler, E., Brunner, R., Wiebel, A., Reck, C., & Resch, F. (2006). Maternal depressive symptoms in the postnatal period are associated with long-term impairment of mother-child bonding. *Archives of Women's Mental Health, 9*(5), 273–278.

Moldavsky, M., & Stein, D. (2003). Munchausen syndrome by proxy: Two case reports and an update of the literature. *International Journal of Psychiatry in Medicine, 33*(4), 411–423.

Montaldo, C. (2005). About.com: Crime/Punishment. Retrieved August 8, 2007, from http://crime.about.com/od/history/p/Letourneau.htm

Moore, J. K., & Smith, J. C. (2006). Abusive fractures. In C. R. Brittain (Ed.), *Understanding the medical diagnosis of child maltreatment* (pp. 49–60). Oxford: Oxford University Press.

Moore, T. E., & Pepler, D. J. (2006). Wounding words: Maternal verbal aggression and children's adjustment. *Journal of Family Violence, 21*(1), 89–93.

Moran, G. F., & Vinovskis, M. A. (1986). The great care of godly parents: Early childhood in Puritan New England. *Monographs of the Society for Research in Child Development, 50,* 24–37.

Morelli, K. (2002a, September 24). Police tell more of abused girl's grim existence. *Tampa Tribune.* Retrieved September 28, 2005, from http://web.lexis-nexis.com

Morelli, K. (2002b, September 26). N.Y. knew of abuse worries. *Tampa Tribune*. Retrieved September 28, 2005, from http://web.lexis-nexis.com

Morrision, C. A. (1999). Cameras in hospital rooms: The Fourth Amendment to the Constitution and Munchausen by proxy. *Critical Care Nursing Quarterly, 22*, 65–68.

Mother faces neglect, drug charges. (2005, May 6). *St. Petersburg Times*. Retrieved September 28, 2005, from http://web.lexis-nexis.com

Mother is charged after 4 die in fire. (1984, December 24). *The New York Times*. Retrieved September 28, 2005, from http://web.lexis-nexis.com

Mullen, P. E., Martin, J. L., Anderson, J. C., Romans, S. E., & Herbison, G. P. (1996). The long-term impact of physical, emotional, and sexual abuse of children: A community study. *Child Abuse and Neglect, 20*, 7–21.

Myers, J. E. B. (1996). A decade of international reform to accommodate child witnesses. *Criminal Justice and Behavior, 23*(2), 402–422.

Myers, J. E. B. (1998). Legal issues in child abuse and neglect practice (2nd ed.). Thousand Oaks, CA: Sage Publications.

Myers, J. E. B. (2002). The legal system and child protection. In J. E. B. Myers, L. Berliner, J. Briere, C. T. Hendrix, C. Jenny, & T. A. Reid (Eds.). *The APSAC handbook on child maltreatment* (pp. 305–327). London: Sage Publications.

National Association of Counsel for Children (n.d.). Children and the law: Child maltreatment. Retrieved August 16, 2005, from http://naccchildlaw.org/childrenlaw/childmaltreatment.html

National Association of Public Child Welfare Administrators. (1999). *Guidelines for a model system of protective services for abused and neglected children and their families*. Washington, DC: American Public Human Services Association.

National Clearinghouse on Child Abuse and Neglect Information (2001). *In focus: Acts of omission: An overview*. Washington, DC: Children's Bureau, Administration for Children and Families, U.S. Department of Health and Human Services.

National Clearinghouse on Child Abuse and Neglect Information (2004). *Child maltreatment 2003: Summary of key findings*. Washington, DC: Children's Bureau, Administration for Children and Families, U.S. Department of Health and Human Services.

National Clearinghouse on Child Abuse and Neglect (2005). Definitions of child abuse and neglect: State statute series 2005. Retrieved August 30, 2005, from http://nccahch.acf.hhs.gov/general/legal/statutes/define

Ney, P. G. (1989). Child maltreatment: Possible reasons for its intergenerational transmission. *Canadian Journal of Psychiatry, 34*, 594–601.

Niccols, G. A. (1994). Fetal alcohol syndrome: Implications for psychologists. *Clinical Psychology Review, 14*(2), 91–111.

Nichtern, S. (1973). The children of drug users. *Journal of the American Academy of Child Psychology, 12*(1), 24–31.

Norton-Hawk, M. A. (1998). How social policies make matters worse: The case of maternal substance abuse. In S. Nolen-Hoeksema (Ed.), *Clashing views on abnormal psychology: A taking sides custom reader* (pp. 185–193). Guilford, CT: Dushkin/McGraw-Hill.

Olds, D. L., Henderson, C. R., Jr., Kitzman, H. J., Eckenrode, J. J., Cole, R. E., & Tatelbaum, R. C. (1999). Prenatal and infancy home visitation by nurses: Recent findings. *The Future of Children, 9*, 44–65.

Olsen, G. (1999). *If loving you is wrong*. New York: St. Martins: True Crime.

Olsen, J. L., & Widom, C. S. (1993). Prevention of child abuse and neglect. *Applied and Preventive Psychology, 2*, 217–229.

Ondersma, S. J., Chaffin, M., Berliner, L., Cordon, I., Goodman, G. S., & Barnett, D. (2001). Sex with children is abuse: Comment on Rind, Tromovitch, and Bauserman (1998). *Psychological Bulletin, 127*(6), 707–714.

Ondersma, S. J., Simpson, S. M., Brestan, E. V., & Ward, M. (2000). Prenatal drug exposure and social policy: The search for an appropriate response. *Child Maltreatment, 5*(2), 93–108.

Osteogenesis Imperfecta Foundation. (2006). Welcome to the Osteogenesis Imperfecta Web site. Retrieved September 19, 2006, from http://www.oif.org/site/PageServer

Ostrea, E. M., Brady, M., Gause, S., Raymundo, A. L., & Stevens, M. (1992). Drug screening of newborns by meconium analysis: A large-scale, prospective, epidemiological study. *Pediatrics, 89*, 107–113.

O'Hagan, K. (1993). *Emotional and psychological abuse of children*. Toronto: University of Toronto Press.

O'Shea, B. (2003). Factitious disorders: The Baron's legacy. *International Journal of Psychiatry in Clinical Practice, 7,* 33–39.

Paltrow, L. M. (1991). Perspective of a reproductive rights attorney. *The Future of Children, 1*(1), 85–92.

Paltrow, L. M, & Newman, T. (2008). South Carolina Supreme Court reverses 20-year homicide conviction of Regina McKnight. *Drug Policy News.* Retrieved July 10, 2008, from http://www.drugpolicy.org/news/pressroom/pressrelease/pr051208ccfm

Paavilainen, E., Åstedt-Kurki, Paunonen-Ilmonen, M., & Laippala, P. (2001). Risk factors of child maltreatment within the family: Towards a knowledge base of family nursing. *International Journal of Nursing Studies, 38,* 297–303.

Paolucci, E. O., Genuis, M. L., & Violato, C. (2001). A meta-analysis of the published research on the effects of child sexual abuse. *The Journal of Psychology, 135*(1), 17–36.

Parks, A. (2004, December 13). Angry father's kick might not equal child abuse, court says. *The Daily Record.* Retrieved July 12, 2006, from http://web.lexis-nexis.com

Parnell, T. F. (2002). Munchausen by proxy syndrome. In J. E. B. Myers, L. Berliner, J. Briere, C. T. Hendrix, C. Jenny & T. A. Reid (Eds.) *The APSAC Handbook on Child Maltreatment* (2nd ed., pp. 131–138). Thousand Oaks, CA: Sage Publications.

Paxson, C., & Waldfogel, J. (1999). Parental resources and child abuse and neglect. *The American Economic Review, 89*(2), 239–244.

Pearl, P. S. (1994). Emotional abuse. In J. A. Monteleone & A. E. Brodeur (Eds.), *Child maltreatment: A clinical guide and reference* (pp. 259–283). St. Louis, MO: G. W. Medical Publishing Inc.

Pecora, P. J., Whittaker, J. K., Maluccio, A. N., Barth, R. P., & Plotnick, R. D. (2000). *The child welfare challenge: Policy, practice and research* (2nd ed.). New York: Aldine de Gruyter.

Pelcovitz, D., Kaplan, S. J., DeRosa, R. R., Mandel, F. S., & Salzinger, S. (2000). Psychiatric disorders in adolescents exposed to domestic violence and physical abuse. *American Journal of Orthopsychiatry, 70*(3), 360–369.

Pelton, L. H. (1994). The role of material factors in child abuse and neglect. In G. B. Melton & F. D. Barry (Eds.), *Protecting children from abuse and neglect: Foundations for a new national strategy* (pp. 131–181). New York: Guilford Publications, Inc.

People v. Stewart, No. M508 197 (San Diego Municipal Court, Februrary, 26, 1987).

Perez, C. M., & Widom, C. S. (1994). Childhood victimization and long term intellectual and academic outcome. *Child Abuse and Neglect, 18,* 617–633.

Peterson, L., Tremblay, G., Ewigman, B., & Saldana, L. (2003). Multilevel selected primary prevention of child maltreatment. *Journal of Consulting and Clinical Psychology, 71,* 601–612.

Pianta, R., Egeland, B., & Erickson, M. F. (1989). The antecedents of maltreatment: Results of the Mother-Child Interaction Research Project. In D. Cicchetti & V. Carlson (Eds.), *Child maltreatment: Theory and research on the causes and consequences of child abuse and neglect* (pp. 203–253). Cambridge, UK: Cambridge University Press.

Pollitt, K. (1990). Fetal rights: A new assault on feminism (laws protecting the fetus from the mother). *The Nation, 250*(12), 409–415.

Polusny, M. A., & Follette, V. M. (1995). Long-term correlates of child sexual abuse: Theory and review of the empirical literature. *Applied and Preventive Psychology, 4,* 143–166.

Poole, D. A., & Lamb, M. E. (1998). *Investigative interviews of children.* Washington, DC: American Psychological Association.

Pope, H. G., & Hudson, J. I. (1992). Is childhood sexual abuse a risk factor for bulimia nervosa? *American Journal of Psychiatry, 149*(4), 455–463.

Prince v. Com. of Mass., 321 U.S. 158(1944).

The probability of injustice; British courts. (2004, January 24). *The Economist (US), 370,* 13.

Rampini, S. K., Schneemann, M., Rentsch, K., & Bachli, E. B. (2002). Camphor intoxication after *Cao Gio* (coin rubbing). *Journal of the American Medical Association, 288*(1), 45.

Ramsland, K. (2007). The McMartin nightmare and the hysteria puppeteers. Retrieved September 5, 2007, from www.crimelibrary.com/criminal_mind/psychology/mcmartin_daycare

Rand, D. C., & Feldman, M. D. (1999). Misdiagnosis of Munchausen syndrome by proxy: A literature review and four new cases. *Harvard Review of Psychiatry, 7*(2), 94–101.

Realmuto, G., Jensen, J., & Wescoe, S. (1990). Specificity and sensitivity of sexually anatomically correct dolls in substantiating abuse: A pilot study. *Journal of the Academy of Child and Adolescent Psychiatry, 29,* 743–746.

Reppucci, N. D., Jones, L. M., & Cook, S. L. (1994). Involving parents in child sexual abuse prevention programs. *Journal of Child and Family Studies, 3,* 137–142.

Rind, B., Tromovitch, P., & Bauserman, R. (1998). A meta-analytic examination of assumed properties of child sexual abuse using college samples. *Psychological Bulletin, 124*(1), 22–53.

Rind, B., Tromovitch, P., & Bauserman, R. (2001). The validity and appropriateness of methods, analyses, and conclusions in Rind et al. (1998): A rebuttal of victimological critique from Ondersma et al. (2001) and Dallem et al. (2001). *Psychological Bulletin, 127*(6), 734–758.

Rispens, J., Aleman, A., & Goudena, P. P. (1997). Prevention of child sexual abuse victimization: A meta-analysis of school programs. *Child Abuse and Neglect, 21,* 975–987.

Robinson, J. (2001). *The Mary Kay LeTourneau affair.* Overland Park, KS: Leathers Publishing.

Rogeness, G. A., Amrung, S. A., Macedo, C. A., Harris, W. R., & Fisher, C. (1986). Psychopathology in abused or neglected children. *Journal of the American Academy of Child Psychiatry, 25,* 659–665.

Rohner, R. P. (1986). *The warmth dimension: Foundations of parental acceptance-rejection theory.* Newbury Park, CA: Sage Publications, Inc.

Roland, B., Zelhart, P. & Dubes, R. (1989). MMPI correlates of college women who reported experiencing child/adult sexual contact with father, stepfather, or with other persons. *Psychological Reports, 64,* 1159–1162.

Romano, B. (2001, June 3). San Jose mom found guilty of making son ill. *San Jose Mercury News.* Retrieved June 21, 2004, from: http: www.vachss.com/help_text/archive/sanjose_mom.html

Rorty, M., Yager, J., & Rossotto, E. (1994). Childhood sexual, physical, and psychological abuse in bulimia nervosa. *American Journal of Psychiatry, 151*(8), 1122–1126.

Rosenberg, J. (1996). Patient by proxy. *American Medical News, 39,* 11–14.

Rosenthal, R., & Jacobson, L. (1968). *Pygmalion in the classroom: Teacher expectation and pupils' intellectual development.* New York: Holt, Rinehart and Winston.

Rudy, L., & Goodman, G. (1991). Effects of participation on children's reports: Implications for children's testimony. *Developmental Psychology, 27*(4), 527–538.

Sagatun, I. J., & Edwards, L. P. (1995). *Child abuse and the legal system.* Chicago: Nelson-Hall Publishers.

Sanders, M. R., Cann, W., & Markie-Davis, C. (2003). Why a universal population-level approach to the prevention of child abuse is essential. *Child Abuse Review, 12,* 145–154.

Sanfranek, L. (2005, June 30). Kids left in car get baby sitter a ticket. *Omaha World Herald.* Retrieved September 28, 2005, from http://web.lexis-nexis.com

Santrock, J. W. (2007). *A topical approach to life-span development.* Boston: McGraw Hill.

Satterfield, J. (2005, June 25). Trying to make 'em pay: ET child's alleged abusers, DCS sued for total of $12.1 million. *Knoxville News-Sentinel.* Retrieved November 1, 2005, from http://web.lexis-nexis

Saunders, B. E., Villeponteaux, L. A., Lipovsky, J. A., Kilpatrick, D. G., & Veronen, L. J. (1992). Child sexual assault as a risk factor for mental disorders among women: A community survey. *Journal of Interpersonal Violence, 7*(2), 189–204.

Saywitz, K., Jaenicke, C., & Camparo, L. (1990). Children's knowledge of legal terminology. *Law and Human Behavior, 14*(6), 523–535.

Schaefer, C. (1997). Defining verbal abuse of children: A survey. *Psychological Reports, 80,* 626.

Schreier, H. A., & Libow, J. A. (1993). *Hurting for love: Munchausen by proxy syndrome.* New York: Guilford Press.

Schumm, J. A., Hobfoll, S. E., & Keogh, N. J. (2004). Revictimization and interpersonal resource loss predicts PTSD among women in substance-use treatment. *Journal of Traumatic Stress, 17,* 173–181.

Sedlak, A. J., & Broadhurst, D. D. (1996). *Third national incidence study of child abuse and neglect.* Washington, DC: U.S. Department of Health and Human Services.

Sedlack, A. J., Schultz, D., Wells, S. J., Lyons, P., Doueck, H. J., & Gragg, F. (2006). Child protection and justice systems processing of serious child abuse and neglect cases. *Child Abuse and Neglect, 30,* 657–677.

Senn, T. E., Carey, M. P., Vanable, P. A., Coury-Doniger, P., & Urban, M. A. (2006). Childhood sexual abuse and sexual risk behavior among men and women attending a sexually transmitted disease clinic. *Journal of Consulting and Clinical Psychology, 74*(4), 720–731.

Shaw, L. E., & Brenner, S. W. (2006). *Federal grand jury: A guide to law and practice* (2nd ed). Belmont, CA: Thomson.

Shelman, E. A., & Lazoritz, S. (2005). *The Mary Ellen Wilson child abuse case and the beginning of children's rights 19th century America.* Jefferson, NC: McFarland & Company, Inc., Publishers.

Sheridan, M. S. (2003). The deceit continues: An updated literature review of Munchausen syndrome by proxy. *Child Abuse and Neglect, 27*(4), 431–451.

Showers, J. (1992). "Don't shake the baby": The effectiveness of a prevention program. *Child Abuse and Neglect, 16,* 11–18.

Sirotnak, A. P. (2006). Emotional maltreatment. In C. R. Brittain (Ed.), *Understanding the medical diagnosis of child maltreatment: A guide for nonmedical professionals* (3rd ed.). Oxford: Oxford University Press.

Slack, D. (2005, August 9). Illness got "out of hand" lawyer says: Mother ordered held for evaluation on neglect charge. *The Boston Globe.* Retrieved September 28, 2005, from http://web.lexis-nexis.com

Slack, K. S., Holl, J. L., McDaniel, M., Yoo, J., & Bolger, K. (2004). Understanding the risks of child neglect: An exploration of poverty and parenting characteristics. *Child Maltreatment, 9*(4), 395–408.

Small, M. A., Lyons, P. M., & Guy, L. S. (2002). Liability issues in child abuse and neglect reporting statutes. *Professional Psychology: Research and Practice, 33*(1), 13–18.

Smalley, S., & Slack, D. (2005a, August 5). Girl found emaciated, near death at home. *The Boston Globe.* Retrieved September 28, 2005, from http://web.lexis-nexis.com

Smalley, S., & Slack, D. (2005b, August 6). DSS probed family in Hyde Park twice: Girl remains in critical condition. *The Boston Globe.* Retrieved September 28, 2005, from http://web.lexis-nexis.com

Smith, M. G., & Fong, R. (2004). The children of neglect: When no one cares. New York: Runner-Routledge.

The Social Security Act of 1935. Act of August 14, 1935 [H.R. 7260].

Spitz, R. (1956). The influence of the mother-child relationship, and its disturbances. *Mental Health and Infant Development, 1,* 103–108.

Stallman v. Youngquist, 531 N.E. 2d 355 (1988).

State v. D. R. H. (1992) 127 N. J. 249, 604 A.2d 89.

State v. Horne, 319 S.E. 2d 703 (S. C., 1984).

State v. Johnson, No. E89-890-CFA (Fla. Cir. Ct. July 13, 1989), affd., 578 So. 2d 419 (Fla. 5th Dist. Ct. App. 1991, No. 77, 831 (Fla. Sup. Ct. May 7, 1991).

State v. McKnight, 576 S. E. 2d 168 (S.C., 2003).

State v. Michaels, 625 A.2d 489 (N. J. Super Ct. App. Div. 1993).

State v. Palabay, 844 P.2d 1 (Hawaii Ct. App. 1992).

State v. R. W., 514 A.2d 1287 (N. J. 1986).

Steiger, H., & Zanko, M. (1990). Sexual traumata among eating-disordered, psychiatric and normal female groups. *Journal of Interpersonal Violence, 5,* 74–86.

Stone, L. (1977). *The family, sex and marriage in England 1500–1800* (Abr. Ed.). New York: Harper Torchbooks.

Stowman, S. A., & Donohue, B. (2005). Assessing child neglect: A review of standardized measures. *Aggression and Violent Behavior, 10,* 491–512.

Straus, M. A. (1992). Children as witnesses to marital violence: A risk factor for lifelong problems among a nationally representative sample of American men and women. In D. F. Schwartz (Ed.), *Children and violence: Report of the Twenty-Third Ross Roundtable on Critical Approaches to Common Pediatric Problems* (pp. 98–109). Columbus, OH: Ross Laboratories.

Stutts, T., Hickey, S. E., & Kasdan, M. L. (2003). Malingering by proxy: A form of pediatric condition falsification. *Journal of Developmental and Behavioral Pediatrics, 24*(4), 276–278.

Tannous, Z., & Abdul-Ghani, K. (2005). Mongolian spot. Emedicine from WebMD. Retrieved September 19, 2006, from http://www.emedicine.com/derm/topic271.htm

TenBensel, R. W., Rheinberger, M. M., & Radbill, S. X. (1997). Children in a world of violence: The roots of child maltreatment. In M. E. Helfer, R. S. Kempe, & R. D. Krugman (Eds.), *The battered child* (pp. 3–28). Chicago: The University of Chicago Press.

Trickett, P. K., Aber, J. L., Carlson, V., & Cicchetti, D. (1991). Relationship of socioeconomic status to the etiology and developmental sequelae of physical child abuse. *Developmental Psychology, 7*(1), 148–158.

Tyler, K. A. (2002). Social and emotional outcomes of childhood sexual abuse: A review of recent research. *Aggression and Violent Behavior, 7,* 567–589.

U.S. Department of Health and Human Services. (2003). National study of Child Protective Services systems and reform efforts: Review of state CPS policy. Retrieved November 6, 2007, from http://aspe.hhs.gov/hsp/cps-status03/state-policy03/

U. S. Department of Health and Human Services. (2007). *Child maltreatment 2005*. Washington, DC: Government Printing Office.

VonHahn, L., Harper, G., McDaniel, S. P., Siegel, D. M., Feldman, M., & Libow, J. A. (2001). A case of factitious disorder by proxy: The role of the health-care system, diagnostic dilemmas, and family dynamics. *Harvard Review of Psychiatry, 9,* 124–135.

Wallace, H. (1996). Family violence: Legal, medical and social perspectives. Needham Heights, MA: Allyn and Bacon.

Warren, A. R., Woodall, C. E., Hunt, J. S., & Perry, N. W. (1996). "It sounds good in theory, but…": Do investigative interviewers follow guidelines based on memory research? *Child Maltreatment, 1,* 231–245.

Watkins, S. A. (1990). The Mary Ellen myth: Correcting child welfare history. *Social Work, 35*(6), 500–503.

Wells, K. M. (2006). Injuries to the head, eyes, ears, nose and mouth. In C. R. Brittain (Ed.), *Understanding the medical diagnosis of child maltreatment* (pp. 79–90). Oxford: Oxford University Press.

Wells, S. (1997). Screening in Child Protective Services: Do we accept a report? How do we respond? In T. D. Morton & W. Holder (Eds.), *Decision making in children's protective services: Advancing the state of the art* (pp. 94–106). Atlanta, GA: Child Welfare Institute.

Wells, S. (2000a). How do I decide whether to accept a report for a child protective services investigation? In H. Dubowitz & D. DePanfilis (Eds.), *Handbook for child protection practice* (pp. 3–6). Thousand Oaks, CA: Sage Publications, Inc.

Wells, S. (2000b). What criteria are most critical to determine the urgency of the child protective services response? In H. Dubowitz & D. DePanfilis (Eds.), *Handbook for child protection practice* (pp. 7–9). Thousand Oaks, CA: Sage Publications, Inc.

Whitner v. State, 1996, WL 393164 (S. C., July 15, 1996).

Widom, C. S. (1989). The cycle of violence. *Science, 244,* 160–166.

Williams, L. M. (1994). Recall of childhood trauma: A prospective study of women's memories of child sexual abuse. *Journal of Consulting and Clinical Psychology, 62*(6), 1167–1176.

Williamson, J. M., & Borduin, C. M. (1991). The ecology of adolescent maltreatment: A multilevel examination of adolescent physical abuse, sexual abuse, and neglect. *Journal of Consulting and Clinical Psychology, 59*(3), 449–457.

Wilson, D., & Morton, T. D. (1997). Issues in decision-making. In T. D. Morton & W. Holder (Eds.), *Decision making in children's protective services: Advancing the state of the art* (pp. 1–11). Atlanta, GA: Child Welfare Institute.

Wind, T. W., & Silvern, L. (1992). Type and extent of child abuse as predictors of adult functioning. *Journal of Family Violence, 7,* 261–281.

Winton, M. A. & Mara, B. A. (2001). Child abuse and neglect: Multidisciplinary approaches. Boston: Allyn and Bacon.

Wodarski, J. S., Kurtz, P. D., Gaudin, J. M., & Howing, P. T. (1990). Maltreatment and the school-age child: Major academic, socioemotional, and adaptive outcomes. *Social Work, 35,* 506–513.

Wolfe, D. A., Reppucci, N. D., & Hart, S. (1995). Child abuse prevention: Knowledge and priorities. *Journal of Clinical Child Psychology, 24* (Suppl.), 5–22.

Wood, J. M., & Garven, S. (2000). How sexual abuse interviews go astray: Implications for prosecutors, police, and child protection services. *Child Maltreatment, 5*(2), 109–118.

Wurtele, S. K., & Miller-Perrin, C. L. (1987). An evaluation of side effects associated with participation in a child sexual abuse prevention program. *Journal of School Health, 57,* 228–231.

Yeatman, G. W., & Van Dang, V. (1980). Cao Gio (coin rubbing): Vietnamese attitudes toward health care. *Journal of the American Medical Association, 244*(24), 2748–2749.

Zuravin, S. J. (1989). The ecology of child abuse and neglect: Review of the literature and presentation of data. *Violence and Victims, 4,* 101–120.

Zuravin, S. J., Bliss, D. L., & Cohen-Callow, A. (2005). Maternal depression and adverse parenting. In K. A. Kendall-Tackett & S. M. Giacomoni (Eds.). *Child victimization: Maltreatment, bullying and dating violence, prevention and intervention* (pp. 10-01–10-19). Kingston, NJ: Civic Research Institute, Inc.

Index